Edward IV's Fatal Legacy

Edward IV's Fatal Legacy

The Restoration and Ruin
of the Courtenays 1479–1558

Hazel Pierce

PEN & SWORD
HISTORY

First published in Great Britain in 2025 by
Pen & Sword History
An imprint of Pen & Sword Books Limited
Yorkshire – Philadelphia

ISBN 978 1 39908 300 3

A CIP catalogue record for this book is
available from the British Library.

Typeset by Mac Style
Printed in the UK by CPI Group (UK) Ltd, Croydon, CR0 4YY.

MIX
Paper | Supporting
responsible forestry
FSC
www.fsc.org   FSC® C013604

The Publisher's authorised representative in the EU for product
safety is Authorised Rep Compliance Ltd., Ground Floor,
71 Lower Baggot Street, Dublin D02 P593, Ireland.
www.arccompliance.com

For a complete list of Pen & Sword titles please contact

PEN & SWORD BOOKS LIMITED
47 Church Street, Barnsley, South Yorkshire, S70 2AS, England
E-mail: enquiries@pen-and-sword.co.uk
Website: www.pen-and-sword.co.uk
or
PEN AND SWORD BOOKS
1950 Lawrence Road, Havertown, PA 19083, USA
E-mail: uspen-and-sword@casematepublishers.com
Website: www.penandswordbooks.com

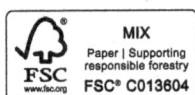

To Brian and Jacob as always, and to Peggy and Seamus with love.

And in fondest memory of my friend Lesley Griffith, my fellow student and friend Andrew (Andy) Downham, and my PhD supervisor and mentor, Professor David Loades, who remain an inspiration.

Contents

Acknowledgements

I have incurred many debts of gratitude while writing this book, the idea for which was born out of my PhD research on Margaret Pole, Countess of Salisbury. First and foremost, I should like to thank my publisher, Pen & Sword History, especially Sarah-Beth Watkins, Senior Commissioning Editor (History), for her patience and support. I would also like to pay tribute to Margaret Westcott for the immense and invaluable research she has conducted on the Courtenay family for which I am more indebted than I can say.

I am extremely grateful to Geoffrey Wheeler for his assistance with the illustrations. His kindness and generous commitment of time is hugely appreciated, and his expertise has greatly enriched this element. I should also like to sincerely thank Elizabeth Dent for her advice on the Royal Window, Canterbury Cathedral, and Livia Visser-Fuchs for her assistance with BL Arundel 26, the account of Elizabeth Woodville's funeral.

Debts of gratitude are also owed to Michael Peter Desmond O'Donoghue, York Herald, for his assistance with sources for the funerals of Katharine and William Courtenay, Chris Broom and Ann Ballard of the Institute of Heraldic and Genealogical Studies for their advice on the Courtenay arms, the staff of the British Library and the National Archives, and Katie Edwards, Collections Manager at Powderham Castle, for her help with Margaret Courtenay's letter. I should also like to thank Bill Zarratt for our helpful discussions about Katharine Courtenay's burial place in St Peter's Church, Dr David Wright for his advice and Latin translations and to Anna Ortiz Talvaz for her translation of Antoine de Noailles' letter.

Sincere thanks go to my great colleagues at Bangor University whose support has been invaluable, to the wonderful team at the University Print Unit, and to my friend Tim Radford for kindly giving of his time to cast a forensic eye over this manuscript. Having made my acknowledgements, any errors are entirely my own.

Most especially, I should like to thank my husband, Brian, for selflessly allowing this family to take over our lives. Without his encouragement, help and unstinting support this book simply would not have been possible.

Part I

Katharine Plantagenet

Daughter, Sister and Aunt of Kings

Chapter 1

1479–1495

King's Daughter, King's Bastard, Queen's Sister

Katharine Plantagenet was born at Eltham Palace between 24 January and 4 February 1479.[1] Her father was the powerful King Edward IV, a man who had claimed his crown on the field of battle. Although ruthless when needed, he was also charming and affable. With his confidence and casual air he easily put others at their ease, one chronicler recalling 'He was so genial in his greeting, that if he saw a newcomer bewildered at his appearance and royal magnificence, he would give him courage to speak by laying a kindly hand upon his shoulder.'[2] Standing at over six foot, he was once regarded as the most handsome prince in Christendom, but not so now. Throughout his reign he had fully indulged himself, 'no man ever took more delight in his pleasures than he did, especially in the ladies, feasts, banquets and hunts' thus becoming 'very fat and gross'.[3] His wife, older than him by five years, was the opposite. The beautiful and poised Elizabeth Woodville had self-control and discipline, keeping both her looks and her health. She was still giving birth to children in her forties, first Katharine in 1479 and her younger sister Bridget in November 1480. Katharine would turn out to be very much her mother's daughter, inheriting that same self-control.

Katharine was Edward and Elizabeth's eighth surviving child. She had four older sisters; Elizabeth aged 13, Mary aged 12, Cecily aged 10 and Anne aged 3. Her sister Elizabeth would become one of the most important people in her life with whom she would form a deep emotional bond. Her three older brothers were Prince Edward, the future king aged nine, who resided in his own household at Ludlow, Richard, Duke of York, aged 6 and George, less than 2 years old who was in his nursery at Windsor when Katharine was born. Sadly, she would never meet him as he died in March, most probably of the plague that was then raging in England. Possibly named after her aunt Katharine Woodville, her mother's younger sister, Katharine's christening took place shortly after her birth and under normal circumstances would have entailed the attendance of a large number of individuals. However, with the outbreak of the plague these were not normal circumstances and her christening was a more scaled down event. It is significant that no account of it survives, when normally it would have been recorded by a herald. Edward was certainly keeping people at arm's length, refusing to allow the newly appointed Abbess of Barking to perform her fealty to him in person because 'great mortality' reigned in the monastery, and he would have exercised similar precautions for his daughter's christening.[4] This took place at Eltham, the wardrobe accounts recording a payment of three pence to Piers Draper for several hundred laten nails 'of him so bought and expended at Eltham about covering of the font at the christening of Lady Katharine the King's daughter'.[5] According to directions for the christening of a prince or princess in the reign of Henry VII, 'the font must be set on height, that the people may see the christening, and press not to near; and the font must be hanged with a rich sele [canopy], and overlaid about with carpets on the steps and other places; and the font must be hanged all about with cloth of gold'. For the procession to church a duchess should precede the child and, for a princess, a countess must carry her train.[6] Katharine's christening, in the middle of an epidemic, was therefore both muted and magnificent, the latter befitting a princess of England whose life promised to be one of status and privilege.

The first mention of Katharine in contemporary records occurs just a few months after her birth.[7] Edward IV, like all rulers, recognised the dynastic importance of his children and the potential, through their marriages, to form alliances with other European royal houses. In 1475 it had been agreed that Edward's eldest daughter, Elizabeth, should marry the dauphin Charles, thus becoming the future Queen of France. Her sister Mary was to stand as reserve in the event of Elizabeth's death, but in 1481 she was betrothed to King Frederick I of Denmark, thus she became the future Queen of Denmark. Princess Cecily was affianced to the future James IV of Scotland in 1473 meaning that one day she would be Queen of Scotland. In 1480, Edward's sister Margaret, Duchess of Burgundy, visited her brother in England to discuss and finalise negotiations for the marriage of Edward's daughter Anne to Margaret's step grandson Philip 'the fair' of Burgundy. This meant that Anne looked forward to becoming Duchess of Burgundy and daughter-in-law to the Emperor Maximillian.[8]

To complement these strategic unions, negotiations for Katharine's marriage began in August 1479 when the king despatched Bernard de la Force and John Coke to Spain to negotiate a match between Katharine and Juan, son and heir of Ferdinand and Isabella of Spain. If this had gone ahead, her sister-in-law would have been a certain Catherine of Aragon. By their own marriage, Ferdinand and Isabella had united the crowns of Aragon and Castille, thus Juan was heir to the crown of Spain. This means that almost from birth, Katharine was being considered as the future Queen of Spain. Edward was very serious about the match and prepared to put his money where his mouth was to secure it. In order to advance the matter de la Force and Coke were given 'many yards of scarlet, crimson, and violet cloth to be distributed among divers lords and magnates of Spain whose help it might be well to enlist'. On 2 March 1482 de la Force, now in company with Henry Aynesworth and Arnold Trussell, returned to Spain, this time to conclude the marriage agreement. Edward again sent inducements including the huge sum of £1,000 'to be employed within the realm of Spain according to our commandment' as well as expensive materials for 'the constable and other lords of Spain'.[9]

On a personal level, marriage to Juan may have brought Katharine happiness as well as position. Born in 1478, he was close in age to her, and as he grew older descriptions of him alluded to 'his beauty, his gracious bearing, his precocious intelligence, his aptitude for learning and manly sports'.[10] His parents' only son, his mother in particular doted on him. She chose the palace of Almazán in Soria as his residence and provided many little luxuries for him including a silver ewer and bowl for washing his hair, a manicure set, silver mirrors and basins along with incense, rosewater and perfumes.[11] Isabella was equally attentive to her daughters ensuring that they had a wider education than was normal for the time, and as her daughter-in-law, Katharine may have benefitted from this. However, the marriage never materialised and Juan went on to marry Margaret, daughter of the Emperor Maximillian, and died from a fever six months after his wedding aged just 19.[12]

For the next few years Katharine remained in the royal nursery with her sister Bridget. In overall charge was Lady Elizabeth Darcy who came from solid gentry stock, and she had a team of nurses who reported to her along with rockers and a wet nurse. To ensure that she was suitably nourished to feed the princess, a physician would have stood over the wet nurse at every meal to monitor her diet.[13] Katharine's nurse was Mrs Joan Colson, wife of Robert Colson, and in July 1480 Robert and Joan 'nurse of the king's daughter Katharine' were granted 'the custody of all lordships, manors, lands and services, and other possessions late of Christopher Bewfere of Hychin, c. Hertford … during the minority of John his son and heir, with the marriage of the latter'. This was a generous grant which enabled the Colsons to receive the revenue from the lands and arrange John's marriage. As the grant was only in force during John's minority, on 5 November Edward further granted the couple £5 a year for life including arrears from Easter. All this suggests he took a close interest in the upbringing of his daughter and was very happy with the care Joan had given her. In fact, Edward habitually treated the nurses of his children generously. This should come as no surprise as Katharine's parents were attentive and not as remote as might be expected. Her mother's apartments were often full of music, laughter and fun as her ladies danced and played games, and sometimes the king himself joined in, one time dancing with his 6-year-old daughter, Elizabeth.[14] The Plantagenet sisters were close, their parents caring and Katharine's early years were spent in this happy and secure family environment. But when she reached the age of 4, everything changed.

On Wednesday 9 April 40-year-old Edward IV died, possibly from a stroke, and although he had been ill for ten days no one expected his death. Katharine's brother Edward was now king, but at 12 years old was just a little too young to rule in person. Henry VI began to exercise his royal prerogative when he was 15 years old, and it was these mere three years that altered the course of history. The shocking events of the spring and summer of 1483 which left 'experienced politicians gasping'[15] and Edward IV's brother, Richard, Duke of Gloucester king, are so well known not to require detailed rehearsal here. What is important to note is that these events changed the lives of Katharine and her family forever and led to one of the greatest mysteries of all time when Edward V and his brother Richard, Duke of York, were placed in the Tower of London and never seen again. As the implosion of the Plantagenet dynasty began in the blood bath of 1483, it revealed that family ties provided no protection, and while this is not the place to discuss the fate of the princes, by 1515 it seems that Katharine herself believed that one, if not both, of her brothers had perished and this profound event made her, understandably, very protective of her own son.[16]

Initially, however, everything proceeded as expected. The royal council including the queen and her eldest son from her first marriage, Thomas Grey, Marquess of Dorset, met and the new king's coronation was set for 4 May. Then shocking news reached the queen; her brother Anthony, Earl Rivers, and her younger son from her first marriage, Richard, had been arrested at Stony Stratford on the orders of Gloucester who had taken possession of the king's person. Elizabeth Woodville had lived through the Wars of the Roses during which her brother-in-law, George, Duke of Clarence, had been involved in the murder of her father and brother, and she had no reason to trust her remaining brother-in-law now. In the early hours of Thursday 1 May, she gathered her children and fled from the Palace of Westminster to the Abbott's Palace within Westminster Abbey to claim sanctuary. All around the abbey grounds people could be seen running, carrying boxes and household items for the queen's use. To enable faster and easier access into the Abbey, walls were broken down and the chaos continued all night. Although 4-year-old Katharine was too young to understand what was happening, she would have been unsettled by the tension and upheaval all around her. Nor could she have known how much her life was about to change, for she entered sanctuary as a royal princess and left it ten months later as a bastard.

Sequestered in sanctuary, the date of Edward V's coronation came and went and on 16 June a deputation, including Henry Stafford, Duke of Buckingham, arrived. Although Buckingham was her brother-in-law and had been brought up in her household, he felt no loyalty towards the beleaguered queen and every persuasion was used to obtain possession of her youngest son, 9-year-old Richard, Duke of York. With Gloucester's men outside, Elizabeth feared that if she refused, her son would be taken by force, and reluctantly she handed him over. With Edward IV's remaining son now under Gloucester's control, the direction of travel changed. On 22 June, Edward IV's marriage to Elizabeth Woodville was sensationally declared to be invalid due to his supposed precontract with Eleanor Butler (née Talbot) and Katharine and her siblings were declared 'bastards, and unable to inherit or to claim anything by inheritance'.[17] On 24 June the queen's brother Earl Rivers and her son Richard Grey were executed at Pontefract and Edward V's reign ended the next day. On 6 July Gloucester was crowned King Richard III at Westminster Abbey and the two princes, Katharine's brothers, gradually disappeared from view until they were seen no more. By December, disaffected Yorkist exiles had accepted Henry Tudor as their candidate for the throne with Katharine's sister, Elizabeth, as his queen, suggesting they believed the princes were dead.[18]

Elizabeth and her daughters were now at the mercy of a man who had shown himself to be both violent and unpredictable, while the Abbott's Palace was completely surrounded by armed guards under the command of John Nesfield so that 'the whole neighbourhood took on the appearance of a castle and fortress'.[19] In 1484 Richard was 32 years old and might rule for many more years, therefore Elizabeth knew that they could not remain in sanctuary and this intolerable situation forever. Thus, in March 1484, after ten long months, Elizabeth and her daughters left sanctuary, and she has been criticised for this, but in reality she had little choice. However, she did her utmost to ensure their safety by forcing Richard to make a public oath, his private assurances not being enough. Swearing on holy relics before 'my lords spiritual and temporal' and the Mayor and Aldermen of London, Richard significantly vowed not to imprison them 'within the Tower of London or other prison'. Aware of how volatile and suspicious Richard could be, he was also made to promise that if 'any evil report be made to me of them or any of them by any person or persons that then I shall not give thereunto faith or credence nor therefore put them to any manner punishment before that they or any of them so accused may be at lawful defence and answer'.[20] To be forced to make such a public oath was not a compliment to any king, but it was a testament to Elizabeth's shrewd judgement as she tried to protect what was left of her family in the only way open to her.

The world in March 1484 was very different to the one Katharine had been born into. She was now the illegitimate daughter of a deceased king whose future no longer lay in the hands of a protective father but in those of a distrustful and potentially hostile uncle. Richard knew that each one of Edward's daughters were possible figureheads for rebellion, which is why he had posted armed guards around the Abbot's Palace to prevent their escape. He now had to ensure that any husband they married would be someone upon whose loyalty he could depend, as their children, especially male children, could pose a dynastic threat. He was certainly aware that support for Henry Tudor was dependent upon him marrying Princess Elizabeth, who was now 18 years old.

It is not known for certain where Elizabeth and her daughters resided during Richard's reign. Agnes Strickland claims that 'some obscure apartments in the palace of Westminster are supposed to have been the place of her abode',[21] while Hall states that Elizabeth Woodville's daughters were received into Richard's palace, and Vergil that they were received into his court. The most likely scenario is that Elizabeth and her daughters were initially brought from sanctuary to nearby Westminster Palace, which was both a royal household and the administrative headquarters of government. Keeping Elizabeth close would make sense if Richard intended to pressurise her, which evidence suggests he did. After emerging from sanctuary, she wrote to her son, Dorset, urging him to abandon Henry Tudor and return to England. Opinions are divided over her actions with some believing she did this willingly as she now saw reconciliation with Richard as the only way forward. Realistically, it is unlikely she would have sought the return of her son knowing the danger he would be in, and more plausible that Richard forced her to write the letter.

After initially being accommodated at Westminster Palace, did Elizabeth and her daughters remain there? Alison Weir has discussed David Baldwin's theory that they might have been sent to John Nesfield's manor of Heytesbury in Wiltshire, the same Nesfield who had been in command of the guard surrounding the Abbot's Palace. Furthermore, in his oath of 1 March Richard pledged to pay 700 marks a year in four instalments for Elizabeth's maintenance, but these funds were to be paid to John Nesfield not to Elizabeth, while Nesfield was also to 'attend upon her'. Residing at Nesfield's manor under house arrest is therefore a credible suggestion. Weir also notes that Princess Elizabeth visited this small village many years later suggesting that she had a link to it, and this indicates that Elizabeth's daughters were allowed to reside with her.[22] These living arrangements mean that for two years Katharine was in the constant presence of her mother, something that would not have happened under normal circumstances, but whether it brought them closer together is not known. More importantly, she was in the company of her siblings and the bond with her eldest sister deepened over this challenging period.

With the death of their father, the marriages of Katharine and her sisters were now in the gift of their uncle and either in 1484 or 1485 Richard III arranged the marriage of Princess Cecily to a member of his household. Ralph Scrope was the younger brother of the king's supporter, Thomas, Lord Scrope of Upsall.[23] He was a much less illustrious husband than Cecily could have once expected, but it was his modest status and loyalty to Richard that were the deciding factors.[24] This marriage reveals the status of husband that Richard was likely to provide for Katharine had he continued to reign, a far less grand match than the future King of Spain. In the end though, it would not be Richard who arranged her marriage but someone much closer to home.

As Richard's reputation continued to plummet and ugly rumours swirled that he had poisoned his wife in order to marry Princess Elizabeth, his own niece, the threat of invasion grew and Richard took precautions. He despatched Princess Elizabeth to his double moated stronghold, Sheriff Hutton Castle in Yorkshire, where she joined her cousins, Edward, Earl of Warwick and his sister Margaret, the orphaned children of George, Duke of Clarence. Whether any of Elizabeth's sisters were sent here is not documented, but as it was imperative that Edward IV's daughters did not fall into the wrong hands it would be surprising if they were not also sent to Sheriff Hutton. If this was the case, 6-year-old Katharine would have found the residence very pleasant and a change from the house arrest she had endured over the past year. Although primarily a military construction, it was also comfortable and grand while the household was presided over by her Yorkist cousin, John de la Pole, Earl of Lincoln, son of Edward IV's sister Elizabeth. When the little group at Sheriff Hutton saw the approach of riders, including Robert Willoughby, in the last week of August 1485, they waited with trepidation to hear the latest news of Henry Tudor's invasion; who was their king, was it Richard or Henry, and how would this affect their future? For some, the outcome would bring stability, even prosperity, for others imprisonment and ultimately death.

The Battle of Bosworth took place on the morning of 22 August 1485. Although it changed the course of history and established the Tudor dynasty, it was all over in no more than two hours. Fighting bravely on foot to the last, the examination of Richard III's skeleton reveals that it was one of two severe head wounds that killed him. While Henry Tudor savoured his triumph, he, nevertheless, faced the same dynastic threats as his predecessor had, and his immediate actions reveal he was fully aware of this. One of the first orders Henry VII gave was to Robert Willoughby. He was sent to Sheriff Hutton to take possession of Edward, Earl of Warwick, the 10-year-old son of the Duke of Clarence. According to Polydore Vergil, 'Henry, not unaware of the mob's natural tendency always to seek changes, was fearful lest, if the boy should escape and given any alteration in circumstances, he might stir up civil discord. Having made for the castle without delay, Robert received the boy from the commander of the place and brought him to London.'[25] Henry had every cause for concern because, by right, Warwick should now have ascended the throne, and it is indisputable that his claim was stronger than Henry's. Warwick was the only direct male descendant of Edward III via his fourth son, he was also descended in the female line from his second son. He had only been prevented from ascending the throne during Richard III's reign by that monarch claiming that Clarence's children were 'barred by his attainder for high treason from any claim to the crown'.[26] But this was questionable, and when judges considered Henry Tudor's attainder under the Yorkists they agreed that 'the King was responsible and discharged of any attainder by the fact that he took on himself the reign and was King'.[27] In comparison, Henry VII's claim was via the illegitimate Beaufort line of his mother, Margaret Beaufort, who was the great granddaughter of John of Gaunt. Gaunt was Edward III's third son, but the Beauforts were the result of his relationship with his mistress, Catherine Swynford. Although Gaunt eventually married Swynford and their four children, born out of wedlock, were declared legitimate by Richard II, it is clear that there were many loopholes to Henry's claim, which could easily be exploited.[28]

Along with Edward, Earl of Warwick, Henry also ordered that the rest of the group at Sheriff Hutton should be conveyed to London. Although he would never publicly admit it, and did everything to prove otherwise, Henry knew that his accession to the throne depended on his promise to marry Edward IV's heir, Elizabeth, thus securing her person was imperative. It was also important to take control of her sisters and the sister of Edward, Earl of Warwick. Thus, the little group was brought to London and placed in the household of someone whose loyalty was beyond question; Henry's mother, Margaret Beaufort, Lady Stanley. On 24 February 1486 a warrant ordered the payment of £200 to Margaret Beaufort because 'our most dear mother, at our singular pleasure and request, of late had the keeping and guiding of the ladies, daughters of King Edward the IVth, and also of the young lords, the duke of Buckingham, the earls of Warwick and Westmoreland to her great charges'.[29] As Polydore Vergil states that Princess Elizabeth 'was brought to her mother in London', we can assume that Elizabeth Woodville had also arrived at Margaret Beaufort's household, Coldharbour, and that it was here that Katharine, her sisters and their mother were reunited.

Meanwhile, Henry VII made his own, more ostentatious way to London as every effort was made to keep the focus entirely on him and not his future wife.

When he approached London in early September the mayor 'and all the citizens came forth to meet him and accompanied him ceremoniously as he entered the city: trumpeters went in front with the spoils of the enemy, thundering forth martial sounds'.[30] In fact, the previously impoverished exile had gone on a bit of a spending spree to assemble a wardrobe fit for a king. Excited merchants hurried across the city with wagon loads of items, and among the luxurious fabrics waiting for him was six yards of cloth of gold, which alone cost the equivalent today of £7,000 per yard. Significantly, three yards of crimson velvet was also ordered to make roses, the Tudor emblem, to decorate his horse harnesses. Altogether, Henry spent the equivalent of nearly half a million pounds in one week![31]

Those first weeks following Bosworth were ones of frenetic activity involving rewards to Henry's allies and friends, arrangements for the coronation and the first meeting of his Parliament. On 30 October Henry was crowned at Westminster but was crowned alone, a move calculated to demonstrate that he ascended the throne in his own right and not by right of his wife. However, when his first Parliament met, the benefits for Elizabeth Woodville and her daughters were immediately apparent. She was restored to her dignity as queen dowager as if 'no act of Parliament had been made against or touching her in the time of Richard III late, in deed and not of right, king of England'. More importantly for Katharine, the act that had declared Elizabeth's marriage to Edward IV invalid and their children bastards, was stated to be 'void, annulled … and of no force nor effect'. The contents of the act were not rehearsed, as was usual, as Henry wanted no part of it remembered. This is understandable as it had compromised his wife's right to the succession and he ordered every copy to be destroyed. Crucially for Katharine, he was not only re-instating his wife's dynastic claims but also her sisters'.[32]

Katharine was a royal princess once again and in 1486 the event that the whole country had been waiting for finally took place. Following 'the humble request of all three estates of the realm', on 18 January King Henry VII married Princess Elizabeth.[33] Although no account of the marriage survives, her sisters and mother would have attended and for Katharine, who had spent the last two years in an atmosphere of fear and uncertainty, it would have been a wonderful moment. As the newly married king and queen smiled and acknowledged the shouts of joy of their subjects, they made an impressive couple. Henry VII, just short of his twenty-ninth birthday, was an attractive man. His 'open, bold and commanding' face had high cheekbones, chiselled features and a little dimple in his chin. His eyes were small, blue and piercing and he boasted a shock of thick red hair. Although not as tall as Edward IV, he was nevertheless of above average height standing at six feet one inches with a slim, well-built and strong physique. Elizabeth, just short of her twentieth birthday, was very pretty with expressive eyes and a face that exuded kindness and serenity. Her hair was long and hung about her shoulders and, like her father and husband, she was also of above average height being five feet eleven and a half inches tall. It is not surprising that she was described by contemporaries, on more than one occasion, as being a 'handsome woman'.[34] Now that Elizabeth was queen, Katharine, her sisters and their mother felt more secure than they had in a long time. They knew she would do all in her power to protect and care for them for she had 'remarkable respect for her parents' and an 'almost incredible love towards her brothers and sisters'.[35] This depth and longevity of feeling is borne out by her privy purse expenses. In 1502, nineteen years after the disappearance of her brother Edward V, she made a gift of cloth to a woman who had been nurse to the prince, and also twelve pence to 'a man of Pontefract' who claimed to have lodged her uncle, Anthony, Earl Rivers, in his house 'in time of his death'.[36]

In March 1486 Henry VII granted Katharine's mother her dower, which had been denied to her by Richard III, and by 26 March she was in possession of 'Cheynegatis' or Cheyneygates, the Abbot's house at Westminster where she set up home with her daughters. On 10 July she signed an eleven-year lease which allowed for her possession from the previous Easter. The lease specified that she was to have the 'mansion' with 'all the houses, chambers, easements and other appurtenances thereunto belonging'. The yearly rent of £10 was reasonable considering its size and location. However, it could be regarded as a strange choice as this was where the family had lived in sanctuary after the usurpation of Richard III, and it must have held traumatic memories for them all. On the other hand, the rent was affordable and it was close to Westminster Palace, which meant she could maintain her own household yet remain in close contact with her daughter, the queen.[37] Cheyneygates therefore became the first settled home 7-year-old Katharine had known since her father's death.[38] The fledgling dynasty and the family's security further increased when, on 20 September, Elizabeth gave birth to a son and heir, Arthur, at St Swithun's Priory, Winchester, having dutifully trekked the sixty miles to the legendary seat of Camelot at her husband's behest.[39] At the prince's christening Katharine's immediate family held prominent roles, including her sisters Cecily and Anne, while throughout the country there were celebrations. In the churchyard at Winchester two pipes, or casks, each containing approximately 126 gallons of wine, were set so that 'every man might drink enough'. As this was equivalent to 1,008 pints in each cask, it can safely be said that everyone would indeed have drunk enough![40] It is hard to believe that just six months after this joyous occasion of family unity, John de la Pole, Katharine's cousin, fled the realm to help raise an army whose aim was to overthrow Henry VII and remove Prince Arthur from the line of succession.

The plot is believed to have involved a young boy named Lambert Simnel who had been trained by a priest to impersonate Edward, Earl of Warwick. As Warwick did indeed have a superior claim to the throne and was the nephew of Margaret, Duchess of Burgundy, this implausible scheme gained her support, and she provided troops. Even though Henry VII had the real Warwick in his possession, and paraded him through London to St Paul's to prove that Simnel was an imposter, this did not deter de la Pole from fleeing the realm and joining the conspiracy.[41] As he knew full well that the real Warwick was incarcerated in the Tower, his actual intention was probably his own accession with Simnel a mere stalking horse. Amid these betrayals and the threat of invasion, Katharine's life was once more turned upside down when her mother was suddenly deprived of her dower lands, barely twelve months after receiving them, and they were re-assigned to her daughter.[42] She also abandoned the home she had established for herself and her daughters at Cheyneygates and retired to Bermondsey Abbey where she would remain until her death.

Some historians have claimed that, due to a variety of motives, Elizabeth Woodville was involved in the conspiracy resulting in the seizure of her lands and expulsion from court by an angry and suspicious Henry VII. However, it is highly unlikely that she would have supported the claims of John de la Pole, or the son of her hated enemy George, Duke of Clarence, over her own grandchild. A more plausible reason is economic. Dower lands were granted by the king to his queen as part of the marriage settlement to enable her to maintain herself and her household, and also to provide support during her widowhood. However, evidence suggests that Henry VII was struggling to provide an adequate dower for his wife. Even after Queen Elizabeth was assigned the lands previously held by her mother, Henry VII had to make further provision for her in 1492 by granting her lands upon the death of her grandmother, Cecily, Duchess of York, because the lands she currently held were 'insufficient to maintain the queen's dignity'.[43] Yet even after this, she was often in debt and sometimes forced to pledge her plate as security for loans. Significantly, the grant of 1492 was made just before Henry VII led an invasion force to France, and was the main reason for it, while in 1487 he was facing an invasion. Therefore in 1487, as in 1492, he was at risk of losing his life in combat and wanted to ensure his queen was provided for should the worst happen. As such, the re-assignment of the lands was probably made with the agreement of Elizabeth Woodville. The fact that she continued to enjoy cordial relations with her daughter and son-in-law until her death, also argues against her involvement in the conspiracy. She continued to receive gifts from Henry and was always addressed in warm terms. In May 1488 he described her as 'our dear mother' and in December 1490 as 'our right dear and right beloved queen Elizabeth mother unto our most dear wife the queen'.[44] In 1489 when the queen had retired to her chamber for the birth of her second child, her mother was with her as she had been for the birth of Prince Arthur, and along with Margaret Beaufort welcomed a French delegation which included one of her de Luxembourg kinsmen, something the king would not have allowed had he considered her a threat.[45] The choice to retire was probably Elizabeth's own, and at around 50 she may have been suffering from ill health. But she was not isolating herself from her family as Bermondsey Abbey was opposite the Tower and not far from the Thames, thus visits could easily be made. The prior and monks were required to support her, as per the deeds of their charter, and she was a pious woman whose will suggests she fully embraced her new religious life at the abbey, her final sanctuary. Eight-year-old Katharine was now fully dependent upon her sister, the queen, who immediately took responsibility for her. Meanwhile, the dynastic importance of this Plantagenet princess was at the forefront of the king's mind.

From the beginning of his reign, Scotland was a belligerent neighbour. As early as September 1485, orders were issued to the northern counties to raise local troops in preparation for a Scottish invasion.[46] This threat from the 'backdoor' of England was something Henry could not afford, and on 3 July 1486 a truce was signed by both parties in London, and ratified in October. The truce contained a clause for a meeting in March 1487, the purpose of which was to prolong it 'and add the tie of a three-fold marriage treaty'.[47] Significantly, one of the proposed brides was Katharine. This is not surprising as Henry only had one child, his son and heir Arthur, as his daughter Margaret would not be born until 1489. Therefore, if he wanted to conduct multiple diplomatic marriage negotiations, he would have to look elsewhere, and this would naturally be to his sisters-in-law. While three marriages were discussed, Katharine's appears to have been the one that was the main focus of negotiations. The marriage proposed was between 'the High and Mighty Prince James Marquis of Ormond, Earl of Ross, Lord of Brechin and Navar' and the 'Right Noble Lady Katharine' daughter of the 'Right Noble Prince Edward the Fourth late King of England Sister to the Right Excellent High and Mighty Princess Elizabeth now Queen of England'.[48] This was agreed in November 1487 and shortly afterwards James was created Duke of Ross and Earl of Edirdale.[49] Because of Katharine's youth, the marriage would not take place for some years, by which time Henry could expect to have more male heirs, be more secure on his throne and therefore less worried about sending his dynastically important sister-in-law off to Scotland. The other two proposed marriages included one between 35-year-old James III and Elizabeth Woodville, and a marriage between James III's heir and one of the remaining unmarried daughters of Edward IV. In November 1487 this was Anne or Bridget as Mary had died in 1482. They were placeholder brides, and the fact that neither princess was named was deliberate. Henry wished to leave the option open for one of his own, as yet unborn, daughters to marry the future King James IV, and this is exactly what happened.[50]

At first glance, the Scottish match appeared to be a good one for Katharine. Born in 1476, James was close in age to her and both were the offspring of a king, James being the second son of James III. As his wife, Katharine would become Duchess of Ross, Marchioness of Ormond and Countess of Edirdale, meaning she would outrank her elder sister, Cecily. Whether she would have been keen to marry into this violent family if she had known all the facts is another matter. Her future father-in-law, James III, ascended the throne aged just 8. When he was 11, he was seized by a group of ambitious magnates who mercilessly dominated him to gain promotions. Once he came of age, he was opposed by his half uncles and his brothers, one of whom died in mysterious circumstances, possibly at James' hands. In 1488 he faced a rebel army whose ranks included his own son and heir, the future James IV, and he was killed on 11 June after a skirmish.[51] James III's death brought an end to the marriage plans and for Katharine's future husband, ended all hope of matrimony. No other wife was ever proposed for him as his brother intended him for high office in the church. In 1497 he became archbishop designate of St Andrews but was never consecrated and died suddenly in January 1504, the second of Katharine's proposed husbands to pre-decease her.[52]

In 1489 Queen Elizabeth gave birth to her second child, Margaret, and on 28 June 1491 the couple's second son, Henry, was born. Prince Henry's christening must have given Katharine the opportunity to carry out her first, high-profile ceremonial role. Just as her sisters, Cecily and Anne, had played important roles at the christenings of Arthur and Margaret, so Katharine, now aged 12, must have done at Prince Henry's christening. Although she could not have known it, her nephew, the helpless baby she may have carried to the font, would prove to be both the saviour and persecutor of her family. Unfortunately, as no record of Henry's christening survives, this significant moment in Katharine's life remains unevidenced. The first time we do 'see' Katharine at a ceremony, it is a much sadder affair, the hurried funeral of her mother who died on 9 June 1492 aged around 55. Elizabeth Woodville's departure from this world is in stark contrast to her sensational arrival on the national stage following her marriage to Edward IV. Her will stipulated that she was to be buried with Edward at Windsor 'without pomp or costly expense done thereabout'. As she had few worldly goods to leave to her children, she could only give them her blessing. However, 'such small stuff and goods that I have', she wished to be used to settle her debts and for the health of her soul, and 'if any of my blood will any of my said stuff or goods ... I will that they have the preferment before any other'.[53]

On Whitsunday, Elizabeth's body was taken from Bermondsey Abbey and transported to Windsor by boat, arriving at the chapel at eleven o'clock at night. There were no bells, no solemn dirge, and she was immediately buried in the vault with her husband where her coffin was discovered in 1789; 'the decayed parts of a stout wooden coffin, a skull, and some bones, were found over the king's coffin'.[54] Two days later her daughters, Anne, Katharine and Bridget, arrived 'by water' accompanied by their sister-in-law, Cecily Bonville, Marchioness of Dorset, and other family members. On Wednesday a requiem mass was held, during which Katharine and her sisters knelt at the head of the hearse with their gentlewomen behind them, and the next day the sisters made their offerings. Anne offered the mass penny on behalf of the queen who was close to giving birth to her fourth child and unable to attend. Katharine and Bridget each offered a piece of gold, approaching the altar and returning to their places while carrying their own trains. However, the herald recording the ceremonies was shocked at this slap-dash funeral. He complained about the make-shift hearse 'there was nothing done solemnly for her saving a low hearse, such as they use for the common people' and instead of poor men in black gowns holding large new candles, there were merely twelve old men holding used candles and stubs. Indeed, Livia Visser-Fuchs and the late Anne Sutton have pointed out that the 'apparent omissions of protocol noted by the herald-narrator are difficult to assess'.[55] Euan Roger has recently proposed that Elizabeth died from the plague which would explain the need for a hasty burial. Having succumbed to a contagious disease, the fear of infection and miasmatic air was the driving force behind the hasty interment. Once this was done, the funeral rites could begin without the body being present for the safety of all in attendance.[56] It was a sad and somewhat shabby end for a woman who had blazed so brightly and been loved and hated in equal measure.

These first tumultuous years of Katharine's life had a lasting effect on the woman she would become. She had been a princess, a bastard and a princess once again, witnessed family betrayals and been in fear of her life. Her composure, wariness and reserve were traits formed over these years, along with a desire to direct her own life, something she would realise many years later.

Chapter 2

1495–1502

Lady Katharine Courtenay

In her young life, Katharine had already been proposed as wife to the future King of Spain, and to the son of the King of Scotland, but in 1495 negotiations for her marriage finally came to fruition. The backdrop to this marriage, and that of her sister Anne, was the advent of another pretender who was to torment Henry VII for six long years. In 1492, 18-year-old Perkin Warbeck began to make claims that he was Richard, Duke of York, the youngest of the princes in the Tower. Initially supported by Charles VIII of France, who wished to deter Henry from defending Brittany against French ambitions, Perkin then travelled to the court of his 'aunt' Margaret, Duchess of Burgundy, who welcomed him with open arms. By 1494 he had also won the support of the Holy Roman Emperor, Maximillian, who was the step son-in-law of Margaret, Duchess of Burgundy.

The year 1495 was a particularly unpleasant one for Henry VII. The discovery that his step-uncle, Sir William Stanley, had flirted with the idea that Warbeck might indeed be the Duke of York and that 'if he were sure that the man was Edward's son he would never take up arms against him'[1] unnerved the king. Tried for treason, his alleged arrogance sealed his fate and he was executed on 16 February 1495. Meanwhile Warbeck was welcomed at the Scottish court by James IV. He arranged an honourable marriage for him to the beautiful Lady Katherine Gordon, provided Falkland Palace as a base for him and his 1400 supporters, and planned an invasion of England in support of his claims.[2] As the bodies of the two princes had never been found, it was impossible for Henry to claim with certainty that they were not alive. This, combined with Warbeck's facial similarity to Edward IV, his height and gentlemanly demeanour, made him a credible pretender. For the queen and her sisters, it was a stressful period and they must have secretly wondered whether he was indeed their brother. While the discovery that he had survived the coup of 1483 would be joyful, it would also threaten the position of the queen's children and the torn loyalties must have been unbearable. It is in light of this threat that the marriages of Katharine and her sister Anne took place. As in 1487, when Henry hastily arranged the marriages of Princess Cecily and Margaret, daughter of the duke of Clarence, to men whose loyalty he could be sure of, he did so again now. Furthermore, if he had married Katharine into the Scottish royal family as once planned, she would now be the sister in-law of James IV and there is no doubt that he would have induced her to recognise Warbeck as her brother. Marriage within England was therefore safer, and the husbands chosen for both princesses were sons of experienced military leaders whose allegiance and expertise Henry needed.

On 4 February 1495, twelve days before the execution of Sir William Stanley, 19-year-old Anne married 22-year-old Thomas, Lord Howard who would become infamous during the reign of Henry VIII as the third Duke of Norfolk and uncle of Anne Boleyn. The Howards had been caught on the wrong side at Bosworth, but the subsequent loyalty of Howard's father, the Earl of Surrey, and his martial experience ensured the reversal of the family's fortunes. In the same year 16-year-old Katharine married 20-year-old Sir William Courtenay, son of Edward, Earl of Devon, in the 'King and the Queens presence where some officers of armes have be present'.[3] A parliamentary ratification detailing the land settlements for the couple were similar to those made for Anne and Thomas Howard. The Earl of Devon granted lands in Devon and Somerset to Henry, Duke of York, Thomas Marquess of Dorset, Edmund de la Pole and others to his use, which were to pass to William and Katharine after his death. This ensured they would pass intact to William and Katharine while providing the earl with an income during his life.[4] However, if William and his father died without male issue the lands were to revert to the king and his heirs forever, and as William was Devon's only son this was a distinct possibility.

Although the final choice of spouses was the king's decision, it was the queen who conducted all the negotiations, made all the arrangements and provided significant financial contributions towards them. It is even possible that it was she, and not the king, who purchased William's wardship and marriage for a sum which required yearly payments. As late as 1535, a payment of £120 was received by William and Katharine's son for 'the wardship and marriage of William Courtenay, son and heir of Edward, late earl of Devon'.[5] The parliamentary ratification was augmented by an indenture which would have detailed any contributions the queen had agreed to make towards Katharine's maintenance, as the couple did not yet have access to any landed income. Unfortunately, only Anne's indenture has survived but as both brides were in similar situations, arrangements for Katharine are likely to have been similar. In Anne's indenture, drawn up between the queen and the groom's father on 12 February 1495, the queen pledged to subsidise her sister. She agreed to pay for her food and drink, eight members of staff, seven horses and also arranged to pay the earl £120 per year, significantly, the same sum paid yearly for William's marriage.[6] Furthermore, we know that by 1 October 1501, if not before, Katharine was a member of the queen's household and in receipt of a generous yearly payment of fifty pounds.[7] The above reveals the considerable on-going expense that the queen was happy to discharge on her sisters' behalf, and the crucial role she played in their lives.

Katharine was now the future Countess of Devon, and as staunch Lancastrian supporters the background of the Courtenays could not be more different from that of the Howards. Several family members had been executed in that cause including William's grandfather, Sir Hugh of Boconnoc, while his father had joined the rebellion against Richard III and fled to Brittany to join the future Henry VII.[8] Knighted on 7 August 1485 before Bosworth, he was created Earl of Devon on 26 October 1485 making him one of the richest and most prominent nobles in that county.[9] From the beginning of the reign he was active in maintaining law and order, especially in Devon, Cornwall and Somerset, and was appointed a Justice of the Peace in every year of Henry's reign, except three. He fought for Henry at Stoke in 1487 and was part of the king's campaign to France in 1492 bringing a retinue of ninety-nine men.[10] Clearly, Henry wished to reward Devon and, through this marriage, maintain his allegiance. Within two years, Henry VII's new brothers-in-law had met the king's expectations, the Howards leading forces against a tax rebellion in Cornwall in June and against the King of Scotland in July 1497. When Perkin Warbeck arrived in Cornwall in 1497, he gained the support of the disgruntled tax rebels, which swelled his small force to 8,000, and on 17 September they besieged Exeter which was ably defended by Devon and his son William. The situation was tense as Warbeck attempted to burn down the gates. The citizens, who could not prevent their destruction, flung 'heaps of wood on the blaze' and 'so increased it that the flames completely filled every approach to the gates and kept the enemy from entry'. Warbeck then attempted to scale the walls with ladders 'hoping that in the meantime the citizens, overcome either by fear or by lack of supplies, would voluntarily surrender the town'.[11] Meanwhile 'lord Edward Courtenay earl of Devonshire and lord William his son, a man of great force and valiantness' and their retinue 'with all speed came into the city of Exeter and helped the citizens, and at the last assault the earl was hurt in the arm with an arrow, and so were many of his company, but very few slain'.[12] Having been repelled, Warbeck's followers began to desert him and by 5 October he was a prisoner in Henry's hands at Taunton Castle.

Although Katharine's marriage was motivated by politics and the couple themselves had little say in the matter, it was genuinely hoped that a bride and groom would be happy with the spouse chosen. Contemporary descriptions of William were positive; he was 'valiant' 'strong in mind and in body', 'brave and noble'. Katharine was dignified, composed, but she combined this with kindness and gratitude, especially to those who served her well no matter how lowly their status. We don't know what William looked like, but we do know that he was athletic with a strong physique. Likewise, no portrait of Katharine survives, although one or more must have been commissioned during the reign of her nephew, Henry VIII. A contemporary representation, but not portrait, of her in glass suggests a woman who was attractive rather than pretty, with strong facial features, a regal bearing and long fair hair.[13] What the couple felt about each other can never be known for sure; no letters survive between them and only small clues are left which might give an inkling. In her will many years later, Katharine remembered her husband, making arrangements for three priests to pray for his soul.[14] She would attend requiem masses in his memory throughout her life, while he made her an executor of his will. When they married in 1495 they already had much in common, such as their unstable childhoods. Following the Earl of Devon's flight to Britany, he was attainted leaving his son, aged just 8, in a vulnerable position. It is not known where William was during this period, but his maternal grandfather, Sir Philip Courtenay, was in favour with Richard III being one of his Knights of the Body, and it is possible that William was with him. Upon the accession of Henry VII, his father returned, and the family were restored to wealth and prominence. To 10-year-old William, the new Tudor king must have appeared a hero, something which is tragic and ironic considering later events.

In 1487 William was created a Knight of the Bath on the occasion of Elizabeth's coronation, and in 1492, aged 17, he accompanied his father as part of the royal army that crossed to France to lay claim to the French crown.[15] In October they laid siege to Boulogne but by 3 November the Treaty of Etaples was concluded, which provided Henry VII with much needed revenue and a promise from the French king that he would give no more support to Perkin Warbeck. William was among those who accompanied several nobles, knights and their interpreters when they rode out to meet and receive the French representatives.[16] Although the fighting had been short, the army Henry VII took to France totalled 26,000 men, and it would have been a heady experience for a young man on his first campaign. In 1494, just a year before his marriage, William was part of a high-profile ceremony in which Katharine's nephew, Prince Henry, was created Duke of York. This creation was strategic, intended to make a statement throughout England and Europe that Prince Henry was the real Duke of York and not the imposter Warbeck who, at the time, was enjoying the hospitality and support of the Emperor Maximillian in the Netherlands.[17] The whole process lasted several days with William taking part on 31 October when he carried the duke's spurs and sword into Westminster Hall for his creation as a Knight of the Bath. On 1 November Henry was created Duke of

York in the Parliament Chamber, and this was followed by a large procession described as 'the best ordered and most praised of all the processions that I have heard of in England'. It included the queen, the king's mother and 'duchesses, countesses, baronesses, and other ladies and gentlewomen'.[18] Katharine, now aged 15, would have been among the queen's ladies and on 9 November several days of celebrations began, marked by jousting, tournaments, suppers, dances and prize giving. Katharine and William were married a few months later, and this occasion would have provided a perfect opportunity to become acquainted with one another.

After their marriage they spent time at the family estates in Devon, where Katharine would one day make her home, and also enjoyed access to a London residence. This was located on Warwick Lane in the shadow of St Paul's Cathedral and was a large and impressive building. It had an outer gate suggesting a court yard, while John Stowe claimed that the earl of Warwick was able to house a retinue of 600 men here in 1457–1458.[19] Over the next seven years Katharine fulfilled her wifely duties by bearing at least two sons and one daughter. Her son Henry and daughter Margaret were very close in age, being born between 1498 and 1499.[20] We don't know who was the elder of the two, but we do know that Henry was the eldest son because his arms, which can be seen in the stained-glass windows of Wimborne Minster St Cuthberga, include the label of three points denoting the eldest son.[21] Edward was the couple's youngest child, born between 1500 and 1501. We would expect Katharine to name her first-born daughter after her sister the queen, so an elder daughter likely died young with the second daughter, Margaret, named after the king's mother.

Upon his marriage, William became brother-in-law to the king and might have hoped for appointment to the royal household or to administrative office, but this did not happen. Thomas, Lord Howard found himself even more underused while the young Duke of Buckingham and the Earl of Northumberland were given no meaningful responsibilities either.[22] We know that Henry liked to have men around him who combined ability with loyalty proven over many years, so perhaps it is not surprising that William and the others were given no role. However, Henry did like 'to have the great peers around him at important occasions of state',[23] and this is where William did find a role. The king was an enthusiastic spectator and judge of tournaments and jousts, and it was in this area that William shone, becoming one of the best jousters at Henry's court. He was such a superstar that he left an indelible impression on the future Henry VIII, which would stand him in good stead many years later.

To be a successful jouster you needed to be athletic, physically strong and courageous. Jousting was dangerous; one of the most serious injuries Henry VIII ever sustained was during a joust, while one of his favourite courtiers, Sir Francis

Bryan, lost an eye. You also had to keep your nerve as there was huge pressure to excel and give reputable and impressive displays. The purpose of the joust, especially when foreign dignitaries were present, was to overawe and impress spectators with the martial prowess and equestrian skills of the nobility; the king's honour depended on it. The marriage of Prince Arthur to Catherine of Aragon in 1501 was one of the most high-profile events of Henry VII's reign, and the fact that William was chosen to joust as part of the wedding celebrations is proof of his skill.

The princess finally arrived at Plymouth on 2 October and began her long journey to London, where she was met outside the city by her future brother-in-law, 10-year-old Prince Henry, accompanied by an impressive retinue of fifty-one nobles and churchmen in their best finery including 'the lord William of Devon'.[24] Accompanying the princess into the city, William would never have experienced anything like it. The London streets were full, people hung out of windows, or were dangerously perched on window ledges, to get a look at the new princess. Several pageants were stationed at points throughout which required the huge snaking procession to stop. Catherine, as gracious as ever, listened intently to the actors earnestly delivering their lines praising her and Prince Arthur, but due to the language barrier probably didn't understand a word they said![25] The wedding itself took place on 14 November at St Paul's Cathedral and the entire area must have had a carnival atmosphere about it, with wine flowing outside for all to enjoy. As she arrived at St Paul's, Catherine's train was borne by Katharine's sister, Cecily, and the wedding ceremony itself was spectacular, with bride and groom wearing white satin. Once the wedding was over the jousting and tournaments could begin, and the first of these took place four days later at Westminster.

The area before the hall and the palace was prepared, with sand put down for 'the ease of the horses' and a tilt was constructed along with a strong, substantially built stage, garnished with hangings and cushions for the royal spectators and their guests. Waiting in the wings were the stars of the show, William and his fellow jousters. First the challengers entered led by Katharine's cousin Edward, Duke of Buckingham, then the defenders, of which William was part, all in a succession of elaborate floats. William arrived 'in a red dragon led by a giant, and with a great tree in his hand' and his friend Henry Bourchier, Earl of Essex 'in a great mountain of green'. The combatants then rode round the field 'doing their obedience and courtesy to the king' and the jousts opened with the 23-year-old Duke of Buckingham running against Katharine's half-nephew, 24-year-old Thomas Grey, the new Marquis of Dorset.[26] The rest of the field then jousted and 'such a field, and jousts royal, so noble and valiantly done, have not been seen nor heard'. Afterwards, the king hosted a banquet in Westminster Hall where Katharine was present and watched her sister Cecily dance with Prince Arthur and Prince Henry dance with his sister Margaret. This joyous celebration was very much a family affair. Two days later another sumptuous banquet took place in the Parliament chamber where Katharine and her sister Cecily sat at the queen's table 'the table of most reputation of all the tables in the chamber'. The illustrious guests were served five courses, each course including seven dishes, followed by fruit, wafers and ipocras. If they were able to move after all this food, there were then disguisings and dances!

There were further jousts over the following days, and on Wednesday the tilt was removed in order for a tourney to take place. This included mounted combatants fighting each other with blunted weapons. William and his friends Essex and Dorset were among the defenders and made an impressive entrance onto the field 'so courageously advancing their horses and coursers' that the sight was 'so pleasureful and so goodly that unto it in times past have not be seen any like'. Using spears, William and his opponent used 'such strength and power that they broke many and divers staves each upon other'. Next they fought with swords 'full eagerly and valiantly' before departing the field to prepare for the next event which entailed fighting on foot with spears over a barrier at waist height. Again, William and his fellow defenders made the most spectacular entrance in a ship which fired gunshots throughout the combat! On the following day, yet more jousts and tourneys took place with the final event involving the dramatic sight of all combatants fighting in the field at the same time 'lashing at each other many strokes …. Some of their swords were broken of two pieces, and some other their harness was hewn of from their body, and fell into the field.' In the evening there was another banquet in Westminster Hall at which William and the rest of the combatants received rewards. These included precious stones and rings of gold for having 'manly upheld and maintained the noble deeds in jousts and tourney the four days past'. Barely had William and his comrades drawn breath after this frenetic activity, than another round of celebrations and jousting began.[27]

On 25 January 1502, at the palace of Richmond, Henry VII's eldest daughter, Princess Margaret, was betrothed to King James IV of Scotland. The ceremony began with a mass and a sermon in the palace chapel. The king and queen were accompanied by a large contingent of lords, ladies and ecclesiastics among whom were 'The Lady Katharine the Queens Sister' along with 'The Lord William of Devonshire'. Afterwards, they processed from the chapel to the queen's great chamber where the proxy marriage took place. Immediately the ceremony ended, the trumpeters standing at the end of the chamber 'blew up, and the loud noise of minstrels played, in the best and most joyful manner'. After those present had dined, the celebratory jousts began. William was part of the team which again included Essex and Dorset, and everyone 'ran so very well, that it was a great pleasure to have seen them'. The following morning Princess Margaret, now known as the Queen of Scots, came into the queen's great chamber. On her behalf, the principal Officer of Arms 'gave thankings to all those noblemen, that had taken pains and charge to joust for her sake, which full well and notable had accomplished the same'. The prizes were then given out, the Officer of Arms declaring 'Rayne de Shezells and Charles Brandon had right well jousted; John Carr better, and the Lord William of Devonshire best.' As such, the 'Queen of Scots, by the advice of the ladies of the court, gave them praise with thankings'.[28]

This was the highpoint of Henry's reign, with two dynastically important marriages secured and his wife by his side. It was also the highpoint of William and Katharine's life together. After this moment their lives changed forever, and in a matter of days William would be arrested and taken to the Tower.

Chapter 3

1502–1509

Traitor's Wife

rather taken of suspicion and jealousy ... than for any proved offence or crime.[1]

WWilliam Courtenay's circle included the privileged young aristocrats who orbited Henry VII's court. This was entirely appropriate, and he could not have imagined the devastating consequences that would result from his choice of friends. Edmund de la Pole, Earl of Suffolk, was the brother of John de la Pole, Earl of Lincoln, who had lost his life at the Battle of Stoke when Edmund was just 15 years old. As the son of John, Duke of Suffolk and Elizabeth, sister of Edward IV, he was Katharine's cousin. Thomas Grey, second Marquess of Dorset, was Katharine's half-nephew and the two would maintain a close bond for the rest of their lives. Finally, there was Henry Bourchier, Earl of Essex, whose mother, Anne, was the sister of Elizabeth Woodville, meaning he was another of Katharine's cousins. Described by S.J. Gunn as a man who 'danced and jousted his way through the reign',[2] he would outlive all his companions and die doing what he loved best, breaking his neck after falling off a young horse in 1540 aged 68.[3] For these young men the world was their oyster. They trained for tournaments together, experienced the excitement and adrenaline rush of danger together, and in the evenings recalled the day's events over good food and wine. These family ties and shared activities created a strong bond between them, but in 1498 something happened which changed everything; Edmund de la Pole committed murder.

According to Hall's Chronicle, Edmund 'being stout and bold of courage, and of wit rash and heady, was indicted of homicide and murder, for slaying of a mean person in his rage and fury'.[4] The person in question, Thomas Crue, was apparently a plaintiff in a case under consideration by Henry VII's council, and the murder was alleged to have taken place in the parish of All Hallows Barking by the Tower. Even worse, William Courtenay and two more of Suffolk's friends, Thomas Neville and William Brandon, were reportedly involved.[5] Whether the murder resulted from an unseemly street brawl that got out of hand, or was connected to a case in the Court of King's Bench involving some Yorkshire lands which had belonged to Edmund's late father, is unclear. If it was related to the land case, it is possible that Edmund's financial desperation had caused him to lose his temper and snap.

Edmund's older brother John had been his father's heir upon whom many manors had been settled. When he was killed in 1487 and posthumously attainted, all those manors and the significant revenue attached to them, were forfeit to the crown. Thus, when Edmund came of age in 1493, he lacked sufficient income to support the dukedom and had to accept an earldom instead. As part of this agreement, Henry VII granted him certain of his brother's manors but charged him the huge sum of £5,000 payable in yearly instalments of £200 to enter his inheritance.[6] Edmund, innocent of his brother's crimes, was paying the price for them. Therefore, almost from the moment he entered the earldom of Suffolk he was financially oppressed by the king.

By 1499 he had been summoned to king's bench twice over the situation with his father's Yorkshire lands, but he failed to appear and incurred a fine, making an already difficult situation worse. The murder of Thomas Crue occurred in the middle of all this and Edmund was indicted, but Henry VII stopped the proceedings which might have been calculated to place Edmund under an obligation to sue for pardon. According to Hall 'because he had been brought to the king's bench … and arraigned' which, 'he reputed to be a great maime and blemish to his honour' he 'shortly after for this displeasure fled to Flanders, without any licence or safe-conduct given him of the king, to the lady Margaret his aunt'. Rather than pride, another reason might have been the financial penalties which he knew would be imposed to obtain such a pardon, and this left him at the end of his financial tether. In 1503 the annual income from his estates was valued at approximately £876 for 1503–1504,[7] meaning the £200 on-going yearly payments for entry into his inheritance accounted for a quarter of his income, let alone further fines.

Whatever the main reason, in July 1499 Edmund fled from England without the king's permission, swiftly followed by Henry's ambassadors who threatened Philip the Fair, Duke of Burgundy, with a trade embargo if he sheltered the earl, and he was forced to return. Although he was not imprisoned, the situation for Edmund and those around him now became much worse. First, he had to grant certain lands to the king until he had paid £1,000 for their release,[8] which heaped debt upon debt as the financial stranglehold in which he found himself continued to tighten. Second, with stealth, Henry VII mobilised his spies and double agents who insidiously began to seep into every part of Edmund's life. According to Polydore Vergil, Henry VII 'dealt gently with the earl after his first flight, so that by maintaining this attitude for a period he might at length acquire information concerning some conspiracy, which he considered had been hatched between the earl and several other persons'.[9] To Henry VII, Edmund was a dynastic threat because he possessed a plausible claim to the throne. Edward IV had become king through the claim of his father Richard, Duke of York. Edmund was the Duke of York's grandson who had connections in high places, his aunt Margaret, Duchess of Burgundy, being the step-mother-in-law of the Emperor Maximillian. Thus, he had potential access to funds and troops should he decide to launch his own claim to the throne, just as his elder brother had.

In November 1499, using a failed escape attempt as pretext, Henry VII executed the innocent Edward, Earl of Warwick, a prisoner in the Tower since the age of 11. Henry had been under pressure from Ferdinand and Isabella of Spain to remove this threat before they would conclude the marriage of their daughter to Prince Arthur. Following Warwick's execution, the Spanish ambassador eagerly informed his masters that 'not a doubtful drop of royal blood remains in this kingdom, except the true blood of the king and queen, and above all, that of the lord prince Arthur'.[10] Clearly, the last thing Henry needed was another Yorkist pretender, thus Edmund's family and friends found themselves under surveillance. His wife's movements were monitored by the Earl of Oxford, a staunch ally of Henry VII who was powerful in East Anglia where Edmund's power base lay, while his servants were interrogated and some fined for not appearing before the king and council to answer questions about Edmund's time overseas.[11] For William, the situation would have been very uncomfortable as loyalty to his friend placed him in a difficult position with an increasingly suspicious king. However, on the surface Edmund appeared to have been accepted back into the royal fold; he was re-appointed to the Suffolk bench and in May 1500 was among those, including William, who accompanied the king and queen to Calais to meet Philip, Duke of Burgundy. Likewise, the following year William received a grant also seemingly suggesting that the king was not harbouring any suspicions of him.

On 15 March 1501, eleven months after Edmund first fled to Flanders, William received the following:

Grant during pleasure to the king's servant, William Courtenay, knight, son of Edward earl of Devon, for his daily and diligent attendance on the king's person, of an annuity of 50 marks a year at the receipt of the exchequer.[12]

Most historians have viewed this as a sign of Henry's favour, but is there another interpretation? First, this grant was in force 'during pleasure' not for life, meaning it could be revoked at any time. Second, William was not appointed to a specific or prestigious post, instead he was just to be in daily attendance upon the king.

Therefore, the purpose of this appointment is more likely to be surveillance. William was to be in the king's presence daily, thus not at the family estates in Devon where he could be plotting to raise men in Edmund's cause. Henry wanted him where he could keep an eye on him, or rather, where his spies could keep their eyes on him. Whether William was aware of this sinister motive is not known, but five months later, in August 1501, Edmund again fled from England. The timing could not have been worse as Catherine of Aragon was due to arrive for her marriage to Prince Arthur within months. Henry had only just eliminated two Yorkist claimants, in the persons of Perkin Warbeck and Edward, Earl of Warwick, to assuage the concerns of Catherine's parents, but now he was faced with the same situation all over again; a rogue Yorkist pretender at large in Europe. It was not only concerning, it was embarrassing. For William and Katharine, Edmund's departure was to have terrible consequences, which would become apparent five months later when William was suddenly arrested.

According to Desmond Seward, Henry VII 'had a feverish obsession with Edmund de la Pole',[13] and this fear is understandable in light of the actions of the Emperor Maximillian. He had told Edmund's friend and fellow jouster, Sir Robert Curzon, that if he 'might have one of king Edward's blood in his hands, he would help him to recover the crown of England and be revenged upon Henry ... Upon this the said duke of Suffolk was by the lord Curzon ascertained, and so departed out of the realm of England.'[14] Sadly for Edmund, he was to be a mere pawn on Maximillian's chess board as the emperor, aided and abetted by his son, Philip, Duke of Burgundy, probably never seriously intended to provide an invasion force for his claim. What Maximillian really wanted was the presence of Edmund in his territories and the leverage this gave him in negotiations with Henry VII. As the king's desperation to get Edmund back intensified, his army of spies, agents and double agents went into overdrive, Sir Robert Curzon joining them. He eventually betrayed Edmund and, as the king's man, became a mole in his camp.

With such subterfuge, it is difficult to be certain of the facts and what William's involvement was, if any. He is only mentioned by name in one mysterious deposition, which included information gleaned, by an anonymous informant, from one of Edmund's associates, William Hussey. Hussey stated that, within five or six nights of his departure in August 1501, Edmund 'banqueted privily in a place in London with lord Marquess, lord Essex, lord William of Devonshire, and left them there and departed, and with him Sir Thomas Green'. This had come to the attention of Henry VII, which is not surprising as William had been under close surveillance since March 1501, and Hussey asked the informant to let Edmund know of this. These four friends often dined together, so that in itself does not prove they were involved in Edmund's schemes. Edmund, when later confronted by the informant, defended them for this very reason 'it happened so often times that we were in each other's company together, but to say they knew of my departing that I p … you they did not, and Sir Thomas Greene was in no such company'. However, the partially legible deposition went on to claim that Edmund told both William and Dorset that he had given them each a horse and issued them with instructions. The suspicion that this was part of the logistics of his departure further implicated William and the marquis. Also embroiled was William's father as the deposition declared 'a little before his departing' Edmund dined with the earl at the Courtenay family residence on Warwick Lane. Not only that, the earl 'came to his outer gate to receive him with great reverence' causing many to suspect that Edmund's planned flight was not unknown to him 'but he was thereunto agreeable', and also that he planned to put land near his holdings in the south-west at Edmund's disposal. When confronted with this, Edmund astutely noted that there was many 'pretty castings of eyes made to any countenance that was showed me'; in other words, anyone who knew him and socialised with him was automatically under suspicion.[15] Unfortunately, a letter Edmund wrote showing concern for those suffering for his actions in England would not have helped matters if it had come to Henry's attention. In May 1502, just over three months after William's arrest, he wrote to Maximillian of 'the danger in which my good friends are, and will yet be every day more and more whilst awaiting my arrival'.[16] In 1506, while William was still in prison, Edmund wrote to Henry himself requesting that his brother 'and all such gentlemen and other persons' in prison for his sake should be released and restored to their goods and lands'.[17] The letter merely drew attention to Edmund's closeness to these individuals and inevitably deepened Henry's suspicions.

There has always been uncertainty over the actual timing of William's arrest, with historians variously believing it took place in February or March 1502. However, evidence suggests it was earlier. On 24 January 1502, the marriage agreement of Princess Margaret to James IV of Scotland was ratified and the betrothal itself was celebrated on Saturday 25 January.[18] William jousted as part of the celebrations immediately following the betrothal and the next day, Sunday 26 January, he was declared to have jousted the best. On Thursday 30 January another joust was held involving a smaller number of combatants. Among those missing were William and his friends, Thomas, Marquess of Dorset, and Henry, Earl of Essex. From 1 February 1502, it is clear from payments made out of the queen's privy purse expenses that Queen Elizabeth was maintaining the children of Katharine and William Courtenay.[19] While she had made gifts of clothing to them prior to this, at Christmas 1500 and Easter 1501,[20] it is questionable whether the queen, whose finances were constantly stretched, would have assumed total responsibility for them prior to William's arrest. It must not be forgotten that their grandfather was the Earl of Devon and in a position to contribute to their support. Therefore, the fact that they were under the queen's care from 1 February 1502 suggests that something dramatic had happened, and this must have been the arrest of their father. Alison Weir, accepting that William was arrested in late February, proposed that Elizabeth knew of this in advance and consequently assumed immediate control of them in early February, prior to his arrest.[21] However, this would have required a considerable amount of deception as she could hardly take charge of the couple's children without some explanation, but neither could she warn them of William's impending arrest. It is doubtful that she was capable of this, especially in light of her close relationship with her sister, and it is more likely that William was arrested soon after Sunday 26 January, which explains his absence from the joust on the following Thursday. Significantly, his friends Dorset and Essex, who had also been accused of 'banqueting privily' with Edmund de la Pole, were similarly missing from the joust, and it is possible that all three had been taken in for questioning. According to Polydore Vergil, William's arrest occurred within a few days of the marriage celebrations for Prince Arthur, which is obviously incorrect. Vergil has clearly got the events mixed up, and it was actually within a few days of the betrothal celebrations for Princess Margaret.[22] The question is: Was William really conspiring against his own brother-in-law, Henry VII?

When William was seized, he was not the only one. Edmund's younger brother, William de la Pole, was arrested at the same time, and later they were joined in the Tower by Sir John Wyndham, Edmund's stepfather-in-law, and Sir James Tyrell, who as deputy of Guines Castle, Calais, had met with Edmund after his flight in 1499. Tyrell and Wyndham were tried and executed on 6 May 1502 and, according to Polydore Vergil, all those arrested were condemned to death except William Courtenay and William de la Pole 'since they were less incriminated'.[23] Hall's *Chronicle*, which describes William as 'a man of great nobility, estimation and virtue' stated that both Williams 'were rather taken of suspicion and jealousy' than 'for any proved offence or crime'.[24] One of the strongest pieces of evidence that William had not acted maliciously against the Tudor regime was the behaviour of Queen Elizabeth. Payments were made from her privy purse expenses on 30 May 1502 for materials and clothing for her brother-in-law. The items included cloth for shirts, a night bonnet, the making of a russet gown and fox fur for the same.[25] Even if Elizabeth was showing kindness to William for her sister's sake, it is doubtful she would have done so if she believed he had been conspiring against her husband, and thus, her children. It does seem unlikely that he was plotting against his wife's family. His situation under Henry VII was materially comfortable and also honourable, his wife being the queen's sister. If Edmund de la Pole took the throne his wife would be merely a cousin of the king and, while he could count Edmund a good friend, friendships can change. A strong motive for his involvement in the conspiracy is therefore lacking.

The extent of his guilt, if any, was no more than a suspicion or knowledge of what Edmund was planning and his failure to inform the king, and he would have been in an invidious position; if he had informed Henry of Edmund's plans, it would have been tantamount to signing the earl's death warrant. Prophetically, his own son would find himself in a similar situation some thirty-six years later. The attainder of 1503–1504 which condemned him concerned the forfeiture of lands held by him on 1 July 1499, meaning the king believed he had knowledge of, and involvement in, Edmund's activities as early as his first flight in July 1499. However, William does seem to have been particularly singled out for reprisals when we consider that the Marquess of Dorset and the Earl of Essex, both of whom were reported to have been at the banquet with Edmund, were not imprisoned and nor was William's father who had also been accused of dining with Edmund and promising support. In 1513, when William's son, Henry, petitioned Henry VIII for restoration to certain lands, the petition stated that his father had been attainted of high treason as a direct result of 'the sinister means and untrue information of certain malicious and evil-disposed persons made unto your most noble father of famous memory'.[26] If there is any truth in this, then it is most likely connected to the Courtenay lands.

When Thomas Courtenay, fourteenth earl of Devon was executed after the battle of Towton in 1461, most of the family lands were forfeit to the crown and the male line of the senior branch was extinguished. In 1485 Henry VII elevated Edward Courtenay, William's father, from a younger branch of the family and bestowed upon him the title and most of the Courtenay lands. However, the fourteenth earl had sisters and one of these, Elizabeth, married Sir Hugh Conway. Conway had been a go-between for Henry VII and his mother while the king was in exile in Brittany and he enjoyed Henry's favour. He became a Knight of the Bath, a Knight of the Body and was employed in Henry's service. It was probably in 1487 that Conway married Elizabeth Courtenay, for in that year Edward Courtenay conveyed eight manors to the couple, possibly at Henry's behest. Significantly, they were to descend to Elizabeth's heirs but, as it is likely she was of a mature age and beyond childbearing, the grant of the manors to Conway would not be permanent. Elizabeth died before 1497 and Conway re-married, but he still retained the lands, including the manor of Hillesden, Buckinghamshire, which he designated his country seat. Around 1500 he began investing considerable amounts of money in Hillesden including the creation of a deer park, commissioning lavish alterations to the adjoining parish church and maybe even building a new manor house.[27] As such, he would not appreciate having to hand over Hillesden to the Courtenay family, and William's arrest and subsequent attainder, which also disinherited his young sons, was very much in Conway's interest. As Edward, Earl of Devon, had no other heir, on his death the estates of the earldom would pass to the crown. As a royal servant who enjoyed Henry's favour, Conway might therefore hope that the lands he currently held on a temporary basis, would eventually be granted to him on a more permanent arrangement. So, could Conway have been one of those 'malicious and evil-disposed persons' who used 'sinister means and untrue information' to bring down William Courtenay for his own ends?

Conway certainly had a rather mysterious career in Henry's service. In 1504 he was appointed Treasurer of Calais, and naturally he travelled there to take up his post. Shortly afterwards, a report reached Henry VII from John Flamank, son-in-law of the lieutenant of Calais, Sir Richard Nanfan. Flamank's report makes damning allegations about Conway's loyalty as it recounts a secret conversation between Conway and several key office holders at the Calais garrison. Apparently, Conway began to speculate about events following the king's death 'for the king's grace is but a weak man and sickly, not likely to be a long lived man'. He claimed to have heard 'many great personages' speak of the succession when Henry was ill some years ago. They mentioned the Duke of Buckingham, Edmund de la Pole, but none mentioned Henry's son, Prince Arthur. On finding out that Conway had not informed the king of this, the others remonstrated with him, but Conway explained 'If you knew King Harry our master as I do, you would beware how that you break to him in any such matters, for he would take it to be said but of envy, ill will and malice.' Conway again speculated on the king's death, mentioning a prophecy that stated Henry would not reign longer than Edward IV meaning he would die in 1507. This shocked his listeners and Nanfan, worried he had heard such words, immediately declared his loyalty to Henry. Conway also expressed doubts about the fidelity of Sir Anthony Brown, Lieutenant of Calais Castle, his wife and Sir Nicholas Vaux, lieutenant of Guines. Flamank then went on to accuse Conway of saying that 'there should be never more popes in Rome after him that is now, neither kings in England after your grace'.[28] The words ascribed to Conway were incendiary, and his arrest should surely have followed, but it did not. In fact, Conway remained in Henry's service, and as Treasurer of Calais, until the end of the reign. This is hard to understand considering Henry's suspicious nature and the shocking things Conway had said. Perhaps this is because, unknown to Flamank, Conway was one of Henry's agents whose words were calculated to test the reaction of his listeners and thus their loyalty. He certainly revealed that he had prior experience of informing Henry about other matters, and the fact that he continued unscathed after such a report points to him being one of Henry's spies. If this is the case, he would be extremely well placed to provide damaging information about William Courtenay. Even if the facts were exaggerated or untrue, Henry might be persuaded to believe the words of one of his own spies, especially one who had served him loyally for many years, and at great personal risk during the period of Henry's exile.

Neither was Conway the only one to cast covetous eyes over the Courtenay estates. Henry VII's hot shot lawyer, Edmund Dudley, generated a lot of income for the king but also for himself. In an indenture of 1508, he purchased the marriage of William Clifford who was intended for one of his daughters 'or such other 'conveable' person' as Edmund might dictate. William was the son of Charles Clifford, who in turn was the son and heir of Jane Courtenay, another sister of the fourteenth earl. She had married first Sir Roger Clifford, Charles' father, and then Sir William Knyvet.[29] On 9 March 1490 Henry VII granted Jane and Knyvet a number of the earldom of Devonshire estates in Somerset and Dorset 'to hold to them and the heirs of the body of Joan', meaning that Charles and his son William stood to inherit.[30] Significantly, the indenture of 1508 stated that 'if it fortune Charles or his heirs to be restored to the earldom of Devonshire or to any lands of the present earl' then provision was to be made regarding a quarter of the lands for the use of his son William and his wife, Dudley's daughter. Stipulations were also included to cover the lands that Hugh Conway currently held in right of his deceased wife. Should these lands come into Charles Clifford's possession after Conway's death, then they were eventually to pass to William Clifford after his father's decease.[31] The vultures were definitely circling the Courtenay estates and while we cannot know for sure who these 'malicious and evil-disposed persons' were, Conway already had motive at the time of William's arrest, while Dudley could have added his voice to the chorus later on when he spied an opportunity for himself.

It does seem that William had been caught up in events beyond his control, and this left his wife and children in a very vulnerable position. Fortunately, they had a powerful defender; immediately after his arrest the queen swooped in and took the Courtenay children under her protective wing. Their father was facing charges of treason, and it could not be guaranteed that their grandfather would not be arrested as the evidence implicated him too. She therefore arranged for Katharine's children to take up residence at Havering-atte-Bower in Essex, a property she was using to rear her horses. Her Master of the Horse Sir Roger Cotton was based there with his wife, Lady Margaret Cotton, and it was Lady Margaret who was put in charge of the Courtenay children. Also sharing the nursery with them was an Edward Pallet, son of Lady Jane Bangham. They also had the use of Sir John Hussey's house within his manor of Dagenhams and

Cockerels which was only four miles from Havering. This meant the children and their servants could vacate one house to be thoroughly cleaned, while they stayed at the other one, which was well under a day's ride away.

In addition to Lady Margaret, the children each had a rocker and were attended by two female servants and a groom. Members of the queen's household also occasionally went to Havering such as Elizabeth Saxilby, one of her ladies.[32] We know this because on 10 May 1502, the queen sent her messenger James Nattres to Havering to bring Elizabeth back. The purpose of Elizabeth's sojourn at Havering might have been to temporarily bolster the staff there until more permanent arrangements were made. Alternatively, she might have travelled there with messages and supplies, and to ensure that the queen's latest instructions were carried out. As a member of the queen's household, Elizabeth Saxilby knew Katharine personally and it would have been reassuring for her to hear directly from Elizabeth how her children were. In addition to staff, the queen also provided various items of clothing for them including a gown of black damask lined with sarcenet and a coat of murrey-coloured chamlet for both Henry and Edward. The children were also supplied with 'hose, shoes, laces, soap and other necessaries'.[33]

While her children remained in Essex, Katharine resided in the queen's household, which provided a safe haven for her during this period of crisis. Unfortunately, the bombshell of William's arrest was followed by another disaster, this time relating to the king and queen. In the early hours of Tuesday 5 April a messenger arrived at Greenwich Palace post haste from Ludlow. The news he brought was so devastating that the council decided only the king's confessor could break it to him. Having gone to the king's chamber and asked all those present to leave, he informed Henry that on Saturday 2 April Prince Arthur had died. The king immediately sent for the queen so they could 'take the painful sorrows together'. When she heard the news and saw the king's 'natural and painful sorrow' she did all she could to comfort him, reminding him 'that God is, where he was, and we are both young enough', meaning they could have more children. Afterwards she returned to her own chamber where her strength failed her, and she collapsed with grief. So inconsolable was she that even her ladies, including Katharine, were unable to comfort her, and they sent for the king who 'of true gentle faithful love' came at once.[34] This terrible loss reveals the closeness that existed between Henry and Elizabeth, and why she was able to act in the defence of her family independently of him. He loved and trusted her, and he knew she would always put his interests and those of their children, first.

True to her prediction that 'we are both young enough', Elizabeth promptly fell pregnant by May 1502 and began to plan a trip to Wales. It has been suggested that this was due to a rift between the king and queen over his arrest of William Courtenay and his reaction to Princess Cecily's second marriage in 1502. This disparaging match had taken place without royal permission and an angry king had stripped Cecily of her lands and banished her from court.[35] It does seem a little unwise for a 36-year-old woman, who had never had the easiest of pregnancies, to travel miles across the country on bumpy roads. However, other evidence points to her closeness to her husband, and perhaps she just needed time away to come to terms with her son's death. She may also have wished to take her sister away from the febrile atmosphere of the court, which was still embroiled in investigations into the de la Pole conspiracy and the identification of guilty parties.

The destination chosen for their visit was Raglan Castle, South Wales, the home of the Herbert family where Henry VII had been brought up as a child. The heir to Raglan Castle was Elizabeth Herbert, cousin to Katharine and the queen through her mother Mary Woodville. In 1502 Raglan Castle was under the control of Sir Walter Herbert, illegitimate brother of Sir William Herbert whose wife was Anne Stafford, another cousin whose sister, Elizabeth, was one of the queen's favourite ladies-in-waiting.[36] The visit would therefore be something of a family reunion, but en-route the party received devastating news after their arrival at Notley Abbey in early July. A messenger from Lady Cotton informed Katharine that her youngest son, Edward, had died.[37] Again, her sister was there for her, paying for the funeral expenses and giving Edward's nurse and rocker payments upon their departure from the nursery. It is unlikely that Katharine attended the funeral, and she was certainly with the queen on 19 July when she handled money for her after they arrived at Woodstock Palace in Oxfordshire. Here more upset occurred when the queen fell ill and one of her ladies became so sick that she was unable to continue the journey. Following so many setbacks, everyone must have wondered whether this ill-fated trip would ever reach its destination, but finally it did. After trundling across the country negotiating muddy rutted roads, the queen, her attendants and cartloads of necessaries finally reached Raglan Castle by 19 August. Here the exhausted visitors had a welcome rest and enjoyed the splendours of the castle and its breath-taking vista for several days. The castle ruins today testify to its former magnificence and allow visitors to enjoy some of the same views as Elizabeth and Katharine did over 500 years ago. Following a pleasant visit, the queen and her ladies took their leave after 24 August and began their slow return to London. In December, Katharine was reunited with her children as the queen had arranged for them to be brought from Sir John Hussey's house to London for Christmas, probably the first time Katharine had seen them in months. Items for their chamber were purchased by the queen, including 'candlesticks, cupboard clothes and other necessaries'.[38]

Once the Christmas celebrations were over, the new year of 1503 did not begin well. Katharine's son Henry fell ill, and it was serious enough for the queen to pay ten shillings on 6 January to 'Richard Bullok surgeon for medicines by him ministered upon the Lord Henry Courtenay'.[39] Fortunately, Henry recovered and Katharine was spared the loss of a second child. By February, the queen and her ladies were at the Tower, and Katharine may have been given permission to visit her husband. If so, it would be the first time they had seen each other in twelve months and the first time since the loss of their son Edward. Looking to the future, they must have hoped that after the birth of her child, the queen would continue to intercede with the king who might relent over William's imprisonment, especially if the child was a boy, which would further secure the succession. Then abruptly, everything changed.

While at the Tower the queen unexpectedly went into labour, and during the evening of 2 February she gave birth to a girl who she named Katharine after the sister who was now her constant companion. Although this was not the hoped-for son, mother and baby seemed fine and the little girl was baptised on Saturday 4 February at the parish church within the Tower.[40] Although no account of the baptism survives, it is almost certain that Katharine attended, probably as godmother to her namesake. Then a few days later to the horror of everyone, the queen's condition suddenly deteriorated. The king immediately sent one of Elizabeth's own messengers, the reliable James Nattres, to Kent for Dr Hallysworth. That Hallysworth was not already in attendance suggests that the decline was sudden, while the requirement for Nattres to travel at night implies real urgency. Nattres needed boat hire from the Tower to Gravesend where the two boatmen were ordered to wait until Nattres returned with the doctor. He also hired horses and two guides because, by the time he reached Gravesend, it had gone dark.[41] While Nattres sped through the night to Hallysworth's house, back at the Tower Katharine and the rest of the queen's ladies tried to keep her comfortable. If Elizabeth was suffering from puerperal fever, at that time a common post-natal complication resulting from lack of cleanliness during childbirth, her suffering would have been acute. The symptoms, which usually occurred a week or ten days after confinement, included a fever, headache and severe abdominal pain caused by the infected and swollen uterus. Finally, she would have become delirious. We can only imagine the atmosphere in the queen's chamber, the stress and anxiety as they tried to sooth their feverish and distressed mistress. Placing cold cloths upon her forehead to ease the fever and headache, holding her hands as she writhed in pain, trying to reassure and comfort her, desperately waiting for Nattres and the doctor, constantly going to the window for any sign of them. It is not known if Dr Hallysworth did arrive in time to treat the queen, but if he did there was nothing he could do for her. She died the morning of 11 February on her 37th birthday and was not long survived by her newborn daughter.[42] For Katharine, Elizabeth's death was one of the greatest, if not *the* greatest, tragedy of her life. She had lost the person to whom she was closest, her sister, her confidant and her protector.

For her husband, Elizabeth's death 'was as heavy and dolorous to the king's highness as hath been seen or heard of'. After appointing the Earl of Surrey and Sir Richard Guildford to attend to the order of her burial, he 'privily departed to a solitary place to pass his sorrows and would no man should resort to him but such his grace appointed'.[43] Before leaving, he did one more thing; he despatched Sir Charles Somerset and Sir Richard Guildford to the queen's household 'with the best comfort to all the Queen's servants that hath been seen of a sovereign Lord with as good words'. By considering the feelings of her servants in this way, he showed remarkable thoughtfulness amidst his own grief. As tradition dictated, the king would not attend his wife's funeral and the 'solitary place' he chose to withdraw to was Richmond. Here, the anxieties of the past year and the immediate emotional reaction to his wife's death became manifest in a physical illness. He developed quinsy, a condition that caused severe swelling and an intensely painful sore throat. Hardly able to swallow or open his mouth, he lay feverish and close to death watched over by his anxious mother who had arrived to nurse him.[44] Meanwhile, arrangements for the queen's funeral reveal that despite her husband's perceived crimes, the king had a certain regard for his sister-in-law. Katharine was appointed chief mourner and she would not have held this crucial position without the king's knowledge and consent. She therefore found herself in the contradictory position of being the wife of a traitor, yet also a royal princess playing a central role in one of the most high-profile events of the period. This was the last service Katharine would perform for her sister, and thousands of eyes would be upon her. While the focus of the funeral procession would be the queen's coffin and effigy, Katharine, travelling behind, would have nearly equal prominence.

On Sunday 12 February, after her corpse had been embalmed and encased in lead within a coffin, the queen's body was moved from her chamber to the Chapel in the Tower. Accompanied by a large entourage, the chief mourner that day was Lady Elizabeth Stafford. At no other point was Elizabeth Stafford named as chief mourner and Katharine would carry out that function for the rest of the funeral ceremonies. As this was just a day after the queen's death, we must accept that Katharine was not in any fit state to fulfil the duties of chief mourner. She would have been up all night with her sister, and then grief-stricken and in shock afterwards. She needed time to compose herself and did not appear as chief mourner until later that day. When she entered the chapel, she was escorted by the Earl of Surrey, father-in-law of her sister Anne, and Henry Bourchier, Earl of Essex, William Courtenay's friend, while Lady Elizabeth Stafford bore her train. Katharine knelt at the head of the coffin alone while the mass was sung then made her offering, followed by the rest of the queen's ladies and 'all the other Ladies and knights with other Gentlemen'. These ceremonies continued every day for the next ten days allowing time for the funeral arrangements to be completed and the effigy to be made. In this period, it was the custom for royal funerals to place a lifelike effigy of the deceased royal personage above the coffin where it would provide 'a focus for the prayers and emotions of the onlookers'. As the queen's death was unexpected, royal craftsmen worked day and night to produce the lifelike, five-foot eleven-inch effigy of Elizabeth of York. The face was carved by Swabian sculptor, Lawrence Emler 'with Fredrik his mate' and a wig was hired for 5s to recreate Elizabeth's hair. The queen's surviving portraiture, based on a lost original painted in the last years of her life 'show a strong facial likeness to the funeral effigy and tend to confirm its status as an extremely accurate portrait'.[45] This is the face upon which thousands looked before bowing their heads, and behind which Katharine rode in that funeral procession over 500 years ago.[46]

After lying in the chapel, the body and effigy were placed in a chariot draped in black velvet and drawn by six horses trapped in black velvet bearing the queen's arms. As the immediate entourage assembled around the chariot, could William see them from his prison? He would have mourned the passing of the queen as she had been kind to him, but he also knew, with dread, that he had lost the greatest intercessor he could have had. As the mourners got into position, Katharine and seven of the queen's ladies mounted their horses which were draped in black velvet and each led by a man on foot wearing a 'demy black gown'. As the procession left the Tower and began the three-mile journey through London to Westminster Abbey, Katharine would have been struck by the thousands of people lining the streets on every side, all there to pay their respects to a queen who had been genuinely popular. Following Katharine and the seven ladies behind her, in horse-drawn 'chairs' were a great number of other ladies, including Lady Anne, Katharine's sister, and the Marchioness of Dorset, wife of her half-nephew Thomas Grey. Next came the citizens of London on horseback and after them a hundred of the king's servants. Preceding them were dignitaries including the Mayor of London, Margaret Beaufort's husband, the Earl of Derby as Constable of England, heralds and a large ecclesiastical contingent. As they made their way through London, from Mark Lane to Temple Bar, it was estimated that 4,000 to 5,000 torches were 'set all the street along of the parish Churches in their best manner'.

Arriving at Westminster Abbey, the coffin was taken inside and placed on a hearse, where several bishops officiated at the obsequies, after which 'the estates and the officers of Arms accompanied the Chief Mourner led by the Lord Marquis and the Earl of Derby to the Queen's Great Chamber to supper'. The next morning at seven o'clock the first mass began. Katharine offered at the first and second masses, and at the third 'accompanied with divers noble ladies', she offered an Angel, before returning to the hearse.[47] Then, without any assistance 'she with the lady Anne her sister went up again and offered for themselves followed by 'the lady Marquess and the lady Elizabeth Stafford and so in order all the ladies mourners two and two together'. The herald describes the presence of 'every of the Queen's sisters' suggesting that Cecily had been allowed to attend despite her disgrace, and Bridget had received special permission to leave her closed order of nuns at Dartford Priory. After the funeral sermon the queen's coffin was lowered into the ground, her chamberlain and gentlemen ushers broke their staffs of office and cast them into the grave and 'there was weeping and sorrowing and so departed'.[48]

The queen's death had left Katharine exhausted and bereft, but help came from an unexpected quarter. By the end of March Henry VII had begun to recover from his illness and he now 'set his mind to reconstructing the future of the kingdom around his second son'.[49] Prince Henry was only 12, and the composition of his household was strictly controlled by his father. It is therefore significant that Katharine joined the young Prince of Wales' household with her attendant groom.[50] This could only have happened with the king's approval, revealing that he did not consider her to be involved in any way with her husband's perceived treason. Her son, the prince's cousin, was also welcomed into the household and was later described as having 'been brought up of a child with his grace in his chamber'.[51] As Princess Mary resided with her brother it is likely that Katharine's daughter Margaret also joined the prince's establishment, especially as there was a strong female presence within it including thirteen gentlewomen.[52] Prince Henry had been very fond of his mother who was more hands-on than most royal mothers. She taught her children to read and write herself, and the prince described the news of her death as 'hateful intelligence'.[53] To help fill this void, Henry VII could think of no one better than the prince's aunt who represented the closest link to his mother. The fact that this also helped Katharine was a bonus, as the king knew this is what his wife would have wanted. A further mark of favour to his sister-in-law occurred on 7 September 1503 when he sent her a gift of £10. In the original accounts he had taken the trouble to insert her surname 'Courtenay' in his own hand to ensure there was no doubt as to which 'lady Katayn' was intended.[54] Katharine's period of residence in Prince Henry's household was happy; she was fond of her nephew and he of her. She is known to have given him two rings as gifts which appear in an inventory of the prince's jewels taken on 14 January 1504. One was a ring of gold and the other 'a little ring with a little triangle diamond'. The prince later gave these away as was his usual practice, and the ring with the triangle diamond was given to Lord Mountjoy, a prominent member of his household who would feature significantly in the lives of the Courtenays later on.[55]

While Henry VII would not go as far as to release her husband, the attainder of 1503–1504 which condemned William Courtenay and others, did include a clause giving the king the option to pardon those named in the bill by letters patent under his great seal. This meant there would be no need for another act of Parliament to reverse the attainder, but any hope that this might happen was dashed when Edmund de la Pole returned to England.[56] In January 1506, on his way to Spain with his wife Juana, Philip, Duke of Burgundy, was blown off course in a storm and forced to land at Falmouth. Henry VII was delighted to welcome the duke to England because he had something he wanted: Edmund de la Pole. While Philip was hosted in style, he was under no illusion that the price of his departure was the earl. And so it was that he agreed to hand Edmund over, although he did extract a promise from Henry that he would be pardoned and restored.[57] Having paid the price of his ticket to freedom, Philip left England taking his tragic wife, Juana, known to history as 'Juana the mad', with him. She had only been allowed a few hours to visit with her sister, Catherine of Aragon, and the two would never see each other again.

On 16 March 1506 Edmund de la Pole was handed over to the king's men at the Calais garrison, and on 24 March he was brought to Dover under armed escort and conveyed to the Tower.[58] Whether William was innocent or not, this would have caused him great concern. Words could be twisted during interrogation, and a person might be induced to say anything if threatened with torture. As he feared, Edmund must have said something incriminating because the situation for William and his friend Dorset deteriorated after the earl's arrival in England. Dorset, who had also dined with Edmund before his departure, was now arrested and on 18 October 1507 both he and William were incarcerated in Calais Castle. With a permanent garrison, this was akin to a maximum-security prison and William's execution now seemed a distinct possibility. According to one chronicler, they 'were kept prisoners in the castle of Calais as long as king Henry the Seventh lived, and should have been put to death, if he had lived longer'.[59] Fortunately for both, Henry VII did not live much longer and with the old king's passing a new reign began, that of Katharine's nephew Henry VIII.[60]

Chapter 4

1509–1511

Reunited

the right noble lord William Courtenay Earl of Devonshire.

Henry VII's death on 21 April 1509 was both painful and angst ridden as he clung onto life in fear for his immortal soul. Emaciated, struggling for breath, he shakily reached out to a crucifix held before him 'enfolding it in his thin arms, kissing it fervently, beating it repeatedly against his chest' before death finally overcame him.[1] Many welcomed the news, looking forward to release from the economic chains with which Henry had bound them, some almost overstepping the bounds of decency in their celebratory tone. Only those who were close to the king, such as his devoted mother, Margaret Beaufort, or those who had glimpsed the more sensitive side of him, mourned Henry VII. Surprisingly, Katharine was one of these. Henry and Katharine had a special bond, their love for Elizabeth of York, and although she resented him for the imprisonment of her husband, she did respect the genuine feelings he had for her sister. He, in turn, had a special regard for her for the same reason and took care of her, not lavishly, but honourably. He did it in part for his wife's sake, but also due to his respect for Katharine in whom he saw something of his queen; amiable, discreet and impeccably behaved. So, Katharine would mourn him, but her priority was the future, in particular her husband's release and the restoration of her son's inheritance.

We can only imagine her disappointment when, on 30 April, an annex attached to the warrant issuing letters patent of general pardon listed all those who were to be exempt from it. At the top of the list were the three de la Pole brothers, Edmund and William who were still incarcerated in the Tower, and Richard who was at large overseas. But the very next name was that of William Courtenay followed by Thomas, Marquis of Dorset. Henry VIII had carefully signed the top and bottom of the list and could not have failed to see the name of 'Will. Cortney, son of the earl of Devon' clearly written there.[2] However, it was only nine days into the new reign and Henry VIII was being advised by councillors who had served his father, and it was probably they who had concerns about William's loyalty. Furthermore, the Courtenay estates were extensive and valuable and, as things stood, they were due to pass to the crown on the death of Williams's father. If Henry VIII restored William he would lose access to them, something which was not to be taken lightly. This was a major decision which Henry needed time to think about, and for the moment Katharine could take comfort from that. Nevertheless, it would have hung over her as she participated in Henry VII's funeral as part of the household of his daughter, Princess Mary.

On 28 May, just two and a half weeks after Henry VII was interred, Katharine's father-in-law, Edward, Earl of Devon, died.[3] This was a disaster because all the Courtenay lands now passed to the crown in accordance with the 1504 attainder against William Courtenay. The earl's will took this into account and made some provision for his grandchildren. Out of the earl's Boconnoc lands, which were not part of the Courtenay inheritance, 50 marks was to be paid annually to Henry until he reached the age of 21 and 50 marks annually to Margaret until she married, on which day she was to receive 1,000 marks. William was to inherit all the Boconnoc lands apart from those set aside to establish a chantry, provided 'he do obtain the king's grace and pardon and be at his liberty ... and keep his due allegiance to the king our sovereign lord and to his heirs kings of England'.[4] While this provision was some consolation for Katharine, it was far less than her son could have once expected. Meanwhile, Henry VIII enthusiastically received the Courtenay estates into his possession, immediately using them as a means of dispensing patronage to his servants, making ten grants between July and October alone. On the positive side, most were granted during pleasure and not for life, but Katharine knew she would need to prepare her approach to her nephew carefully. While nothing could be taken for granted, she was in a strong position. She was the king's aunt and he was fond of her, while her 11-year-old son idolised the king who would want to protect his future. But the biggest problem was gaining Henry's attention amidst so many distractions, and none more so than the one that occurred unexpectedly on 11 June when he married Catherine of Aragon. Prophetically, on 24 April a member of Henry VIII's council had informed the Spanish ambassador that it was unlikely the king would marry her 'because from what they knew of Henry it would burden his conscience to marry his brother's widow',[5] in fact it would take twenty years for those doubts to surface.

Henry VIII's coronation procession on 23 June was a vivid feast of colour, the sides of the streets were hung with rich materials including arras, cloth of gold, velvets, silks of scarlet, crimson and murrey colours.[6] Katharine's cousin, Margaret Pole, had become a close friend of the new queen during their time together at Ludlow where Margaret's husband, Sir Richard, had been Prince Arthur's chamberlain. She was delighted to be recalled to court from the wilderness of her widowhood, and she proudly took part in the coronation procession. Katharine herself was absent, probably because she was with Margaret Beaufort who had hired a house in Cheapside to observe the proceedings in private with Princess Mary. Her sister Anne, Lady Howard, may have been with them as she too was missing from the procession.[7] What none of them could have known is that within a week 66-year-old Lady Margaret would be dead. Perhaps her grief for her son combined with the exertions of the past few weeks had taken its toll. Another suggested cause was the eating of a cygnet, so perhaps food poisoning. Ironically, she had just taken a lease on Cheyneygates, the very residence that Elizabeth Woodville had leased in 1486.[8] With the demise of Lady Margaret, the baton was decisively passed to King Henry VIII and a line firmly drawn under the previous reign.

On 1 July 1509 Henry VIII's household book recorded 'to my lady kateryn upon a Warrant signed for her Reward' the sum of £40, which probably relates to Katharine's services to Princess Mary throughout recent events.[9] Later the same month both Katharine and Margaret Pole were granted annuities to be paid during the king's pleasure. Margaret received £100 and Katharine, described as 'wife of William Courtenay, the King's aunt' received 200 marks, or £133.[10] While the king wished to be kind to his kinswoman, Margaret Pole, her immediate return to royal favour was due to her close friendship with the queen. However, the favour shown to Katharine was the result of her relationship with the king; nevertheless, her husband still remained in Calais. On 10 July the king despatched Sir Thomas Lovell to bring the Marquis of Dorset back to England, and this was followed on 26 August by an invitation for the marquis to sue for pardon.[11] It must have been a gut-wrenching experience for William to witness the departure of Dorset while he remained behind. Furthermore, a letter from Sir Richard Carewe, Captain of Calais Castle, to Thomas Ruthall, Bishop of Durham and secretary to the king, provides no evidence of regal warmth towards him as yet. In the letter, which has an air of desperation about it, a cash-strapped Carewe reminded Ruthall 'as your lordship knoweth right well I have the lord William of Devonshire here in keeping to mine great charge and I have nothing for the keeping of him and my charge nevertheless wherein I beseech you at your goodly leisure to have me in your remembrances unto the king's highness'.[12] Behind the scenes Katharine continued to petition for her husband's release and by the following June, much to the relief of both, William was finally free.

On his arrival back at court, William knew what was expected of him. Henry VIII was an enthusiastic jouster who was determined to excel at the sport, and he wanted talented men around him to compete in the tournaments he would organise. He remembered watching in awe as William carried the field at the celebrations for Princess Margaret's betrothal in 1502, and he wanted to use this superstar in the lists. William, obligingly, put himself through a rigorous regime to regain the fitness and strength needed to live up to the king's expectations. On 1 June 1510 he appeared as an answerer to a standing challenge at the barriers, which involved competing with a blunted casting spear and target, and engaging in one-to-one combat with a blunted sword.[13] His opponent was Sir Thomas Knyvet who at 25 years old was ten years younger, and this bout at the barriers was just the start of a gruelling programme of training to get himself jousting fit. To his credit, in just seven months he had achieved it. On 1 January 1511 Catherine of Aragon gave birth to a son who was named Henry for his father, and William was selected to play a prominent role in the celebrations that followed. A spectacular two-day tournament, the most expensive of Henry VIII's reign, began at Westminster on Wednesday 12 February to celebrate the baby's birth.[14] Four unknown knights with assumed identities issued the challenge: Ceure loyall [Loyal heart], Vailliaunt desire [Valiant desire], Bone voloyr [probable meaning Good valour] and Joyous panser [probable meaning Good hope or Joyful thoughts]. The star of the show was Henry VIII [Ceure loyall], but his co-stars were Sir Thomas Knyvet [Vailliaunt desire], Sir Edward Neville [Joyous panser] and Sir William Courtenay [Bone voloyr]. Looking at the ages of those who made up Henry's top team, Henry himself was 19, Knyvet was 26 and Neville probably around 29. At 36, William was by far the oldest challenger, yet the training he had put in had paid off.

Day one began with a blaze of colour and carnival as the challengers entered the field concealed in a pageant car. On arriving before the queen who was watching from a raised gallery with her ladies, including Katharine, horns sounded and the king and his companions emerged. The answerers then entered the field with equal display, among them was the Marquis of Dorset, William's old friend.[15] That day William and Edward Neville rode about ten courses, the king and Knyvet far more, and it was Knyvet who carried off the prize as best jouster. But Henry stole the show later when he rode his courser before the queen and 'turned the feet of the horse against the tilt and caused him to fling and beat the boards with his feet that it redounded about the place as it had be shot of guns'. After this display he turned to Catherine and 'made a lowly obeisance' and rode sedately into Westminster Hall. Elated by the events of the day and his love for Catherine, he then jumped off his horse and ran to her tent where, Hall reported, he could be seen 'kissing and clyppyng [embracing] her in most loving manner'.[16]

The second day's events have been recorded in the magnificent Westminster Tournament Roll created by the College of Arms, where it is still kept. Apart from its exquisite drawings and vivid colours the roll, nearly sixty-foot-long, is important for another reason; it includes the only known contemporary depictions of William Courtenay, even though they depict him in full armour and helmet that hides his face. On this second day each challenger entered beneath a pavilion which was held above them by footmen and each is depicted on the roll in the following order: first came Edward Neville followed by William Courtenay, then Thomas Knyvet and finally the star of the show: the king. Membrane 9 records William's entrance, which is one big splash of colour. He rode beneath a pavilion surrounded by five footmen, two in front and three behind. The footmen wore doublets that were half grey and half yellow, their yellow caps sported brown or white feathers and their yellow hose was finished off with black shoes. In their hands they carried green and white batons. William himself looked spectacular, clad head to foot in silver armour over which was a blue surcoat set with large gold letters K, for his queen. His magnificent steed was dark grey, the detail of the drawing even revealing the studs in the horse's shoes to prevent it from slipping. Silver armour covered the front of the horse's face, continuing along the top of its neck to its withers, while three large feathers were attached to the top of the bridle between its ears. The front of the decorative bard worn by the horse was red and the back was blue. This was also adorned with large gold letters K and William's chivalric name along the bottom. The pavilion borne above him was made up of panels of crimson and blue damask again set with golden letter Ks. William is depicted once more in the roll, on membrane 24. Here three of the challengers, William, Neville and Knyvet, are lined up at the end of the tilt watching their team mate, the king. William sits upon his horse between the other two, the bridle and reins are red and the lining of the bard is green. The two other challengers are similarly adorned, but the king's appearance is far more ornate and ostentatious enabling him to stand out from the rest.[17]

William's performance on day two was better than day one and he completely trounced Thomas Lucy. Thundering down the tilt he broke two lances on his opponent's body and achieved two attaints [blows], one on Lucy's body and one on his head. In return, the unfortunate Lucy only managed one attaint on William's body. If this was the Sir Thomas Lucy born in Charlecote, Warwickshire, in 1488, then William had defeated a much younger opponent. However, it was a much closer run thing with his next opponent, John Molton. Molton broke two lances on William's body and also gained one attaint on the body. William matched Molton with two broken lances and one attaint on the body, and narrowly took the match by achieving one more attaint on the body.[18] William's performance was respectable, and certainly on a par with Edward Neville's, but compared to the much younger king the difference is clear. Henry ran far more courses, breaking twelve lances and scoring nine attaints to the body and one to the head. In fact, that day it was the king who was awarded the prize for having jousted the best among the challengers.[19] He was brave and chivalrous, he had a wife he adored and now a son and heir. As Henry VIII retired to bed that night he could not have known that he had probably enjoyed the happiest day of his entire life.

Nine days after the jousts Prince Henry died and the 'mirth and gladness' was replaced by sorrow and despair. His small lead coffin was brought by river from Richmond and interred with great ceremony in Westminster Abbey. It lies unmarked on the north side of the Sanctuary area near to the entrance of the chapel of St Edward the Confessor. According to Sydney Anglo, Catherine 'grieved deeply but Henry took the blow philosophically', but this is not the case.[20] According to Hall, his main concern was to comfort Catherine and so 'like a wise prince … he dissimulated the matter, and made no great mourning outwardly'. However, a letter from the French ambassador to the Treasurer of France on 8 April 1511 reveals Henry's true feelings. Carrying a letter of condolence from the French king to present to Henry, the ambassador was advised by Richard Fox and the rest of the Council not to 'present the King's letter touching the death of the Prince or say a word about it at present, as it would only revive their king's grief'.[21]

Although little Prince Henry's death was a severe blow, by May more jousts were being planned as part of the ceremonial rhythm of the court. At the same time, William and Katharine continued to negotiate for full restoration of the Courtenay estates, and Katharine had a trump card up her sleeve. As a daughter of Edward IV she had a claim on the estates of the earldom of March that had only been absorbed into the crown estates on the accession of her father. These lands belonged to the Yorkist family and should have descended to the heirs of Edward IV, but Henry VIII wished to retain them.[22] He revealed that he was prepared to strike a bargain when he came to an arrangement with Katharine's sister and her husband Lord Howard on 1 July 1510.[23] He was also prepared to come to an arrangement with Katharine and her husband, and this was detailed in an indenture dated 12 April 1511. It was agreed that before September 1511 he would restore William and Katharine to the lands of the earldom of Devon, create William Earl of Devon and reverse the act of attainder against him at the next Parliament. William and Katharine were also entitled to those lands held by Sir Hugh Conway and Sir William Knyvet in reversion, meaning that when Conway and Knyvet died the lands would fall back into the earldom estates. In return, Katharine and William were to 'renounce all claim to lands belonging to the earldom of March and Ulster and all other lands purchased by Edward IV'.[24] As it had been passed by act of Parliament, Henry could not simply reverse William's attainder so, as a mark of consideration, he made interim provision until the next Parliament met. On 9 May he reversed the act of attainder by letters patent 'as much as is legally in our power' and the very next day he created 'Sir William Courtenay, husband of the king's aunt' Earl of Devon by Royal Charter.[25] Both these documents were countersigned by Sir Thomas Englefield, a lawyer and trusted adviser of the king who had been assisting the Courtenays in their negotiations.[26] Shortly afterwards Katharine appointed Englefield Steward of Colyton, Devon, 'for good and faithful service rendered'.[27]

As these developments progressed, William continued to take part in the jousts organised for that month. On 1 May, dressed in crimson satin trimmed with green velvet, he was one of the answerers in a two-day joust and took third prize as best jouster, only beaten by the king and his old friend, Henry Bourchier, Earl of Essex.[28] On 15 May there were more jousts, and it is possible that William was again among the combatants. At this time William and Katharine were residing at court where apartments were set aside for them. In late May the court was at Greenwich Palace, and it was here that Katharine must have begun to notice that something was wrong. William became tired, his head ached and he felt uncomfortably hot. Worse of all he began to experience a severe pain on one side of his chest, which became worse when he tried to breath in deeply. After a few days, breathing became more of a struggle and William was forced to take to his bed. Doctors were called, but try as they might they could not alleviate his symptoms, which were getting worse. It became more and more difficult for him to breath, his face was deathly pale and his lips livid while any attempt to move in bed or talk only increased the discomfort. His anxiety and distress became acute as he literally struggled for every breath in a desperate attempt to avoid suffocation. On 9 June William could fight no more and his death, when it came, must have been a relief. He was 36 years old and yet to be formally invested with the earldom he had waited so long to attain.

Polydore Vergil tells us that he died of pleurisy, a condition that was rare in England at the time, which explains his doctors' inability to give him any kind of effective treatment.[29] Although bacterial or viral infection are the most common causes of pleurisy, it can also be caused by trauma to the chest. If this was the cause of William's pleurisy, then the most likely way he sustained such an injury was on the jousting field, either in one of the recent tournaments or in training. The whole point of the joust was to land a blow on your opponent's head or body. The force of such a blow, coming at the end of a lance propelled by a large horse weighing more than half a tonne and travelling at speed, was considerable. It was something a suit of armour could not fully mitigate against. It is a cruel twist of fate that it was this very activity at which William strove so hard to excel, for his family's future and his place in Henry's favour, that probably caused his traumatic demise.

Despite the formal investiture never taking place, Henry VIII declared that William was to be buried as an earl. His body was taken from Greenwich by boat to St Paul's Wharfe. Here many gentlemen and friars were waiting to accompany the coffin to the Friary of the Blackfriars, which lay on the banks of the Thames next to Baynard's Castle. William's standard, helmet and crest, last seen on the tournament field, were now borne before his coffin. His coat of arms was carried by Lancaster Herald, followed by Norroy King of Arms and Garter King of Arms who walked immediately before his coffin. On arriving at the imposing Blackfriars Church a heraldic roll of his ancestors, including his marriage to a princess of England, was on display along with his arms and badges. After the dirge the mourners retired and the coffin was watched all night 'by his servants and friars with lights' and 'at times accustomed an officer of arms with a high voice said ye shall pray for the soul of the right noble lord William Courtenay Earl of Devonshire'.

Appropriately, the chief mourner was Thomas Grey, Marquis of Dorset, while the other mourners come as no surprise being a mixture of friends and associates. These included fellow jouster Sir Thomas Knyvett, Sir Edmund Carew who had fought alongside William in the defence of Exeter in 1497, Sir Thomas Englefield and Sir John Arundel of Lanherne, steward of several of the earldom manors in Cornwall, a position he would hold for many years.[30] John Rowe had been surveyor to William's father and, as a sergeant at law, he would be retained for his legal expertise by Katharine and her son.[31] Richard Fox, Bishop of Winchester, an associate of the Courtenays was also present but, on this occasion, was attending as the pope's ambassador. Following the offerings Dr Standish, warden of the Greyfriars, delivered the sermon during which 'he named him Earl and excused him of all infidelity against his sovereign lord and that he was falsely accused counselling all princes and other great lords not to give hasty credence without sure ground'. William's body was then gently lowered into its final resting place and 'lieth on the south side of the high altar'.[32] At the end of one of the accounts of the funeral is a list of his executors. Unsurprisingly, this included several of the mourners mentioned above but, revealing his confidence in his wife, at the top of the list is written 'The lady Katherine fourth daughter of King Edward the fourth countess of Devon.'[33]

Chapter 5

1511–1519

Widow and Mother

After her husband's death, Katharine's material prospects were not diminished as she now came into sole possession of the earldom of Devon lands for life. This was in accordance with the indenture of 12 April 1511, and the grant was formalised on 3 February 1512.[1] At a stroke, this made her one of the most powerful, wealthy and influential figures in the south-west of England. Paradoxically, the situation was to the detriment of her son who, when he came of age and succeeded to the earldom, would hold the title but not the lands to support it while his mother lived. When William died Katharine was well aware of what she was to receive as outlined in the indenture, and this explains the action she took on 13 July 1511, just over a month after her husband's decease. On this day Katharine stood before Richard FitzJames, Bishop of London, the same bishop who had sung the third mass at William's funeral, and made the following solemn vow:

> In the name of the Father, the Son and the Holy Ghost I Katerine Cowrtneye Countes of Devonshire widow and not wedded ne unto any man assured do promise and make a vow to God and to our Ladye and to all the Companye of Heven in the presence of you worshipful father in God Richard Bishop of London for to be chaste of my bodye and truely and devoutly shall kepe me chaste for this time forwards as long as my life lastith after the rule of Saint Paul. In nominee Patris & filii & Spiritus Sancti.[2]

Some have seen Henry VIII's hand in this as a condition of her restoration to the earldom. By ensuring she was taken off the marriage market it would prevent any ambitious nobleman from benefitting from her wealth and dynastic lineage should she re-marry. However, around the same time Henry also restored Margaret Pole, daughter of the Duke of Clarence and niece of Edward IV, creating her Countess of Salisbury in her own right, and there is no evidence that Margaret was required to take a similar vow. Of course, Katharine, at 33 was of child-bearing age but so technically was Margaret. Although she was 39 years old, it should be remembered that Elizabeth Woodville was still bearing children into her forties. This therefore suggests that the vow was Katharine's decision and Henry allowed her, rather than forced her, to take it. If she remarried, her husband would take control of her lands and her children's futures, and this was something she was not going to allow. In fact, one of the first things she focussed on following her restoration was arranging suitable marriages for her children, neither of which turned out to be straightforward.

In 1514 Henry Courtenay, now aged 15 or 16, received the exciting news that he was to accompany his cousin, Princess Mary, to France where she was to wed the French king, Louis XII. Princess Mary herself was not happy. Aged around 18 or 19, she already had a crush on 30-year-old six-foot alpha male, Charles Brandon, the newly created duke of Suffolk. In comparison, her prospective bridegroom was a 52-year-old man in declining health. Mary's revulsion can only have increased if we believe Peter Martyr's mocking account of their first meeting as he described Louis going out 'to meet his bride like a gay bridegroom, perched elegantly on a fine Spanish war-horse … licking his lips and gulping his spittle'.[3] Louis' eagerness to meet his bride is unsurprising as Mary was one of the most beautiful women in Europe, with golden hair and dainty facial features. While Mary grappled with her feelings and steeled herself to do her duty, Henry Courtenay eagerly prepared for his trip to France unaware that Mary's marital exploits would directly influence the identity of his own bride.

Granted 100 marks pension 'to give his daily attendance upon the French Queen [in] the parts of France' during the king's pleasure,[4] Henry Courtenay and the wedding party left England at four o'clock in the morning on 2 October 1514.[5] On 8 October, Mary and her entourage entered Abbeyville amid a large procession of between 2,000 and 3,000.[6] Henry was part of this ceremonial entry, and the following day he witnessed his cousin's marriage to the French king taking part in the celebratory banquets and dancing that followed. Having survived her wedding night, after which Louis crudely claimed to have 'crossed the river' three times, Mary had to deal with her husband's capriciousness when he dismissed several of her female attendants who had accompanied her from England. Distraught, she sent letters desperately hoping her brother would help but there was nothing he could, or would, do. Respecting a husband's authority over his wife, when he said goodbye to her at her departure, Henry had consigned her 'to the governance of the French king her husband'.[7] However, Louis did allow some of her English attendants to remain, and heading the list of these was Henry Courtenay 'Le Conte de Nonshere'. Also included was Arthur Pole, Margaret Pole's son, and Mary Boleyn.[8]

Things became more difficult for Mary when Charles Brandon arrived two weeks after her wedding. He had been sent to attend her coronation, organise the celebratory jousts and discuss arrangements for a future meeting between Henry VIII and Louis.[9] On 25 October, Louis received him lying in bed with gout while Mary sat obediently beside him. As Suffolk strode in and knelt down by his bedside, the difference between the two men could not have been more marked.[10] The contrast was brought sharply into focus again at the jousts in November to celebrate Mary's coronation. While Louis reclined on a couch in the spectators stand wincing in pain from gout, below Suffolk led the English team in a particularly furious and violent set of combats in which he excelled and the English emerged victorious.[11] Then, just a month later on 31 December, Louis died.[12] Mary was now in a very difficult position. The new king, the womanising Francis I, was showing more interest in the beautiful young widow than was appropriate while starting to select a range of French husbands for her. Henry VIII, aware of her vulnerable position, immediately sent Suffolk back to France to bring her home. According to Mary, before her marriage she extracted a promise from her brother that if Louis predeceased her she could choose her next husband.[13] However, she began to doubt whether he would keep this promise and, if we are to believe Suffolk, took matters into her own hands by insisting that the duke marry her. Writing to Wolsey, he explained that on his arrival in France 'the Queen would never let me be in rest till I had granted her to be married; and so, to be plain with you, I have married her heartily and has lain with her, in so much as I fear me less that she be with child'.[14] Wolsey informed Suffolk that when the king was informed he took the same 'grievously and displeasantly'.[15]

Henry Courtenay, who was in France while all this was going on, would have been one of the first to find out, no doubt sending letters to his mother informing her of everything. What Katharine felt about her niece throwing herself away on an oafish cad with a marital history as chequered as Suffolk's can only be imagined, but what we do know is that she saw it as an opportunity for her son.[16] In 1512 Suffolk had obtained the wardship and marriage of Elizabeth Grey, who was Lady Lisle in her own right.[17] Lady Lisle's lands were worth around £800 per year and due to his friendship with the king, Suffolk obtained her wardship on very favourable terms agreeing to pay a total of £1,400 in instalments over seven years.[18] Lady Lisle was too young for marriage but contracting to marry her at some point in the future was all that was required for Suffolk to be created Viscount Lisle in her right, and this occurred in 1513 along with a grant of twenty marks a year.[19] Although this intention of marriage was well known,[20] it seems he planned to leave his marital prospects open for as long as possible in case a more advantageous bride presented herself. This was the situation when he married Princess Mary in 1515. Katharine, knowing that Suffolk could not now marry Lady Lisle, immediately approached the king for her hand as a bride for her son. While Suffolk kept his head, the couple were subjected to extreme financial penalties for their transgression and one of these was the surrender of Lady Lisle's wardship. It is not clear if this was the king's idea or whether Katharine's approach prompted the surrender. Whatever the reason, Suffolk relinquished the wardship of Lady Lisle to the king who then sold it to his aunt. Lady Lisle's lands lay in eleven counties including Devon, Cornwall and Somerset, and were worth even more than the Boconnoc inheritance. Together with those lands and the earldom lands, the estates of Lady Lisle would make Henry Courtenay one of the wealthiest nobles in England, and one of the most powerful.

On 3 July 1515, Suffolk surrendered the wardship and marriage of Lady Lisle in favour of Katharine and her son, and on 11 July the wardship was officially granted to them.[21] However, the financial arrangement to purchase the wardship was finalised at Easter which fell in early April that year, just two months after Suffolk and Mary had wed and even before they returned to England, proving that Katharine acted very quickly.[22] Henry VIII, knowing the Courtenay lands could bear the cost, charged a far higher but a more realistic price than the £1,400 demanded of Suffolk.[23] Katharine was required to pay £4,000 in instalments, £166 13s 4d twice a year in February and June, but if she defaulted on the payments the king was to receive the profits of certain manors, including the manor of Sheviock, Cornwall, currently held in trust to meet the instructions contained in her will.[24] Furthermore, she was to receive the wardship of Lady Lisle, 'on surrender (as far as regards the said wardship) by Charles Duke of Suffolk'.[25] This meant that while Suffolk surrendered the wardship and marriage of Lady Lise, he kept her lands and would not be required to relinquish them until she came of age and took livery of them.[26] Therefore, in the short-term Katharine did not gain any economic benefit but did take on a huge financial commitment. She discharged this by using the income from the lands of the Boconnoc estates. These were held in trust for her son and were currently providing him with an annuity of £100.[27] If Henry came of age in his mother's lifetime, these were the estates he would inherit, but they were now under a heavy financial burden and how he felt about this is not known. He would surely have had an opinion about it, but may have had little say in the matter.

In 1515 Lady Lisle was 11 years old, and due to her youth would have been taken to live with Katharine in Devon until she was old enough to marry Henry. During this period, she would have been brought up to become the next Countess of Devon, taught by her able mother-in-law. Katharine had already brought up one daughter, while evidence suggests that her household was a happy one, and this was probably a period of welcome stability for young Lady Lisle. Her father, Sir John Grey, died on 6 September 1504 aged 23 when she was just eight weeks old, placing her birth around July 1504.[28] Her mother, Muriel, was the daughter of Thomas Howard, Earl of Surrey, and sister of Thomas, Lord Howard, Katharine's brother-in-law. Proving that they wished to exercise control over the Lisle lands, the Howards had held the wardship of John Grey whose marriage to Muriel made this influence more secure.[29] Their eagerness to maintain control after John Grey's death landed them in trouble, and in July 1506 a pardon was granted to Thomas, Lord Howard, his brother Edward and others for 'entries without licence' on the manor of Payneswyke, Gloucester, 'lately belonging to John Grey viscount Lisle, deceased'.[30] However, their persistence paid off and in 1507 they were permitted to lease the Lisle lands to the use of Muriel and her second husband, Sir Thomas Knyvet.[31] Knyvet, as we have seen, was a rising star at the court of Henry VIII and a jousting companion of William Courtenay, he was also popular within the Howard family, especially with Edward, Muriel's brother. Knyvet's marriage to Muriel was a happy but tragic one. On 5 August 1512, he drew up his will making her his main beneficiary and appointing her his sole executor.[32] Five days later he was killed, aged just 27, in appalling circumstances when his ship caught fire during an engagement against the French when hundreds of lives were lost. Edward Howard's determination to avenge his friend's death led to his own the following year. When Muriel received the news of Knyvet's death she was six months pregnant with their sixth child. On 13 December 1512 as the birth of her child approached, Muriel made her own will and died in childbirth shortly afterwards. Her will focussed on the futures of her children with Knyvet but no mention was made of her eldest daughter, 8-year-old Elizabeth, Lady Lisle, possibly because her future had been arranged just before her mother's death when Suffolk was granted her wardship on 3 December.[33] As a result of this grant, the Howards were forced to surrender to Suffolk the Lisle lands they had leased.[34] With Suffolk's marriage to Princess Mary, the possibility of obtaining Lady Lisle's wardship and taking possession of the Lisle lands once again must have crossed their minds. Whether they felt Henry VIII's price was too high is not known, but equally their ambitions may have been thwarted by Katharine to whom it was ultimately granted.

There is little evidence of contact between Henry, who now lived predominantly at court, and his future bride who was based in Devon, but a set of his accounts for the period January to March 1519 do include one reference to Lady Lisle. On 3 January he purchased six yards of yellow satin at 7s 6d per yard 'for my young lady'.[35] Shortly after this, at some point before 12 May the unfortunate

Lady Lisle died. On this date her aunt, who was her heir, took livery of her lands and it was to be her husband, Katharine's half-brother Arthur Plantagenet, who would eventually hold the title, Viscount Lisle. Although Katharine would have taken care of Lady Lisle's funeral expenses, we would expect to see some costs in relation to her death incurred by Henry, but none appear. Therefore, as the accounts cover the period to the end of March, Lady Lisle must have died between 1 April and 12 May 1519 when she was aged just 14. There is no record of her burial, but it probably took place in a church near one of her mother-in-law's Devonshire residences. Lady Lisle's death meant that the considerable expense charged against the Boconnoc estates was all for nothing, as Henry never benefitted from either the Lisle lands or the title. While Katharine can hardly be blamed, Henry's next bride was a lady of his own choosing, and it was a choice in which, significantly, his mother had no say.

Turning now to Katharine's daughter, Margaret Courtenay, this lady has received little attention from historians yet she was a granddaughter of Edward IV, sister of the Earl of Devon and someone who expected to occupy a prominent position within the Tudor nobility. Katharine began to look for suitable husbands for Margaret from as early as 1511–1512 when she informed her councillors and legal advisors Lewis Pollard, John Rowe and Sir John Arundel 'that Margaret her daughter was then above thirteen years old, and that by the Grace of God she intended to purvey for her a convenient marriage'.[36] Indeed, by 1515 Margaret was on the radar of the international marriage market. On 16 February Sir Robert Wingfield, English ambassador to the Emperor Maximillian, wrote to the king from Innsbruck that if 'my Lady of Devonshire, the King's aunt, or the Lady Saly[sbury], have marriageable daughters' he believed that the Duke of Milan 'would rather be joined with the King's blood than with any other'.[37] However, arrangements for Margaret's marriage to another gentleman were already well underway in 1515, after an embarrassing rebuff the previous year.

John de Vere, thirteenth Earl of Oxford, had been one of the most important men during Henry VII's reign. He was an experienced battle commander who was powerful enough to keep East Anglia in order,[38] something that became especially important following Edmund de la Pole's treason. Even the christening of Prince Arthur was delayed by three hours to ensure the earl could attend.[39] Another family of approaching prominence in the locality were the Howards. Bosworth had been a disaster for them, but despite his power and prominence in the region, Oxford never took advantage of their plight. He was protective of the Countess of Surrey during her husband's imprisonment, and this generous approach continued throughout the Howards' journey back to favour. As James Ross notes 'his magnanimous actions in the aftermath of Bosworth earned him the respect and goodwill of the Howard family'. These good relations culminated in the betrothal of his nephew and heir, John de Vere, to Anne, daughter of the Earl of Surrey in 1511, with the marriage taking place in 1512.[40] The marriage was a sensible course of action for all, aimed at ensuring peace and stability in the region once Oxford was dead, which occurred a year later in March 1513. Then, something unexpected happened.

In August 1513 the young earl reached his fourteenth year[41] and at some point after this, possibly early in 1514, Henry VIII suddenly threatened to overturn his marriage. He offered him the option of repudiating Anne and taking another wife, and the alternative wife he proposed was none other than Margaret Courtenay. A grant to the Duke of Norfolk dated 29 May 1514 includes the following:

> And whereas the espousals between the said earl and Anne his wife were, during the life of the said late earl, celebrated according to the laws of the Church, the said earl then and after the late earl's death being within marriageable age, viz., within 14 years, it pertains to the King's prerogative to offer him another woman for wife, and the King lately offered him Margaret Courtenay.[42]

Henry was able to do this because the marriage had been conducted when the earl was under the age of 14. According to canon law, now aged 14 he could reject it as it had taken place when he was not old enough to give his consent.[43] The action threatened to disadvantage Thomas Howard, the hero of Flodden, who only a few months earlier had been created Duke of Norfolk with accompanying grants of lands outside East Anglia as reward for his military efforts. It is certain that Katharine was involved in these moves as it was her daughter's hand that was being offered. She would naturally have been keen for such an advantageous match, but the choice was Henry's. While he was fond of his aunt and happy to promote the interests of his cousin, he would not have taken such a decision against his own better judgement. His motives, however, remain unclear. Did he want to bring the new and very wealthy Earl of Oxford into his own family through marriage to his cousin? Or was it part of his plan relating to the advancement of his friend Charles Brandon, who had been elevated to the dukedom of Suffolk at the same time as Surrey to the dukedom of Norfolk? Suffolk, with title and lands in east Anglia was being built up to replace the disgraced and dangerous de la Poles.[44] Did Henry believe he had a better chance of doing this if he was not overshadowed by the Howards? Perhaps he also felt it was unwise for any one family to be too dominant in East Anglia? Whatever the reason behind this astonishing intervention, the marriage did not take place because the young earl refused Margaret's hand. In fact, he didn't just refuse her, he 'utterly' refused her.[45] Of course, he may have been coerced by the Duke of Norfolk, and once the marriage with Margaret had been refused Norfolk was confirmed in his possession of his son-in-law's wardship and the Howards 'inherited Oxford's dominant position in Norfolk and Suffolk, maintaining it for most of the sixteenth century'.[46] Although this might have been a humiliating experience for Margaret, when the young Earl of Oxford came of age in August 1520, both mother and daughter realised she had had a very lucky escape. Within a mere three or four years of this weak and self-indulgent man taking control of his estates, the king and Wolsey had to step in to protect his lands from 'decay' and ensure the correct treatment of his wife.[47]

Despite this rebuff, Margaret was not long without a husband. On 15 June 1514 Pope Leo X issued a dispensation 'for the marriage of Henry Somerset, lord Herbert and Margaret Courtenay'.[48] Lord Herbert was the heir of Charles Somerset, Earl of Worcester, the king's Lord Chamberlain. This meant that one day, like her mother, Margaret would be a countess. In addition, royal blood flowed through Somerset's veins. He was the illegitimate son of Henry, second Duke of Somerset, who was first cousin to Margaret Beaufort. In fact, Edward III was the three times great grandfather of both Somerset and Katharine. Somerset fought for Henry VII at Bosworth and enjoyed a successful career during his reign. Following his marriage to the Herbert heiress, Elizabeth, the king built him up to be 'the most powerful man in south Wales and the crown's principal agent for its government'.[49] It was hoped that Lord Herbert would one day step into his father's shoes and grants had already been made to Somerset and his son jointly for life. It was Somerset, along with Sir Richard Guildford, who had been sent to Elizabeth of York's household in 1503 to give comforting words after her death, and following the decease of his friend Sir Richard Pole in 1504, Somerset took out a loan with his widow, Margaret, to pay for Sir Richard's funeral. It is most likely that Sir Richard had appointed him one of the executors of his will and he was acting in that capacity, and as good lord to his late friend's widow.[50] Somerset was therefore a man prominent within Katharine's extended family and the marriage would serve to strengthen these existing ties of kinship. Following the dispensation issued on 15 June 1514, the marriage took place the following year. In the accounts of 1513–1514 for the Boconnoc estates, it is recorded that £666 13s 4d [equivalent to 1,000 marks] had been delivered to Katharine, and this was evidenced by a bill dated 26 February 1515 testifying that the money was for the marriage of her daughter, Margaret.[51] As previously noted, Edward Courtenay, Margaret's grandfather, had stipulated in his will that she was to be given 1,000 marks on the day of her marriage.[52] But what of the lady herself, what is known about Margaret Courtenay? Until recently, very little, until an extraordinary letter was discovered in the archives at Powderham Castle that briefly illuminates this elusive daughter. As no other letter sent by Katharine's children to their mother has survived, and as it is the only piece evidence which provides any clue to Margaret's character, it deserves to be considered in full.

We know from court documents that Margaret Courtenay, referred to as Lady Courtenay, had been appointed as one of the queen's ladies and had taken her place at court by 1513. As the new year of 1513 dawned, Margaret took part in a magnificent revel for the feast of Epiphany on 6 January. This involved 'the Ryche Mount', obviously a pun on Richmond, which was a huge rock or mountain of gold covered in precious stones, adorned with red and white Tudor roses and planted with broom to signify Plantagenet. Drawn by two 'wildmen', when the structure was opened it revealed six ladies 'in gold and rich clothes'. Margaret was one of these ladies, and only she and Princess Mary were provided with cloth of gold for their garments, clearly identifying them as members of the royal family. For the Epiphany revels in 1515, Margaret again took part receiving, along with three other ladies, a crimson satin gown embroidered with yellow 'from the King's store'. As headdresses they wore purple velvet bonnets and gold wrought cauls for their hair.[53] The letter written to her mother was written at Greenwich and dated 5 January, the day before the epiphany revels, but no year is specified. We know that the New Year celebrations of 1513 and 1515 were held at Greenwich, but in 1514 they were held at Windsor.[54] Furthermore, the contents of the letter means it cannot have been written earlier than 13 December 1512 or later than 1515 when Margaret became Lady Herbert, thus, it must have been written on 5 January 1513 or 1515.[55]

The letter opens with a traditionally respectful form of address to her mother 'Most entirely beloved lady and mother I commend me in my most humble manner unto your grace. Beseeching your grace of your daily blessing.' However, rather than write it herself, Margaret dictated it, and at a time when 'it was considered polite, respectful, and a sign of deference to write personal letters in one's own hand'.[56] Of course, she may have struggled with literacy, but we would expect her to at least be able to sign it herself, but she does not. She then makes a very blunt request, beseeching Katharine 'to be a good lady and mother unto me that I may have my money of my lord my grandfather's bequest Which is 50 marks by year Whereof sithens his death I had never but £20'. The sum of 50 marks is equivalent to £33, thus £20 is less than the bequest, but it is not clear if she is claiming to have received only £20 per year or £20 in total. More significantly, Margaret knew the detail of her grandfather's will and exactly what she was entitled to. She then requested Katharine and her council to 'call upon the executors to see that I may content of the whole sum which is behind'. To ask Katharine and her council to act was clever, as one of her mother's councillors, John Rowe, was also one of the executors of the will. However, the will actually stipulated that the 50 marks was to be 'distributed to and for the exhibition of Margaret Courtenay … till such time as she be married'.[57] So it did not preclude Katharine retaining control over the money, giving her daughter an allowance and using the remainder towards her expenses. But this is clearly not what Margaret wanted and she felt empowered enough to approach her mother and demand to have her own money to spend as she wished.

We now get to the real purpose of Margaret's letter, and perhaps the reason for Katharine's reluctance to give her daughter control over her money. Margaret explained that 'I have made a bargain with my lady of Surrey for certain stuff and jewels which lately were my lady Lisle's Which will draw nigh 100 marks' and trusted, that by her mother's help 'I shall have money to pay for it.' Her next words would have angered her mother, a woman to whom discretion was everything. Margaret informed Katharine that 'there be divers about the queen that love your grace right well counselled me to write unto you herein showing me that if I let it slip I should not fortune upon such another bargain of long year'. In other words, Margaret had revealed her financial difficulties to the queen's ladies and then used them to endorse her request by repeating their apparent advice that 'if I let it slip I should not fortune upon such an other bargain of long time'. This really was poor judgement on Margaret's part, which would only have convinced Katharine that she had been correct to maintain control over her daughter's bequest.

But what of this bargain and who was 'my lady of Surrey' and Lady Lisle? In 1513 Lady Surrey would have been Agnes Tilney, married to Thomas Howard, future second Duke of Norfolk, but in 1515 it would have been Elizabeth Stafford who was married to Thomas Howard, future third Duke of Norfolk. We know that Elizabeth Grey, Lady Lisle, would become Margaret's sister-in-law, but in 1512 her wardship had been purchased by Charles Brandon who would not relinquish it until July 1515. Are we to believe that he would have allowed one of the Howard women to retain Lady Lisle's jewels and stuff and then sell them on? It is hardly likely. It is therefore clear that the Lady Lisle referred to here is Muriel Howard, mother of Lady Lisle who, as we have seen, died in December 1512. Even after her marriage to Sir Thomas Knyvet Muriel continued to be known as Lady Lisle, and in her will describes herself as 'Dame Meryell, Viscountess Lisle'.[58] If this is the case, it is implausible that Elizabeth Stafford would have had the right to sell her deceased sister-in-law's items in 1515. In that year she was very much the junior Howard lady. It is far more probable that Margaret struck this bargain with Agnes who was Muriel's stepmother and therefore likely to have possession of these items and permission to sell them. This therefore dates Margaret's letter to 5 January 1513 when she was about

15 years old and Agnes was still Countess of Surrey. However, the timing of this would only have increased Katharine's distaste for the whole affair. Muriel had died in childbirth in December 1512 leaving her children orphans, and it is unedifying that her stepmother and Margaret were haggling over her stuff and jewels less than a month after her death. It is hard to imagine what Agnes was trying to achieve here? She was certainly a sharp operator having married Thomas Howard, aged 20 to his 54, a mere four months after his first wife's death, bringing little dowry with her. Although her household would become notorious during the fall of Catherine Howard in 1541, by 1513 she was a seasoned courtier and her motivations are hard to fathom. Did she feel sorry for the cash-strapped Margaret? Was she attempting to raise money for Muriel's children? Or was she taking advantage of a naive young girl's desperation to have fine jewels and clothes? We cannot know, but the whole episode would not have pleased Margaret's mother. By complaining to the ladies of the queen's household, she had implied that her bequest had been illegally withheld from her, a situation her mother had done nothing to rectify despite one of the executors being her own legal counsel. Her grumbling also indirectly accused her mother of not catering to her needs, which had led her to barter for a dead woman's 'stuff and jewels', which hardly seems fair. As one of the queen's ladies, Katharine would have ensured she was honourably attired. Furthermore, the day after she wrote this letter, and following the revels, Margaret received those rich items of clothing she had worn during the celebrations, it being recorded that the ladies 'kept their corresponding articles of attire'.[59]

While we do not know the outcome of Margaret's request, it does reveal that she had inherited her mother's independent spirit but not yet her good judgement. She had a robust personality that she was not afraid to give expression to and the letter is a fascinating insight into the relationship between mother and daughter. The fact that she made this bold approach to Katharine might suggest that she had been a more indulgent mother than not; her daughter was clearly not afraid to express her opinions to her. Whatever the outcome, Katharine spent the next couple of years attempting to identify an honourable match for her, culminating in her marriage to Lord Herbert in 1515. We might imagine that Margaret was pleased with this as one day she would be Countess of Worcester, would enjoy the same rank as her mother, and all the fine clothes and jewels commensurate to that station!

Despite an erroneous story that Margaret died young after choking on a fish bone, she actually went on to enjoy several years of married life.[60] Relations between her husband, Lord Herbert, and his new in-laws, were warm. In 1519, payments to Herbert can be seen in Henry Courtenay's expenses of that year, one entry describing Herbert as 'my lord's brother'.[61] However, after the letter of

1513 and her attendance at the 1515 revels, there is only one further reference to Margaret, which occurred in January 1519 when her brother Henry gave 'my lady Herbert' 6s 8d.[62] A later potential reference of 1520 has caused confusion among historians, but in all probability does not relate to Margaret.[63] This means that the last known reference to her was in early 1519, after which nothing more is heard of Margaret.[64] Following her marriage, she may have suffered a combination of miscarriages, still births and infant deaths as she left no surviving children, and by 1526 she had died, possibly in childbirth or from illness and still only in her twenties. Her husband married soon afterwards and his second wife promptly bore him four sons, the eldest being born around 1526/1527. This suggests that the problem had been with Margaret rather than him. When Herbert died in 1549 he chose to be buried in St Mary's Church, Chepstow, with his second wife Elizabeth, the mother of his children, and no record of Margaret's final resting place survives. This lively and forthright young woman never had a chance to fulfil her potential, and we can only speculate how she might have reacted during the 'king's great matter'! Although she appears to have disappeared without trace, there was one person who did remember her; in her will of 1527 her mother instructed a priest to pray for the souls of several family members, included among them was her daughter, Margaret.

By 1515 Katharine had successfully arranged honourable marriages for both her children, but something else should be noted here. Two of these marriages, in the space of a year, threatened the interests of the Howards. First, Katharine was complicit in trying to obtain the marriage of the earl of Oxford, an attempt which the Howards managed to frustrate, then she obtained the marriage of Lady Lisle, whose lands the Howards had gone to great lengths to retain. It is important to remember that Thomas, Lord Howard had been Katharine's brother-in-law for around sixteen years. A man of slight build, small and wiry with dark hair, his work ethic has to be admired as he was still leading men into battle aged 81. While he is certainly not the ignorant boor of film and TV fame, speaking French fluently and displaying an amiable charm when he wanted to, he had a vicious, even sadistic, temper when his ambitions were thwarted. Much to the disgust of Chapuys, beheading was not enough for his disgraced niece, Queen Catherine Howard, instead he wanted her burnt alive, and he drew further gasps when he was seen laughing as the sentences of hanging, drawing and quartering were handed down to Dereham and Culpepper, the men accused with her.[65] This is a man who apparently tried to stab Cardinal Wolsey for daring 'to speak some insulting words' against him, and showed the most ruthless self-interest when he testified against his own son who subsequently went to the block in 1547.[66] His biographer has observed the 'rough manners' and 'taste for cruelty' of the third duke of Norfolk during Henry VIII's reign, speculating that during the reign of Henry VII he 'may already have been a rather unpleasant character'.[67] When his second marriage to Elizabeth Stafford broke down from the late 1520s, she accused him of physical violence, and we know for sure that he did threaten violence against her in a letter to Cromwell.[68] Unfortunately for Katharine's sister, by 1508 Howard's dynastic legacy was under threat. After thirteen years of marriage, he still had no male heir. Two sons had been born to the couple, Henry and Thomas, but both had died, the latter on 4 August 1508.[69] Howard was now aged 35, his wife Anne 33, and he knew it was extremely unlikely he would have a living son by her, something that could have put a strain on the marriage. Whether Howard's treatment of her reflected this is unknown, but when she died in 1511 he regarded it as an opportunity not a tragedy. In fact, a letter written many years later by Anne's successor provides the unedifying scene of Howard eagerly choosing his next bride while his current wife lay dying. As soon as Anne had taken her last breath he 'immediately' approached the Duke of Buckingham and by Shrove Tide 1512 had resolved to marry Elizabeth Stafford.[70] If Anne's life was made a misery by her husband and her sister knew about it, that would give her a strong motive to show Howard and his family little concern. While she was too shrewd to move against them in open enmity, if her actions happened to discomfort them, then all the better. Of course, without firm evidence the above must remain speculation, while Katharine's main priority would have been the suitability of the marriages. But circumstantial evidence does point to a lack of consideration towards the Howards, which remains intriguing.

Once her children's marriages were arranged, Katharine could concentrate more fully on running the earldom estates, although, as the king's aunt, she still had occasional responsibilities at court. In February 1516 she attended the christening of her great niece, Princess Mary, and was chosen as one of the godmothers. She maintained contact with the princess thereafter and regularly sent her New Year's gifts.[71] In May 1516 Henry VIII's eldest sister, Margaret, Queen of Scotland, arrived in London. As her only surviving aunt, it would be surprising if Katharine was not at Greenwich to greet her and attend the two-day joust held in her honour. However, this was not a triumphal state visit. Like her sister, Mary, Margaret had made some questionable choices. Following her husband's death at Flodden, after which she became regent, she rashly took a second husband which cost her the regency, and her children, who were taken away from her. In September 1515, heavily pregnant, she fled to England, gave birth to a daughter, the future Margaret Douglas, fell seriously ill, and it was in the aftermath of all this that she arrived in London in May. The tarnish was also starting to show on Henry VIII's once shiny new reign. His marriage to Catherine of Aragon, whose looks were already beginning to fade due to her numerous pregnancies, had still not produced a male heir. This fuelled the dynastically insecure king's suspicions and on 17 May 1521 Katharine's cousin, Edward Stafford, Duke of Buckingham, was executed. This was a man she had known all her life, whose sister Elizabeth Stafford she counted as a friend, and his downfall was a stark reminder that no one was safe once the king's affection and trust was lost. If not before, Katharine would now be certain she had made the right decision to leave court and the backbiting with which she was so familiar.

Chapter 6

'My Ladys Grace'

The Countess of Devon

While Katharine now based herself primarily in Devon, this was no retirement. Her servants were regularly sent to the capital on business and there was on-going communication with her son Henry, earl of Devon. For example, in 1526 they were involved in granting a lease to Anthony Harvey and his wife, one of Henry's most trusted servants.[1] The grant was most likely made at Henry's behest with his mother's agreement, and reassured Harvey that after the countess' death the grant would be honoured. This arrangement of Katharine in Devon and Henry at court worked well. In his position as earl of Devon and a member of the royal family, maintaining good relations with the king was imperative and this could only be achieved effectively by direct contact with him. Henry had a permanent base at court, which he took full advantage of, despite spacious properties nearby that were available to him. He also followed the king on progress and joined him in pastimes such as hunting and hawking. Occasionally, he was absent from the royal presence when visiting family, friends or attending to business, but the majority of his time was spent within the king's orbit.[2] Katharine, on her side, earned provincial loyalty and developed regional networks in her role as resident landlord.

The income from the earldom lands generated around £2,750 per year.[3] It was Katharine's responsibility to maintain this large estate and she appears to have viewed her role very much as a custodian. As Margaret Wescott notes 'the Earldom inheritance which Henry Courtenay received in 1527 was identical in size and form with that which had been granted to his mother in 1511'.[4] Unlike the early 1500s when Katharine was powerless to protect her son's inheritance, she could now afford the best legal advisers, some of whom sat on her council. The council was an advisory body and Katharine's included heavyweights like Sir Lewis Pollard from Bishops Nympton, Devon, who was also the king's sergeant at law and kinsman of the judge and speaker of the House of Commons, Sir John Pollard.[5] John Rowe, sergeant-at-law, hailed from Totnes and was one of those both she, and later her son, retained for his legal advice. As someone who had been surveyor to Henry's grandfather, Edward, Earl of Devon, and executor of his will, Rowe's in-depth knowledge of the Courtenay estates was invaluable.[6] Katharine's attorney general was a gentleman called Charles Hopping, and she kept him very busy. One of the first actions she took once restored related to the manors held by Sir Hugh Conway and Sir William Knyvet, revealing Katharine's absolute determination to repossess them. The matter was confirmed by two acts of Parliament in 1512, but it had taken a great deal of wrangling to get there. On 27 October 1511, just four months after her husband's death, Katharine and Conway entered into an indenture but only after the mediation of Richard Fox, Bishop of Winchester, Thomas Dowkra, Prior of St John's of Jerusalem, Richard Broke, sergeant-at-law and Lewis Pollard. The indenture allowed 'a full end and peace to be continued and had from hence forth between the two parties'. It stipulated that Conway would retain the Buckinghamshire manors for term of his life, after which they would revert to Katharine and her heirs. The Courtenay manors in Somerset, Berkshire and Hampshire he surrendered immediately in return for an annual rent of £176 18s 9d. We cannot know if Katharine ever suspected Conway of informing against her husband, but if she did, this was sweet revenge. A similar indenture of 27 November 1511 was entered into by Katharine and Knyvet concerning the manors he held. Again, arbitration was necessary, this time involving William Warham, Archbishop of Canterbury, Richard Fox, John Fyneux, chief justice of the king's bench, Richard Elyot, the king's serjeant-at-law, Lewis Pollard, Richard Broke and 'Thomas More Gentilman'. In his case, Knyvet agreed to relinquish all the manors he held in return for an annual rent.[7] Katharine's resolve to protect the lands of the earldom is again demonstrated by the number cases she brought to Common Pleas. Between 1513 and 1515, of the cases brought by members of the nobility, Katharine brought twelve, the fourth highest number. Of these twelve cases, eleven of them concerned trespass and this was by far the greatest number of trespass cases in that period. The £4 6s 6d she paid Charles Hopping between 1513 and 1514 for dealing with various matters in London most likely related to these cases,[8] and between 1522 and 1523 she spent nearly £6 on 'Costs of the law'. Katharine pursued her legal rights with vigour, and in April 1523 a John Darche of Wiveliscombe, Somerset, was granted a royal pardon for having escaped from Ilchester gaol 'where he was imprisoned by the bailiff of Katharine countess of Devon'.[9]

As head of 'the richest and most influential house in Devon',[10] Katharine had responsibilities to the king which included providing men for his wars. Unlike her male counterpart she could not lead the men herself, but she could raise them. In 1513 lists of the ships, captains and masters with the numbers of solders and mariners on board, was drawn up in preparation for the king's offensive against France. The men Katharine raised embarked upon the 800-ton

Marie de Loreta, a former merchant ship built for size.[11] With a crew of 604, it also carried men furnished by the city of Exeter and Sir Amyas Paulet, who was also one of Katharine's stewards. Katharine provided 200 men, the city of Exeter 100 and Paulet 25.[12] The following year, in response to the king's letters, Katharine sent a certificate signed 'Kateryn Devonschyr' confirming she could provide 100 men.[13] This extremely capable woman was Elizabeth Woodville's daughter indeed, and taking control of such a large estate did not daunt her.

Heading up her own household far from court gave her the sense of security she had always craved. Nevertheless, she did not forget her royal lineage and was determined that no one else should either. Everything about the way Katharine lived proclaimed her to be a woman of very high status, from official documents, to her internal accounts and to the very food that she ate. In her household accounts she was referred to not as 'my lady' but as 'my ladys grace', and in her official documents was styled 'daughter, sister and aunt of kings', and this was often preceded by the designation 'Princess Katharine, Countess of Devon'. In fact, her elevated station was such that her rank was overstated in a grant of November 1524. Receiving the wardship of Richard Chudleigh, she was referred to as 'Katharine, Duchess of Devon, the King's grand aunt'.[14] When she arrived in Devon it must have caused great excitement, she was a royal princess and therefore something of a celebrity, but there was more to it than this. To gain her patronage provided unequalled opportunities for advancement, not only for local gentry but right down to merchants and tradesmen, and to their delight, Katharine bought local. Of course, this was the sixteenth century so she had to, but she was lucky. In 1520, the city of Exeter was one of only six cities outside of London that had more than 7,000 inhabitants[15] and everything she needed was there or thereabouts, only rarely did she need to use craftsmen from outside the local area. So how did she live and where did she live? What was her household like, who did she socialise with and what networks did she develop? To go some way towards answering this, it is necessary to rely on three major sources. E36/223 held at the National Archives is a set of Katharine's household accounts for the year 26 September 1523–29 September 1524. Unfortunately, a lot of the writing has faded and some of the pages are mere fragments, but together with an edited copy in the *Letters and Papers of Henry VIII*, a summary of the accounts for the previous year, and an inventory of her possessions at Tiverton Castle in 1527, they provide a fascinating glimpse into Katharine's life in Devon.[16]

Katharine had three main residences; Tiverton Castle, some twenty miles or so from Exeter was the most northerly, then south lay Columbjohn about five miles from Exeter. Some twenty-seven miles south-east was Colcombe Castle, which lay the furthest from Exeter and nearer to the coast than the rest. Katharine used these three residences on rota, moving her household from one to the other to allow the most recently vacated property to be thoroughly cleaned, refreshed and repaired. Moving from Tiverton to Columbjohn could probably be completed within a day, but moving to Colcombe would require one or two overnight stays. Katharine and her entourage would travel sedately, almost like a royal progress, and it would be a treat for locals to see this royal princess passing by. From the small amount of information we have about Katharine's movements, we have enough to propose a scenario about how she would have lived in and used these properties.

The winter months and Christmas were spent at Tiverton Castle. Tiverton is important because Columbjohn and Colcombe have all but disappeared, but Tiverton is still lived in today and parts that existed in Katharine's time have survived.[17] Standing high and proud on the east bank of the River Exe, it had been the main seat of the Courtenay family for hundreds of years. It's initial purpose had been defence, hence its elevated position. Tiverton was described as a 'large and rich demesne for hospitality' which was 'the head and chief mansion house, moated, walled and embattled round like a castle with all manner of houses of offices and lodgings within the same, well kept and repaired, and fair gardens to the same belonging …'.[18] It was arranged around a courtyard, and four strong walls twenty to twenty-five feet high surrounded the entire area, estimated to have extended to about an acre. To the east was a gatehouse which jutted out from the wall, with a corresponding tower behind it jutting inwards towards the courtyard. The gatehouse was flanked by guardrooms with accommodation above. Within the middle of the wall on the western side which stood sixty feet above the river was a tower. Another tower, originally designed to include the lord and lady's private rooms and sleeping quarters, stood at the south-west corner and provided unrivalled views over the river and surrounding countryside. A round tower was located at the south east corner, and each tower was described as having battlements and being about thirty-five feet high, while a moat provided additional defence. According to James Dugdale who viewed the remains of the castle in 1819, the best apartments were probably located towards the north wall, which have not survived, and those above the gatehouse 'which remain almost entire, and are regular, lofty, and spacious'.[19] The location of the hall where Katharine entertained and received visitors and petitioners is not known, but the chapel may have been located along the south wall, possibly above the domestic offices. That wall is directly opposite St Peter's Church, which is next door to the castle.[20] In addition to commodious accommodation, it had 'fair gardens' and 'two parks for pleasure', Ashley Park and the smaller Newpark, the latter of which adjoined the castle.[21] The 1734 engraving by

Samuel and Nathaniel Buck allows us to see what the castle looked like some 200 years after Katharine had lived there.

Records reveal that it had several areas associated with the preparation and storage of food, including the buttery where alcoholic drinks, vinegars, oils and other liquids were kept. Considering that Katharine bought several hundred gallons of ale and beer every week, this room was very necessary! The ewery stored Katharine's napkins, towels and tablecloths along with the ewers and basins, proudly displaying her arms, which were used by diners to wash their hands between courses. Salt was an expensive commodity that would be prominently displayed on the table while dining, and Katharine possessed several ornate salt cellars of various sizes. One was a great salt cellar wreathed with leaves, one was of gold, and another had an enamelled red rose on the cover. These were kept in her pantry along with spoons of silver and gilt, and knives. She had a dry larder, which was used to store pulses and nuts, including the almonds she purchased, and the 'great coffer for fish' would have sat in the wet larder. Katharine, as befitting her wealth, had a separate bakehouse boasting 'a great furnace' in which pastries were cooked and bread was baked using the wheat she purchased every week on a Tuesday. As it made the best bread, it was naturally the most expensive grain and certainly beyond the reach of the poor.[22] Tiverton also had an armoury where chain mail and armour was stored while 'in the gate of the place two great guns' reminded visitors that this was indeed a fortified residence.

The castle also housed several stables including the 'great stable' comprising 'ten great stalls for horses to stand in with rack and manger'. Katharine was known to have possessed twenty-five horses, and in 1527 the horses at pasture in her two parks at Tiverton were recorded. At Ashley park was a 7-year-old bay mare standing at eighteen hands with her foal. This was a very large horse, even by todays' standards, and was probably one of Henry Courtenay's jousting horses. Another horse at Ashely was 'a great horse' that Henry Courtenay had sent to be 'put to the use of a stallion'. This valuable horse was brought down by 49-year-old Petty John who, as a 'breaker of horses', was one of Henry's most experienced stablemen. Furthermore, over at Chulmleigh Park, another manor within the earldom, was found 'a roan stallion of my lord's called Parker'. Horses were crucial in this period and Katharine and her son not only purchased them but also bred and broke them in via experienced horsemen like Petty John.

Seven miles away lay Columbjohn where Katharine and her household spent the spring and summer months. It was positioned next to the meandering River Culm which provided a range of fresh fish for Katharine's table, including eels. Described as a 'fair house with diverse lodgings within the same', Katharine loved Columbjohn and ensured that repairs were regularly carried out and the garden well maintained. She covered the cost of lodgings for her gardener, John Toke, to stay near Columbjohn from March through to September 1524 so he could tend to it, paid a woman to provide additional labour and someone else to weed it. She possessed everything necessary to maintain her residences including ladders of various sizes, scaffolding, tools, slates and other materials. It is tempting to think of Katharine spending long, lazy summers in this green meadow land, but lazy would be the wrong word as most of the visitors she received in 1524 were hosted here. At the end of July the long line of horses and heavily laden carts snaked its way nearly thirty miles to Colcombe Castle near Colyton where the household would reside before moving back to Tiverton ready for Christmas. Like Columbjohn, it was described as 'a fair large house with diverse lodgings in the same, well-kept and repaired, set standing and being within the park'.[23] John Leland writing in the 1540s, noted that about a mile before reaching Colyton 'I could see from a hill the Lord Marquis of Dorset's excellent manor house on the hillside at Shute, with a fine, large park beside it.' He also noted the River Coly which flowed from below Colyton past Colcombe Park, giving the impression of a delightful aspect.[24]

These three residences were commensurate to a woman of Katharine's status, but what of her furnishings, her clothes and her servants? Unsurprisingly, as a devout woman no expense was spared on the necessaries for her household chapels. On entering, a visitor's senses would have been assailed by the vivid, vibrant colours, costly, shimmering materials and items of silver and gilt. Vestments in the chapel at Tiverton included one of blue, one of black and one of green velvet, and on every one was embroidered a cross of crimson velvet. Other vestments included one of cream damask with a cross of blue velvet, with the Courtenay arms and Mary Magdalen embroidered on it. There was an altar cloth of crimson velvet and satin embroidered and fringed with red, yellow and green silk and another of crimson and green satin fringed with red, white and green silk with a crucifix in the middle. Upon the altar stood two 'great candlesticks' of silver and gilt and a 'great chalice' of gilt. She also possessed a silver and gilt pyx [vessel] to hold the consecrated bread and a canopy of black velvet fringed with black silk to bear over the sacrament. There was a lectern at which to sing Mass and a sacring bell which was rung during the elevation of the Host and chalice. Katharine's two matins books including psalms and readings for the service, were covered with velvet and held closed with clasps of silver and gilt. On 6 March 1524 the Prior of the Black Friars, Exeter, would have used these items when he preached a sermon before Katharine in her chapel at Columbjohn. The Courtenay family had longstanding links to the friary where rooms were set aside for them, and which her son would personalise with his own furniture.[25]

Unfortunately, no contemporary portrait of Katharine is known to have survived, but the few details we have about her clothes suggests that she dressed conservatively. Unlike her father, bright, bold colours did not appear in her wardrobe but more muted ones such as black and tawny. One item that recurs regularly in Katharine's accounts is the 'sloppe'. A sloppe was most commonly described as trousers, and we might imagine that these were worn by Katharine as part of her underwear, but the materials used argue against this. In fact, 'slop' was also used to describe a loose jacket, tunic, mantle, cassock or gown, and in Katharine's case 'sloppe' probably refers to a gown. Gowns were worn over the kirtle, which was usually visible by the gown being cut away at the front from the waist down. Katharine's slopes, or gowns, were decorated with a variety of furs including black lamb skins and pampillion, a fur commonly used at this time for lining and trimming garments. Other furs included 'lettys skins', a whiteish, grey fur, and also ermine which declared her royal lineage. One sloppe was known to have been of tawny velvet. She had a little matching purse of tawny velvet lined with buckram to stiffen it, which had a drawstring of tawny silk. We also know that she had a partlet of black velvet, a small sleeveless garment worn to cover the neck and shoulders. Katharine's was decorated or lined with black rabbit fur and if worn with her tawny gown would have provided an attractive contrast. Katharine's kirtles were made from a variety of costly materials including velvet and black satin. To complete the look, Katharine would have worn a placard. This was a decorative, detachable panel that was fixed over the front lacing of the gown and held in place with pins.[26] These tiny pins were easily lost while dressing so, to ensure she always had plenty, in 1524 she purchased 1,000 white and 1,000 black pins for 15d. One charming departure from this sober dress was a hat that she paid to have covered in white sarcenet, a silklike material, which was obviously for summer wear – her summer hat! In 1522–1523, the total amount she spent on her 'apparel' was £32, which is not an excessive sum, revealing that she dressed honourably but not extravagantly.

The dress of a Tudor noble woman was intricate with detachable pieces and lacings. As such, assistance was needed when dressing and undressing, and we know the names of five of Katharine's gentlewomen, each of whom received 13s 4d every quarter for their wages. Mistress Agnes Beare may have been the daughter or wife of William Beare, who was eventually appointed steward of Boconnoc manors in Cornwall by Katharine's son. Mistress Courtenay may have been a relative of Robert Courtenay who was surveyor of the earldom of Devon lands in Berkshire and Hampshire,[27] while evidence suggests that 52-year-old Margaret Brown was something of a family retainer. She attended upon Katharine's daughter-in-law after she had given birth in 1524, and after Katharine's death had the honour of being loaned 'my ladys graces white palfrey' to ride to London upon. In 1538 66-year-old Margaret 'Brewne' 'a poor woman not having many friends' was one of the gentlewomen serving Henry Courtenay's wife and likely to be the same lady. Mistress Motton's identity is unclear, but she may have been related to the 'Motton of Exeter' who Katharine rewarded in July for bringing cherries and strawberries. Certainly, there was a John Motton who was a tailor of Exeter in 1528,[28] and it is likely that the Mottons were successful Exeter merchants. Nothing is known about Mistress Elizabeth Fynes, but she may have been a member of the family of Thomas Fiennes, Lord Dacre, whose main seat was in Sussex. Apart from Elizabeth Fynes who might have been related to a baron, the ladies Katharine chose to wait upon her were of middling status, most with links to local officials employed by the Courtenay family. They would have been women with whom she felt comfortable and whose company she enjoyed. In addition to helping her dress, they would be present in her chamber, would embroider with her, ride with her, prepare her for bed and basically be in attendance upon her. We know that Katharine possessed three pairs of clavichords, a small, square, piano-like instrument usually with a four octave keyboard. It produced a softer sound than the harpsichord and was easily transportable. Katharine and her ladies would have played these clavichords which, for want of a better expression, produces the traditional Tudor sound, and her chamber would have been a pleasant environment full of music and chatter.

Another valued member of Katharine's household who was of much lower rank was the laundress, and Katharine's relationship with her laundress reveals more about how she operated as mistress. Katharine's laundress, who was called Phillippa, looked after her undergarments including the linen smocks she wore to prevent her skin from being rubbed by the thick materials of her outer garments. They also protected the expensive but unwashable apparel from sweat and the stench of body odour. Phillippa also washed her linen nightgowns, and her hose, which was a stocking extending to above the knee and held in place with garters. We know that Katharine felt the cold because she paid for sixteen pairs of 'double hosen', obviously bought for winter. More sensitively, the other items that needed to be washed were the linen rags that Katharine used when she was on her period, and she may have used some kind of girdle to keep them in place in the same way as it is believed her great-niece, Elizabeth I, did. The laundress' role was one that required tact and discretion and Katharine would need to be certain she could trust the person who was responsible for her underwear and sanitary items. Henry VIII certainly appreciated his laundress, to whom he made generous grants, as did Elizabeth I, and Katharine was no different.[29]

We are fortunate that in the year 1523–1524 Phillippa decided to get married, because the care Katharine took to ensure she had an adequate trousseau demonstrates the value she placed on her service. In total, Katharine spent nearly £7,000 in today's money on Phillippa's wedding, a generous gift indeed. First, she gave her £5 13s 4d for her 'marriage money', paid 3s 4d for her wedding ring, while the rest was spent on clothing, a pin case and two knives. Katharine paid for her wedding dress to be made, consisting of a gown, kirtle, petticoat and smock. The materials used were very expensive including velvet, ribbon, lace, linen, buckram for stiffening, and aglets made of silver or other metal which were attached to the end of laces. She was also supplied with a cap, two head kerchiefs to cover her hair, two neckerchiefs and two aprons. Katharine was also very generous to 'Andrew of the kitchen'. She bought him a pair of shoes and had a doublet and hose made for him, along with the repair of another pair of hose. As Andrew worked in the kitchen and therefore knew Phillippa, it is tempting to wonder whether Andrew was her intended. Phillippa was a trusted member of Katharine's household who would have travelled with her between her residences, and Katharine's attention to her trousseau reveals her to be an appreciative and generous mistress. This is further demonstrated by the presentation of New Year's gifts to her officials and household servants. For New Year 1524 she gifted three yards of black satin to Nicholas Fortescue, one of her bailiffs, and gave rewards to all of her household staff, which meant that the entire household, from the highest to the lowest, would be celebrating the festivities!

As stated, one of Katharine's key roles as Countess of Devon was to develop good relations with those individuals who held positions of power and influence in the region and we can see evidence of this throughout her accounts. Katharine was well aware of the importance of patronage, and this formed a major outgoing in 1522–1523 with 'Rewards for presents and other' costing £50 8s 5d. Among the most expensive items she gave, in a category all of its own, were the New Year's gifts for the king and queen. In 1524 Katharine spent an enormous £20 on the king and queen's gift, and she gave generous rewards to the royal servants who brought their gifts to her. Touchingly, the gift in which most time and thought was invested was that to her son. In April 1521 Henry had been elected to the chivalric order of the garter, and Katharine ordered elaborate garters to be made for him. Commissioning a craftsman called Peter John, buckles, pendants, studs, hoylettes and aglets were used along with gold and enamel. Henry was very particular about his appearance and, like his grandfather Edward IV, loved clothes, and Katharine knew her son well. In turn, Katharine received a large number of gifts from those who courted her favour and wished to pay their respects to the most powerful landowner in the county. At Christmas 1523 she received a boar from Lady Martyn, an ox from her legal adviser John Rowe, and a boar and two swans from Thomas Chard, Abbot of Forde Abbey. Forde

Abbey was a wealthy Cistercian monastery located near Colcombe. It was regarded as a centre of learning, which is not surprising as Thomas Chard was a scholarly man who was energetically engaged in re-building and improving the abbey. Katharine would no doubt have visited Forde Abbey while she was in residence at Colcombe. She also received gifts from John Ellys, abbot of the large Cistercian abbey of Newenham, near Axminster, also not far from Colcombe.[30]

To be invited to visit the Countess of Devon was a great honour, and those who visited her included family, friends and individuals whose goodwill was important. As little is known about Katharine's socialising and networking, it is important to look at these guests. On 19 December 1523 she was visited by 'My Lady Zouche' who stayed until the following day. It is not absolutely clear which of the Zouche ladies this was, but it is most likely Dorothy, Lady Zouche. She had married John, eighth Lord Zouche before 1510 and her cousin was Sir John Arundel, who was linked to Katharine by service and marriage. His first wife, who died before 1507, had been Eleanor Grey, Katharine's half-niece, daughter of Thomas Grey, first Marquis of Dorset, and Arundel was an influential figure in the region being receiver general of the duchy of Cornwall.[31] He had been one of the mourners at Sir William Courtenay's funeral, and in July 1511 Katharine appointed him joint steward of the earldom manors in Cornwall, Devon, Dorset and Somerset with her half nephew, Thomas Grey, Marquis of Dorset. They were also appointed masters of all wild beasts in her parks and chases except for Okehampton.[32] On 23 December John Veysey, Bishop of Exeter, arrived and presented two oxen to her, no doubt staying to dine. Veysey, like Chard, was a learned man, so much so that Henry VIII used him as a diplomat, and he accompanied the king to the Field of the Cloth of Gold. In 1522 he was involved in welcoming the emperor Charles V to England and in a few months would be tasked with greeting the pope's ambassador.[33] This courtly man, at ease in the presence of royalty, would have made an interesting dinner guest and Katharine clearly enjoyed his company.

In the summer, a flurry of guests were entertained at Columbjohn, beginning with the arrival of Mr Bamfyld and his wife on 17 May. This was almost certainly Sir Edward Bamfyld of Poltimore, Devon, and his wife, Elizabeth [née Wadham]. Poltimore was a mere three miles from Columbjohn and the Bamfyld family had been established there since at least the fourteenth century. They were prominent members of the local gentry and Edward Bamfyld's grandfather had been sheriff of Devon, a position his son Richard would also hold.[34] They stayed at Columbjohn for two days, dining on lamb, chicken, rabbit, beef, venison, various fish and strawberries. They must have had a very enjoyable visit because during their stay the king's servant arrived 'with a harper and a tumbler'! To return the favour, Katharine also visited them at Poltimore on 13 June where she 'dined and suppeth' and also made an offering. This would have been a great honour for the Bamfylds and suggests that Katharine genuinely enjoyed their company.

The most important visitor of the year was Katharine's half-nephew, Thomas Grey, Marquis of Dorset, the third highest-ranking noble in the realm who arrived at the end of June. Although he was her half-nephew, Dorset was actually two years older than Katharine, and she had known him all her life. He would be another informative dinner companion as he had been involved in leading raids across the Scottish border the previous year as part of the king's French offensive. While he took the opportunity to relax at Columbjohn with his aunt, she would be keen to hear the latest news and perhaps reminisce about her husband with a man who had been his close friend. The proliferation of entries in her accounts relating to his visit reveal the time and effort that went into preparing for it. Six loads of rushes were delivered to ensure the floors were clean and sweet smelling. Wine was carried to Columbjohn 'against my Lord Marquis coming' along with cinnamon, while the bailiff of Sampford Peverell brought fish. Motton of Exeter was rewarded for 'cherries, strawberries and his labour when my Lord Marquis was here', Mr Chichester was re-imbursed for two dozen gulls purchased 'against my Lord Marquess coming' and further expenses of £3 14s 1d were incurred.

As the visit drew closer, a servant arrived post haste from Sir George Speke 'bringing off a letter off knowledge off my lord marquess coming'. From 1525, Sir George Speke was the steward of the earldom lands in Devon[35] but may already have been in post. As one of Katharine's most important officials he had a chamber set aside for him at Tiverton Castle, and no doubt at her other residences too. He held the manor of Dowlish Wake, Somerset, some seventeen miles from Katharine's residence at Colcombe, which had been in the hands of the Speke family since the fifteenth century.[36] While the household waited in anticipation as the marquis approached, Katharine may have ridden out to meet him as a mark of honour and genuine pleasure to see him. She had recently ordered velvet 'for making of the broad rein of my lady's grace bridle' along with a fringe for it. During his stay they dined on a variety of food including salmon, venison, chicken and pheasant, along with a pudding that was sent as a gift 'to my lady's grace against my Lord Marquis was here'. Katharine also made gifts of venison to several individuals who were probably among the guests invited to dine with them. These included the bishop of Exeter and Sir George Speke but also Edmund Specot, one of Katharine's stewards whose wardship she had been granted in 1518.[37] Mr Forest, her physician, whose services she valued greatly, was also included along with Nicholas Fortescue, one of her bailiffs, and Richard Haydon, one of her stewards and auditor of her son's Boconnoc inheritance.[38]

It may be surprising to hear that this reserved lady certainly knew how to enjoy herself. For example, in August, Katharine took some time out for herself and travelled to Marshwood Park in Dorset, which was held by Catherine of Aragon.[39] The queen's Keeper of the Park, John Agavut and his family, fell over themselves to welcome the countess and make her stay enjoyable, and she gave him a total of 73s 4d in reward, plus 14s 10d to 'his wife for meat and drink and her labour and his servants' and 5s 8d to his daughter and his servants. Katharine and her companions stayed for several days to hunt red deer in the park and had quite a party! Not only did she send for two more horses 'for a gentleman and a woman to ride upon with my ladys grace', she also rewarded a John Parry 'for fetching of wine to John Agavutts at night' instead of wisely waiting until day light when it was safer to transport such a valuable commodity. Parry was followed by Richard Lambprey, John Blakmore and Richard Red 'each of them with a horse to Marshowd vale with carriage of ale'. With an eye to detail, Katharine also ensured that her nephew's visit would be equally enjoyable.

Two figures feature regularly in the life of Katharine's household; these were Dick and Mug, her fools.[40] Their routines were obviously very boisterous and slapstick as their clothes constantly needed washing, mending and replacing! In June Mug had been sent to her son in London, who was no doubt planning to entertain guests himself, but Dick remained with Katharine. In preparation for Dorset's visit, new stockings were made for him and his clothes repaired. His routine must have been as lively as ever as a Mr Selwood was paid for washing Dick's coat 'when my Lord Marquis was here'. A payment around this time to Lord Daubeney's minstrels for mending one of her instruments suggests that they were also present for the visit.[41] Further entertainment was provided by several of Katharine's servants who were summoned to wrestle 'before my Lord marquis', receiving 20d in reward. Wrestling was considered a warlike sport and therefore an acceptable one to take part in. It was a sport that Henry VIII enjoyed very much, and a wrestling match is known to have taken place between the English Royal guard and the Bretons at the Field of the Cloth of Gold. As 'wrestlers from Devon and Cornwall were considered the best',[42] we can imagine that the servants put on a good performance for the marquis.

Following his visit, a succession of guests arrived throughout July including a Mr Carant who stayed for two days, probably a member of the Carent family of Somerset and Dorset that had been prominent in local affairs during the previous century.[43] Next to arrive was Sir Thomas Stukeley and his wife who stayed for four days, also accompanied by the Bamfylds on their second visit. This was most likely 'Thomas Stucle', son and heir of Nicholas Stucle esq of Devon, Somerset and Dorset, whose wardship had been granted to Thomas Wode and Thomas Englefield in 1489.[44] Englefield, of course, had assisted

Katharine and William in their negotiations for the reversion of the earldom and was steward of her manor of Colyton, Devon. Stukeley attended the Middle Temple and had served as J.P. (Justice of the Peace) since 1504 and as sheriff of Devon 1520–1521.[45] Furthermore, he had links to the Marquis of Dorset, being a witness to the will of the marquis' mother. These guests were joined by a Dr Chasleigh, probably Dr Peter Casely, canon of Exeter, vicar of Pitt, Tiverton and of Broadclyst, the parish in which Columbjohn was located.[46] On Saturday 26 July, Katharine's half-nephew, Lord George Grey the younger brother of the Marquis, stopped by for breakfast. Grey was in holy orders and also active in legal matters, often named with family members on enfeoffments to use.[47] As Grey left, Mr Sydynar, Mr Rowe and Sir John Kirkham arrived to dine with Katharine on 27 July. While the identity of Mr Sydynar is not clear, John Rowe, as we know, was one of Katharine's retained legal counsel while Sir John Kirkham of Blagdon was a member of a long-established Devonshire family who, the previous year, had been appointed sheriff of Devon.[48] On 6 August, shortly after her arrival at Colcombe, Sir Thomas Stukeley and his wife again called to see her, remaining for two days, and on 10 August the accounts recorded that there were 'dyvers staying'. The above reveals that Katharine's life in Devon was not a quiet and isolated one, with the summer involving a frenetic round of socialising and entertaining.

There is one more visitor who arrived at Colcombe in the second week of September, and he is of special significance. Like the Marquis of Dorset, Henry Pole, Lord Montague, was an important visitor. The son and heir of Katharine's cousin, Margaret Pole, Countess of Salisbury, he stood to inherit substantial lands, a large number of which were located in Devon, Somerset, Dorset and Cornwall.[49] He may have been visiting some of these properties, something that would become more regular after his mother was re-appointed governess to Princess Mary in 1525. As with the marquis, Katharine made special preparations for Montague's visit. At Christmas she had managed to secure the Exeter waites [the city musicians] to play for the household, but for Montague's visit entertainment was to be provided by no less than the king's own players 'English and his company' while Dick the Fool was lodged nearby at Colyton. A fresh load of rushes were delivered, two stags and a buck were brought, and two barrels of Malmsey wine transported from Columbjohn. Again, Sir George Speke's servant was on stand-by and received 8d 'for bringing word against my Lord Montague coming'. Although Katharine remained in contact with her son, that was no substitute for actually seeing him, but Montague could go some way towards filling that gap because he did see him, and regularly. The two sons of Katharine and Margaret enjoyed a genuinely close friendship; it was unbreakable and not based on self-interest like most formed at the Tudor court. It is poignant that her last recorded visitor of 1524 was Lord Montague whose friendship with her son, in a cruel twist of fate, would contribute to the destruction of everything she held dear.

The accounts of 1523–1524 provide a fascinating insight into the life of this female magnate who spent most of her life away from court. One of two royal grand-dames of the Tudor period, Katharine Courtenay, like Margaret Pole, ran vast estates and was served by hundreds of officers, the majority of whom were men at a time when the subservience of women to men was the norm. Whereas Margaret held a key royal appointment as governess to Princess Mary necessitating long periods away from her estates, Katharine remained in Devon where she devoted all her energies towards maintaining the fortunes of the Courtenay family, both in terms of land and local influence. She also maintained the family's standing through her religious and ceremonial duties. For the Maundy Thursday ceremony on 24 March, thirteen purses each containing 20d were 'given by my ladys grace to poor folks' along with thirteen pairs of shoes. Sometimes this number might reflect the benefactor's age, but in this case it probably refers to the thirteen years since her husband died and she took a vow of chastity, revealing how significant a stage in her life it was to her.

Her son, who spent most of his time at court, could not possibly have developed the relationships that Katharine, based in Devon, was able to do. She cultivated links with a network of local families who, themselves, wielded regional influence and this required energy, diplomacy, authority and charm. Her generosity to her household servants and estate administrators, and the longevity of service she enjoyed from them, points to her success as an employer and mistress. Members of the ap Howell family provide evidence of this. Thomas ap Howell gave life-long service to the Courtenay family. It was he, as a young man of 24, who was sent by the queen to the earl of Devon in 1502 to inform him of Prince Arthur's death, being described with Robert Bailly as 'late servants to Lord William Courtenay', thus ap Howell had been present at some of the most critical moments in Katharine's life. One of her household officials, he was also the keeper of Newpark at Tiverton, and in 1517 she appointed him bailiff of the manor of Exminster, positions he retained under her son. Other members of his family were also in Katharine's employ, including his son, and this is a compliment to her 'good lordship' and ability to inspire and maintain loyalty, a trait her son also possessed.[50]

Katharine was a Plantagenet with Woodville blood in her veins, and she could be ruthless, vengeful even if pushed, but she was a fair and gracious employer. As a widow who had taken a vow of chastity, she presented herself as such, wearing sober, modest colours, but life in Katharine's household was far from dull. Dick and Mug provided regular rowdy entertainment, while she enjoyed music, dancing, hawking and hunting, with the occasional indulgence of apple fritters and apple tarts, her favourite deserts! Katharine's role as countess of Devon was as guardian of the earldom lands and of Courtenay influence in the west country. This allowed her to live life on her own terms, providing the peace, security and, dare we say, happiness she had lacked for most of her earlier life. It is fitting to close this chapter in the words of Sir Thomas More, who had been part of her negotiation team for the recovery of lands against Sir William Knyvet in 1511. He aptly sums up her tortuous journey to the safe haven she had at last found:

Katherine which long time tossed in either fortune, some time in wealth, oft in adversity, at the last, if this be the last, for yet she lives, is by the benignity of her nephew, King Henry VIII, in very prosperous estate, and worthy her birth and virtue.[51]

Chapter 7

1527

Daughter, Sister and Aunt of Kings

as it shall beseem and become our estate and degree to be.

On 2 May 1527 Katharine, surrounded by familiar faces including her steward, Sir George Speke, and her comptroller, Humphrey Colles, signed her last will and planned her detailed departure out of this life.[1] In the very same month her nephew, Henry VIII, surrounded by Cardinal Wolsey, William Warham, archbishop of Canterbury and several lawyers, planned his departure from his marriage.[2] This momentous step set in train events that 'marked the line of the watershed between the old way of life and the new'.[3] The tribunal, held in secrecy at Wolsey's London residence, York Place, was to ascertain if the king would submit himself to trial for having lived in sin with his late brother's wife. Henry was more than willing but the other defendant, the queen, was kept entirely in the dark; but not for long. Despite all those involved being sworn to secrecy, she found out about it in less than twenty-four hours.[4] And so, the first seeds of Henry's paranoid suspicion were sown; grown in the fertile ground of fear, frustration and rage which, over the coming years, would reach towering and murderous heights.

We cannot be certain about what Katharine knew at this stage. The young woman 'that did set our country in a roar' was already on the scene, currently in transition from potential royal mistress to future wife and queen. The king had been pursuing Anne Boleyn since 1526, but he had had mistresses before, and he liked to keep these matters private. Henry Courtenay, one of the king's closest companions, would have known about the king's latest infatuation, but this does not mean that he wrote to his pious, widowed mother about it. However, when it became clear that Anne was not going to be a mere mistress and gossip began to emerge about the king's intentions in June 1527, it is hard to believe that Katharine would not have heard about it. Although she, of all people, would have empathised with the king's need for a legitimate male heir, especially one that would reach adulthood before his death, she must surely have felt sympathy for the queen. When Catherine of Aragon told the Spanish humanist, Juan Luis Vives in 1523 that she 'preferred moderate and steady fortune to great ups and downs of rough and smooth',[5] Katharine, more than most, would have understood.

The will that Katharine signed in May 1527 was an updated version of an earlier will, necessitated by the deaths of trustees previously named.[6] She now appointed her son her sole executor and placed manors in Cornwall, Devon and Somerset in trust for the performance of her will. Significantly, she stated that 'we now be in bodily helthe and perfitte mynde'. If she was suffering from a physical ailment we would expect her to say so while asserting that, mentally, she was fit. The fact that she did not suggests that in May she was well. Previous bouts of illness had occurred in winter months but had abated in the summer. In October 1523 her gardener, John Toke, was sent to fetch Mr Parkhouse 'when my lady's grace was sick'. Then on 31 October the bill of Mr Forest, the physician, was paid, which amounted to £7 15s 8d, but by November she had recovered enough to celebrate All Hallows' Day and All Souls' Day. In March 1524 she fell ill again, seriously this time. Local doctors were not sufficient and 'Mr Morys the physician' was sent for from Cornwall, with Robert Adrow despatched to bring him to Columbjohn at considerable cost. Through April Katharine's ill health continued and Mr Forest was paid £5 'for medicines for my ladys grace'. However, by May that year she had recovered, perhaps helped by the warmer weather.

Following the signing of her will in May 1527, Katharine's health began to deteriorate. When this started, we do not know. It could have begun in the autumn as a recurrence of one of those previous bouts that this time took a stronger hold. Certain items she possessed do suggest that she had suffered a severe decline. In the inventory of her possessions taken in 1527 was a litter covered in black velvet. Litters enabled the occupant to travel sitting, or lying down. We know that Katharine was an accomplished rider, so her possession of a litter does point to increasing physical discomfort and weakness.[7] In addition was the presence of 'a great hears and a bere which my ladys grace was carried to church upon',[8] suggesting that, at some point, she had become too ill to walk. During the autumn and winter of 1527 Katharine was residing at Tiverton Castle, and it was here that her illness really took hold. Communication must have passed between her and her son as per usual, but there is nothing to suggest that Henry made the long journey to Tiverton to visit her. We also don't know if the king wrote to his aunt who represented the last link to his beloved mother. By now, Henry was totally preoccupied with Anne Boleyn and the annulment of his marriage, thus his ailing aunt miles away in Devon was not a priority.

In October 1527 when 'the divorce is more talked of than ever',[9] Katharine's son was busy moving many personal items from his London residence to

Greenwich Palace.[10] Meanwhile, Greenwich Palace itself was a hive of activity where men had been working 'day and night' repairing and painting the 'Revelling Chamber' within the tilt-yard, and cleaning the Banquet Chamber. These preparations were in anticipation of an important event that formed part of England's rapprochement with France. On 1 November 1527 a French delegation installed Henry VIII in the French chivalric order of St Michael.[11] Bringing 'a collar of fine gold of the order' and robes that were 'wondrous costly and comely, of purple velvet richly embroidered' Henry VIII was adorned with them and then processed to Mass[12] observed by his courtiers including Henry Courtenay. As a form of reciprocation, Francis I was elected to the Order of the Garter. On 10 November, as Katharine's struggle to overcome her illness at Tiverton continued, at Greenwich there was merriment as revels and a banquet were held to honour the French visitors. For the celebrations and dancing the king, Henry Courtenay and other lords wore jolly bonnets, each boasting three ostrich feathers.[13] However, the king's marital difficulties were still at the forefront of his mind, and an important meeting planned for 15 November caused the queen great alarm. On 19 October she had written to her nephew, Charles V, that the purpose of the November meeting was to 'discuss whether I am, or am not, his lawful wife' and begged him to 'confer so great a favour on me, since it is doing God's service, as to win over the Pope to our side'.[14]

The 15 November meeting, like the secret tribunal, took place at Wolsey's residence, York Place. It was a crucial moment and therefore a tense one, but happily for the king the outcome was what he had hoped for as the bishops and lawyers agreed 'he had good reason to be troubled and that the matter should be submitted to the Pope'.[15] As this key meeting drew to a close in London, at four o'clock in the afternoon in Devon, as the light of day began to fade, Katharine, Countess of Devon, took her last breath. Thus departed the last of Edward IV's daughters, sister of the 'Princes in the Tower', niece of Richard III, her passing lost in the 'noise' of Henry VIII's 'Great Matter'. No member of her family was present, but those who had become something of a second family to her during her years in Devon, were, and they would ensure that her last wishes were carried out to the letter.

Tried and trusted procedures for dealing with the funeral of a member of the royal family immediately came into play, while other relevant individuals sprang into action. First, the chandler arrived to prepare the body, bearing in mind that it would be more than two weeks before the burial could take place. The entrails were removed and the body was washed and treated with fragrant spices. It was then tightly wrapped in cloth coated in wax, before being further wrapped in lead, and finally placed in a coffin which remained in her chamber. Meanwhile, messengers were sent to London to inform her son and the king of her death. The College of Arms was also informed as representatives would need to be present at her funeral to ensure that all was done correctly and to record the proceedings. Katharine's funeral was not going to be anything like the haphazard burial of her mother, Elizabeth Woodville. Accordingly, Norroy King of Arms, incidentally the same King of Arms who had officiated at William Courtenay's funeral, and Richmond Herald were despatched to Devon and left London on 24 November. Battling the winter weather and poor roads, they must be commended for covering the 180 or so miles to Tiverton in four days, arriving on 28 November. The burial could now proceed, thirteen days after Katharine's death.[16]

First, the chapel at Tiverton was hung with black cloth bearing her coat of arms, as was the great chamber and gate house. Her body was then brought down from her chamber and laid in the chapel, where there was 'daily singing' and twelve poor men in black gowns and hoods were present bearing twelve torches. Twelve tapers burnt day and night 'about the said corpse' and continual watch was kept. Meanwhile, St Peter's Church was hung in black cloth bearing her arms, and a hearse prepared for her body to lie upon. On 2 December, four days after the heralds arrived, her body was moved in a large and sombre procession to the church.

Led by two men in black gowns with black staves in their hands 'as conductors', the cross of the church was carried behind followed by 'many priests and clerks'. Next came twenty-four gentlemen walking in pairs, behind whom were doctors, priors and abbots including Thomas Chard. These were followed by Katharine's chaplains, her officers including her comptroller, Humphrey Colles, and her steward Sir George Speke'[17] and then 'the officers at arms in the king's coats of arms'. Following directly behind was Katharine's body borne by 'six tall gentlemen' in black gowns and hoods accompanied by four assistants in gowns and hoods, these being Sir Thomas Dynes, Sir John Bassett, Sir William Carew and Phillip Champernown. These gentlemen form a roll call of those to whom Katharine and the Courtenay family had longstanding links. Sir William Carew of Mohuns Ottery, Devon, was the eldest son of Sir Edmund Carew who had fought under the banner of Edward Courtenay at the relief of Exeter in 1497, and ridden a horse into Blackfriars at the funeral of Katharine's husband, William.[18] Furthermore, Sir William's son, George Carew, married as his first wife, Thomasin, the daughter of Lewis Pollard who had been a member of Katharine's council. Philip Champernown, sheriff of Devon, was Sir William Carew's brother-in-law.[19] Sir John Bassett held considerable lands in Cornwall and Devon and was prominent in local administration. At this time he was married to Honor Greville, but after his death in 1528 she would go on to marry Katharine's half-brother, Arthur Plantagenet, the illegitimate son of Edward IV. It is their correspondence that would find fame as 'The Lisle Letters'. Sir Thomas Dynes is most likely Sir Thomas Denys who was steward of Margaret Pole, Countess of Salisbury's manor of Pyworthy, Devon, and Princess Mary's comptroller from 1526. An influential figure in Devon, he was a known friend of both branches of the Courtenay family and in 1537 was accused by Thomas Cromwell of 'hanging at the Courtenay's sleeve.[20]

As Katharine's body made its way slowly to the church a canopy of black velvet was held above it by six esquires named as John Chichester, John Fullforde, Andrew Hillesden, John Fortescu of 'Preleston', Bartholomew Fortescu and John Whitinge. Several members of the Fortescue family were among Katharine's servants, while the Fulfords were an established local family with longstanding links to the Courtenays. John Chichester is probably the Mr Chichester referred to in Katharine's household accounts of 1523–1524. At every corner of the canopy a banner was borne by four further esquires in black gowns. The Trinity banner was held by George Carew, son of Sir William Carew, mentioned above, Our Lady banner by Nicholas Ashford, St Edward banner by Richard Chydley, whose wardship Katharine had been granted in 1524,[21] and St Katherine's banner by Alexander Wood, whose servant Katharine had rewarded on 20 October 1523 for bringing her a dozen partridges.[22] A further eight banners, or pennants, were also carried by eight gentlemen in gowns and hoods, four each side. Philip Courtenay and Edward Speke, probably a relative of Sir George Speke, walked in pairs as did Richard Fortescue and Richard Yerd, perhaps the son of William Yerde who was named as one of Henry Courtenay's servants in 1519. The remaining four were Richard Strode, Henry Waliron, Humphrey Ayore and Roger Blewett.

Immediately following Katharine's body came the chief mourner, and as this was the funeral of a female, the chief mourner also had to be female. Katharine's chief mourner was Lady Carew, and it is most likely that this was Lady Joan Carew, wife of Sir William Carew.[23] She was also a member of the Powderham branch of the Courtenay family, being the daughter of Sir William Courtenay of Powderham[24] and, as such, of sufficient standing to be Chief Mourner to the Countess of Devon. Furthermore, she had known Katharine for some years.[25] Assisting her was Sir Piers Edgecombe, a member of Katharine's council, while her train was borne 'by one of her gentlewomen in a black gown and hood'. In addition to Lady Carew were six female mourners, walking two by two. Four of these ladies, Agnes Bere, Mistress Motton, Mistress Courtenay and family retainer, Margaret Brown, had served Katharine for years. Mistress Colles was probably the wife of Humphrey Colles and Mistress Fortescue's family, as we have seen, had a track record of service to Katharine. Following them were 'other gentlewomen in black'. Then 'officers and servants with all other and so proceeded to the Church' where the abbots and suffragans were waiting for them. This group no doubt included Mug the Fool who was still part of her household.[26]

Katharine's body was carried into the church and laid within a hearse covered with cloths of velvet and tissue, adorned with lighted candles and her banners. Following the dirge and other ceremonies, the mourners returned to Tiverton Castle 'where was all things honourably prepared for them for that night'. Meanwhile the candles remained burning around Katharine's body over which watch was kept all night. At seven o'clock the next morning the mourners 'with all other aforesaid' returned to the church, and the mass of our Lady began with Lady Carew, as chief mourner, leading the offerings. The mass of the Trinity was sung next by Thomas Chard, and then the mass of Requiem. Lady Carew and the six ladies of Katharine's household made offerings first, followed by 'the steward, the Treasurer and Comptroller with knights and esquires and gentlemen, and the mayor with the aldermen of the City of Exeter and divers other of the said town and country that would'. After this Dr Peter Carsley, who had visited Katharine in the summer of 1524, gave the sermon with the theme 'Manus deo tetigit me' [The hand of God touched me]. Following the sermon and masses the mourners returned to the castle while 'the suffragen with all other abbots and priors and prelates in pontifical did execute the ceremonies of interment'. Below the hearse a vault had been prepared and Katharine's body was lowered into it using 'towels of linen cloth'. As was the custom, her officers 'with a sad and dolorous countenance, brake the staves of their offices and cast them into the sepulchre, some weeping'. After the interment was complete, they returned to the castle to join the other mourners and 500 people sat down to dine. The funeral would have been a jaw-dropping sight for the locals of Tiverton, who had probably never seen anything like it, and the whole area must have come to a standstill. This was, after all, a royal funeral complete with hundreds of mourners including heralds, local gentry, the king's officers of arms, burning tapers, banners and heraldic flags on display.

Back in the church Katharine's banners, along with those of the saints, were displayed while 'under the hearse a presentation of the corpse covered with a rich cloth of gold of tissue' was lain. This tells us that like her sister the queen, a funeral effigy of Katharine had been prepared. The herald then goes on to record that at Katharine's feet was prepared an altar with double barriers hanged with black cloth garnished with scutcheons which were to remain there until her son 'has caused to be made on the side of the high alter, a chapel with a tomb and a presentation of that noble woman whose soul God assoylle [pardon]'. Katharine, however, had made extensive provision for her soul and the majority of her will was concerned with this.

First, she directed that £21 per year was to be paid to 'three honest priests' in perpetuity. Two of them had already been appointed by the will of her father-in-law, Edward Courtenay, to sing or say masses in the church or in the 'Chapel of our Blessed Lady, standing in the churchyard without the church aforesaid' and Katharine's will supported a third. The priests' purpose was to sing or say three masses 'in the said two chapels in Tiverton aforesaid'. As only Greenway's Chapel and the Chapel of Our Blessed Lady were mentioned in her will, Katharine must be referring to these. It would be expected that one of them would be Greenway's Chapel as that is where she intended to be buried.[27] Katharine then gave explicit instructions about which masses should be sung in the Greenway Chapel and on which days, and further directed that the three priests were to come together once a week in the Greenway Chapel 'at the tomb where the said countess body shall rest' and say together dirige and commendations. She further ordained that they should pray for the souls of her parents, her father-in-law, her husband, her daughter Margaret, her own soul and 'all Christian souls'. Most poignantly, in light of events to come, she asked them to pray for 'the good preservation, health, good and prosperous estate of our said wellbeloved son, of Henry, Lord marques of Exeter, Earl of Devonshire, long to endure, to God's pleasure'.[28]

For her servants, especially her household servants, Katharine's death was a cause of sadness and worry. Sadness because she had been a fair and generous mistress, and worry because their employment, and thus their financial security, had come to an end. Katharine, well aware of their predicament, had made provision for them. She instructed that all her household servants currently in her employ should have, from the day of her death, one year's wages, unless they were taken into the employment of her son. She further willed that her servants be allowed to remain in her household and should enjoy 'meat, drink and lodgings' as they were accustomed to for one month after her death. She was clearly making sure that none of them were suddenly going to find themselves without a roof over their head. But it was not only her servants who were affected, after her death Tiverton and the other areas where she had resided, changed. Her son would not be the resident landowner that she had been. The bustle and excitement generated by her presence, which saw her households visited by nobles, local dignitaries and the king's officers, ceased. So did the opportunities for merchants who had benefitted from her custom and others who had sought her patronage. Locally, there would have been genuine regret at the passing of the Countess of Devon.

Katharine's life had been one of extreme ups and downs, and her determination to preserve the independence she had been granted by Henry VIII reflects the turbulence of her earlier life. More her mother's daughter than her father's, she demonstrated an iron will and a steely self-control. This kept her and her children safe during the final years of Henry VII's reign, and by her vow of chastity, ensured that the lands of the earldom of Devon remained very firmly under her control. She had a keen eye for detail and was certainly not afraid to take swift legal action in defence of her rights. But she was also astute and knew how to deal with people, even earning the grudging respect of Henry VII. She charmed local dignitaries who flocked to pay court to her and knew how to handle her nephew, the mercurial Henry VIII. When he requested that she relinquish her rights to the lands of the earldom of March, she immediately acquiesced unlike her counterpart, Margaret Pole, Countess of Salisbury, who argued with Henry VIII for years over possession of lands to which she had a weak claim.[29] Katharine knew that her nephew took great offence at any sign of ingratitude, and Margaret Pole's behaviour proved to be a dangerous misjudgement.

Katharine's relationship with her children, Henry and Margaret, is more difficult to understand due to lack of contemporary evidence. She kept a firm hold on the purse strings, but this was more likely prudence borne of previous experience than meanness. Residing together in Prince Henry's household for six years, the children saw more of their mother while growing up than was common at the time. Both were headstrong individuals, and the fact that Margaret felt able to write such a letter to her mother in 1513 indicates that she allowed them to express their opinions to her. She was certainly generous to her son, sending him £200 per year to ensure he could fund his expensive lifestyle at court, while her will demonstrates that her daughter's soul and her son's future were at the forefront of her mind.

Fortunately, Katharine never lived to see the consequences of Henry VIII's determination to marry Anne Boleyn, the reverberations of which enveloped the country until 'the daily life of a whole people rocked with its commotion'.[30] She never had to face the horrors that her son Henry and her cousin Margaret Pole did, and it is not known how she would have behaved in those circumstances. In light of her devout piety, her nephew's course of action would have caused her great pain, leaving her conscience in turmoil. Mercifully, Katharine never witnessed those tides of change, which would overwhelm her family within just eleven years. Her death, at 48, spared her that, and she died, as she had not always lived, in peace and in the belief that her family's future was secure.

St Peter's Church, where her body lies at rest, is a vibrant church that is attended and visited regularly. In addition to its church services, it hosts concerts, organises afternoon teas and coffee mornings, has its own choir and an active bell ringing group. In addition to the main church, weddings are also conducted in the exquisitely beautiful and serene Greenway Chapel, when chairs are brought in and flowers fill the air with the scent of spring and summer. So in death, as she was in life, Katharine remains at the very heart of Tiverton's community.

Part II

Henry and Gertrude Courtenay
The Rise and Fall of a Royal Power Couple

Chapter 8

The Marquis and Marchioness of Exeter

The first half of Henry VIII's reign were halcyon years for young Henry Courtenay. Just 10 or 11 years old at the king's accession, he received many gifts of apparel from his generous cousin in these early years. Items included a crimson gown furred with black, three satin doublets of yellow, of crimson and of tinsel, French and Milan bonnets and six pairs of double-soled shoes. Henry became an accomplished jouster, and this burgeoning ambition was also catered for when he received two saddles and two horse harnesses one of red leather and one of black velvet fringed with black silk. Another change was his graduation to king's servant by March 1511 when he was 12 or 13 years old.[1] Henry was becoming established at court and thoroughly enjoying himself, but in 1513 a hiatus occurred.

Henry VIII was preparing for war against France and was going to lead the army himself. As preparations gathered pace throughout the first few months of 1513, a disgruntled Henry, probably accompanied by his sister Margaret, was removed from court and sent to stay with his mother in Devon, no doubt at her request.[2] As Henry VIII still had no heir, if any harm should befall him the prospect of a disputed succession loomed. The king was well aware of this, demonstrated by the sudden execution of Edmund de la Pole just before he left. In this event, Katharine did not want a repetition of 1483, this time involving her son. Henry VIII and Henry Courtenay were the only surviving grandsons of Edward IV, meaning her son had a strong claim to the throne. However, he was only a year or two older than her brother Edward V had been when Richard III usurped the throne. If the king did not return, there was another candidate who Katharine knew would advance his claim: her cousin the Duke of Buckingham. While both Buckingham and Henry Courtenay's claims came via two sons of Edward III in the female line, Henry was out-matched in that Buckingham was an adult male aged 35, experienced in battle and had previously been mentioned as a potential claimant. Involved in the invasion of France, he conveniently had men already under his command, raised for military action. Katharine therefore withdrew her children to Devon, probably Tiverton, which was moated and fortified with two great guns in the gatehouse. We should not doubt for a moment that if it came to it, Katharine would defend her children and use her position as Edward IV's daughter to generate support. Her son, though, was merely frustrated that he had been sent to his mother in Devon rather than being allowed to accompany the king to France. He was permitted one visit to Bishop Richard Fox, who was provisioning ships at Southampton, to experience the excitement of the preparations for war, but apart from that had to rely on letters from the battlefield. On 2 September one of the Courtenay servants who was overseas with the army, probably a member of the ap Howell family, wrote a detailed and colourful letter to him. This contained everything a teenage boy would be interested in; the taking of Therouanne, the bravery of the English, the honour shown to Henry VIII, the rich clothes worn and the incredible fortifications of Therouanne 'Verily, my lord, it was a stronghold'![3]

Fortunately, the king returned unscathed and Henry was soon back at court where, on 21 February 1516 he attended the christening of Princess Mary, carrying the basin supported by his new brother-in-law, Lord Herbert. Henry's royal profile was also increasing. As part of negotiations with France and Scotland, Henry VIII drafted articles to invite the man who was now regent of Scotland, John, Duke of Albany, to meet him. In order to assure Albany of his safety, Henry VIII considered sending to Boulogne the son of the Duke of Norfolk 'and the Earl of Devonshire, who is of the blood royal'.[4] Although the meeting never took place, significantly it was Henry VIII himself who described Henry Courtenay as 'of the blood royal'. The young earl's international standing is further evidenced by immediate activity following his first wife's death. Hardly was Lady Lisle cold in her grave when an approach was made regarding his marriage. A series of three letters between June and July 1519 reveal that William de Croy Lord of Chièvres, minister to Charles V, had raised the prospect of a marriage between his niece and Henry, authorising the English ambassador in Spain, Thomas Spinelly, to advance the proposal with the king. Ungraciously, Chièvres informed the ambassador that his niece 'is not handsome' but assured him that her dowry would be. However, his next words conjure images of the earl of Oxford and his disastrous marriage. He told Spinelly he had heard 'the youth is of evil rule' and in the event of the marriage taking place did 'beseech' Wolsey to 'put to her husband and her such persons as unto the same shall be thought good'.[5] Obviously, these criticisms are concerning and will be looked at later, but for now the marriage negotiations continued. The king was approached and was initially supportive, thus Wolsey was ordered to instruct Henry Courtenay to halt the current negotiations of marriage he was engaged in for a different bride as 'there is a far better offer made him'.[6] The king obviously wanted time to think about the proposal, but having done so he started to get cold feet. Spinelly was ordered to 'find out secretly for what reason Chièvres makes the proposal; whether he looks to any chance of the Earl's succession to the crown of England'.[7] This was the sticking point for Henry VIII, revealing his on-going concerns for the succession, and the marriage negotiations went no further.

But what of Chièvres' concerns? Was Henry Courtenay 'of evil rule'? The answer is no. What seems to have happened is that Henry's reputation became caught up in something known to historians as the 'Expulsion of the Minions'. Greg Walker has shown that several young men, who were members of Henry VIII's Privy Chamber, had been on embassy to France in the autumn of 1518 and while there had behaved badly. Egged on by Francis I himself, Nicholas Carew, Frances Bryan and others rode in disguise through Paris throwing eggs and stones at the citizens. On their return to England they acted obnoxiously, mocking anything that was not French and became overfamiliar with the king. Furthermore, the Duke of Norfolk complained that they had been the cause of the king's 'incessant gambling, which has made him lose of late a treasure of gold'. As a result, the council, with the king's agreement, removed four of them from the Privy Chamber and temporarily sent them to overseas posts. This caused much speculation in Europe; the Venetian ambassador reported it, the French king grumbled about it and it quickly reached the ears' of the Imperial court. It is significant that Chièvres described Henry Courtenay as 'being of evil rule', while the Venetian ambassador described the minions as 'youths of evil counsel', virtually the same phrase.[8] Henry was not one of these young men but, like the king, he was led astray by them.[9] For example, between 7 and 10 February he accompanied the king on a visit to Nicholas Carew's residence, Beddington Place, during which he gambled with the king and Carew culminating in one of the largest sums he ever lost gambling, £3. Clearly, Henry's friendship with some of the 'bad boys' at court had led Chièvres to find him guilty by association.

A set of accounts covering the period from January to March 1519 provide a snap shot of his life at this time.[10] It reveals a young man who was energetic, boisterous, indulged but charming. He played tennis with opponents including life-long friend and servant Anthony Harvey, Thomas Manners, great-nephew of Edward IV, and William Carey, whose family held lands in Devon and who would marry Mary Boleyn the following year. At one shuffleboard session involving Arthur Pole, he drafted in a Yeoman of the Guard to keep the score! He was regularly hosted at the tables of the great and the good including his relations Thomas Grey, Marquis of Dorset, Lord Leonard Grey, the marquis' younger brother, Charles Somerset, father-in-law to his sister Margaret, and also enjoyed the hospitality of Cardinal Wolsey. On an overnight visit to Stepney to dine with experienced solder and Battle of the Spurs veteran, Thomas, Lord Darcy, he thought nothing of sending his unfortunate servant, Bennett, all the way back to Greenwich to fetch his night cap!

Although Henry was currently a little too young and inexperienced for any serious political or administrative post, he was nevertheless used by the king in the area of 'soft power'. It was he who was often sent to meet and greet ambassadors and other foreign dignitaries, and it is easy to see why. As a member of the blood royal his mere presence was a mark of honour to those he was meeting. The fact that he was repeatedly used in this way suggests he was very good at it. Not only was he amiable and engaging, he must also have been discreet as any mistaken word, or inadvertent revelation of English plans, could be embarrassing or worse. We can imagine that at dinner with Wolsey he would be briefed on what the government was trying to achieve and what should and should not be said to the ambassadors. As part of the Treaty of London, which involved the return of Tournai to France, eight distinguished French 'hostages' were sent to England.[11] More like honoured guests, it was important to put on a good show for them as they would report all they saw and experienced in England on their return to France. Part of this charm offensive was Henry Courtenay who dined with them on 16 March. At the same time, ambassadors arrived from the queen's nephew, Charles. His grandfather, the emperor Maximillian, had died in January 1519 and Charles was canvassing for election as Holy Roman Emperor. On 9 March Henry incurred costs for his drink and for a man to walk his horses when he went to meet Charles' ambassadors at Crayford. On 17 March he was despatched to meet and accompany them to Greenwich and three days later he travelled to Kew to dine with them. It is clear that the king trusted his cousin and was fond of him, it is in this year that the famous snowball fight at Charlton near Greenwich occurred, when Henry Courtenay rewarded 'a lad … for lending his cap to my lord when the King and his lords threw snowballs'. At the culmination of this milestone decade in Henry Courtenay's life three significant events occurred: he came of age, he became a widower, he took a new wife. Just two or three months after the death of Lady Lisle, Henry Courtenay was deeply involved in negotiations for the hand of Gertrude Blount. If she was a great heiress we could understand such speed, but she was not. This strongly suggests that, on Henry's side, it was a love match. As such, we can imagine his despair in July 1519 when Wolsey told him to halt these negotiations as 'there is a far better offer made him'. Gertrude's feelings are harder to discern because she would have been very foolish to turn down such a spectacular match. However, their subsequent life together reveals that Gertrude did love, or grew to love, her husband. But who was Gertrude Blount, the woman who captured the heart of England's most eligible bachelor?

She was certainly beautiful. We know this because, in order to outshine the ladies of the French court, Catherine of Aragon was expected to bring only the most beautiful of her ladies to the Field of the Cloth of Gold in 1520 'the cream of English beauty', and Gertrude was among them.[12] She also played a prominent role in the now famous Chateau Vert of 1522 in which Mary and Anne Boleyn also participated. Only attractive ladies who could dance with elegance and poise were selected for such masques, and the ladies participating in the Chateau Vert revel were 'the crème de la crème of the Tudor Court', led by the king's sister Mary.[13] But it was not just her physical attractions that drew Henry and others to her. Gertrude was a charismatic woman who combined beauty and intelligence, courage and conscience. Henry respected his wife and they operated as equals within their marriage. Because she spent so much time with her husband, either at court or in later years at their residence at West Horsley, his friends became her friends. With her strong personality she became the centre of this close network of friends who orbited her husband. Like him, they treated her as an equal, Lord Montague adored her, Sir Nicholas Carew tried to protect her at risk to himself, and all held her in the highest regard. No wonder Henry was smitten by this captivating young woman who knew her own mind. It is not known what Henry's mother felt about her son's marriage, little evidence of contact between the two women has survived, but as the earl of Devon and cousin to the king he could have aimed higher. Nevertheless, Gertrude's family and connections, while not in the higher echelons of the aristocracy, were honourable.

Through her mother, Elizabeth, Gertrude was descended from the Say family of Essex and Hertfordshire. They were a respectable gentry family who had enjoyed royal connections for years. The family wealth was established by Gertrude's great grandfather, Sir John Say, whose life and career can only be described as dramatic. An MP who was elected speaker of the commons three times, he was 'unique in having been Speaker in both Lancastrian and Yorkist parliaments'. He was an esquire of the Body to Henry VI, progressing to the position of Chancellor of the Duchy of Lancaster in 1450 and then membership of the royal council by 1454. While he slowly but surely worked his way up in local and central administration, his life was unavoidably caught up in the struggle between the Lancastrians and Yorkists. His first patron, William de la Pole, Duke of Suffolk, was murdered in 1450 while a satirical ballad of the time referred to Say as the hated duke's creature.[14] The same year he nearly lost his head during Jack Cade's rebellion which demanded the 'dismissal and punishment of Suffolk's "false progeny and affinity"' of which Say was one. The first Parliament he attended witnessed the arrest of Humphrey, Duke of Gloucester, followed within days by his death amid accusations of foul play, and in 1478 he sat in the Parliament that secured the attainder of George, Duke of Clarence, Edward IV's brother. Say was Oxford educated and an astute man of Cromwellian abilities possessing 'a good head and sound nerves in time of crises'. He didn't, however, bear grudges or seek revenge on fallen opponents, and it was these attributes that allowed him to survive the overthrow of the Lancastrian dynasty and move smoothly into the service of the Yorkist regime. This transition was also facilitated by Say's connection to the Bourchier family, the head of which was Henry, first Earl of Essex, an alliance that would extend into the sixteenth century.[15] Despite the volatility of the period, Say built up an impressive property portfolio through purchase and royal favour. He also contracted a marriage that seems to have been genuinely happy. His wife was Elizabeth Cheyne, widow of Sir Frederick Tylney, and through a daughter of that first marriage was great grandmother to both Anne Boleyn and Catherine Howard. She bore Say at least seven children of which William, Gertrude's grandfather, was the eldest. Incidentally, their daughter Anne married Sir Henry Wentworth and their daughter, Margery, married Sir John Seymour of Wolf Hall, meaning that Gertrude's great aunt Anne was the grandmother of Jane Seymour.

When Elizabeth died in 1473 she was buried in the Say Chapel in St Augustine's Church, Broxbourne. The tomb inscription describes her as 'a woman of noble blood and most noble in good manners'. John's second wife was wealthy widow Agnes Danvers who brought to her husband 'a handsome jointure',[16] but he was unable to replicate the happiness of his first marriage. In his will he stipulated that his wife should 'have and peaceably enjoy' all the goods and chattels she had possessed before their marriage on the condition that 'she not trouble nor vex mine executors after my decease'.[17] Sir John died in 1478 and was buried in accordance with his wishes 'by the body of Dame Elizabeth late my Wife'. In his will he remembered both kings he had served giving truth to Edward IV's description of him as 'the truest and the faithfullest man that any christian Prince may have'.[18] Sir John Say died possessed of an impressive collection of twenty-two manors, the majority in Hertfordshire[19] with others in Essex, Norfolk and Rutland. It was a selection of these that would descend to his great granddaughter, Gertrude.

Sir William Say, Gertrude's grandfather, was aged 26 years and more when he succeeded to the estates[20] and at first appeared to follow in his father's footsteps. In 1478–1479 he became Sheriff of Somerset and Dorset and between 1482 and 1489 Sheriff of Essex and Hertfordshire. Made a Knight of the Bath at the coronation of Richard III, he went on to enjoy a steady but unremarkable career under Henry VII. He may have been a member of the king's council established at the beginning of the reign,[21] and from then on sat regularly on Commissions of the Peace and Gaol Delivery for Hertfordshire. While he also sat as MP for Hertfordshire in 1491–1492 and 1495, he failed to emulate his father and did not obtain any royal offices.[22] Nevertheless, he managed to extend his land holdings, building on the fine estate left to him.[23] Perhaps unsurprisingly, William's ambitions brought him into conflict with Sir John Fortescue of Punsborne, near Hatfield, Hertfordshire.

Fortescue enjoyed the favour of Henry VII having joined him in exile before fighting for him at Bosworth. Remembering such past loyalties, the king appointed him a Knight of the Body and Butler of England and also granted him several manors, one of which was in Essex. Fortescue naturally assumed a position of authority locally, serving as sheriff of Hertfordshire and Essex in 1486,[24] and sat on Commissions of the Peace for Hertfordshire, often alongside William. Furthermore, William's seat at Baas was in the same part of Hertfordshire as Fortescue's seat at Punsborne, and both men evidently decided that the area wasn't big enough for the both of them. While generally William seems to have been an amiable individual, this was not the case in his relationship with Fortescue, and both men resorted to force of arms in the course of their dispute. What it was about is unclear, but it was serious enough to warrant the personal intervention of the king. He wrote identical letters to both men, but only the letter to William has survived. It makes clear the king's anger, having heard that they were both going to attend the next sessions at Hertford with 'unlawful assemblies' the intention of which was 'the affraying of our peace and the disturbance of the same sessions'. He therefore commanded them to absent themselves from the sessions and not do anything 'repugnant to the equity of our laws or rupture of our said peace, at your uttermost peril'. They were also, immediately upon receipt of the letter, to present themselves before the king 'to know our further mind and pleasure in the premises'. We do not know when the letter was written, but as Fortescue died in 1500 it was earlier than that. As Henry VII had endured uprisings and rebellions in both decades prior to 1500, any disturbance and fracas in Hertfordshire, which was close to London, was extremely unwelcome. The fact that Fortescue's favour with Henry VII did not protect him from the king's anger, reveals the seriousness with which the situation was regarded. What the outcome was is not known, but both men were lucky to have received nothing more than a rap on the knuckles.[25]

In addition to his purchases, William's strategic marriages added more lands to the portfolio. He had married, in his father's lifetime, heiress Genevieve Hill, but she died without surviving issue in 1480. His second wife, and Gertrude's grandmother, was the formidable Elizabeth Fray, one of the daughters of his stepmother, Agnes Danvers, and the widow of Sir Thomas Waldegrave.[26] Elizabeth was wealthy, being co-heiress of her father Sir John Fray as well as enjoying her widow's jointure, and she was in no rush to relinquish her independence. In 1474 she turned down more than one proposal from an apparently lovesick John Paston III, who was not only attracted to her wealth but to Elizabeth herself.[27] In fact, Elizabeth did not re-marry until several years later when she took Sir William Say as her husband. She knew William, she knew the household, having visited it often to see her mother, and she was happy that this situation would suit her. Elizabeth bore her husband two daughters, Elizabeth, Gertrude's mother, and Mary, and the couple enjoyed fourteen years of married life until Elizabeth's death in 1494–1495.[28] Her death meant that William was left to arrange marriages for his two daughters without the in-put of his capable wife, an in-put that might have helped to avoid the protracted legal action that followed.

As co-heiresses to desirable estates in the home counties, the Say girls were attractive propositions on the marriage market. As a result, the Say family's position in society reached a pinnacle when William was approached by none other than Henry Bourchier, second Earl of Essex, friend and jousting companion of Sir William Courtenay. Not only was Essex a member of the aristocracy, he was also a member of the royal family. His mother was Anne Woodville and his great-great-grandfather was Thomas 'of Woodstock', youngest son of Edward III. His father was also first cousin to Edward IV through Essex's grandmother Isabel. Both girls were unmarried when Essex made his approach and so he was able to choose which of them to marry. It has been speculated that the elder daughter, Elizabeth, was less attractive as Essex chose the younger daughter, Mary, as his wife.[29] Clearly, the inheritance of each daughter would need to be sorted out, and as this was primarily a dynastic land transaction for Essex, he was keen to select the most strategic of William's manors for himself and Mary. The indenture drawn up ahead of the marriage dated 12 March 1497, stipulated that lands worth 300 marks per year would be allocated as Mary's share.[30] Two months later Essex was called away to serve the king against the Cornish rising that broke out in May, and thus the wedding was delayed.[31] In the meantime, William was dazzled by the approach of another prospective bridegroom, this time for his daughter Elizabeth.

The erudite and well-connected William Blount, fourth Baron Mountjoy, also wanted to obtain the most lucrative and geographically valuable lands as his wife's share, and William found himself offering manors to Mountjoy that he had already promised to Essex, in particular Lawford [then known as Lalford Says]. If he hoped that his sons-in-law would sort this out after his death, he was mistaken and by 1505 both had begun legal action.[32] Suing to William Warham, Archbishop of Canterbury and Lord Chancellor, Mountjoy claimed that Essex had agreed to Lawford being part of his wife's inheritance. In response, Essex denied that he had ever agreed to such a thing and stated that Sir William had no right to make such a promise to Mountjoy, the manor already being part of his marriage settlement. Finally, he requested that the case be dismissed with costs and damages awarded to himself 'for his wrongful vexation and trouble sustained in this behalf'.[33] It is difficult to understand how William allowed such a situation to arise. If his will is anything to go by, it was out of character as that document took into account almost every eventuality, including future outbreaks of the plague! Perhaps he was overawed by two men so senior in rank and unable to say no to either during negotiations. It was not until 1515 and following the mediation of Wolsey, that things were finally settled. What is remarkable in all of this is that the three men involved managed to remain on good terms. Mountjoy and his wife were often in the company of William Say, and probably resided with him part of the time, while the location of their London properties made Mountjoy and Essex close neighbours.

The final settlement of 1515 is important because it decided which manors would pass to Gertrude, as her parents' only child, and formed the inheritance that she brought to her husband. There were seven manors in all, three in Essex [Lawford, Wikeham Hall, and Hooks and Pinnacles], three in Hertfordshire [Mylkeley also called Mentley, Ayott St Laurence also called Laurence Eyot, and Bedwell] and one in Rutland [Market Overton].[34] Together they were worth around £153, revealing that Gertrude's inheritance was far less than Lady Lisle's. Nevertheless, four of them were conveniently located near London, and what she lacked in lands Gertrude made up for with her personal charms and family connections. We have already seen on her mother's side that she was descended from a respectable gentry family, and her aunt Mary was the Countess of Essex. Her father, Lord Mountjoy, was one of the leading scholars of the age who had something money couldn't buy: favour with the royal family.

Mountjoy's wedding to Elizabeth Say took place shortly after 11 June 1499. Gertrude was their only child and may have been born within a year or two of their marriage, meaning that she was close in age to her husband. There is a tantalising entry in the privy purse expenses of Elizabeth of York for 4 July 1502 when her servants, Thomas Woodnote and John Feld, were paid three shillings 'for their costs riding to the christening of my Lord Mountjoy's child by the space of three days'.[35] Could this be Gertrude's christening? Frustratingly, details about the child are not given so it is impossible to be sure, neither do we know how many children the couple had, but only one survived and that was Gertrude. Sadly, her parents' marriage was short-lived as Elizabeth died before 1 July 1506 and, although Mountjoy outlived her by about thirty years and took three further wives, he never forgot her and the marriage appears to have been happy.[36] She was buried in the parish church of Essenden, Hertfordshire, but her father always intended to move her, probably to the Say Chapel that he had built in 1522 in Broxbourne Church. As such, no stone was placed over her resting place, but as her body was never actually moved, in his will of 1534

Mountjoy stipulated that 'a fair large and convenient stone with scriptures upon it' be laid over her.[37]

Mountjoy's family came from Barton Blount in Derbyshire and his father, John Blount, died in 1485 when he was just seven. The Blounts had a history of holding office in the pale of Calais and in November 1484 William's uncle, James, who was in charge of Hammes castle, freed his prisoner John de Vere, Earl of Oxford, and both fled to join Henry Tudor in France.[38] He was knighted at Milford Haven and continued to receive rewards for his loyalty. On 1 February 1488 he received 'for services rendered at great bodily risk and expense, in favouring and supporting the king's title to the crown' various manors in Warwick, Leicester, Northampton and Derby which had been forfeited by Richard III's supporters.[39] The family's standing within the Tudor regime continued, and Mountjoy went on to make his own mark as a result of his academic abilities. He was both the pupil and patron of the humanist scholar and reformer, Erasmus. He first studied under Erasmus when he was in Paris prior to his marriage and when he returned to England he persuaded Erasmus to accompany him. The two enjoyed a regular correspondence throughout their lives, and Erasmus wrote in glowing terms of Gertrude's father. He described him as 'so kind, so gracious, so amiable' and declared that he would follow him 'by heaven, to the grave itself'. Mountjoy's home became a centre of learning and here Erasmus met Gertrude's mother, Elizabeth, and grandfather Sir William Say, referring to them as 'his generous lady and kind father-in-law'.[40] After his father's death, Mountjoy's mother married twice more, her last husband being Thomas Butler, Earl of Ormond. Ormond held the position of Lord Chamberlain to Elizabeth of York, who was primarily responsible for the education of her younger children. It was probably through Ormond that Mountjoy was brought to the attention of the royal parents, leading to an honourable and prestigious appointment by 1499 as young Prince Henry's academic mentor [socius studiorum, companion of studies].[41] No greater compliment could have been paid to him, selected by the queen 'as a man of the world: educated, cultured and well rounded' who would be 'a positive role model' for her son.[42] Indeed, Mountjoy would become one of the most important and formative figures in Henry VIII's life.

While in the prince's household he would have met his future son-in-law, Henry Courtenay, and may even have tutored him. Where Gertrude was living following her mother's death is not known, but she too may have spent some time in the prince's household. As to her education, we know that Mountjoy took great care with his son, Charles', studies and employed the best tutors. Although, in accordance with the mores of the time, he would give more attention to the education of his son, this does not mean that such a scholar as he would have neglected the education of his daughter, especially his eldest daughter who was his only child for quite some years. It is reasonable to expect that Gertrude had an excellent education, which equipped her for a life at court. This would include skills such as dancing, singing and playing musical instruments, also reading and the ability to debate appropriate subjects, ensuring she was an interesting and engaging companion. Linguistically, she must have spoken French fluently, possibly even Latin, as these were the preferred languages of the imperial ambassador, Chapuys, who arrived at the English court in August 1529.[43] Gertrude and Chapuys would strike up a relationship in the 1530s, forged by their support of Catherine of Aragon, and their clandestine conversations must have taken place using a language in which both were fluent to avoid misunderstandings or the presence of interpreters.

In the first year of Henry VIII's reign, Mountjoy was appointed Master of the Mint and the almost hereditary Blount post of Lieutenant of Hammes Castle. He was also appointed to posts in Tournai following its capture, and made periodic visits to discharge these overseas duties. In July 1509 he joined his protégé in the state of matrimony when he married, as his second wife, Inez de Venegas who had been one of Catharine of Aragon's attendants when Princess of Wales. In 1512, Mountjoy took up his most prestigious and influential position, that of Lord Chamberlain to the queen. This meant that his daughter almost certainly obtained a position in the queen's household, as his son Charles would later do.[44] Gertrude was also in the queen's care, especially when her father and stepmother were overseas, and it is easy to see where the devotion that Gertrude felt for Catherine began. In some ways, Catherine was more of a constant in her life than her stepmothers. Inez had died by 1515 when Mountjoy married as his third wife, Alice Keble, who gave birth to his son Charles and several other children. In 1521 she too died, and Mountjoy married for the fourth and last time in 1523. Dorothy, the widow of Robert, Lord Willoughby de Broke, was the daughter of Thomas Grey, first Marquis of Dorset, and it is likely that the marriage came about through Mountjoy's connection to the Courtenay family.[45]

The lives of this young couple had criss-crossed each other's over many years; first probably in the household of the young Prince Henry, and then in his court. Gertrude was one of the queen's ladies, Henry one of the king's men, and they would have met at the various revels and masques which Henry Courtenay loved. He had his own 'masking gear' and once danced so vigorously in the queen's chamber that he lost his hat, which was never found! The young men of the king's household were accustomed to visit the queen and her ladies in her chamber, and this allowed more time for acquaintance. During these visits, Gertrude and Henry would have had the opportunity to talk and get to know one another, all under the watchful eye of the queen. At first it would have been conducted innocently, within the bounds of courtly love with no prospect of anything more, but with Lady Lisle's unexpected death Henry was suddenly free to marry, and things moved at pace. Of course, Henry needed the king's permission, and he was only too happy to grant it. Gertrude had no royal blood in her veins, so the marriage was not a dynastic threat, and she was the daughter of a man he greatly admired. In fact, so happy was he that he paid for their wedding celebrations!

On Tuesday 25 October 1519 Henry and Gertrude were married at Greenwich Palace in the presence of the king and queen.[46] Five days earlier Henry VIII had spent the huge sum of £200 4s 9d on jousts to celebrate the forthcoming nuptials.[47] These also took place at Greenwich and involved the groom himself, along with friends including Nicholas Carewe, Henry Norris, William Carey and, of course, the king. Two days later, the king's benevolence continued when he granted the newlyweds an annuity of £66 13s 4d.[48] For quite some time they must have felt as though they were on an extended honeymoon especially when, eight months later, they travelled to France to attend the Field of the Cloth of Gold. The purpose of this meeting between Henry VIII and Francis I was to maintain peace, and it enabled Gertrude to make her international debut as Henry's wife and Countess of Devon.[49] Henry, as an earl, was accompanied by three chaplains, six gentlemen, thirty-three servants and twenty horses; his wife by three gentlewomen, four menservants and eight horses. It is no exaggeration to say that those attending the Field of the Cloth of Gold enjoyed a once-in-a-lifetime experience. The splendour and opulence was breathtaking, the workmanship staggering and the newly-weds must, like everyone else, have gasped when a 'dragon' appeared in the sky, a large kite-like construction breathing smoke via pyrotechnics! However, the young earl of Devon was not there to simply spectate. Just as his father had been an outstanding jouster, the same was now required of his son. Joining other jousting luminaries such as the Duke of Suffolk and his kinsman, the Marquis of Dorset, Henry led a jousting team comprising English and French contestants. Among the English contestants were kinsmen and friends including Lord Montague and his brother Arthur, and brother-in-law Henry, Lord Herbert.[50] Although the whole purpose of the meeting was to maintain peace and amity, for the two kings it was an opportunity to compete and attempt to out-do one another in absolutely everything. Unsurprisingly, after the meeting came to an end Henry VIII was on his way to Gravelines to meet Francis I's enemy, Charles V. Among the large entourage attending him was the earl of Devon accompanied by six servants on horseback. Charles and his aunt, Margaret of Austria, then returned to Calais where Charles' other aunt, Catherine of Aragon, was waiting. It is likely that Henry Courtenay had met Charles in May 1520 when he paid a flying visit to England, spooked by the impending Anglo French meeting, but we know for certain that in July 1520 Henry was at the meetings in Gravelines and Calais, and was definitely in the emperor's presence.[51] Henry could not have known that the man towards whom he was now showing such deference and courtesy, would one day do everything in his power to bring about the death of his only son, Edward; fortunately, all were in ignorance of the future to come.

Back in England, with apartments set aside for them at each royal residence,[52] Henry and Gertrude spent the majority of their time at court. As already noted, the earl of Devon was used extensively in the arena of soft power and this continued, strengthened by his charming wife. One example occurs in 1527 when a betrothal of marriage was contemplated between Princess Mary and either Francis I or his son, Henri, duc d'Orleans. In March, Henry was part of an elite group including the king, Wolsey and the dukes of Norfolk and Suffolk, that dined with the French ambassadors[53] and in May, a performance was staged for them in the great hall at Greenwich. A curtain at the far end fell down to reveal a 'verdant cave' approached by four steps. Within the cave 'were eight damsels of such rare beauty as to be supposed goddesses … They were arrayed in cloth of gold, their hair gathered into a net, with a very richly jewelled garland, surmounted by a velvet cap, the hanging sleeves of their surcoats being so long that they well nigh touched the ground.' At the sound of trumpets, the 'damsels' then descended from the cave 'the first of them being the princess' who was hand in hand with Gertrude. Presenting themselves to the king, they then danced which was 'very delightful by reason of its variety, as they formed certain groups and figures most pleasing to the sight'.[54] As part of the same negotiations, when the Lord Steward of France, the Bishop of Bayonne and the Chancellor of Alencon arrived in England in October 'the King of England treated them with all possible honour; he sent his cousin … and many other noblemen to meet them at the seaside'.[55]

Since 1519 Henry had enjoyed informal membership of the Privy Chamber and by June 1520 this was formalised. Apart from a couple of temporary expulsions, he retained membership for the rest of his life and in 1532 assumed a senior position. To ensure that the king always had an appropriate number of gentlemen to serve him, two teams of six gentlemen, one under Henry's leadership and the other under George Boleyn, were to serve for six weeks alternately.[56] Henry's membership of the Privy Chamber reflected his close relationship with the king. It was here that the king could enjoy 'quiet, rest, comfort' and no one was allowed to enter except those the king called for and those appointed to attend upon him.[57] By May 1521, Henry had also been appointed a member of the king's council. Significantly, this meant that he had access to the king in both public and private spheres, and this constant attendance on the monarch gave him the potential to be very influential indeed.[58]

Henry's income from the Boconnoc lands was clearly insufficient to support his prominent role at court and position as Earl of Devon, so in addition to the £200 a year he received from his mother, the king made a series of grants of lands and offices to him over the next few years, most of which were in the west country. They not only provided funds but bolstered Henry's influence in the area where his power base lay by providing opportunities for patronage, as he was able to appoint household servants and others he wished to reward to lower-level posts associated with the offices.[59] A swathe of grants were made in 1523 including appointment as Steward of the Duchy of Cornwall 'and of all lands belonging to the duchy in Cornwall and Devon', and keeper, or warden, of the stanneries in Cornwall and Devon.[60] These appointments were valuable assets and there is evidence that Henry jealously guarded his rights. The Cornish and Devon tinners were organised into different areas of jurisdiction, known as 'stannaries', and as warden Henry was the crown's representative responsible for making appointments to the stannary courts and enforcing the stannary laws, which sat outside of normal manorial jurisdiction.[61] In 1529 a dispute over a tinwork in Cornwall got out of hand leading to an assault, but Henry was most put out when the case was taken out of his jurisdiction. When one of those involved complained to Wolsey and the king's council, Henry immediately sent a letter of objection. The decision, he argued, 'appeareth to me to be a thing again the customs and old usages used in the said stannary out of time of mind', which resulted in the 'derogation and hindrance of mine office of Wardenship'.[62]

As he got older, Henry was expected to play a greater role in government, but he was eased into this slowly and we can probably see Wolsey's hand here. Wolsey had known Henry since he was a teenager; he knew his strengths and weaknesses and was likely acting in a kind of mentoring role to the young earl. There is certainly plenty of evidence of contact between the two over the years, whether dining together, riding together or the various errands Henry ran for the cardinal, such as taking fresh minted crowns from Wolsey to Henry VIII in August 1526.[63] In 1522 Henry was appointed to his first Commission of the Peace for the counties of Devon and Somerset,[64] and he sat regularly thereafter and for additional counties, until 1536. The year 1523 saw him taking an active part in the Parliament of that year when he was appointed a trier of petitions from Gascony and parts beyond the Sea. This entailed dealing with petitions which usually did not concern the Crown's affairs thus allowing Parliament to concentrate on its core business. Not considered as important as being a trier of petitions from England, by 1529 Henry had 'graduated' to being one of those higher-level triers, and this shows him progressing as he gained experience.[65] One of the more unwelcome roles he carried out was as a member of the panel of peers that condemned his mother's cousin, Edward, Duke of Buckingham in 1521. Henry, along with every other peer on the panel found Buckingham guilty, and this would have brought home the reality and brutality of the Tudor court in which he was now complicit.

In addition to lands and offices, Henry received marks of honour that reveal the royal favour he enjoyed. In April 1521 he was elected to the Order of the Garter, and the king seemed delighted to welcome his cousin into the order, telling him it was expected 'that his virtue which had already begun with such a lustre would increase from that time, and his nobility would shine out more and more in him every day'. He then ordered the Marquis of Dorset to tie the garter about his left leg, but the king himself 'put on him the collar, adding also the George'. Due to Buckingham's trial, Henry's official installation and the feast of St George were delayed until 9 June, but before the feasting could begin all were required to watch the deceased duke's ceremonial expulsion from the order. The crest, banner and sword of the once greatest nobleman in England were thrown from the loft of St George's Chapel into the choir, then dragged through the church and out the west door where they were contemptuously dumped in a ditch.[66]

Four years later, in June 1525, Henry received the greatest honour of his life when he was created Marquis of Exeter. At the time the only other marquis in England was his mother's half-nephew, Thomas Grey, second Marquis of Dorset. The ceremony was to take place on 16 June at Bridewell Palace, but before this Henry and Gertrude took a trip into Devon, perhaps to celebrate his elevation with his mother and to show himself and his wife to the locality. After visiting various parts of the earldom including Chulmleigh Park where many of his horses were at grass, their return began in early June. By 12 June they had reached the Vyne, the splendid home of Lord Sandys near Basingstoke where they drank with Gertrude's father, Lord Mountjoy, and Henry's friend Thomas Manners, Lord Roos. They had a lot to celebrate as Manners would be created earl of Rutland in the same ceremony. In preparation, Henry had already purchased a number of costly materials for his robes including three yards of gold ribbon, damask, black satin, tinsel, purple velvet and a gold and silk tassel for his coronet. Thirty servants were dressed in the Courtenay colours for the elevation, including longstanding servants such as Anthony Harvey, Jasper Horsey and Lewis ap Howell.[67] Several elevations took place that day, the most important being that of Henry Fitzroy, the king's illegitimate son, who was created duke of Richmond and Somerset. When it was Henry Courtenay's turn, he was led into the king's presence between the Duke of Suffolk and the Marquis of Dorset, the sword was carried by the Earl of Northumberland and the cape and circlet by the Earl of Oxford. To support his new title, the king granted him the manor of Dertyngton, Devon, followed in August by a fine

London house at St Laurence Poultney called The Rose, which had belonged to the Duke of Buckingham. This impressive residence was described as being large and superb, located on the banks of the Thames 'with very delightful gardens'.[68] The marquis was very proud of his London home and commissioned James Redam, 'one of the king's master carpenters' to make improvements to it. The main alteration was to build a new gallery along three sides of the garden, with twelve bay windows, fitments for hangings and 'a convenient chimney' in the south end part. A summer house was built under the gallery on the south side 'well plastered paved and latticed'. The house itself had a gate house, a great chamber and a hall, and was certainly a residence fit for a marquis and his marchioness.[69] Gertrude was now the highest-ranking lady within her family and one of the highest-ranking ladies in England; she even out-ranked her own mother-in-law. But one thing the couple desperately needed was an heir to inherit his father's wealth and title, and this is one area in which they were not blessed.

If we accept Whitley and Kramer's persuasive hypothesis that Henry VIII's problem producing a male heir was due to a genetic condition inherited in the female line from his great grandmother, Jacquetta of Luxembourg, we might suspect that Exeter had the same condition, as Jaquetta was also his great grandmother.[70] Gertrude stated in 1533 that she 'had had children before which lived not after their birth' and a pregnancy that year also failed to lead to the birth of a living child.[71] However, in the summer of 1524 Gertrude did give birth to a child which may have survived infancy. In May her mother-in-law's comptroller rewarded Simon Plant, one of Exeter's servants, 'what that my young lady was brought abed with child'. In June the huge sum of £200 was given by the countess to her son 'towards his business against that my lady should have child', and in the same month family retainer Margaret Brown was despatched from Devon to London, probably to care for Gertrude and her child, and she was still there in September.[72] Exeter's accounts of 1525 reveal that the couple did have a living son at that point, but unfortunately he is unnamed and referred to only as 'my young lord'. He is likely the child born the previous year as items associated with him suggest he was very young. One son, Edward, did live to adulthood but the only evidence we have for his age is provided years later and points to his birth taking place between 1525 and 1526. The 'young lord' referred to in 1525 may have been their son Henry, most likely their eldest son as he was named after his father and after the king. He died in childhood and was buried in Essenden Church where his grandmother, Elizabeth Say, was buried.[73] The accounts of 1525 provide details about the life of this 'young lord' revealing that Henry and Gertrude were attentive parents. He had 'a chariot to learn my Lord to go', probably a sixteenth century version of a baby walker, and a 'horn garnished with silk and ribbons' for him to blow. His clothes were luxurious and included a coat of green velvet with a matching hat and a pair of velvet shoes. Evidence suggests that he resided mainly at the manor of Bedwell under the care of Mrs Knighton. This delightful manor, complete with deer park, was owned by Gertrude's grandfather and formed part of her inheritance. When the court stayed at nearby Hatfield in August 1525, Gertrude visited her son at Bedwell, receiving a gift of a partridge from one of the locals, and arrangements were also made for her son to join them at Hatfield.[74] Henry's death, when it occurred, would have been a deeply personal tragedy, as well as a dynastic one.

From the 1530s, the marquis and marchioness of Exeter began to spend more time at their residence West Horsley, and it is the inventory taken here in 1538 that tells us more about their lifestyle and interests. The pastimes they enjoyed were typical of their class. They loved music and owned various musical instruments including one double pair of virginals, one great pair, two small pairs of regalles and nine viols. Their household was full of individuals who could play them, and in 1538 they were taught by Master of the Musicians, 33-year-old Hugh Browne.[75] Anne Browne, one of Gertrude's ladies, could 'play well upon the virginals and lute', Thomas Harrys, one of the Yeoman Waiters, could sing and play the viol and other instruments, while Welshman William Boothe could sing in three-man songs, producing beautiful harmonies. Thomas Whight not only sang and played the harp but could also juggle 'and make pastimes'.[76] The sports they enjoyed included archery and hawking, the latter of which appears to have been Henry's favourite sport and at Horsley he kept his hawks in a tower attended by four falconers.[77]

Their clothes also reflected their status with Gertrude's wardrobe including gowns of black velvet furred to contrast with grey or white miniver, crimson velvet and crimson satin lined with cloth of gold.[78] Henry's wardrobe was vivid and contained doublets of white taffeta, jackets of yellow velvet and black velvet all fringed with gold and a jacket of cloth of silver and gold tissue. One of his hats was a splendid red silk one trimmed with gold.[79] Henry was very particular about his appearance; he had his own barber, 30-year-old Edmund Tyrell who was described as being 'very good' and 'can do all things that be incident unto the same science'.[80] However, when he was travelling and didn't have his barber with him, there are numerous occasions when he rewarded others for shaving him, including his father-in-law's barber, and he even rewarded George Boleyn's servant for bringing him a hair comb! The furnishings in their household were luxurious including hangings of cloth of gold and crimson velvet for their beds, expensive tapestries and silver and gilt tableware displaying the Courtenay arms. However, it is the less ostentatious items that are far more revealing. Recorded in their household in 1538 were four cushions, two of crimson velvet and two of green velvet, all embroidered with the initials H and G. Among other items were two cradles, one of purple velvet and the other of scarlet, and '3 pieces that belongeth to the birth of a child one of purple velvet with powdered ermines one with crimson with powdered ermine and the other of red damask embroidered with gold and silver'.[81] The poignancy of these items needs no explanation.

In 1527 Henry's mother died and he finally succeeded to the lands of the earldom of Devon, which made him one of the wealthiest nobles in England. Thus, by the summer of 1528 after nearly ten years of marriage, the couple appeared to have everything: affluence, status, royal favour and an heir. However, the spectre of Anne Boleyn was already hanging over the court, and as if to reflect the fearful changes to come, Gertrude almost died. An epidemic of the sweating sickness occurred in the summer and in late June she fell ill. The king was terrified and ordered that 'all such, as were in my said Lord Marquys company, and my said lady, to depart in several parcels, and so not continue together'.[82] This was a perilous situation; the disease caused headaches, a virulent fever, palpitations and dehydration. It was fast working with those who contracted it either recovering or dying within a mere twenty-four hours. It swung a scythe through the court, with Wolsey and Anne Boleyn both going down with it but surviving, while major court figures such as Sir William Compton and the Exeters' friends Sir William Carey and Sir Arthur Pole, all lost their lives. Fortunately, Gertrude pulled through, but this fearful brush with mortality ominously marked the beginning of the next decade and provided a taste of things to come.

Chapter 9

1528–1536

The Start

serpentine enemy about the king.

For the Marquis and Marchioness of Exeter the years 1528–1538 could not be more different to the previous decade. Over those early years the king's affection towards them was something they felt assured of, but over the next decade that changed. The unexpected collapse of Henry Courtenay's relationship with his cousin must have been the biggest regret of his life. The unprecedented events of the 1530s, the choices individuals were forced to make, enables us to see them in a way that would not be possible otherwise and Henry and Gertrude were forced to make some very difficult choices indeed. These were years of tension, fractured relationships, dramatic scenes and violence, and no one, from the highest to the lowest, was immune.

Despite Henry VIII's genuine need for an heir and the spent political value of the Spanish marriage, once it became known that Anne Boleyn, rather than a foreign princess, was to become his wife no one believed in the sincerity of his motives. This belief was strengthened when Henry asked the pope to issue a dispensation to marry a woman whose sister he had slept with, while at the same time claiming that the pope had exceeded his authority by issuing a similar dispensation allowing him to marry a woman who, he claimed, had slept with his brother. The beleaguered Pope Clement VII alternated between rocking with laughter when assured that Henry was only acting according to his conscience and wallowing in self-pity at being dragged into this unsolvable situation, weeping and wishing he were dead.[1] The pope was in a difficult position as he could not risk offending the emperor Charles V, Catherine of Aragon's powerful nephew. Therefore, banking on the mercurial king eventually losing interest in Anne Boleyn, he delayed making any pronouncement for or against the king's marriage, but this did more harm than good and drove Catherine to distraction. She complained bitterly and declared that these delays would cause her to 'die of grief, under the stigma of having been the King's concubine'.[2] The imperial ambassador, Eustace Chapuys, agreed with her, but even his eyebrows must have shot to the top of his forehead when an equally frustrated Cromwell raged that the pope would never do the king justice and 'resolved to give His Holiness a good slap on the face'.[3]

Anne Boleyn's hot temper is well known and this became worse at every setback prompting angry threats against Catherine and Mary. When scandalous rumours about Anne began circulating in Italy, a furious king blamed Catherine for spreading them claiming to recognise her style of writing.[4] Anne's insecurity was not helped as relations with her own family broke down. Her uncle, the Duke of Norfolk, called her a great whore, claimed that the devil was behind 'this accursed situation' and complained that she heaped more insults on him than a dog. Even the flexible conscience of the Duke of Suffolk found the situation intolerable. He hated Anne Boleyn, as did his wife, and when a fracas broke out between their servants one of Suffolk's men was killed. The person who suffered most was Princess Mary. Once Henry's 'jewel' now his rejected 'bastard', the teenage princess was often hysterical. Even Chapuys was not immune as his nerves became as shredded as everyone else's. In May 1533 he revealed the pressure he was under from those disaffected individuals who expected him to find a solution, writing dramatically to Charles V that everyday 'I am visited by people of quality, who break my head with speeches and writings'.[5]

Life at court for Henry and Gertrude was no longer a round of dancing, jousting and fun but one of stress, suspicion and developments that threatened the very fabric of their lives. Their friend, Sir Edward Neville's description of the Privy Chamber in this context is easy to understand: 'the king keepeth a sort of knaves here that we dare neither look nor speak, and [if I were] able to live, I would rather live any life in the world [than] tarry in the privy chamber'.[6] The Exeters shared his disillusion and sometime before June 1530, Gertrude's devotion to Catherine prompted Anne Boleyn to demand she be 'dismissed from Court and sent home'.[7] This toxic atmosphere led the couple to spend more time at their family residence, West Horsley in Surrey, but as they had previously spent the majority of their time at court their absence did not go unnoticed.[8]

The break with Rome is so well known not to require detailed rehearsal here, but what is important to understand is how Henry and Gertrude reacted at different stages. Henry Courtenay was a crucial figure throughout this period, using his unique position as close relative and friend of the king to provide a voice of reason while striving to protect Catherine and Mary. Gertrude also played a significant role as the main communicator of a group that expressed their dislike of the king's actions. Their reliance on her was so great that Lord Montague reportedly declared 'that if the wisdom of my Lady were not, he would not be able to bear this world'.[9] It has been claimed that Gertrude ran her own spy network during the 1530s, and she was certainly capable of it.[10]

Her father had spies when in charge of Calais so she was familiar with the concept, while spies were common at the Tudor court. However, it is unlikely that Gertrude ran a spy network in that sense, instead she relied on information provided by her husband and a small circle of trusted friends. This system was more robust, relying as it did on mutual trust and shared values rather than money, patronage and self-interest. The Marquis and Marchioness of Exeter kept their circle very close and this circle consisted of the following, with their approximate ages given in 1530.

Thirty-eight-year-old Henry Pole, Lord Montague, son and heir of Margaret Pole, Countess of Salisbury, was the future earl of Salisbury who expected to inherit substantial lands in the south near to the Courtenay estates. Montague was Henry and Gertrude's closest friend who they trusted implicitly, and he them. At 48, the tall, auburn-haired Sir Edward Neville was the oldest member of the group. He had been in favour with Henry VIII, whom he physically resembled, since the early years of the reign and, like the marquis, was a member of the Privy Chamber. He was accustomed to visiting the Exeters regularly, and might even have had a chamber set aside for him at West Horsley.[11] He was a talented singer, no doubt joining in with the singing sessions performed by the Exeters' talented servants. Neville was also close to Montague who had married his niece, Jane, daughter of his elder brother Lord Bergavenny. Like Exeter, 35-year-old Sir Nicholas Carew had been brought up with the king since childhood and was a member of the Privy Chamber. The dashing jouster and one-time inveterate gambler was one of Henry VIII's most trusted companions.[12] Finally, there was 26-year-old Sir Geoffrey Pole, Montague's youngest brother. Geoffrey enjoyed a joke and was well liked by most who knew him, but he lacked sound judgement and by the late 1530s had debts that were spiralling out of control. Consequently, his admittance to this inner circle was intermittent. Whenever Geoffrey was in royal favour and in direct contact with the king and Cromwell, he was excluded due to concerns that he might reveal sensitive information. While Henry and Gertrude kept their circle of intimates small, members of this group had additional friends in whom they confided. Carew was close to his brother-in-law, Sir Francis Bryan 'the Vicar of Hell', while Montague and Geoffrey often discussed matters with their mutual friend, Elizabeth Darell, mistress of the poet Sir Thomas Wyatt. From 1537 Wyatt was ambassador to the emperor Charles V but, revealing the complex relations and loyalties at court, he was also a man under Cromwell's patronage. Geoffrey also counted George Croftes his friend who, by 1538, was Chancellor of Chichester Cathedral. However, the core group around the Exeters consisted of Montague, Neville, Carew and, intermittently, Geoffrey.

In practice, the flow of information centred around Gertrude. Her husband, as a member of the Privy Chamber and the Privy Council, was present at nearly all crucial discussions during the 1530s, and he would impart any information of importance to Gertrude. If this concerned Catherine and Mary, Gertrude informed the imperial ambassador, Chapuys, as the person best placed to help them. Usually this was by letter but on one occasion she went to Chapuys in person such was the gravity of the situation. They also kept Montague informed via numerous letters written by Gertrude and through personal meetings. Nicholas Carew, exploiting his privileged relationship with the king, also provided information to the Exeters and directly to Chapuys, while Neville from his position in the Privy Chamber was another source of information. It is important to note that when the group's disaffection with the Henrician regime came to light, it was not due to a clumsy slip by Gertrude or Henry. With assassination attempts being made against Lord Montague's other brother, Reginald Pole, and emotions running high, it was the gossiping of servants in and around the household of the Countess of Salisbury that finally reached the ears of Cromwell's spies. The question is, why did Henry and Gertrude act against character by betraying the king's confidence and what did it cost them?

Initially, Henry VIII tried to obtain an annulment within the parameters of the church and rested his case on a passage in Leviticus which said that if a man had carnal knowledge of his brother's wife, it was an unclean thing and they would be childless. Henry interpreted childlessness as a lack of legitimate sons. The fact that Deuteronomy said the opposite, that a man should marry his brother's widow to avoid her being remarried to a stranger outside the family, did not shake his conviction. This was strengthened when John Stokesley, Bishop of London, solved this contradiction by interpreting Leviticus as divine law and Deuteronomy as moral law.[13] According to the king, Catherine had consummated her marriage to his brother Prince Arthur and therefore their marriage was prohibited by God, for which they were punished by a lack of sons. As the prohibition was God's law, no pope could dispense against it, and this remained Henry's stance. Catherine, however, maintained that her marriage to Arthur had never been consummated, while the pope was reluctant to set a precedent by ruling that his predecessor had exceeded his authority. This was the impasse that remained throughout, and when Henry could not obtain a solution within the bounds of papal jurisdiction, he began to look beyond it.

The first big political earthquake occurred with the failure of the legatine court at Blackfriars in June 1529, which led to Wolsey's fall. Most historians have claimed that Exeter was among the cardinal's enemies and was part of the cabal that destroyed him. According to them, Wolsey had tried to remove Exeter from the Privy Chamber via the Eltham Ordinances of 1525 because he was his enemy, and he was also part of the 'aristocratic heavy mob the cardinal feared most'.[14] However the evidence, slight as it is, suggests that in the dying throes of his administration Exeter was one of the few who remained loyal to Wolsey and did not attempt to benefit by trying to push himself into the power vacuum left by the cardinal.[15] Following the failure of the legatine court and Wolsey's fall, the next tactic used between 1529 and 1530 was the canvassing of university theologians whose opinions Henry VIII could present to the pope in support of his suit. Among those he tasked with this was Reginald Pole, Lord Montague's brother who Exeter knew personally. He was sent to Paris in October 1529 and, at this time, was fully supportive of the king's cause. Bribes were used on both sides, but positive responses began to be declared in Henry's favour from early 1530, and in June the king called a meeting to discuss a letter, or rather a petition, to the pope which he required the nobility and prelates to sign. This would urge the pope to grant Henry's request and point out 'the evils' which would arise from delay. Encouraged by the responses from the universities, the meeting was asked why the king should not marry at once without waiting for papal consent. This suggestion was met by stunned silence until 'one of the King's chief favourites' threw himself on his knees and implored the king to take into account 'the slight symptoms of disaffection appearing in many parts of the kingdom ... which the slightest provocation might kindle into a flame' continuing, that if he was determined to go ahead without papal approval 'he should at least delay it until winter, when the general excitement might have somewhat subsided'. It has been suggested that 'the one most likely to dare express such opinions' was Exeter, and this is plausible. As the king's near kinsman, he was one of the few who could take such a risk. His words struck home and, for now at least, the matter rested and in July he, along with many others including Montague and Lord Mountjoy, signed the petition to the pope.[16]

Nevertheless, the atmosphere at court was deteriorating, perhaps not helped by the arrival of Thomas Cromwell who was sworn a member of the council towards the end of 1530. In May 1531 the Duke of Norfolk fell into conversation with Exeter, describing the queen's courage as 'supernatural, that showed neither care nor anxiety at the course of affairs'. Exeter's reply 'that it must be thought that she felt assured in her conscience of the justice of her cause' reveals his true feelings, and as the court became increasingly polarised Exeter was suddenly ejected from the Privy Chamber after more than ten years of constant attendance.[17] On 17 July Chapuys informed Charles V that Exeter had 'been forbidden to appear at Court for some time to come, having been charged with recruiting men in Cornwall and the adjacent counties'. However, he continued, 'The Queen fancies that this has been designed by the Lady, [Anne Boleyn] owing to the said Marquis being a good servant of hers.'[18] Exeter was distraught at this first breach with his cousin, nothing having grieved him 'so much in all his life as the putting out of the Privy Chamber'. Gertrude was supportive and angry on her husband's behalf, complaining that 'men of noble blood were put out and the King taketh in other at his pleasure'. Lord Montague was also sympathetic, telling his brother Geoffrey 'it was a pity the lord Marquis was so handled, and that he had a just suit depending in the law for that matter'.[19]

The cause of Exeter's expulsion as described by Chapuys, being the recruitment of men in the south, is correct, but a certain William Kendall inflamed the situation. An unpopular and divisive character, Exeter used him as 'a skilful and ruthless agent' in the south-west,[20] but Kendall had little regard for Cromwell and didn't care who knew it. Kendall's enemy, Sir William Courtenay informed Cromwell in 1535 that Kendall 'makes many cracks in your name at Launson' and the following month described him as 'that wretch Kendall'.[21] The unpopularity of Kendall led those with an axe to grind to use the increasingly uncertain times to make claims against him which compromised his master. On 10 September 1531 Chapuys reported that Kendall had 'been sent to the Tower on the charge of having tried to seduce some of his comrades, … to take up the part of their master, telling them … the Marquis could not fail to be king of England in time'. The words were incendiary at a time when the king had no legitimate heir to succeed him.[22] While Exeter had been allowed to return to court, Chapuys presciently noted that this was 'more to be under vigilance and some kind of arrest than otherwise'.[23]

What seems to have precipitated all this probably started in 1530, when Kendall was tasked with retaining men for Exeter who wished to support his father-in-law in a private dispute with Sir Anthony Willoughby. Mountjoy and Willoughby were linked by marriage as Mountjoy had married Willoughby's stepmother, Dorothy. Dorothy had six children with Willoughby's father and about August 1530 her daughter Anne married Lord Mountjoy's son and heir Charles, the son of his third wife, Alice.[24] It is likely that the dispute, which was sparked around this time, was over land and competing claims following Charles and Alice's marriage. When Kendall began recruiting men for Exeter who were required to be 'in readiness at an hour's warning', gossip swirled. Peter Corrington claimed Kendall's servant 'Quynterell', declared that the marquis 'was heir apparent, and in case the King should die or marry, the marquis should be King'. Three other men testified that Quynterell stated that 'if the king's Grace marry my lady Ann, there will be need of such good fellows' while one of Kendall's servants was heard saying that 'We care not and the King taketh Sir Anthony Willoughby's part, for our master shall wear the garland [crown] at the last.' During a fracas between the servants of Mountjoy, Exeter and

Willoughby, a Thomas Rede was killed and there was even a suggestion that Exeter interfered in the inquest via his servant John Philip, forcing them to find that Rede 'died of God's visitation and not murdered'.[25]

Exeter could not afford to let such accusations go unchallenged, especially in light of his dynastic claims when even the Venetian ambassador described him as 'next in succession to the Crown'.[26] He therefore sued Peter Corrington for slander declaring that, as a result of Corrington's words, 'Henry VIII had conceived such suspicion of him that he could no longer enter the royal presence and for three months he had been shunned by the rest of the nobility.' He won both his cases, one in Common Pleas and one in King's Bench, and for the latter was awarded substantial damages of £3,000 against Corrington.[27] These cases were the 'just suit depending in the law' to which Montague had referred. Despite Exeter's success, it left an indelible stain on his relationship with the monarch. Henry VIII was a deeply suspicious man who never forgot a transgression, real or imagined, while Exeter's confidence in his cousin's character and judgement was shaken. The Exeters were not the only ones with reservations and 'through 1530 and 1531 there was a steady growth of opinion at court and in the council which was hostile to the marriage'.[28] Reginald Pole was now among them, and this led to his departure from England in January or February 1532. He later claimed that the last nobleman he visited before leaving was Exeter. The marquis could not have known how detrimental his departure would be for those left behind, for once he was safely overseas, Reginald was only too happy to give his honest, unvarnished opinion of the king's break with Rome and marriage to Anne Boleyn.

Reginald was fortunate to leave when he did. A bill called the Supplication of the Ordinaries submitted by the commons, ultimately led to the submission of the clergy on 15 May 1532. This resulted in the surrender of the church's judicial independence and Sir Thomas More resigned as Lord Chancellor the very next day. This watershed, combined with Henry's activities during 1532, caused Catherine's supporters to fear that Henry and Anne were actually planning to marry without waiting for the pope's decision on the matter. These fears increased as plans for a meeting with Francis I at Calais gathered pace and Anne's status was elevated by her creation as Marquis of Pembroke in her own right. On 11 October the king, Anne and their attendants arrived at Calais, and a reluctant Exeter and Montague were among the entourage forced to honour her. It would prove to be a challenging situation in more ways than one as Montague's brother, Geoffrey, had recklessly stowed away on board and only revealed his presence on arrival. As he had been specifically excluded from the meeting his discovery would have seriously compromised his brother and Exeter. He therefore remained hidden in his brother's chamber during the day and never went out except at night, although he did claim to have been present in disguise at the meeting between Henry and Francis, which seems incredible and can hardly have been with Montague and Exeter's knowledge. He then threatened to go to Spain to offer his service to Charles V 'and would have gone in warfare' had his brother not prevented him.[29] An exasperated Montague managed to persuade him to return to England and inform Catherine of Aragon that 'nothing was done at that meeting touching the marriage with the lady Anne, and that the King had done his best but the French king would not assent to it'.[30] It is in the aftermath of the Calais interview that we see clear evidence of Gertrude corresponding with Chapuys, but the familiarity with which Chapuys refers to her message suggests that this was not the first time she had passed information to him. Gertrude's correspondence with Chapuys makes clear that the Exeters' motivation was primarily the protection of Catherine and Mary, and this would remain their motivation throughout. Obviously, this was dangerous as Chapuys was the ambassador of a potentially hostile state, and one that was directly opposed to the annulment of the king's marriage.

In contradiction to Geoffrey's message to Catherine, the king did get something from the Calais interview. While Henry needed French support for the annulment, Francis wanted English support to curb Habsburg power in Germany and as a result of the meeting Francis despatched Cardinals Grammont and Tournon to the pope. They were to threaten to call a general council of the Church and remind him that the two monarchs 'were so closely united that their interests were the same'. But they had a secret commission too and it was this that prompted Gertrude's approach to Chapuys. On 10 November the ambassador informed Charles V that the 'marchioness of Excet' had sent him a letter, unsigned 'but which must have been written either by her husband, the Marquis, or by the Grand Squire' [Nicholas Carew]. It revealed that the cardinals' 'principal commission' was to demand that the pope allow the matter to be tried in England 'otherwise both kings were determined to abrogate in their respective Kingdoms all papal authority'. Therefore, the unsigned letter urged Charles V 'to hasten the decision of the suit at Rome, upon which the writer says the delivery of the Queen from the purgatory she is now enduring … entirely depend'.[31] But it was all too late. Shortly after their arrival in England, Henry and Anne secretly married and she fell pregnant almost immediately. On 25 January 1533 they underwent a second more public, but still very private, ceremony and on 9 April, with Anne visibly pregnant, a mortified Exeter was sent as part of a delegation to inform Catherine that the king 'had already taken another wife, and that in future she must abstain from calling herself or being addressed as queen'.

While Exeter brooded, Cromwell and the king seethed over information leaks from the Privy Council and on 16 April, in a meeting with the Venetian ambassador at which Exeter was present, the king made an ominous remark. He told the ambassador, 'You have made a law prohibiting any one – under pain of capital punishment – from daring to divulge what passes in the Council of Ten and in the Senate; the Signory governs most prudently, and this decree was most sage, for I assure you that the greater part of your affairs were known.' Following Exeter's expulsion from the Privy Chamber, this must be seen as a second warning shot across his bow. Henry VIII and Cromwell knew that details of discussions and decisions taking place in the Privy Council were being leaked, a serious and dangerous betrayal, and this incident suggests that Exeter was already one of their suspects. In addition, on 7 May Chapuys was left in no doubt that some of his letters were being intercepted, meaning Gertrude was putting herself and her husband in grave danger by corresponding with him.[32]

Following the pronouncement on 23 May, by the new archbishop of Canterbury, Thomas Cranmer, that Henry's marriage to Catherine was invalid and his marriage to Anne was lawful, her coronation inevitably followed. Taking place on 1 June, a reluctant Gertrude was required to attend, although her husband managed to avoid it as he was lying sick at Horsley. She later rather poignantly recalled 'that though her person was at the coronation yet her heart was at home with her husband'.[33] She had to watch as Anne travelled from Greenwich to the Tower in Catherine's barge, from which her coat of arms had been 'torn off and cut to pieces'. An anguished Chapuys disgustedly remarked, 'May God permit that she may henceforwards be contented with possessing the barge, the jewels, and the husband of the Queen, without attempting … the life of the Queen and Princess.'[34]

Anne Boleyn was six months pregnant at her coronation, and Gertrude also believed she was in the early stages of pregnancy. Her desire to give her husband more than one male heir never left her, and after fourteen years of marriage appears to have made her desperate. Elizabeth Barton, known as the Nun of Kent, had been known in the highest circles for at least the previous five years due to her devout life and the seeming accuracy of her prophesies. However, in the 1530s she began to criticise Henry VIII and most dangerously predicted that if he should marry Anne Boleyn 'that then within one month after such marriage he should no longer be king of this realm'.[35] Despite the obvious risks, following Anne Boleyn's coronation Gertrude made contact with the nun. Swapping clothes with one of her ladies, Contance Bontayne, she travelled to Canterbury disguised as a servant while Constance played the part of mistress. They were escorted by four servants including Jasper Horsey who had served the Courtenays for years and held several appointments including, by 1538, treasurer of the household. On arrival Gertrude dined with Barton and Dr Bocking, the nun's confessor. According to Barton, after this visit 'upon the Friday after midsummer last' which was 30 June 1533, Gertrude sent two of her servants to Syon Abbey, where Barton was then staying, and desired the abbess to send Barton to her at Horsley. The abbess advised Barton 'to go unto the said Lady Marchioness saying that she was an honourable woman', which Barton did, and met Gertrude the following day 'in a chamber apart'. According to both Gertrude and Barton, the main reason for the nun's visit was 'forasmuch as she [Gertrude] had had children before which lived not after their birth that supposing herself to be with child again she said Dame Elizabeth should pray for her to our lady that she might have issue as fruit that might live'. During the conversation Barton said 'it was thought that we should have war which if so it should chance then the said lady Marchioness should pray her to pray for my lord her husband if in case he should go over that he might return safely and if it were possible that he might not go himself …' There is no reason to doubt that Gertrude summoned the nun due to her pregnancy, but inviting a notorious figure who had made treasonous statements to her own home, while her husband was in residence due to his sickness, was a serious and uncharacteristic lapse of judgement. Perhaps this is revealing of the stress that she, like everyone else, was under, but this reckless act would come back to haunt her.[36]

Despite the nun's predictions promising disaster if the king married Anne, the pregnant queen's position had never been stronger, while Catherine's was dire. On 3 July Gertrude's father, the long-suffering Lord Mountjoy, led a delegation to Ampthill where he reluctantly informed her that she may no longer use the title of queen to which she replied 'that she was not Princess Dowager, but the Queen, and the King's true wife'. Mountjoy was then reduced to threatening her daughter, for if her disobedience continued it would cause the king to 'withdraw his fatherly love' from the princess, but she remained defiant.[37] Meanwhile, Lord Russell wrote to Lord Lisle on 6 August that he never saw the king 'merrier of a great while than he is now … And for cheer, what at my Lord Marquess of Exeter's, Mr Treasurer's, and at Mr Weston's, I never saw more delicate nor better cheer in my life.'[38] While Henry and Gertrude outwardly smiled and made merry with the king, privately they were appalled at the mission Mountjoy had been forced to carry out. The king, of course, had every reason to be happy for Anne was about to enter her confinement and both were prepared for the birth of a son.

In the event, Anne gave birth to a daughter, Elizabeth, on 7 September and the celebrations were immediately toned down. However, she had conceived immediately so there was no reason to doubt, yet, that she would produce a son. The christening took place at Greenwich on 10 September at which Exeter bore a taper of virgin wax and Gertrude stood godmother at the confirmation. Five days later, ignoring the king's earlier indirect warning over leaks, Exeter informed his wife of discussions in the Privy Council, which Gertrude duly passed on to Chapuys. On 15 September Chapuys informed the emperor that Gertrude 'who is the only true comforter and friend the Queen and the Princess have' had informed him that 'the frequent and almost daily meetings of the Privy Council are for no other purpose at present than to decide how much and in what manner the household of the Queen and Princess, and their rank and estate are to be reduced, and yet the same lady writes that the King's Privy Councillors had not yet found a solution to the affair'.[39] One of those who had had enough of all this was Gertrude's father. Still smarting from his interview with Catherine in July, when he received letters from the king on 6 October ordering him to provide the names of those in Catherine's household who had refused to address her as Princess Dowager, it was the final straw and he wrote to Cromwell asking to be allowed to resign. He was not prepared to name names 'nor to vex and unquiet her, whom the King's grace caused to be sworn unto, and truly to serve her to my power'. He lamented the 'sore words' he had had from Catherine 'for the messages which I have brought her, and executing of commandments' and that he would rather serve the king in any cause 'if it were very dangerous, than further to meddle in this'.[40] We can only imagine the disillusion that Mountjoy must have felt at his protégé's deterioration from the chivalrous king he had promised to be, but how fortunate that he avoided witnessing the tragedy that would soon engulf his daughter for he would die, just over a year later, aged around 56.

While the Privy Council met repeatedly about Catherine and Mary, things suddenly took a worrying turn for Gertrude when the Nun of Kent was arrested in November 1533. The king deployed his privy councillors to try and discover if Catherine had ever contacted her, but Exeter, as one of those privy councillors, knew that his wife had and that it was bound to come out. Knowing the king as he did, and that a confession before being presented with evidence was the best chance of obtaining mercy, the likely scenario is that Exeter advised Gertrude to admit to her contact with the nun and throw herself on Henry's mercy. In fact, jottings in Richard Pollard's hand in 1538 might actually refer to this earlier incident. Although mutilated, it refers to Sir Nicholas Carew labouring to the king 'for a letter of comfort unto the lady Marques upon the knowledge of her offence thereof. And likewise the lord Marques hath afore thys tyme k … the same offence to the Kyng' k possibly being the start of the word 'knowledged'.[41] It was good advice for the nun did admit to meeting Gertrude at Horsley, while further damning evidence also emerged. It was claimed that Hugh Riche, guardian of the Observant house next to Richmond palace, and a Father Riseby both informed Gertrude of Barton's prediction that the king would not remain king after marrying Anne Boleyn, while Cromwell personally added in the testimony of Henry Goold, a priest, who admitted telling Exeter's chaplain, John Stephyns, and other of his servants.[42] Much to her relief, on 25 November Gertrude received the king's pardon, and her letter in return offers complete abasement. She used her sex to explain her offences, being 'a woman, whose fragility and brittleness is such as most facilely, easily, and lightly is seduced and brought into abusion' and described the nun as 'that most unworthy, subtle, and deceivable woman'. The reason she had not reported what she heard was because she thought them to be 'so full of folly and untruth' that they weren't worth reporting. She went on to describe her 'great agony of mind' and exonerated her husband by describing his displeasure with her who she feared 'hath not zeal, like love, and affection towards me as afore I thought myself assured of'. She then begged the king 'to require my said good lord and husband that he, for his part, will also to remit and forgive me mine offences'.[43] Her exoneration of Exeter, who knew all about her contact with the nun, was important. While Henry VIII might accept her failures due to her sex, the consequences for her husband would have been far more serious.[44] The following day Gertrude wrote to Cromwell re-iterating her obedience and gratitude to the king. She then added, 'I write to you as my Lord's very friend, that if the King speak of this matter you will answer for me that he had no more obedient subject.' She ended by trusting the king would realise it is hardly surprising that she, a woman, had been deceived considering 'so many wise persons have been equally abused'. The letter reveals the underlying tension in the relationship between Cromwell and the Exeters. Gertrude did not beg, or even ask him to assure the king of her obedience, she told him to do so, and the difference in tone between the two letters is marked. Gertrude had been in real danger, bearing in mind that the nun was executed the following year along with Hugh Riche, Dr Bocking and others, while John Fisher had been charged with concealing treason.[45] Despite this, while she was prepared to 'humbly prostrate at the feet of your royal majesty', she could not bring herself to grovel to Cromwell.

Meanwhile, Catherine and Mary's on-going resistance to Henry's demands left the court in a continual state of tension. First, Princess Mary's household was broken up amid distressing scenes. Having been separated from her mother, Mary was now separated from the woman she considered her second mother, her governess, Margaret Pole. The countess' offer to follow and serve Mary at her own expense was rebuffed, and the distraught 60-year-old returned to her residence at Bisham where she suffered some sort of collapse, while Mary was sent to join the household of her new sister, Princess Elizabeth, still refusing to accept that she was no longer princess.[46] A reluctant Duke of Suffolk was then

King Edward IV, Katharine's father, was once regarded as the handsomest prince in Christendom. (*Public domain*)

The earliest known portrait of Elizabeth Woodville (1513–1530), 'lovely looking ... and her wit so pregnant, when she allured and made subject to her, the heart of so great a king'. This portrait shows a marked resemblance to her grandsons, Prince Arthur and Henry VIII. (© *Royal Collection Enterprises Limited 2024 | Royal Collection Trust*)

Richard III, Katharine's uncle. When he took the throne in 1483 Katharine and her siblings were declared bastards. (*United States public domain*)

Elizabeth of York, Katharine's sister, to whom she had a deep emotional attachment. (*United States public domain*)

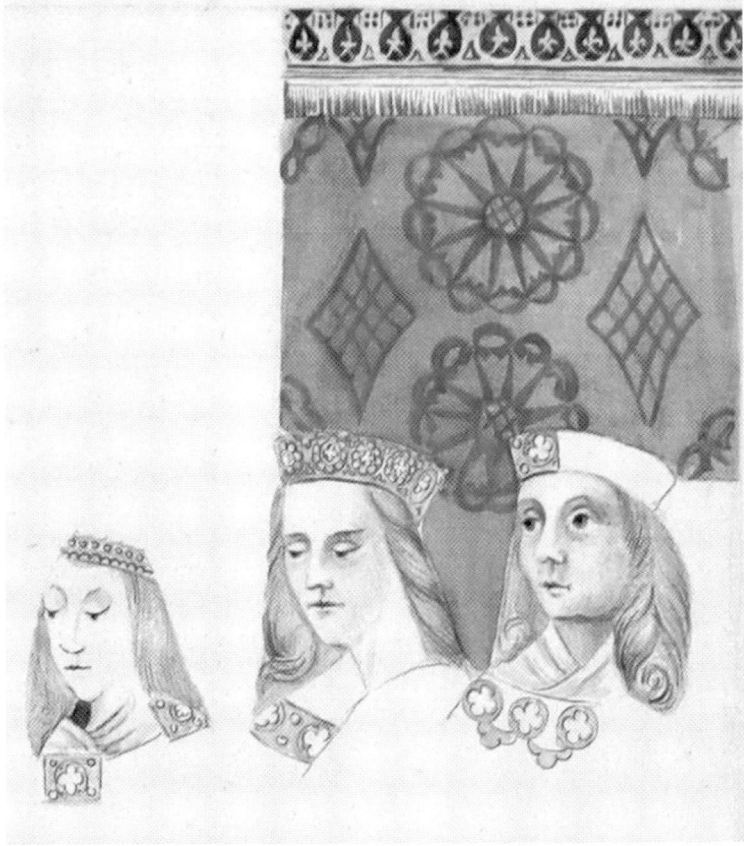

Detail of the 1789 watercolour by Jacob Schnebbelie showing the original stained glass head depicting Katharine (centre) in the Royal Window, Canterbury Cathedral. (© *The Society of Antiquaries of London*)

Bust of King Henry VII by Pietro Torrigiano, 1509–11. Katharine had a complex relationship with her brother-in-law. (© *Victoria and Albert Museum, London*)

The remains of the funeral effigy of Elizabeth of York. (*Copyright: Dean and Chapter of Westminster*)

Henry VIII aged 29. A year earlier he had spent £200 on jousts to celebrate the wedding of his cousin, Henry Courtenay. (*By Unknown Anglo-Netherlandish artist oil on panel, circa 1520. NPG 4690. © National Portrait Gallery, London*)

Catherine of Aragon. Henry VIII was deeply in love with his first wife during the early years of his reign. (*United States public domain*)

Katharine was quick to take advantage of the reckless marriage between her niece, Princess Mary, and Charles Brandon, Duke of Suffolk in 1515. (*United States public domain*)

Thomas Howard, 3rd Duke of Norfolk c. 1539 aged 66. Katharine's brother-in-law for sixteen years, relations between them may have been strained. (*United States public domain*)

1734 engraving of Tiverton Castle by Samuel and Nathaniel Buck. The castle was one of Katharine's three main residences in Devon. (*United States public domain*)

1795 watercolour of Colcombe Castle by Rev John Swete. Katharine normally resided here from late summer to early autumn each year. (*United States public domain*)

The Greenway Chapel, St Peter's Church, Tiverton, the final resting place of Katharine, Countess of Devon. (*Courtesy of William Zarrett, reproduced with the kind permission of St Peter's Church, Tiverton*)

Lady Elizabeth Say, Gertrude's indomitable grandmother. (*Chris Parkinson, reproduced with the kind permission of Holy Trinity Church, Long Melford*)

The tomb of Sir William Say, Gertrude's grandfather to whom she was close. Erasmus described Sir William as kind. (*Lynda Dray, reproduced with the kind permission of St Augustine's Church, Broxbourne*)

Sketch of an unknown lady by Hans Holbein the Younger c. 1532–43. Could this be Gertrude Courtenay, Marchioness of Exeter, wearing the IHS brooch? (© *Royal Collection Enterprises Limited 2024 | Royal Collection Trust*)

Catherine of Aragon wearing the IHS brooch c. 1525 aged 40 by Lucas Horenbout. (*United States public domain*)

Anne Boleyn, charismatic and sharply intelligent, she captivated Henry VIII for 10 years. (*United States public domain*)

Margaret Pole, Countess of Salisbury, mother of Henry Pole, Lord Montague, Henry and Gertrude Courtenay's closest friend. (*Unknown woman, formerly known as Margaret Pole, Countess of Salisbury by Unknown artist, oil on panel, circa 1535. NPG 2607. © National Portrait Gallery, London*)

Sir Nicholas Carew, a member of Henry and Gertude's inner circle during the 1530s. (*United States public domain*)

Eustace Chapuys, Imperial ambassador to England. Gertrude secretly passed information to him during the 1530s. (*United States public domain*)

Thomas Cromwell c. 1537, the year of the Pilgrimage of Grace. There was gossip that Henry Courtenay had drawn a dagger on the Lord Privy Seal in December. (*By the studio of Hans Holbein the Younger, watercolour and bodycolour on vellum, circa 1537, NPG 6311. © National Portrait Gallery, London*)

Henry VIII in 1537 aged 46, a year before he sent his cousin to the block. (*United States public domain*)

Artist's impression of West Horsely Place c. 1500, Henry and Gertrude's family home throughout the 1530s. (© *West Horsely Place and Michael Goddard*)

Jane Seymour, Henry VIII's much underestimated third wife, wearing the IHS brooch. (*United States public domain*)

Portrait of Edward Courtenay, Earl of Devon by Stephen van der Meulen. Described as `the handsomest and most agreeable gentleman in England', it may have been painted in 1555 when he was 29. (*United States public domain*)

Holcombe Court, Devon which still stands today. The marital home of Gertrude's half-sister Dorothy Bluett from 1547, Gertrude probably visited her here. (*TuckDB Postcards: https://www.tuckdbpostcards.org/ items/28200-holcombe-court/picture/3*)

Edward Courtenay, Earl of Devon after Pastorino de Pastorini plaster cast of lead medal, 20th century, based on a work of circa 1556. NPG 2085a. (© *National Portrait Gallery, London*)

Mary I in 1554 age 38. (*United States public domain*)

Philip II of Spain c. 1554- 1558. Mary's decision to marry him damaged her relationship with Gertrude. (*United States public domain*)

The Holy Roman Emperor, Charles V, cousin of Mary I. He exploited her reliance on him for his own purposes. (*United States public domain*)

Simon Renard, Imperial Ambassador during the reign of Mary I. He believed that she would never be safe while Edward Courtenay lived. (*United States public domain*)

Stephen Gardiner, Bishop of Winchester.
(*United States public domain*)

Sir Peter Carew, one of the conspirators
involved in Wyatt's rebellion. (*United States
public domain*)

Artist's impression of Fotheringhay Castle, the Yorkist stronghold where Edward Courtenay was imprisoned
between 1554–1555. *(Fotheringhay Castle by Julian Rowe, reproduced by kind permission of Peter Hammond)*

Sir John Mason, English ambassador to the emperor from a painting of 1607. He sympathised with Edward Courtenay. (*United States public domain*)

Presumed portrait of Ercole II d'Este, Duke of Ferrara. He welcomed Edward Courtenay to his duchy and encouraged him to assume leadership of the opposition to Mary I. (*United States public domain*)

1786 sketch of all that remained of the original buildings that were part of Gertrude's residence at Canford. (*Hazel Pierce*)

Gertrude's last surviving letter to her son dated 8 November 1555 and written in her own hand. She ends the letter 'if you come into England I trust I shall see you, or else I will shortly write to you if I be alive. By your most assured loving mother Gertrude Exeter'. (*The National Archives, ref. SP11/6*)

Stained glass window at Wimborne Minster showing the arms of William and Katharine Courtenay (bottom left) and Henry and Gertrude Courtenay (top right). (*Gordon Edgar, Wimborne Minster*)

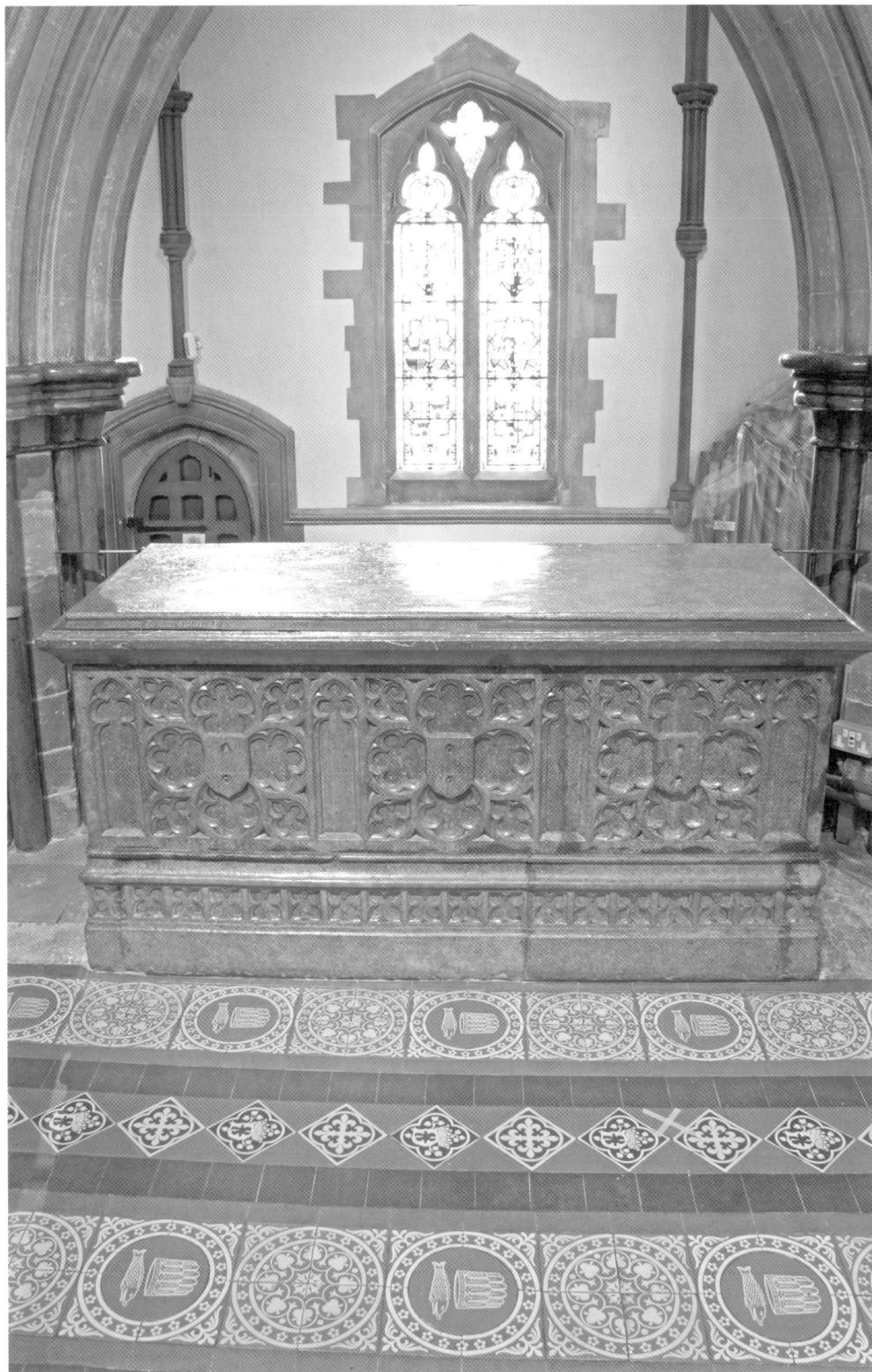

Gertrude's tomb of purbeck marble in Wimborne Minster, Dorset. (*Gordon Edgar, Wimborne Minster*)

despatched to remove Catherine from Buckden to Somersham before Christmas but was met with complete refusal. She locked herself in her chamber, forcing Suffolk to shout to her through a hole in the wall, while outside a crowd of angry villagers began to gather. On 19 December Suffolk informed the king that the only way to assure compliance would be to 'bind her with ropes, and violently enforce her thereunto'.[47] The disobedience of his wife and daughter was an affront to Henry's authority, and his wife's nagging over his handling of the situation was driving him to boiling point. On 29 December, just before the New Year's celebrations, he exploded and the unfortunate Marquis of Exeter was once again in the firing line. Henry raged at him, blaming the emperor for encouraging Mary's obstinacy but assuring Exeter that 'he would bring her to the point'. He feared no one, not even the emperor, especially if Exeter and the other nobles were loyal to him 'as he thought they would be'. He then added, menacingly, 'they must not trip or vary for fear of losing their heads, and he would keep such good watch that no letters could be received from beyond sea without his knowing it'.[48] This was even more of a direct threat than the two previous warnings Exeter had received.

The following year, 1534, the Act of Succession was introduced, which required the king's subjects to swear an oath that the Boleyn marriage was valid and the children of that marriage were the legitimate heirs to the crown. The act also included a preamble that declared Henry's first marriage invalid and entailed repudiation of papal supremacy.[49] This preamble caused a problem for men like Thomas More who could not agree to it, and he was arrested and imprisoned on 17 April, with John Fisher following on 26 April. The act also threatened Catherine and Mary, and throughout this year their supporters were in a state of agitation. On 15 May Chapuys was summoned to Westminster at seven in the morning where he found Norfolk, Exeter and others waiting for him. Dr Edward Fox, one of the most ardent supporters of the break with Rome, proceeded to speak at length in Latin informing Chapuys, untruthfully, that the act had been approved by all his subjects except two; 'Madame Katharine and Madame Mary' and that if they continued in their refusal the king would proceed against them. This was followed by a dramatic message from Catherine to Chapuys on 23 May informing him that a delegation had arrived to see her. They had used 'rude and harsh words' and threatened her 'with the penalties contained in the said statute, telling her it involved death' if she did not take the oath. This resulted in a distressed Chapuys rushing to Richmond, unannounced and against all protocol, to ascertain the truth of this from an astonished Henry VIII. Raising the temperature further, in June 'a gentleman worthy of credit' sent the stressed ambassador word that Anne Boleyn had threatened 'to cause the death of the princess by the sword or otherwise whatever the consequences to herself'.[50] In the middle of all this, news reached England that Pope Clement was seriously ill. Again Exeter, this time with the Duke of Norfolk, misread the signals and when they tentatively suggested that Henry might be happy to obey a new pope, he told them 'that no one should mock him by advising such a thing' and when news of Clement's death arrived on 11 October, it gave the king the 'greatest pleasure in the world'. Cromwell went further 'saying several times in public that this great devil was dead, and it seemed as if he was very sorry he could find no worse name for him than devil'.[51]

Cromwell's priority was to protect the royal supremacy, and he continued to drive through measures to achieve that while attempting to suppress all opposition; and there was plenty of opposition to suppress both overt and concealed. One such individual involved in covert treasonous activities was Geoffrey Pole. Following his clandestine attendance at the Calais meeting of 1532, Geoffrey asked his brother to help him obtain a position in the king's service, but Montague replied that he would take Exeter's advice first.[52] Both were concerned that if Geoffrey was at court and in the king and Cromwell's presence, his recklessness might lead to the discovery of the communications with Chapuys and their true feelings about the king's 'great matter'. As they would not help him, he took matters into his own hands and wrote to Cromwell in April 1533. It worked and he was appointed a server at the coronation of Anne Boleyn, while in July Cromwell gave him £40 for no specific reason.[53] It is possible that Cromwell was hoping to use Geoffrey as an informant, but for now, he was to be disappointed. For one thing, Geoffrey no longer enjoyed the confidence of his brother or the Exeters who distanced themselves from him as soon as he joined the king's service. Second, despite his outward loyalty, Geoffrey was still adamantly opposed to the Boleyn marriage and the break with Rome, no doubt exacerbated by the arrest of family friend Sir Thomas More. In November 1534, he was honoured with an appointment to the commission of Sewers for Sussex, but in the same month was visiting Chapuys' regularly. The ambassador informed Charles V that Geoffrey 'would visit me almost every day, had I not dissuaded him from doing so, on account of the danger he might run', again highlighting his lack of judgement especially as one of Chapuys' neighbours was none other than Cromwell himself, the two living within walking distance of each other![54] During his visits Geoffrey 'like many others' continued to beg Chapuys to inform Charles V 'how very easy the conquest of this kingdom would be, and that the inhabitants are only waiting for a signal'. Fortunately, due to their temporary estrangement, these visits and dangerous discussions took place without the involvement of Montague or the Exeters.

The stand-off between Henry, Catherine and Mary continued throughout 1535 and Mary was not afraid to complain about her situation, loudly and dramatically, whipping her supporters up into a state of frantic worry. It was at this time that Chapuys reported to the emperor that Exeter 'only regrets that he has no opportunity of shedding his blood in the service of the Queen and Princess'. He would be given that opportunity, but first came the executions of More, Fisher and the Carthusian monks which caused widespread condemnation abroad. At home, the horror and disgust felt by many could not be openly expressed, but it was felt none the less. Both Exeter and Montague were reluctantly involved in the trial of the monks, while Montague was forced to take part in the process for More's trial, and his execution affected him badly. He collapsed in London immediately afterwards and was so ill that he received absolution, while it was widely reported that he had died. It took two weeks before he was 'walking' again.[55]

Anne Boleyn knew that the blame for these executions would be levelled at her, but she pressed on nonetheless. She could not risk the king weakening at such a moment when powerful opposition still existed. In March she discovered that she was pregnant again, and in May Chapuys described her as 'fiercer and haughtier than ever she was' no doubt reflecting the confidence she felt at her pregnancy. She went on to tell Henry that Catherine and Mary should have been punished as traitors and that he should be grateful to her because he was 'cleansed from the sin in which he was living' and was also 'the richest monarch that ever was in England'. However, when Anne miscarried in June her position was again exposed and she reacted accordingly.[56] On 23 July Chapuys reported that Anne was 'incessantly crying after the King that he does not act with prudence in suffering the Queen and Princess to live, who deserve death more than those who have been executed, and that they were the cause of it all'.[57] What Chapuys and the rest of Catherine's supporters feared, was that the king would become brutalised to the point where he would be capable of executing his wife and daughter. The ambassador made their concerns clear 'should this King lose all shame, and get used to such cruelties, it is to be feared that the lives of both Queen and princess will be in jeopardy'.[58] They had every reason to be concerned because Henry's actions show that he was indeed getting used to 'such cruelties'. It is in light of this that Exeter and Gertrude were prompted to act in ways that posed much more of a risk to their own safety.

In late October 1535 Henry and Anne returned from their royal progress and by early November the council was sitting in Westminster.[59] On or before Saturday 6 November, Gertrude sent a message to Chapuys that contained words which the king had only said 'to some of his most confidential councillors'. Clearly, Exeter was among these councillors and he had immediately informed his wife. The message concerned the king's threat to deal with Catherine and Mary at the next Parliament. 'The Marchioness declares this as true as the Gospel'

Chapuys informed the emperor, 'and begs me to inform your Majesty and pray you to have pity upon the ladies, and for the honour of God and the bond of kin to find a remedy.'[60] Then something happened that prompted Gertrude to take an even greater risk by donning a disguise and visiting Chapuys in person. A face-to-face meeting had more force, and the purpose was to affirm what she had previously said in her message of the 6 November and to 'beg and entreat' Chapuys 'with the greatest possible speed' to write to Charles V and ask for 'a prompt and efficacious remedy to these many evils'. She explained that when the king noticed that some of those to whom he affirmed his determination to deal with Catherine and Mary began to cry, he was moved not to pity but anger declaring that 'the case was not one for crying and grimacing, for, though he should lose his crown through it, he would insist upon the said measures being carried at once into effect'. His renewed determination to deal with Catherine and Mary and remove any doubt over the succession was probably prompted by his discovery that Anne was pregnant again. Chapuys was flabbergasted and could hardly believe it, yet in light of previous threats and recent events he considered 'the danger imminent'. Gertrude also informed him that four or five days earlier the king had warned that he was going to make an example of Mary to show that no one was above the law. She concluded by begging Chapuys not to keep the knowledge of these threats from Catherine and Mary but to inform them in case they wished to 'send an express messenger' to Charles V themselves.[61] Extracts of Gertrude's reports spread like wildfire. By 1 January 1536 Dr Pedro Ortiz, Catherine's solicitor at Rome, wrote to the empress Isabella, wife of Charles V, that the measures being prepared in Parliament against Catherine and Mary were 'of such cruelty that those who witness them can hardly believe their eyes' continuing, 'though he may lose his crown in consequence, they shall be subjected to the same penalty as other traitors'.[62] Sincerely believing that Anne was the cause of all this, when an opportunity to remove her presented itself it is not surprising that Catherine's supporters grasped it with both hands.

Chapter 10

1536–1537

False Hope

nor to desire to be great about princes for it is dangerous.[1]

I t was a confluence of events that brought down a queen of England between January and May 1536. Christmas 1535 was spent at Greenwich Palace where Henry and a pregnant Anne enjoyed all the usual festivities. At Horsley, Exeter was ill once again but this time Gertrude 'almost [despaired o] f' his recovery 'he was so sick',[2] while ninety miles away at Kimbolton Castle Catherine of Aragon's life began to slip away. Chapuys had, with royal permission, dashed to her bedside and remained with her for four days. As she appeared to rally, he left and returned to London where he heard the news of her death on 9 January. The ambassador was distraught, especially as he had not been with her when she died, something she had wished. He recounted to Charles V that after she thanked him for his service and kindness in visiting her at a time when God might choose to take her to Himself 'it would at least be a consolation to die as it were in my arms, and not all alone like a beast'.[3] Over the next few days he found it difficult to function 'being in such agony of mind' while over at Greenwich Henry and Anne greeted the news with a mixture of relief and pleasure.[4] For Henry there was the opportunity of an imperial alliance 'now that the real cause of our enmity no longer exists'.[5] As part of the celebrations to mark his former wife's death, Henry took part in a joust during which his horse fell and he was knocked unconscious. It is perhaps fitting that the joust held to celebrate her death also ended his career in the lists. Shortly afterwards, Anne suffered a miscarriage leaving Henry in no better position than he had been when married to Catherine. In typical manner, he began to brood.

On 29 January 1536, Chapuys received a message from Gertrude and her husband which passed on information heard 'from the lips of one of the principal courtiers', probably Nicholas Carew. Apparently, the king had confided 'as if in confession' that he had been forced in to this marriage by 'sortileges and charms' and as such he held it to be null, and that God had shown his displeasure by denying him male children. 'He, therefore, considered that he could take a third wife, which he said he wished much to do.' Chapuys often commented on the credibility of his sources, and in this case he considered them to be 'sufficiently authentic' as he had enough experience of the Exeters to know whether they were reliable informants or not. However, he still considered this latest report 'almost incredible'.[6] Nevertheless, by 10 February he was able to mention the name of a certain Mistress Semel to whom the king had given presents, and a month later described Anne Boleyn's 'intense rage' that this amour was still going on.[7] Anne's position was weaker than ever, not only due to the miscarriage but because Catherine's death meant that if Henry chose to repudiate her, he would not be under any pressure to return to his first wife. This increased vulnerability coincided with the king's growing interest in Mistress Semele who was, of course, Jane Seymour.

Princess Mary's supporters moved quickly to take advantage of the situation and were soon working closely with Jane and her family to promote her to a more permanent position than royal mistress. What Anne Boleyn had once done so could another woman if she held her nerve, and they began to advise and coach Jane on how to handle the king. But could the Exeters and Carew trust the Seymours and vice versa? How did this alliance come about so quickly? The answer lies in Gertrude's relationship with Jane. Gertrude's grandfather Sir William Say, to whom she had been close, was the elder brother of Jane's grandmother, Anne Say, thus Gertrude and Jane were second cousins. Jane had served Catherine of Aragon and the two women would have been familiar with each other from that period. It has been claimed that prominent courtier Sir Francis Bryan, brother-in-law of Nicholas Carew and a kinsman of Jane, was the one who brought her to court to serve Anne Boleyn, but David Loades has noted that her arrival in Catherine's service is a mystery and that whoever her patron was they were 'obviously a person of great influence'.[8] It is most likely that this person was Gertrude. She was one of the highest-ranking ladies in England, married to the king's own cousin, and it would be expected that the Seymours would try and make use of their kinship to her to advance their daughter. Furthermore, Gertrude had influence with Catherine while her father was the queen's Lord Chamberlain, meaning he was in charge of her household above stairs. Gertrude knew that Jane had been an admirer of Catherine and was sympathetic to her daughter; she was therefore a much safer option as queen than the hostile Anne Boleyn.

Towards the end of March, Chapuys hosted a dinner party attended by several guests including Lord Montague and members of Exeter's family; Henry Grey, third Marquis of Dorset and his aunt Elizabeth, dowager Countess of Kildare. During the meal Montague, in an unguarded moment, complained of the bad state of affairs in the country and then mentioned that a new marriage for the king was being spoken of. As Chapuys wrote his report about the dinner party conversation to Charles V on 1 April, he received a message from Gertrude explaining that the king had sent Jane a purse of sovereigns with a letter, which she kissed but did not open. Instead, she returned it to the messenger and fell on her knees, stating that she would not lose her honour for a thousand deaths and if the king wished to make her a present of money 'she requested him to reserve it for such a time as God would be pleased to send her some advantageous marriage'. Her refusal did exactly what it was intended to do and 'marvellously increased' the king's love for her, and he dramatically declared that he would not converse with her in future unless one of her relatives were present. Chapuys also reported that she had been 'well tutored', warned not to succumb to Henry's advances and to take every opportunity to criticise the Boleyn marriage, especially in the hearing of high-ranking nobles who could add their voices to hers. Chapuys wholeheartedly endorsed this course of action 'as it would prove a further security for the person of the Princess'.[9] Jane's supporters certainly picked up the pace and on 29 April Chapuys informed the emperor that Nicholas Carew 'is daily conspiring' against Anne Boleyn and 'trying to persuade Miss Seymour and her friends to accomplish her ruin' and that four days earlier he, and others of the king's chamber, had written to Mary 'to take courage, for very shortly her rival would be dismissed'. Geoffrey Pole, who had dined with Chapuys the day before, also told him that John Stokesley, Bishop of London had been asked by a courtier whether the king could 'abandon' Anne. Stokesley sensibly refused to give an opinion unless the king himself asked for it.[10] Meanwhile, Cromwell was having his own problems with the queen.

Anne and Cromwell had fallen out about the use of monastic income, a row that Anne made public when her almoner, John Skip, preached a sermon likening Cromwell to an evil counsellor from the Old Testament who was hanged for his deception. In addition, the negotiations for an imperial alliance, in which Cromwell had invested so much, were being undermined merely by Anne's presence as Henry's queen. According to Chapuys, Cromwell later informed him that it was at this point that he 'planned and brought about the whole affair', referring to Anne's downfall.[11] He was already aware of Jane Seymour and the activities of her supporters, having given up his rooms to her brother and his wife, which enabled the king to visit Jane in secret via a private linked passage. He therefore opened communications with Jane's adherents and through Chapuys gained approval from Princess Mary for, what was at the time, plans for a divorce from Anne. Chapuys 'employed various means for the accomplishment of the said affair' speaking to Cromwell about it 'and others as seemed to me most fit for the purpose'.[12] Then, when she needed it most, Anne's nerve cracked under the pressure of the previous five months and interaction in her Privy Chamber got out of hand. Her lute player, Mark Smeaton, overstepped the bounds of propriety by allowing his crush on her to manifest itself in lovelorn signs and downcast looks, earning a deserved reproval. Then Anne herself sparked a row with Henry Norris, the king's Groom of the Stool, by suggesting that should the king die Norris would look to marry her. These incidents sent court gossip into overdrive and Cromwell heard about them almost immediately. He now had the means to remove Anne permanently, and he may have been waiting for just such a slip as the legal machinery had already been put in place; divorce was no longer an option.[13]

On 1 April Cromwell had told Chapuys that he had never been the cause of the Boleyn marriage but 'seeing the King determined upon it, he had smoothed the way'.[14] He would do so again now, except this time for a different wife. Found guilty of adultery, Anne went to the block on 19 May, the execution of her five alleged lovers, including her brother George, had taken place on 17 May. At the same time her marriage to the king was annulled and her daughter declared illegitimate. While Anne had never been universally popular, hardly anyone believed the truth of these charges, including Chapuys. In contrast, the king ranted and raved that she had been unfaithful with over 100 men. To avoid any scandal attaching itself to Jane, she had been carefully curated during all of this and sent away from the drama to Nicholas Carew's residence at Beddington before her betrothal to Henry VIII on 20 May. Many historians have judged her harshly for this, as she apparently waited in the wings until her predecessor was despatched before eagerly stepping into her blood-spattered shoes. However, the excitement she was supposed to have felt at the thought of becoming queen was more likely to have been apprehension. After all, on 20 May she agreed to marry a man who, the day before, had sanctioned the judicial murder of his second wife after gleefully celebrating the death of his first in January. But Jane was to prove her worth and reveal that she was far more than the meek non-entity most historians consider her to be. She showed remarkable courage by speaking up in support of Mary's reinstatement even before her marriage and gave a measured and steadfast response when the king snapped that 'she must be out of her senses to think of such a thing'.[15] Jane was not the only one speaking up for Mary and, as joy at Anne's removal emboldened her supporters, Cromwell rubbed his hands, sat back and waited. The more vocal they became in her support, the closer they came to being in breach of the Treason Act of 1534 as supporting Mary's restoration could imply acceptance of the papal verdict in favour of Catherine of Aragon's marriage.[16]

Gertrude, Exeter and Carew had miscalculated by underestimating Henry VIII's commitment to the royal supremacy, with or without Anne Boleyn by his side. Princess Mary shared their unrealistic optimism, writing letters to the king and Cromwell in which she pledged her obedience, within reason, then waited to be invited to court. Instead of an invitation, she received a delegation headed by the Duke of Norfolk. To her horror, the king demanded her complete submission, meaning she must accept the royal supremacy and the invalidity of her parent's marriage. This highly charged interview ended with her complete refusal, and she was now exposed to the full penalties of the treason act. Upon hearing of her disobedience, the king 'grew desperate with anger' once again suspecting that her servants had encouraged her obstinacy, and several were interrogated. Meanwhile, the council went into emergency session, meeting from morning to night over several days. As one of Mary's staunchest supporters, Exeter once again felt the full force of Henry's wrath. He was expelled from the council along with the Treasurer of the Royal Household, Sir William Fitzwilliam. In truth no one, including Cromwell, wanted the princess's execution, realising the public outcry that would follow and the disastrous effect it would have on Anglo–Imperial relations. He had been gently guiding Mary behind the scenes to ensure her appropriate acquiescence, which was the price of her father's favour. Her refusal, therefore, threatened even him, and the king swore 'in a great passion, that not only the Princess should suffer, but also the Marquis, Cromwell, and several others'.[17]

Exeter and Carew now did all they could to persuade Mary to capitulate and save herself. Carew wrote to her that he and all 'her friends' besought her '[for] the love of God' to obey the king and rashly pledged that at the next Parliament they were sure the king would 'make her heir apparent' until he had other issue.[18] Under this pressure and faced with threats, not only to herself but to her friends and supporters, Mary signed a set of articles and a letter of submission to her father. At a stroke, she had accepted the royal supremacy and acknowledged that her parents had lived in sin; it would haunt her for the rest of her life. Although the immediate crisis was over, Exeter, Gertrude and Carew were extremely disappointed that the removal of Anne Boleyn had not achieved more. Later, it was claimed that fresh from his bruising exclusion from council, Exeter told Lord Montague that he liked the proceedings of Reginald Pole but not of this realm, that he trusted to see a change of the world and 'to have a fair day upon these knaves which rule about the king'.[19]

As we have seen, Reginald Pole left England in 1532 and in 1535 Henry VIII demanded that he give his opinion on the Boleyn marriage. Reginald's letters in response were positive, and in October 1535 he actually wrote to Cromwell asking him to assure the king 'of my readiness to do him service at all times', and expressing gratitude for his generosity in supporting his education. Naturally, this gave the king hope that he would write in support of the royal supremacy, and in June 1536, in the immediate aftermath of Anne Boleyn's fall, Reginald's long-awaited opinion arrived in the form of a 'letter', but no one was prepared for what it contained. Safe in Europe, Reginald gave full vent to the feelings he was too afraid to express while in England. His fury at the executions of More, Fisher and the Carthusian monks is clear, as he described himself as hardly being able to write for tears when talking about More's execution 'having known the man' as he did. He then went on to liken Henry VIII to a beast, accused him of being incestuous, a reference to the Boleyn marriage, and appealed to the emperor to protect thousands of Christians from a far greater danger than the Turk. This is a king who bears 'most untruly the name of defender of the Faith' a king who 'did not merely kill but tore to pieces all the true defenders of the old religion in a more inhuman fashion that the Turk'. He then warned Henry that 'the Pope is urgently entreated to expel him from the Church as a rotten member, nor can Henry expect his subjects to keep faith with him when he has broken it so shamefully with them'.[20] The king was incandescent with rage, and both the Countess of Salisbury and her son Lord Montague wrote letters of admonishment to Reginald, no doubt intended to be seen by the king's council, but his actions had left them in an invidious position.

There were many others who shared Reginald's views and in October the north erupted into rebellion. The Pilgrimage of Grace came the closest of any rising to toppling Henry from his throne with around 30,000 men up in arms under the leadership of Yorkshire lawyer, Robert Aske. Their demands included a return to Rome, the restoration of the suppressed abbeys, that Princess Mary be made legitimate and Cromwell punished. While the Duke of Suffolk was in overall command, Norfolk was also appointed to lead troops with Exeter as his second in command.[21] Despite Henry's suspicions of both Norfolk and Exeter, they showed scrupulous loyalty. Norfolk marched north with 3,000 men and Exeter with 2,000, intending to join the northern forces of George Talbot, Earl of Shrewsbury, but the organisation of supplies and the issuing of orders from the king and council was chaotic. Cromwell, a man whose attention to detail is well known, on this occasion floundered 'frantically scrabbling to finance this totally unexpected and deeply expensive eventuality'.[22] On 17 October Norfolk wrote a letter to Henry VIII, also signed by Exeter and others, which reveals the confusion 'considering the letters now sent from my lord of Suffolk, I beg to know whether he or I shall set forward towards my lord Steward [Shrewsbury], for I think you will not have both go'.[23] Meanwhile, Shrewsbury wrote to the king and Norfolk that he needed Norfolk, Exeter and their companies to be at Doncaster in under a fortnight, but this was impossible Norfolk explained, 'for our horses are too weak to go more than 20 miles a day'. Furthermore, the mustered troops were in different regions while 'the 10,000*l.* sent us will not despatch the army here and pay those who go northwards till Sunday next. We cannot advance further than they may be paid, without disorder ensuing.'[24] The lack of funds and the king's refusal to pay more than 8d per day for each man meant that Norfolk had to divide the troops and put them under captains and 'If the men grudge upon reasonable ground for lack of money, will cause the captains to give them money out of their own purses.'[25] The chaos continued and on 19 October, addressing his grievance to Cromwell directly, Norfolk wrote in exasperation, 'Where you, my lord Privy Seal, write that in ten days I shall have a sufficient sum to vanquish these rebels, neither my lord Marquis nor I will be able to keep our companies so long without money.' Furthermore, he informed Cromwell that he had already spent £1,500 of his own money to maintain control over his troops.[26] By 20 October both Norfolk and Exeter were en route north, Norfolk ahead of Exeter, but again the provisioning of funds was mishandled. Wriothesley wrote urgently to Cromwell on 21 October that, 'All the said 1,200l. is gone with my lord of Norfolk, so that my lord Marquis, being behind, has not a penny to convey himself and his train toward my lord Steward. You had better send him 400l. or 500l. with all speed.'[27]

While Exeter marched north, his wife showed the same anxiety for his safety as she had expressed to the Nun of Kent three years earlier. She was visited by Sir Edward Neville who asked her how she was and whether she was merry. She replied, 'How can I be merry? My lord is gone to battle, and he will be one of the [foremost].' Neville tried to console her by telling her, 'Madame, be not afeared of this, nor of the second, but beware of the third.' But Gertrude was in no mood for such cryptic advice responding, '[Ah] Mr. Nevell, you will never leave your Welsh prophesies, but one day this will turn you to displeasure.'[28] Meanwhile, by 25 October Norfolk, his son and 30 gentlemen were at Welbeck where he received an urgent message from Shrewsbury summoning him to Doncaster as he had arranged to treat with the rebels. The wiry 62-year-old duke rode the fourteen miles to Doncaster post-haste arriving at two in the morning.[29] Before leaving, he begged the king that 'If it chance to me to miscarry … be good to my sons and to my poor daughter.' At some point before the initial truce was finally agreed on 28 October, Exeter arrived at Doncaster and was among those who negotiated with the rebels and signed an undated address to them.[30] It had been a close shave, but the rebels naïve trust in the king's promises meant the immediate threat was over.

Not long after his return Exeter received, probably in recognition of his service, the dissolved priory of Breamore which included manors in Hampshire, Wiltshire, Dorset, Somerset and Devon. In 1535 the priory had been valued at nearly £155 pa and as Exeter already owned the manor of Braemore this was a beneficial acquisition.[31] It was also a poisoned chalice as he was required to surrender the annuity of £66 13s 4d he had been granted on his marriage, while it made him further, and visibly, complicit in the rejection of papal authority by his acceptance of dissolved monastic property. It certainly pricked his conscience, and he was challenged on this very point shortly afterwards. While riding home to Horsley, he bumped into Geoffrey Pole and they fell into conversation. Exeter told him about the grant to which a shocked Geoffrey responded 'What! ... be you come to this point to take abbey lands now?' Exeter reassured him it was 'good enough for a time; they must have all again one day'.[32] In fairness, Geoffrey had no right to challenge Exeter as he would waive conscience aside in 1537 to purchase various items from the dissolved abbey of Durford on credit from the royal commissioners.[33]

Uncomfortable over the grant, unsettled that he had had to oppose a rebel army with whose aims he sympathised, and angry at Cromwell's mismanagement, by the end of 1536 Exeter was thoroughly disillusioned. When he marched north he was fully prepared for combat and possible death knowing he would face a rebel army of overwhelming numbers, and while this might be called a pilgrimage, some of the participants were far from saintly. During the first Lincolnshire rising one of Cromwell's servants was lynched and the other wrapped in the hide of a newly slaughtered calf and thrown to a pack of bull-baiting dogs, which savaged him to death.[34] Exeter knew he faced this situation with inadequate supplies and underpaid troops of doubtful loyalty. Meanwhile, the man he blamed for this mess, Cromwell, remained safe in the south. He also suspected, probably quite rightly, that Cromwell was behind a series of false rumours that cast doubt on Norfolk's actions during the campaign. While he was not a close friend of the duke, both men had been in the field and slanders by Cromwell, who had not, merely inflamed Exeter's simmering resentment. In June 1537 a butcher of Somerset, John Howell, was accused of gossiping about an argument between Exeter and Cromwell two weeks before Christmas 1536. This included claims that Exeter 'had drawn his dagger on my lord Privy Seal, who was protected by the harness on his back; and that the latter had ordered the former to the Tower'. Howell then boasted that if Exeter 'had been put there ... he would have been fetched out again, though the best of the realm had said nay'.[35] While Exeter pulling a knife on Cromwell is unlikely, there could easily be a kernel of truth to a heated argument taking place between them over the mismanagement of provisions for the military response, none of which would have improved Exeter's standing with the king or his chief minister. As if to block out these events, Exeter began obsessing about obtaining a hawk from his half-uncle, Lord Lisle, and wrote repeatedly throughout December and into January as if nothing else mattered; the strain he was under was beginning to show.[36]

Events of the following year would not have calmed Exeter's nerves as the king despatched agents to assassinate Reginald Pole, who was in turn trying to raise support for action against England, while on 31 March the pope announced a crusading indulgence that would be granted to anyone who attempted to overthrow Henry VIII.[37] All this raised the temperature further and sparked frantic messages among the Exeters' circle. Elizabeth Darrell told Geoffrey Pole that Peter Mewtas had been sent to kill Reginald, at which Geoffrey raged, 'By God's blood, and if he [Meotes] had slain him I would have thrust my dagger [in] him [althou]gh he had [been] at the King's heels.'[38] He then raced over to see his brother at Bockmer where he found him in the garden and told him he had heard that 'our brother beyond the sea shall be slain', but Montague calmed him, reassuring him that he had received letters telling him that on this occasion he had escaped. Geoffrey believed those letters were from Elizabeth Darrell or Gertude, but as he had just come from Elizabeth Darrell it is more likely that the letters had been sent by Gertrude.[39] Pole family servant, Morgan Wells, also heard rumours about plans to assassinate Reginald and angrily told John Collins, Montague's chaplain, that he would kill with a hand gun Peter Mewtas or anyone else who would kill Reginald.[40] Even Sir Edward Neville sang about Mewtas' mission in the garden at Horsley when he went to visit Gertrude.[41] If this was supposed to be a secret mission, then something had gone very wrong as it seemed everyone was gossiping about it. Deeply concerned, Geoffrey went further and asked his man, Hugh Holland, who was going to Flanders to sell wheat, to take a message of warning to Reginald, specifically that Francis Bryan and Peter Mewtas had been sent to kill him with a hand gun. As it turned out, Reginald had already been warned, possibly by a member of Francis I's Privy Chamber who was friendly with Francis Bryan, one of the assassins.[42] During this tense period Montague ordered his chaplain Collins and Geoffrey, who was once again in his brother's confidence, to keep all their conversations about the king, Reginald, abbeys and a change of the world, secret.[43] Despite these precautions, Reginald's successful evasion of the king's assassins caused Henry VIII and Cromwell to begin suspecting Montague. These doubts were expressed during one council meeting prompting Exeter to stand up and offer to be bound body for body for him. This act of loyalty was duly reported to Montague by Gertrude, in one of the many letters she sent him.[44]

Amid all this drama, Gertrude at least found herself in a position she had once held in happier times, that of one of the queen's ladies. On 24 October 1536 a letter sent to Cardinal du Bellay revealed that 'Madame Marie is now the first after the Queen, and sits at table opposite her, a little lower down, after having first given the napkin for washing to the King and Queen. And the marchioness of Exeter gives the water.'[45] Gertrude also received gifts from the queen, including a girdle, and her influence is evidenced by Honor, Viscountess Lisle's attempts to obtain a position in the queen's household for her daughter, and her identification of Gertrude as someone who might help.[46] In January 1537, Honor sent gifts to the queen and to Gertrude and her agent, John Husee, informed her that Mr Coffin, the queen's master of the horse, had specifically advised approaching Gertrude by whose means a positive outcome might be achieved.[47] Gertrude's standing with the queen is not surprising; she was her kinswoman, had assisted her to the throne and the two women had shared aims including a dislike of the religious changes and concern for Princess Mary. At Christmas, Gertrude despatched her loyal servant, Constance Bontayne, to present the Exeters' New Year's gift to Mary, who gave Constance a sovereign, an extremely generous reward in this context to signal her affection for two individuals who had showed unwavering loyalty to her.[48] Jane's period as queen provided a welcome contrast to the hostility Gertrude and Mary had both experienced at the hands of the previous queen. However, Jane was also in need of their support for early in the new year it became clear that she was pregnant, and she was terrified.

By February 1537 Jane and her pregnancy became the focus of unrelenting scrutiny, including bonfires in London when the baby moved, and gun salutes at Calais. Jane knew what was expected of her, but what if she gave birth to a daughter, or worse, miscarried? Would she suffer the same fate as her predecessors? The pressure and resulting stress can be seen in an incident in July when she was six months pregnant. At that time sickness was prevalent in the country and Bold, one of Cromwell's servants, had fallen ill. As Bold had not had direct contact with Cromwell, the king was relaxed about it, informing his minster that he could come to court in a day or two. Comptroller of the royal household, John Russell, who was more observant and sensitive than his monarch, noticed that Jane was 'afraid' and went to Henry who acknowledged that she was 'somewhat afraid'. This prompted him to change his mind and Henry now suggested that Cromwell might stay at one of his nobles' houses from which he could meet the king daily at hunting.[49] Ten days later John Husee informed Lady Lisle 'your Ladyship would not believe how much the Queen is afraid of the sickness; yet the mortality is not so great as last year', clearly revealing Jane's fears for her unborn child.[50]

On 16 September the queen began her confinement at Hampton Court. The labour was prolonged but at 2.00am on 12 October an exhausted Jane finally gave birth to a son who was named Edward. The celebrations immediately began and at eight o'clock in the morning Te Deum was sung in St Paul's and other churches in London, bonfires were lit in every street and there was wine and music. The bells of every church were rung until ten at night, over 2,000 guns fired at the Tower and messengers were despatched to spread the good news. On Monday 15 October the prince's christening took place in the Chapel Royal and Gertrude, her husband and many of their friends were in attendance. Nicholas Carew was one of those in charge of the font in advance of the ceremony while in the procession the Earl of Essex, married to Gertrude's aunt, bore a salt of gold along with the Earl of Sussex who carried a pair of covered basins supported by Lord Montague. There was a difficult moment for Montague when his brother Geoffrey arrived at court and suffered the humiliation of being refused entry. Although this could have been due to concerns about the sickness and a desire to restrict numbers, it was more likely due to Geoffrey being once again out of royal favour. He was by now in considerable debt and had been told explicitly by Cromwell not to come to court.[51] Finally came the prince himself bourn beneath a canopy by Gertrude who was supported on one side by the Duke of Suffolk, and on the other by her husband. No doubt Jane was happy with the roles given to the marquis and marchioness, but the first choice to carry the prince had been the dowager Marchioness of Dorset, who was only prevented from doing so by the sickness prevalent in the area where she lived.[52] The canopy under which Gertrude walked with the baby prince was borne by six members of the Privy Chamber, including Sir Edward Nevill, while the prince's lady mistress, nurse and midwife hovered nearby. Following Gertrude came Princess Mary who was the prince's godmother. At the font Lord Montague uncovered the basins, and also the spice plate when princesses Mary and Elizabeth were served with spices, wafer and wine. Significantly, the godfathers were Thomas Cranmer, Archbishop of Canterbury and the dukes of Norfolk and Suffolk, but not, as we might have expected, the king's first cousin, the Marquis of Exeter. That Gertrude was a substitute rather than first choice to carry the prince and Exeter was passed over as godfather, points to the king's lingering suspicions and the on-going strained relations between them. However, as Gertrude enjoyed good relations with the queen, the couple no doubt planned to make use of this going forward, but then disaster struck.

A few days after her extremely arduous labour Jane became unwell. Five days after Edward's birth things had got so bad that she received the last rites but then seemed to rally. Sadly, hopes for her recovery were dashed when she suffered a relapse and prayers were said for her. Jane's life began to slip away on Wednesday 24 October, and she died around midnight, twelve days after the birth of her son. There was genuine grief for her loss as she was the wife who had finally provided Henry with the heir he had waited nearly thirty years for, but the person most affected was Princess Mary. She knew how much effort Jane had made to reconcile her with her father, and she had always been kind to her. The princess was more than happy to call her mother, addressing one letter to 'the Queen's grace my good mother' and signing it as 'Your grace's most humble and obedient daughter and handmaid', something that would have been unthinkable with Anne Boleyn.[53] So distressed was Mary that she could not immediately carry out her duties as chief mourner, an echo of the grief felt by Katharine, Countess of Devon at the death of her sister Elizabeth of York. Appropriately, it was Gertrude who stood in for her until she had composed herself. On the journey to Windsor for Jane's interment, Princess Mary rode directly behind the hearse while Lord Montague and Lord Clifford rode alongside her.[54] Gertrude's half-brother Charles carried one of the banners that were borne around the hearse on which Jane's body lay, and she was laid to rest in St George's Chapel on 12 November.

The repercussions of Jane's death were profound, certainly for the Exeters. As the mother of the king's son and heir, who might provide her husband with more healthy sons, her position would have been unassailable. With the enhanced influence this would have given her, her voice of reason might have been listened to by the increasingly unpredictable and suspicious king. But with her death and the immediate possibility of begetting another son erased, the birth of Edward only served to make the king more paranoid. At the moment of her burial, Exeter and Gertrude had great need of Jane's help as the marquis once again found himself under suspicion. This might explain why neither he nor Gertrude were listed among the mourners who travelled to Windsor with Jane's body. Between 31 October, when Gertrude stood in for Princess Mary, and 12 November when Jane's body was taken to Windsor, something had happened and Cromwell's remembrances for that month includes the following written in his own hand, 'To remember the examination of my lord Marquis' bearward and Payn his fellow.'[55]

The bearward was one William Parr and his fellow was John Payne.[56] Evidence about what was going on here is scant, but both were arrested and imprisoned in the Tower where, significantly, Cromwell would interrogate them personally. What we do know, is that following Jane Seymour's death Exeter returned to London. This might have been on the king's orders who would have been briefed by Cromwell about the situation with the bearward. The two men were accused of treason and no charge could be more serious. Someone else who had heard about this was Privy Chamber favourite Sir Edward Neville, who immediately sought to warn the marquis. Following his arrival at his London residence, an oblivious Exeter was informed by Neville that 'a bearward of his was taken in the West country, and advised him to look to it, as it was much against his honour'.[57] Perturbed, Exeter immediately sent his trusted servant Anthony Harvey to Cromwell to find out what was going on. However, he was completely unprepared for what happened next. The day after Harvey's visit,

Cromwell told the king, and the king ordered Cromwell to command Exeter 'upon his allegiance' to declare who had told him his bearward had been arrested. The marquis was completely taken aback, 'the most a]ppallyd ma[n]', but to his credit maintained his composure and replied that he would rather die than disclose his friend 'if it touched not the King'. He then produced a servant 'who said it was told him in P[au]les, but of whom he could not [te]ll'. The story was a fabrication, but Exeter reassured Neville that he had 'satisfied' Cromwell with this explanation.[58] In February 1538, Parr and Payne were sent to Gloucester to be tried by ambitious lawyer, Edward Montague, recently appointed king's serjeant at law.[59] On 26 February he eagerly informed Cromwell that 'Today Wm. Parr, the marquis of Exeter's bearward, and John Payne were attainted of high treason, before Mr. Porte and me, at Gloucester, by the verdict of Sir John Brydges, Sir John Huddelston, and others.' He reminded Cromwell of the debt owed to those who had informed on Parr, 'Mr. Panter and five of his neighbours did the King service therein, which it were well to recompense.'[60] Parr and Payne's execution took place shortly afterwards with Bishop Roland Lee, lord president of the council in the marches of Wales, informing his close friend Cromwell that their 'heads and quarters shall be sent to eight of the best towns of the shire'.[61] As the fateful year of 1538 began, the marquis' days were already numbered; he had less than twelve months to live.

Chapter 11

1538

The Fall

he will be watched till your further pleasure is known
whether to take him alive or kill him.

In the cold early months of 1538 Thomas Cromwell ordered that his red deer be moved from Kenilworth to Essex. Many died along the way, succumbing to the biting weather, until just a stag and one hind were left. The hind, too, died, an occurrence which Cromwell took 'in good part'. The stag, however, survived and was discovered 'poor and weary' by a servant of Richard Gyffard who looked after the Marquis of Exeter's park at Lawford Hall. Taking pity on the stag, he let it into the marquis' park, but it broke through a hedge and took refuge in a great wood. The neighbourhood was mustered and attempts were made to capture the beast with 'nets and other engines'. Beleaguered on all sides, he nevertheless managed to evade them and made his escape into another great copse two miles away. As everyone paused and waited, while keeping the noble creature under surveillance, Cromwell's pleasure in the matter was sought and he was asked just one question: 'whether to take him alive or kill him'.[1]

The breakdown of Exeter's relationship with Henry VIII left him vulnerable. He no longer enjoyed the king's confidence and laboured under an aura of suspicion, which left him open to the malice of others. On 15 June 1538, just three months after the execution of his bearward for treason, he was again subject to damaging accusations. Lawyer John Hull, a man who kept Cromwell 'informed on affairs in Devon' wrote to the king's chief minister from Exeter. Hull was actively supporting a scheme to widen and dredge the river Exe, which was becoming difficult to navigate, thus threatening the economy of Exeter. This brought him into conflict with property owners along the bank of the Exe, including Exeter, and Hull turned to Cromwell for support.[2] 'There is a great retainer in our country which causes much mischief and must be redressed. I pray you remember the expedition of my bill, for there shall be much sinister labour made to the King on behalf of Ant. Harvy, surveyor to the marquis of Exeter.' Describing Exeter as a 'great retainer' had echoes of the William Kendall affair of 1531. However, there was more to it than a clash over the river Exe. Hull went on to complain that his wealthy aunt, 88-year-old Lady Martyn, had asked him to manage her affairs, and in return she promised to come and live with him and leave him 'the profit of her lands', naming him sole executor of her will. Lady Martyn was of sufficient standing to have sent a servant with a gift of a boar to Exeter's mother, the Countess of Devon, on 21 December 1524.³ Hull was obviously keen to get his hands on the old lady's money, but while he was visiting London Sir Hugh Paulet and two of Lady Martyn's servants took advantage of his absence and 'craftily' persuaded Lady Martyn 'to be governed by Sir Hugh and his assignees'. This, Hull complained, is 'to my great hindrance'. Sir Hugh Paulet had links to the Courtenays; Sir Hugh's father, Sir Amyas, had been one of the stewards of Katharine, Countess of Devon, and Sir Hugh's father-in-law was Sir Lewis Pollard, who had been one the countess' legal council. Sir Hugh's son, also called Amyas, would marry Anthony Harvey's daughter, Margaret, in 1557. With such powerful backing, it was in Hull's interest to use Cromwell as a counterpoise to the marquis. He ended with a request and a promise 'I trust you will send letters in my favour to the said Sir Hugh and to lady Martyn, and will "acquite" your Lordship with such a pleasure as ye shall be pleased. You will hear more of my mind by the bearer …'⁴ By asking for Cromwell's help in curbing the marquis' power, he was pushing at an open door for, unbeknownst to him, Cromwell was already involved in a covert investigation that was about to explode.

Already suspicious of Exeter and the Pole family, Cromwell's agents and spy network were active. Lord Montague's mother had the misfortune of appointing a loose-tongued gossip with leanings towards the new learning, Richard Ayer, as head of a surgeon house she maintained near her seat, Warblington Castle in Hampshire. Ayer disapproved of goings on in the countess's household and of rumoured correspondence with Reginald Pole, by now a recognised traitor to the crown. Smatterings of Ayer's gossip finally reached the ears of the Lord Privy Seal, who sent one of his spies, Gervase Tyndall, to the source. Arriving at the surgeon house in the summer, he pretended ill health and gained admittance. After that, it was easy to tease out of the gossiping Ayer sensational claims. At Tyndall's offer to arrange an interview with Cromwell, Ayer's words spilled out of him and Tyndall couldn't believe his luck. According to Ayer, Hugh Holland, Geoffrey Pole's man, had conveyed letters to Reginald Pole meaning all the secrets of the realm were known to the pope. Ayer also introduced Tyndall to a previous member of Margaret's household who had been dismissed due to his adherence to the new religion. He gave information about John Helyar, the countess' chaplain and an admirer of Reginald Pole who Ayer described as scarcely the king's friend. He had left the realm without licence in 1535 with the help of Hugh Holland and Geoffrey Pole.

Tyndall's arrival aroused the suspicions of some of the local priests and the constable, but when they confronted Tyndall he revealed his shock that the constable appeared not to take seriously the information he had heard. Attempting to smooth things over Geoffrey Pole, as a local Justice of the Peace, stepped in and summoned Tyndall before him, assuring him he could tell him all he knew as he was the king's friend. Tyndall was more than happy to do so, confidently declaring that all he had said was the truth. A now seriously concerned Geoffrey confided in his mother's devoted comptroller and receiver-general, Oliver Franklyn, who advised him to go direct to Cromwell with Holland and Ayer to explain, which he did. He was relieved when Cromwell appeared to accept his explanation, but Geoffrey had only told Cromwell about letters to Helyar. He was unaware that Tyndall had been told about Holland taking letters to Reginald and England's secrets being disclosed to the pope. Shortly after Geoffrey's visit Tyndall's report arrived on Cromwell's desk, and this did include the allegations about correspondence with Reginald facilitated by Hugh Holland. These damning accusations were received in June along with the letter from John Hull that described Exeter as a great retainer. As these separate pieces of evidence implicated the Poles and cast suspicion on Exeter, Cromwell moved quickly and Hugh Holland was arrested in a scuffle at Bockmer, Lord Montague's seat, while both brothers were in residence.[5] Geoffrey, terrified that the incriminating letters that lay in his study at Lordington would be discovered, immediately despatched Montague's chaplain, John Collins, to burn them. Exeter, Gertrude and their group of friends realised they were in danger, but there was still hope. Holland was a hard man, used to living on the edge, it was possible he would resist intimidation and keep his mouth shut. However, they must have doubted this when, between 20 and 28 July, Cromwell sent his nephew Richard to Exeter and offered him the chance to be 'frank and plain in certain things'. The marquis' courageous and characteristic reply that he 'would open nothing to the hindrance of his friend', showed admirable loyalty but did nothing to earn the king's trust, or Cromwell's.[6]

While Exeter and Gertrude tried to remain calm following Holland's arrest, they suffered another set-back that could not have come at a worse time. At some point before August their son's schoolmaster, Oxford-educated Robert Taylor, left their household without permission and fled to the University of Louvain. No destination could have been worse. It was here that the Countess of Salisbury's chaplain, John Helyar, had secretly come and where he might have met Reginald Pole, while George Croftes, Chancellor of Chichester Cathedral and Geoffrey Pole's friend, had matriculated here.[7] All these men were opposed to Henry VIII's religious changes, and it is likely that Taylor was too and found like-minded individuals at Louvain. If the Exeters hoped to keep Taylor's departure quiet, they were to be disappointed. On 24 August Sir Richard Gresham wrote to John Hutton in Flanders informing him that Taylor had left England. Both Gresham and Hutton were the king's men. Gresham was doing a roaring trade asset-stripping and selling monastic properties, and in 1537 was appointed Lord Mayor of London at the king's request, with Cromwell among the guests at his mayoral feast. Hutton was the king's agent in Flanders and busy in the campaign against Reginald. In May 1537 two of his spies had informed him that Reginald's man, Michael Throckmorton, had, or was about to, take letters to Reginald's friends in England.[8] Both men would have had little sympathy with conservatives such as Exeter.

Following Gresham's letter, Hutton sprang into action and discovered that Taylor was at the University of Louvain. On 29 August Hutton wrote to the marquis from Antwerp informing him of the latest situation regarding Taylor. Sensibly, Exeter had expressed his desire for Taylor to return, but he was under no illusion that Gresham and Hutton were working on behalf of Cromwell and the king. Realising that he 'could not come by him by force', Hutton invited two English gentlemen 'to come to me and make good cheer and bring with them any students of our nation'. The next day they did, and it was clear that Taylor was among them. Saying nothing during the meal, after supper he 'took Mr. Taylor by the hand and told him privately your Lordship's wish that he should return to England, and that you wondered at his sudden departure'. Taylor explained that 'it was to avoid further displeasure, for he had been threatened by some young gentlemen of your Lordship's household for ministering correction to your son; but he consented to return'. It was a plausible excuse, as many tutors found themselves at loggerheads with their pupil's friends who preferred to see young noblemen on horseback instead of inside studying books, but that is probably what it was; an excuse.[9] The quietly efficient Hutton instructed the bearer of his letter to Exeter, Andrew Dyar, 'to keep company with Mr. Taylor and not leave him till he had brought him to your Lordship', which he did, and Taylor was back in Exeter's household by September.[10] The Taylor affair was the latest in a succession of occurrences that had consistently compromised Exeter. Then, on the very day that Hutton wrote to Exeter about Taylor, 29 August, Geoffrey Pole was arrested. It was now certain that Holland had not kept his mouth shut. In fact, Holland had revealed just how closely involved he and Geoffrey had been in Helyar's unlicensed departure, and Geoffrey's on-going correspondence with him. More damaging were his revelations that he had taken messages from Geoffrey to Reginald Pole, while he also testified to communication between Lord Montague and Reginald's man, Michael Throckmorton.[11]

Following Geoffrey's arrest there was nothing to do but wait. The Countess of Salisbury wrote to her son Lord Montague advising him 'to serve your prince not disobeying God's commandments as far as your power and life will serve you'.[12] Worryingly, one of Montague's most trusted servants, Jerome Ragland, had also been taken in for questioning revealing the direction of the investigation as it slowly and inevitably spread, like ink in water, towards Montague and his friends. Geoffrey's initial interrogation concentrated on discovering who else might be involved in this conspiracy, and while he mentioned ten individuals, including Lord Montague and Exeter, he tried to vindicate them of any treason.[13] But his examiners wanted to know if Montague had told Exeter of news, letters and messages sent to him from overseas.[14] Certain that others were involved, Geoffrey's examiners now threatened torture. The desperate message Geoffrey sent to the king supports this, as he pledged that if he could have 'good keeping and cherishing' he would then 'fully open all that he did know or may remember whomsoever it touch, whether it be mother, brother, uncle or any other what so ever he be'. His acceptance that betrayal of his family and friends was inevitable led him to attempt suicide as the only way to avoid the horror.[15] Outside the Tower walls word spread of Geoffrey's collapse which occurred in October. When Constance, Geoffrey's wife, mentioned to Montague the rumour that Geoffrey 'was in a frenzy and might utter rash things' he replied that it 'forceth not what a mad man [speaketh]', in other words, he hoped he would not be believed; he hoped in vain.[16]

Geoffrey's words spilled out of him including claims that Montague said 'none served the King but knaves' and his wish that he and Geoffrey were overseas for the 'world would one day come to stripes'. He also asserted that Throckmorton sent a message to Montague via Holland assuring him that when 'he would come over seas' Throckmorton would come and fetch him. His testimony also implicated Exeter and Gertrude when he said he saw letters from Gertrude to Montague informing him that her husband had pledged in council to be bound body for body for him, thus revealing the closeness between them and their propensity to confide in each other.[17] Augmenting this was the evidence of Jerome Ragland who admitted that Montague often sent his servant, George Tyrell, to Exeter and lamented the pulling down of the abbeys, especially Bisham Abbey where his forebears were buried. Ragland heard talk of it being a meet marriage for Reginald to marry Mary, remembering that the person who said this was a servant of Montague. Ragland's testimony also revealed Montague's personal dislike of the king. He reportedly criticised him when he broke his word to the pilgrimage of grace rebels, complaining that in times past a king's words could be believed and that if the commons rose again they will 'trust no fair promise nor words'. Upon the king's threats to leave the kingdom and go with the 'Lubekks', Montague remarked that 'we should be well rid of him' and described the king as 'full of flesh and unwieldy' who could not long continue with his sore leg. Ragland also testified to the close friendship between Montague and Exeter, and that Montague had praised his brother Reginald, who he thought 'ordained by god to do good'.[18] His evidence listed locations at Bockmer where Montague talked with Geoffrey and his chaplain, Collins, including the garden, the woods adjoining, 'a place called the Long Rowe' and the great chamber. Ragland's interrogators would be aware that Montague was ensuring his conversations were not overheard, begging the question; what did he have to hide?[19] With such testimony, subsequent arrests were inevitable.

It was on a cold winter evening, Monday 4 November, when they came for the family. Arriving at Horsley, the king's men bundled the marquis from the house ten days after his nineteenth wedding anniversary and Gertrude would never see her husband again. This was also the last memory their son Edward had of his father, separated from him in the most traumatic of circumstances, and it would affect him for the rest of his life. As he was taken away, Gertrude and Edward remained at Horsley for a short time before following, first on horseback, then completing the final stage of this fateful journey by boat, arriving at the Tower early the next morning.[20] Gertrude's thoughts would have been with her husband, for whom she had always shown concern, but her thoughts would also have turned to her son, unprotected and vulnerable and on the way to the Tower at just 12 years old. Upon arrival, mother and son were separated, and over the next week or so there was frenzied activity as interrogations took place, with further arrests and a succession of witnesses brought in. Lord Montague and his 12-year-old son were also at the Tower having been arrested on the same day as the Exeters, followed by Sir Edward Neville on the 5 November. Geoffrey had already testified that Montague had burned many letters at Bockmer and that Gertrude had written to him in her own hand.[21] Not surprisingly, her interrogation focussed on the content of those letters and she confessed that she had told Montague that her husband had been warned to avoid his company due to the suspicion in which they were held, and that the king had sent to him in London regarding the bearward. She also confessed that Edward Neville had said 'divers times, and sometimes [sing]' that he trusted the world would amend and honest men rule one day, for which she admonished him. Gertrude's evidence against Neville corroborated Geoffrey's which also claimed that Neville trusted the world would amend one day.[22]

As the examinations progressed, what becomes clear is the large amount of correspondence between the Exeters and Lord Montague, but particularly Gertrude and Montague, and these letters formed a significant part of the evidence against Exeter and his wife. Montague himself stated that he received letters from Gertrude, while Gertrude's servant, Contance Bontayne, testified that 'my lady hath sent often times letters and received letters from the lord Montacute'. William Brent, one of Montague's most trusted servants, claimed that he had seen 'the superscription of letters directed by lord Montacute to the lady Marquis which one Tyrell used to carry'. John Collins stated that 'George Tyrell was often sent from Lord Montacute to the lord Marquis, but he knows not what letters or messages Tyrell carried' while Morgan Wells, Montague's servant, believed 'if any man went to the lord Marquis it was Tyrell, who would never say where he went, but always declared he would be home the same night'. Wells and Brent also stated that they saw Thomas Footeman, servant to Exeter, at Montague's residence, with Wells claiming that he had seen Footeman many times at Bockmer, especially this last summer.[23] Although the name of Thomas Footeman does not appear among Exeter's servants, the likely individual referred to was 40-year-old Thomas Hendrye 'otherwise footman', who served the marquis at Horsley. He was described as a 'tall man' and received a wage commensurate to a position of responsibility.[24]

We don't know whether Hendrye was ever questioned, but Tyrell was. His evidence confirmed the regular exchange of letters between Gertrude and Montague over the past three years. Although the purpose of some of the letters were to enquire about Exeter's health, he admitted that for the majority he did not know their contents. When asked if any conversation took place when he delivered the letters, Tyrell replied that it was 'generally to give commendations and to deliver the letters', adding that he never spoke to the marquis more than twice. This confirms Exeter and Gertrude's *modus operandi* as Gertrude had the time and space to write the letters, whereas Exeter was often in attendance upon the king in the Privy Chamber and the Privy Council. More ominously, Brent admitted seeing Montague 'many times burn letters, and has had letters of his in keeping which he delivered to the said lord Montacute, who used to burn or cast into the jakes [latrine] many of them'. Montague himself admitted he told Geoffrey that his correspondence 'shall hurt no fry[nde] of mine for I have bur[ned all] my letters'. The fact that Cromwell did not find any letters that he could produce confirms that they had been destroyed, and this naturally aroused suspicion. In his notes of the evidence, Cromwell recorded that Geoffrey Pole said if the letters burned at Bockmer and Lordington had been discovered, they would have revealed 'all the intelligence' between Montague and Exeter and Montague and Gertrude, while in the margin crown lawyer Richard Pollard wrote that it appeared 'there was contained treason in those letters that were burned'.[25]

As the interrogations progressed, evidence against Lord Montague continued to reveal his deep dislike of Henry VIII with Geoffrey claiming that his brother rejoiced at the prospect of the king's death saying 'he will one day die suddenly;

his leg will kill him and then we shall have jol[ly] stirring'. Montague also described the king's mood swings and angry outbursts, believing that he 'would be out of his wits [on]e day, for when he came to his chamber he would look angerly, and after fall to fighting', claims corroborated by those independent of this enquiry, such as Chapuys. In addition to this were accusations that Montague 'trusted the world would amend' and 'a time' would come, and that he feared the Marquis of Exeter 'would die before the time'.[26]

Montague's alleged support of Reginald Pole, who had been actively urging hostile foreign powers to invade England, was explosive, and added to this was the damning evidence that Holland had taken letters to Reginald Pole containing the secrets of the realm. Indeed, this formed one of the charges against Holland, that he 'promised Sir Geoffrey to do errands to his brother, cardinal Pole, being traitor beyond the sea, and show him the King's acts and secrets of the realm'. Furthermore, Geoffrey claimed that Montague knew all that was done in Council when Exeter was there. He was able to prove this by telling his interrogators that Montague informed him that many times the Privy Council were at their wits' end with such matters as they had in hand.[27] Suspicion inevitably fell upon Exeter as the leak, or one of the leaks, of information from the Privy Council. He had a direct link to Reginald via his close friendship with the cardinal's brother, Montague, a man he had refused to betray when previously given the opportunity. Their friendship was not a secret, and following one of the king's summer visits to Horsley some of Exeter's friends had warned him to avoid Montague's company. Their closeness was further confirmed by various witnesses. Constance Bontayne saw 'the Marquis use great familiarity with the lord Montacute, and thinks he reckoned him his assured friend' while Montague described Exeter to Ragland as 'a noble man'. Despite feeling that 'he could trust few men nowadays' Ragland believed Montague 'had great trust' in Exeter, and testified to his often resorting to the marquis at Horsley and his residence in London. John Collins also heard Montague 'very much praise the marquis of Exeter, saying that he was a very noble man and one of very good mind and good courage'. Collins believed that 'if any change should have been, lord Montacute would have had a very assured friend of the lord Marquis'.[28]

The questions drawn up for Exeter naturally focussed on this mentioned change of the world and his links to Montague. Questions included whether he had told Geoffrey Pole, or anyone else in Geoffrey's presence, that he disliked the proceedings of the realm and wished for a change, what conversations he had had with Montague and whether 'they agreed to take one part'. He was also asked if any letters were sent from Gertrude to Montague, whether she 'made you privy to their contents' and did he tell her that he had offered in council to be bound body for body for Montague. Finally, he was asked whether he held up his fist and told Geoffrey, 'Knaves rule about the King. I trust to give them a buffet one day.'[29] Suspiciously, Exeter's answers, unlike Montague's, Gertrude's, Geoffrey's and others, are missing. Did he refuse to answer? Were his answers so convincing in his defence and that of his wife and friends, that the government found them embarrassing and destroyed them? Or was the paper on which they were written simply damaged over time or lost? Frustratingly, it is impossible to know.

In addition to evidence gleaned from the prisoners and various witnesses, the wife of Robert Couper, a London goldsmith, came forward. She claimed that one 'Eleys', the marquis' master of the horse, often used to visit her husband's shop to order decorations for horse harness. Forty-six-year-old Roger Elys was a tall and imposing man and during one such visit, accompanied by some of Exeter's other servants including George Gatte, yeoman of the stable, he embarked on an angry rant.[30] Knowing the Coupers to be supporters of the new learning, he told Mrs Couper that a day would come when 'there shall be no more wood spent upon you heretics, but you will be tied together, sacked, and thrown into the Thames'. When she replied that she wished Exeter 'would read the Gospel in English, and suffer his servants to do the same', Elys swore, and shouted that 'If my Lord know any of his servants either to have any of these books in English, or to read any of the same they shall never do him any longer service.' Elys really should have known better than to be so indiscreet as he was an experienced and longstanding member of Exeter's household who had also served his mother.[31] Mrs Couper, afraid for her own safety if she did not report Elys' outburst, duly informed the authorities on 12 November.[32]

Cromwell now had enough evidence to proceed and as the indictments were prepared, the William Kendall affair of 1531 was rehearsed, while Cromwell wrote a five-page document of charges against the marquis. These included that he said 'he trusted to [see a new] world one d[ay]e' and that 'knaves should not rule about the King'. Then Cromwell jotted down a question 'why should the Marquis have s [ecret?] intelligence with the lord Montacue who ... l[ok]yd for an alteration'. The question ends with 'and that ey[ther of] them should burn others letters'.[33] The final indictments charged Exeter with telling Geoffrey Pole at West Horsley and Montague at London that he liked the proceedings of Reginald Pole but not of this realm and that he trusted to see a change of the world. Furthermore, Exeter 'well knowing Henry lord Montague to be a false traitor, held divers treasonable conferences with him in divers parts of the realm', on 25 August 1536 at West Horsley and on 20 August 1537 in London. In addition, he threatened 'to have a fair day upon these knaves which rule about the king', trusted to see a merry world one day and said, '"Knaves rule about the King" but [extending his clenched fist] "I trust to give them a buffet one day.'[34] Lord Montague's indictments included his support for Reginald Pole, words spoken against the king and, significantly, his wish to dwell in the west 'for in the West parts the lord Marquis of Exeter is strong.'[35]

Lord Montague's trial took place on Monday 2 December and the Marquis of Exeter's on Tuesday 3 December at Westminster Hall. As Exeter faced the peers who were to judge him he saw family and also friends. Among them was the earl of Essex, the marquis of Dorset and, worse of all, young Charles Blount, Lord Mountjoy, his 22-year-old brother-in-law. Also present were Lord Sandys and Thomas Manners, Earl of Rutland, with whom he had been friends for years.[36] These individuals would now declare him guilty and by doing so, sentence him to death. For Sandys, who also enjoyed a connection to the Pole family through kinship and service, a guilty verdict would demonstrate his loyalty, important for a man who himself had been implicated during the investigation by the evidence of Sir Henry Owen.[37] Lord Montague had been found guilty the day before and Sir Edward Neville, Sir Geoffrey Pole, George Croftes, John Collins and Hugh Holland were found guilty at their trial on 4 December, although Geoffrey Pole's life was spared and he was later pardoned.[38] On Monday 9 December, George Croftes, Chancellor of Chichester Cathedral, Hugh Holland, one time pirate and agent of Geoffrey Pole, and John Collins, chaplain to Lord Montague, were drawn to Tyburn, hanged and quartered, their heads set on London Bridge and their quarters on various gates around London. Following their executions, Exeter, Montague and Neville took their last journey together to Tower Hill, and here the three friends were beheaded. Their bodies were then conveyed to the Chapel of St Peter ad Vincula where they were buried, and where they lie to this day, still within the walls of their Tower prison.[39]

Reactions abroad to the destruction of these two noble families were unfavourable, prompting the government to explain itself. Initially, they based their explanations on actual evidence such as correspondence from Reginald, and Montague and Exeter's wish for a change of the world. However, as the situation with France and the empire was on a knife edge, their claims soon descended into outrageous nonsense as they strove to justify their actions and prevent any further deterioration in relations. Cromwell claimed that Exeter had planned to marry Mary to his son and usurp the kingdom, while it was made known in Brussels that Exeter had been a traitor for the last twenty years and had planned to take the king's place and kill all his children.[40] Nevertheless, despite the shocking brutality of the debacle, especially the execution of the marquis who was the closest thing to a brother the king had, there was logic to the government's actions.

By 1538 Henry was 47 and had just one baby son whose parents had married while England was in schism, meaning that in the eyes of the Catholic Church Edward was not legitimate. In light of this, what the government really feared was a rising in support of Princess Mary and witnesses during the investigation were questioned on this very point. The Pole family's devotion to Mary was well known, as was Exeter's, whose loyalty to her led to his expulsion from council in 1536. To those who did not accept the royal supremacy, Mary was Henry's only legitimate successor and one who might also enjoy the support of the emperor, her cousin. Furthermore, England's diplomatic isolation was made glaringly obvious when a ten-year treaty between France and the Empire was signed in June 1538, the very month when Hugh Holland was arrested. The following month Francis I and Charles V met in person and agreed 'to co-operate in defending Christendom and bringing heretics back into the church'.[41] Significantly, this peace that was viewed as a serious threat to England, had been furthered by none other than Reginald Pole. This meant that by 1538 the 'government was genuinely afraid that there might be an invasion, with Reginald Pole playing a prominent role and possibly looking to find an entry point around the southern coast'.[42] The southern coast was where Exeter and Montague's mother had considerable landholdings, including areas of coastline. If the king trusted Exeter, Montague and the Countess of Salisbury to defend the south, then he could be reassured, but clearly he did not. It is not unreasonable for him to suspect that if Reginald arrived with an invasion force, he would find an entry point through the lands of either his mother or his kinsman and admirer, Exeter. It is for this reason that the countess, against whom very little could be proven, was imprisoned and attainted thus bringing her lands under royal control. The same was true for Exeter's lands, with the first grant of one of his southern manors not made until October 1539 to the staunchly loyal and reliable John, Lord Russell.[43]

Of course, the actions of Exeter and the Poles in the event of an invasion remain unknown. Montague might have moved as he had no love for Henry VIII, but the ease with which he and his mother were removed casts doubt on whether they could have generated adequate support. The same can be said for Exeter, whose arrest triggered no great outcry despite the boast of Thomas Holman of Sherborne, Dorset, that the men of Devon and Cornwall would not suffer Exeter's imprisonment and death.[44] Furthermore, even if Exeter could have replicated his success in raising thousands, as he did against the Pilgrimage of Grace, whether he could have brought himself to take up arms against his royal kinsman, for whom he still had affection, remains open to question. The key point, and what is more important than anything else, is what Henry VIII feared they might do and that was the deciding factor in their destruction. The king knew the Poles had been communicating with Reginald, that Exeter was keeping Montague informed of confidential discussions in council, that they wished for a change and were staunch supporters of his daughter, Princess Mary. Crucially, when he offered his cousin the chance to save himself and be 'open and frank in certain things', Exeter refused to betray Montague. It was this staunch loyalty to Montague that was of concern; if an invasion army approached, who would Exeter support, the king or Montague? The king regarded Exeter's faithfulness to Montague as disloyalty to him and combined with other instances, real or otherwise, of Exeter's untrustworthiness from the 1530s onwards, he now considered him a threat. While it can be argued that the king's actions against the backdrop of a possible invasion are understandable, his propensity for self-pity and self-righteous indignation which erased all regret for his cousin's death, are less palatable. While the man he had known since childhood, one of his closest family members, faced trial and execution, Henry partied at Westminster. It was here that he entertained guests including his and Exeter's aunt by marriage, Honor Lisle, showing them 'all the pleasures of his house'. He was, as a contemporary noted, 'never merrier'.[45]

Exeter's fate has always been overshadowed by the executions of more high-profile individuals such as Anne Boleyn, the wife the king had loved, and Sir Thomas More, his mentor and friend, yet Exeter's execution is one of *the* great tragedies of the reign. The king had been genuinely fond of his young cousin who was always in his company. He was both amused and charmed by his exuberant enthusiasm, whether dancing, masking, jousting or throwing snowballs. In turn, Exeter had idolised the king since childhood and even when Henry changed and Exeter became disillusioned, his affection remained. The evidence of 1538 makes this clear. While others such as Montague and Neville insulted the king, Neville calling him a beast and worse than a beast, Exeter never did. He blamed those around Henry, like Anne Boleyn and Cromwell, but never Henry himself. It was they, he believed, who were at fault, and it was they who had come between him and his royal cousin and soured their relationship. Exeter was a rarity at the court of Henry VIII where disloyalty and self-serving betrayal were the norm. He was a loyal friend who knew what was at stake when he refused to betray Edward Nevill in 1537 and Lord Montague in the summer of 1538, and the relationships he enjoyed is testament to his character. His servants remained in his employ for years and none are known to have spoken against him in 1538. His friendships were longstanding and his marriage one of affection and respect. When he decided to marry Gertrude, he committed to her completely and loved her for the rest of his life. Lord Montague could not speak more highly of anyone and was devoted to his friend. Fifteen years later, Reginald Pole told Exeter's son that his father and Lord Montague had been 'so linked by God in sincere affection throughout their lives, He would not at the last hour allow them to be separated, both dying together for the same cause'.[46] Shortly before his execution, an independent observer listed in blunt and often uncomplimentary terms twenty members of the nobility. The majority were dismissed as having little wit, some enjoyed power some did not, some had wealth while others did not and the military prowess of a small number was praised, but only one was described as 'specially beloved'; that was Henry Courtenay, Marquis of Exeter.[47]

Part III

Edward Courtenay, Earl of Devon

Chapter 12

1539–1553

Survival

deliver me out of this miserable captivity.

Gertrude's reaction to her husband's death has gone unrecorded, but there is no reason to doubt that she would have grieved deeply for the loss of he who had been her constant companion for the last nineteen years. She would also have mourned her friends, Henry, Lord Montague and Sir Edward Neville. Of that small circle, only Sir Nicholas Carew had emerged unscathed, but now he, too, became a target. Cromwell was well aware of Carew's closeness to Exeter's circle having seen them in action in the run up to Anne Boleyn's fall. Indeed, one of the questions for Geoffrey Pole was whether Lord Montague had confided in Carew.[1] Cromwell also knew how much more hostile to him the influential Carew would be now. Indeed, it is possible that Carew expressed criticism during the legal process. Appointed to receive the Surrey indictment against Exeter, he reportedly exclaimed, 'I marvel greatly that the indictment against the lord Marquis was so secretly handled and for what purpose, for the like was never seen.'[2] It has been claimed that longstanding Courtenay servant Jasper Horsey informed on the Marquis of Exeter, revealed by the grants he subsequently received and his burgeoning royal service.[3] However, the evidence does not support this. The only known evidence Horsey gave against his master and mistress concerned, in the main, Gertrude's contact with the Nun of Kent, something of which the government was already aware. He said no more than Constance Bontayne, and she was not considered a traitor by Gertrude, remaining in her service afterwards.[4] What is more likely is that Horsey was used by Cromwell specifically to provide evidence against Carew. Significantly, of all the known testimonies given during the autumn of 1538, Horsey was the only one who mentioned Carew, stating that he had seen 'the lord Montacute, the Master of the Horses [Carew], and Sir Edward Nevelle, many times resort to the said house [West Horsley], as well when the Marquis was at home as when the lady Marquis was at home and the Marquis absent'.[5] Furthermore, Jasper's elder brother, Sir John, was close to Cromwell who may have used him to 'encourage' his younger brother to provide evidence against Carew, using threats, but also promises of reward.[6]

Carew was arrested on 31 December and Chapuys heard that this was due to the discovery of a letter he had written to Gertrude informing her of conversations that had taken place in the king's chamber. This letter had been found in a coffer belonging to Gertrude and is believable considering the contact between them. Finding Carew's letter, if indeed they did, prompted his arrest, but clearly the coffer was not discovered when the inventory was taken at Horsley on 15 November.[7] Therefore, could Horsey, as controller of Exeter's household, have directed Cromwell to this coffer? Very possibly, and as has been noted, his subsequent grants and appointments do look very much like rewards. Less than two months after Carew's arrest he was appointed a gentleman usher of the king's chamber and on 22 February 1539 was granted leases of part of Carew's lands.[8] In May 1540 his position as Keeper of Dartington which he had held under Exeter was continued and in July a grant of premises in Townstall, Devon, made by the marquis in 1536, was honoured.[9] His career continued to prosper when he was appointed steward to the household of Anne of Cleves following the annulment of her marriage. His salary of £26 13s 4d a year was more than double the salary he had received from the marquis.[10] The clearest evidence of the royal favour he now enjoyed, and independently of Cromwell, came in 1544 when he was appointed Chief Gentleman of the Privy Chamber to Prince Edward.[11] Following that, he was granted a generous annuity of £66 13s 4d, chillingly the exact same amount which had been granted to Exeter and Gertrude following their marriage in 1519.[12]

If Horsey had indeed delivered Carew to the authorities, Cromwell did the rest. Carew's examination focused on correspondence with Gertrude and her husband, as well as with Lord Montague, Sir Edward Neville, Catherine of Aragon and Princess Mary.[13] In addition to his exclamation that Exeter's indictment had been secretly handled, Carew's indictment included conversations and correspondence with Exeter in 1536, while knowing him to be a traitor, and the accusation that he burnt letters from Exeter in October 1537 and September 1538.[14] The verdict was a foregone conclusion for on 13 February Henry VIII told Sir Thomas Wyatt that after the executions of Exeter and Lord Montague 'it was found, by their letters, that Sir Nicholas Carew was one of the chief of that faction'.[15] Duly found guilty of treason on Friday 14 February, Carew was beheaded on 8 March, those nights of merriment and gambling at Beddington long forgotten.[16] Shortly afterwards William Kendall, Exeter's controversial agent, finally lost his ninth life when he was executed along with his man, Quintrell.[17]

Gertrude was alive, but in a perilous position. Cromwell told Chapuys that Gertrude and her husband were behind Princess Mary's obstinacy in 1536, and had encouraged her to refuse to accept the royal supremacy. Furthermore, it was known that the marquis 'and his accomplices' had been informing Chapuys 'for it had been found several times that your Majesty [Charles V] was informed beforehand of their [the government's] intentions'.[18] Gertrude's ordeal was not over and she continued to be interrogated even after Carew's execution. On 19 April, Cromwell informed the king that on 'receipt of the letters of the Council, the Marquise has been examined. She pretends ignorance who reported the tale, but admits that much like words have been told her. Will persist till the bottom of her stomach is disclosed, and all conspiracies unravelled.'[19] It seems that Gertrude was holding her own as Cromwell was not finding it easy to extract information from her. What he was trying to discover is not clear, but according to the Duke of Norfolk, after her release she sent word to him via her brother that Cromwell had examined her 'more straitly of me than of all other men'.[20] Considering Cromwell's animosity towards the duke this is plausible as he would have been delighted to take Norfolk down with Carew. In April the attainder against Gertrude, her husband and many others including the Countess of Salisbury, went through Parliament. Curiously, the attainder only accused her of abetting Nicholas Carew.[21] For Gertrude and the countess, sentence of death could be exacted upon them at any moment, and indeed it would be for the countess in 1541. As Marillac, the French ambassador put it, their bodies were 'reserved for the King to punish or pardon as he will' and reported that 'it is commonly said that sentence of death has been decreed' against them.[22]

With a death sentence hanging over her, Gertrude remained in the Tower along with her son and Lord Montague's son, neither of whom had been included in the attainder. The countess was held at Cowdray, the residence of William Fitzwilliam, earl of Southampton, but she had arrived at the Tower by November. £9 6s 8d was spent per month on Gertrude's diet and that of her two gentlewomen and £4 per month for the diet of her son. Her imprisonment was not comfortable, both she and her gentlewoman, Constance Bontayne, were short of adequate clothing, and she was unable to pay the wages of her servants.[23] However, within Cromwell's remembrances, Gertrude's name recurs several times in this period, either 'to remember' her or for 'her delivery' and on 21 December 1539 she was pardoned 'for all offences committed before 1 July 31 Hen. VIII [1539]'.[24] Not only this, early in the new year she received a £100 reward followed by a grant of £163 15s 11d per year.[25] This outcome is surprising considering she was as guilty as her husband and far guiltier than the elderly Countess of Salisbury. On the other hand, Henry had no incentive to be magnanimous to the mother of Reginald Pole. Furthermore, Gertrude had no royal blood in her veins, was no threat to him and her release enabled him to appear benevolent by his generosity towards a defenceless widow. He would do the same for Nicholas Carew's widow.

As she walked free, she knew she could not return to Horsley as the king had taken that for his own use, his large blood-stained fingers rifling through their most prized possessions including the four little cushions bearing their initials. Their clothing was also appropriated including all of her husband's doublets and hose of satin and his Garter and Parliament robes, which were unceremoniously dumped in the royal wardrobe to be worn by various participants in masques and revels to entertain the king.[26] For the remainder of Henry VIII's reign Gertrude avoided the court, even after Cromwell's bloody execution in 1540, and would not serve any of his queens. When the king took Katherine Parr as his sixth and final wife in 1543, Gertrude was unable to make use of the kinship ties that existed between them through the marriage of Katherine's brother, William, to Gertrude's first cousin, Anne, daughter of her aunt Mary and Henry Bourchier, Earl of Essex. Due to the state of the Parrs' relationship, it was in Gertrude's interest to avoid drawing any attention to her kinship with Anne! William was blatantly unfaithful to his wife throughout their marriage, but she got her own back when she eloped with a former prior, lived openly with him and gave birth to two children, making her husband a laughing stock.[27] Fortunately, there were others Gertrude could rely on in these wilderness years, including faithful servant and friend Anthony Harvey. He had been general surveyor of the earldom of Devon estates and due to his quiet efficiency, the king re-appointed him to the post.[28] Harvey was devoted to Gertrude and would remain so until her death. Princess Mary also kept Gertrude in her thoughts, but had to be cautious regarding contact with her for both their sakes. Nevertheless, in March 1543 the princess gave her a large cask of wine worth 54 shillings, while Gertrude sent Mary a velvet partlet with a wrought lining for her New Year's gift of 1544.[29]

Gertrude was a Blount and she had a number of half-siblings to whom she could also turn. Her brother Charles, the fifth Lord Mountjoy, was a gifted scholar and a patron of learning and he had enjoyed warm relations with his sister and brother-in-law. In 1535, aged 19, he had been appointed one of several feoffees, including Lord Montague, to hold certain of Exeter's lands to the use of Exeter and Gertrude.[30] We know contact with his sister survived Exeter's execution because she despatched him with a message to the Duke of Norfolk following her release. Charles was a sensible choice as he was close to Norfolk's daughter, Mary, and allowed her to reside in his London home on Silver Street. However, Charles died in 1544 aged just 28 at a time when, it could be argued, Gertrude had most need of him. Charles' sister, Katherine, also seems to have enjoyed a warm relationship with Gertrude, despite sinister manoeuvrings around plans for her marriage that had threatened Exeter. In March 1538, barely three weeks after the execution of his bearward and just eight months before his arrest, the beleaguered marquis was obliged to write to Cromwell concerning Katherine's marriage. The letter reveals that Exeter believed himself to be the victim of false reporting. Apparently, the king had been told that Exeter was responsible for paying £1,000 towards Katherine's marriage out of certain lands assigned for that purpose. In addition, the king had been informed that her mother had secretly delivered plate and jewels to Exeter, also worth £1,000, for the same purpose. In a letter to Cromwell Exeter defended himself, politely but vigorously, declaring that the information the king had been given was untrue, that he had neither lands appointed to him nor jewels and plate. He stated he would prove this before the king and 'he or they that hath made this report of me unto the king's highness and also unto you … I shall fully prove them untrue therein'.[31] Evidence does support Exeter's claim, and the whole affair probably formed part of Cromwell's ongoing moves against the marquis.[32] On 9 February 1538 Cromwell's 'client', Sir Anthony Denny, had married Joan Champernown while the marriage in question for Katherine was to Joan's brother Sir John Champernown.[33] It would naturally be in Champernown's interest to gain a generous marriage settlement and in Cromwell's to discomfit the marquis. If this is the case, Exeter's staunch defence and threats to expose these untruths, ultimately caused the Lord Privy Seal to back off. As an innocent bystander, the affair did not damage Katherine's relations with her sister. After Sir John Champernown's death in 1541, she married Sir Maurice Berkeley, a former member of Cromwell's household.[34] More significantly, from 1539 Berkeley had been a gentleman usher of the king's Privy Chamber, and he held this position for the remainder of the reign. In close proximity to the king, it is possible that on occasion he solicited the king on his sister-in-law's behalf. Gertrude certainly gave testament to their amiable relationship in her will. Describing her as 'my sister Katherine Barkeley' she bequeathed her a black wrought velvet gown with fur trimming along with a diamond ring, the only bequest of jewellery that she made.[35]

Gertrude also enjoyed good relations with her siblings from her father's fourth and final marriage to Dorothy Grey, dowager Lady Willoughby de Broke. In 1547, Dorothy's daughter, also called Dorothy, married John, the son of Sir Roger Bluett of Holcombe Rogus. The Bluetts were a prominent Devonshire family and Sir Roger had attended the funeral of Katharine, Countess of Devon. Their delightful seat and Dorothy's marital home, Holcombe Court, still stands today. Holcombe Court was a mere fifteen miles from Columbjohn, where Gertrude would reside in later years, and we can imagine that the sisters visited each other regularly. In her will Gertrude left a furred velvet gown and a cup of silver and gilt 'to my sister Blewett'. Dorothy's brother John was also remembered, with Gertrude bequeathing her 'brother Mr John Blount £20 with a cup of silver and gilt'. Someone else who was remembered was 'my cousin Sir Richard Blunte knight' who was a member of a cadet branch of the Mountjoy Blounts. An experienced royal administrator, he was a valued member of the family. Gertrude's father had named him one of the executors of his will, as had her brother Charles.[36] From 1537, Richard held the position of gentleman usher of the Privy Chamber, and he was thus a colleague of Sir Maurice Berkely and someone else who was in a position to speak in Gertrude's favour.[37] She no doubt called upon his administrative experience regarding her affairs and showed her gratitude by leaving him a standing gilt bowl with a cover in her will. It was these individuals upon whom Gertrude now relied for support.

On 28 January 1547 the man who had played such a large part in her life, for good and ill, died. It is impossible to speculate about her feelings at the death of Henry VIII, but relief must have been among them. His successor, nine-year-old Edward VI, was her kinsman through their shared Say descent. More importantly, the man appointed lord protector and governor of the king's person was his uncle, Edward Seymour, created Duke of Somerset in February 1547. This powerful man was Gertrude's second cousin, and she had every reason to hope for his favour. She had been close to his sister whose marriage to the king she had advanced, leading ultimately to Somerset's exalted position. Thus, on 2 July 1547 the pension granted to her by Henry VIII was honoured, and on 14 March 1550 at a session of the Privy Council presided over by Somerset, she was granted the manor of Columbjohn for life 'without paying any thing for the same'.[38] This was the first grant of property she had received since the fall of her husband, and it was here, in what had been one of her mother-in-law's favourite residences, that she made her home from 1550. She was protective of her new acquisition, and her behaviour in a related court case reveals that her spirit had not been broken despite the trauma she had endured.

At some point after 19 January 1552, Thomasine Everleigh, widow, and her son Edmund Wanell submitted a bill of complaint.[39] They claimed to have been granted various pieces of land within the manor by Exeter and had enjoyed them for the last twenty-four years until Anthony Harvey, on Gertrude's orders, had expelled them. Thomasine needed redress, stating that Gertrude and Harvey were 'of great power and substance and your said orators but very poor folk' and feared she would not receive justice without the 'help and favour' of the Chancellor of England. In a robust defence, Gertrude, with the faithful Harvey by her side, declared that Thomasine's claims were 'matters of untruth devised only of malice', that the lands were part of the demesne lands of the manor and as she 'doth continually keep her family and household at the … manor of

Columbjohn ... the said demesne lands ... are so necessary for her provision and for the continuance of her hospitality' that without them she cannot 'keep her family and hospitality'. She further explained that she and Thomasine had gone to arbitration, the conclusion being that Thomasine should occupy the lands until the feast of St Michael after which Gertrude would take possession. Thomasine naturally cast doubt on all Gertrude's statements and accused Harvey of threatening her.[40] While we cannot be certain of the outcome of the case, it reveals that Gertrude had not lost any of her courage and was still prepared to staunchly defend her rights. However, although her situation had clearly improved since Henry VIII's death, her constant fear for the fate of her son must have run through her like a vein through marble.

Edward, innocent of any crime, was still imprisoned in the Tower. In April 1540 shortly after Gertrude's release, the French ambassador, Marillac, ominously wrote that 'the male children shall remain there, lest some day they should trouble this Crown'.[41] Although a generous £4 per month was spent to cover Edward's food, and he received occasional grants of clothing, he was straitly kept and not given the opportunity to exercise much or mix with anyone. We don't know how aware he was of the disappearance of his fellow captives, but in May 1541 67-year-old Margaret Pole, Countess of Salisbury, was hustled outside to a small block and executed at the hands of an inexperience executioner who 'hacked her head and shoulders to pieces in the most pitiful manner'.[42] A month later, Marillac speculated on the fate of her grandson, Henry Pole, son of Lord Montague, believing him to be in danger of being executed 'though he is very young and innocent'.[43] Henry VIII did not execute 15-year-old Henry, but his hatred for Reginald resulted in the boys being treated very differently. From this point Edward was allowed to go outside more and a teacher was appointed to educate him. In stark contrast, Henry Pole, Reginald's nephew, was 'poorly and strictly kept and not desired to know anything'.[44] Due to the closeness of their fathers, it is likely that Edward and Henry had been friends, especially as they were exactly the same age. However, any contact between the two following their arrest would have been prohibited, and as Edward's life improved, that of his friend got worse. In September 1542, £4 each was again paid for their diets, and this is the last we hear of 16-year-old Henry Pole. Whether he died of natural causes or from the rigours of his imprisonment, we don't know, but his demise would have left Edward in no doubt of his own vulnerability.[45]

Very little is heard of Edward over the following years until June 1546 when he fell seriously ill. Whatever was ailing him, it required doctor John Burgies' 'continual attendance ... about Courteney' over a period of months, along with medicines prepared by Burgies' apothecary, all of which cost the huge sum of £20.[46] His sickness was such that it even moved the king to pity, and on 4 June he allowed Edward to access the garden and gallery as it 'should much confer to his health'. However, the Lieutenant of the Tower was warned to ensure 'that one sober man at the least should be always in company with him to see that no man should confer with him secretly'.[47] Henry VIII, in the final months of his life, with a 9-year-old son to inherit the crown, still feared for his dynastic security.

Henry VIII had reason to be cautious for the minute Edward gained more freedom, an unscrupulous individual, the first of many in his life, moved to take advantage of the situation. On 23 January 1546, a Spaniard calling himself Don Pedro Pacheco was imprisoned in the Tower. Falsely claiming to be a relative of the Duke of Albuquerque and carrying a forged letter of introduction from him, he was regarded with suspicion by Henry VIII's council and by the imperial ambassador, Francois van der Delft.[48] As Edward walked in the gallery and garden as part of his convalescence, he crossed paths with this smooth conman who managed to inveigle himself into the confidence of the well-educated but unworldly young man. How he managed to gain access to Edward is unclear, considering that he was to be accompanied at all times by at least 'one sober man'. Nevertheless, Pacheco did manage to communicate with him, and on several occasions. Eventually, realising the danger in which this placed him, Edward wisely decided to confess before discovery. On 22 September 1546, the Lieutenant of the Tower spoke to the Lord Chancellor, Thomas Wriothesley, explaining that Edward 'was very desirous' to speak to Wriothesley 'for the opening of matter that touched his allegiance'. Wriothesley, unsure of what this entailed or the gravity of the situation, asked William Paulet, great master of the king's household, to meet him at the Tower 'that we might hear him together'. Edward informed them about his contact with Pacheco and was 'very humble and desirous to make some amends for his late folly'. In addition, he presented them with a letter he had written, which Wriothesley included in the despatch he sent to the councillors located with the king. This letter, written in September 1546 when he was 20 years old, allows us to hear Edward's voice for the very first time. Written in the most courteous and respectful terms, Edward informed them that 'the Spaniard who is at this prison here prisoner ... hath sundry and many times been in hand to persuade me to break prison'. He continued that as it touched 'all mine whole allegiance' and 'considering the abundant mercies and manifold goodness which I have received at his grace's hands I thought it my most bounden duty by some means to declare the same unto your honourable lordships'. He ended the letter by beseeching them to 'be means unto the King's most excellent majesty that it may please his highness of his mercy and special grace to have pity and compassion on this my miserable imprisonment'.[49] He could easily have faced the block, but despite reported urgings from some of the council to execute him, Edward survived and in November a warrant was sent to the great wardrobe for apparel for him.[50] He was extremely lucky, considering the fate of others around this time. In December the duke of Norfolk and his eldest son, the earl of Surrey, were arrested and joined Edward in the Tower, but Surrey did not remain there long. On 19 January, this gifted poet and scholar was beheaded, just nine days before the death of the king, which would have saved him. His father was luckier, the king dying on the day scheduled for his execution, and he remained a prisoner for six years. While a dejected Edward remained captive within the Tower the Spaniard, Pacheco, walked free as part of the coronation celebrations for Edward VI.[51]

Like his mother, Edward also hoped for better treatment from the Edwardian regime, especially as he was related to the king through both mother and father. In addition to descent from the Say line, he and Edward VI were the only surviving great-grandsons of Edward IV, but it was probably for this very reason that he was excluded from the general pardon at the beginning of the reign.[52] However, he did not give up hope and focused his attention on the power behind the throne, Somerset's indomitable wife, Anne Stanhope. Edward was gifted academically and he had thrown himself into lessons during his imprisonment. He was fluent in several languages, including Italian, and decided to use his linguistic skill to translate an Italian religious tract, which he would dedicate to the duchess. The 'benefit of Christ's Death' was a reformist work regarded with suspicion by the Catholic church, but Edward chose it as he knew it would appeal to the Protestant duchess. It was completed in 1548 and in the dedication he described himself as 'the sorrowful captive' and carefully detailed his plight without apportioning blame to Henry VIII.

He had, he explained, 'through the guilt of my own natural parent [I being innocent of the same]' not only lost all 'the possessions of this world' along with everything else which 'should have descended to me by rightful course of inheritance' but had also been deprived of his liberty. He had been 'secluded and shut up in prison … from the company almost of all men'. In desperation and 'driven by this miserable captivity' he had decided to 'speak and write for remedy of the same yet being destitute of all good learning and experience'. After apologising that his translation 'be not so exactly done as so worthy a matter requireth', he beseeched the duchess to remember 'the miserable state and dolorous life that I so long time most wretchedly have sustained' that she might 'plead my Lord's grace of his manifold and abundant goodness, to deliver me out of this miserable captivity'. If he were freed, he begged to be taken into the Duke of Somerset's household as his servant where he could learn 'perfect duty, both to god and to the world' and also demonstrate 'the true and faithful obedience of my heart'.[53] Edward was desperate for freedom and who could blame him? But he took a risk by compromising his perceived religious orthodoxy in order to gain the duchess' favour. Edward's true religious beliefs have eluded the understanding, not only of contemporaries but historians and, perhaps, even Edward himself. Brought up a traditional Catholic by his parents, the education he received in the Tower from 1538 onwards would have been reformist, and this may have left an unresolvable confusion deep within him. Although his translation was well received, including by the 11-year-old king who wrote two godly messages in the copy, Edward remained in prison. However, greater freedom within the Tower was now allowed, and this led to him meeting someone who was to have a significant effect on his life.

On 30 June 1548, Stephen Gardiner, Bishop of Winchester, arrived at the Tower where he was imprisoned for his intractable opposition to future religious change. Here, he struck up a friendship with Edward, taking on the role of mentor to the young man. He certainly made an impression on Edward, who would refer to him as 'father'. Gardiner was a gifted academic, a forensic lawyer and a shrewd politician. The fact that he had kept his head throughout Henry VIII's reign, unlike so many of his contemporaries, is testament to his abilities. But he was also a teacher. He had been Master of Trinity Hall Cambridge where his pupils had included Wriothesley, now Lord Chancellor, and William, Lord Paget. When he entered the Tower, Gardiner was in his early fifties and it is easy to understand why 22-year-old Edward would become enthralled by this statesman-like figure and educator who was his only real window into the outside world. Gardiner was a conservative at heart, but practicality had demanded his support of the king's great matter, he had even written in defence of John Fisher's execution. He was dynamic, ruthless, generous, a man of huge contradictions, and his presence was felt throughout some of the most turbulent years of English history. In fact, so outstanding a figure of Tudor politics was he, that even Henry VIII was proud to declare that 'I myself could use him, and rule him to all manner of purposes as seemed good to me' when no one else could.[54]

For Gardiner, Edward was a kinsman of Reginald Pole, a man he admired. His father, a grandson of Edward IV, had died for his loyalty to Princess Mary and adherence to the old religion, thus Edward had impeccable ancestry. He was also scholarly, like his grandfather Lord Mountjoy, and eager to learn. Although the friendship could be viewed as opportunistic on both sides, there must have been a genuine element too. Over the next five years the charismatic Gardiner, a man who 'always wanted to speak and shout and gain the upper hand' spoke, and the impressionable Edward listened.[55] But Edward was not quite as malleable as Gardiner believed. As noted above, his true religious feelings were never made clear and as time would tell, he would not always behave as Gardiner wished. In fact, Edward was quite as capable of dissembling as Gardiner, learnt from years of imprisonment when staying alive depended upon apparent conformity.

Then, on 6 July 1553, something monumental happened. The 15-year-old Edward VI died in agony of a suppurating pulmonary infection, which led to septicaemia and renal failure. Stripped of all regal dignity, the young king was a shadow of his former self. His hair had fallen out and his nails had dropped off, his emaciated body was covered in scabs, his lower body swollen, and all the while he coughed up foul-smelling sputum caused by two abscesses in his lungs.[56] All Henry VIII's efforts, and all the deaths along the way to ensure his son would succeed him had ended in failure, but for 27-year-old Edward Courtenay, after fifteen years of imprisonment, it was a new beginning.

Chapter 13

1553

Great Expectations

like someone who has lived in a tower all his life and now enjoys
great freedom, he can never have enough of its delights.

Edward Courtenay was 'a weakling and a poltroon', a man of 'childish petulance' and 'foolish ambition'. These negative opinions expressed by G.R Elton and E.H. Harbison have generally been accepted by most historians and even some contemporaries. While there are elements of truth in these descriptions, they are not the whole picture. According to M.A. Overell, once released Edward 'had his big chance but he wrecked it'.[1] If this is the case, he had a lot of help in doing so, and from those who should have known better.

Following the death of Edward VI, John Dudley, Duke of Northumberland tried to establish his daughter-in-law Jane Grey as queen but miscalculated badly. Princess Mary, rather than surrendering, showed great fortitude and was prepared to use force to claim her birthright. As she gathered troops, Northumberland left the capital with an army in search of her. However, Henry VIII's will, the authority of Parliament, the traditional line of succession and Mary's personal popularity, prevailed. During Northumberland's absence a group of councillors came to their senses and, to jubilation, proclaimed Mary queen in London on 19 July.[2] Receiving the news of her accession the next day, Queen Mary began a leisurely progress from Framlingham to London during which many flocked to her; among them was Gertrude. There is no record of their meeting, but Mary must have welcomed her with open arms and when they reached London on 3 August, Gertrude was part of her entourage. Dressed in violet velvet with her skirts and sleeves embroidered in gold, Mary was escorted by great numbers of the nobility and over 1,000 men-at-arms. Riding directly behind her was Princess Elizabeth and behind her came Gertrude.[3] In the August sunshine the atmosphere was heady with celebrations and orations along the way, and shots from the guns at the Tower. To Gertrude, and perhaps Mary too, it must have seemed like a dream, or rather that they were waking from the nightmare of the past twenty years, and when they reached the Tower, all Gertrude's hopes were realised. As the queen dismounted and made her way to her private apartments, 'she came upon a number of prisoners strategically positioned to beg mercy from her'.[4] Lined up were Stephen Gardiner, Thomas Howard, third Duke of Norfolk, Anne, Duchess of Somerset and Edward Courtenay. Hearing their pleas, Mary answered that 'they had done nothing for which they should sue for mercy, and she was sorry that they should have suffered and been detained so long. She gave her full consent to their liberation'. In fact, Edward had been released on 21 July, just a day after the queen received news of her proclamation revealing that his release was a priority.[5] However, Edward's return to the outside world was challenging from the start.

When 'Lord Courtenay' emerged from the Tower on Friday 21 July 1553, he entered into what we today would describe as a media storm. He was inexperienced in worldly affairs, institutionalised, brutalised and traumatised. He needed careful handling, sound advice and a quiet introduction to this new life of freedom. Instead, his name was on everyone's lips; every ambassador, courtier, council member, even foreign monarchs knew the name of Edward Courtney, and his every move was reported on in letter after letter. But why the sudden interest? The reason is simple; this is the man that many believed would soon be King of England by his marriage to Queen Mary. Despite some historians dismissing the idea, contemporaries, including those who knew the queen well, sincerely believed this would happen. On 12 August Cardinal Farnese actually wrote to Reginald Pole congratulating him on Edward's release and 'expressing confidence that the young man would marry Mary'.[6] A queen regnant was a new and untried concept but, as with a male monarch, everyone believed that the queen must marry and produce an heir. To those who feared a foreign match, which might lead to foreign domination, as the lines of authority between husband and wife, queen and king consort were untested, an English match was safer. However, such a man would have to be of sufficient status to marry a queen and the only plausible candidate in England, everyone agreed, was Edward Courtenay as the great grandson of Edward IV. Even before Edward VI died, Edward's marriage to Mary was being discussed. On 11 June as the king's condition worsened it was reported that 'Mr. Courtenay, of the blood royal, … has been put out of the way, or is about to be, in order to checkmate the plan of those who would like to marry him to the Princess [Mary].'[7]

His personal attractions also ensured that attention remained focussed upon him. It was widely recognised that 27-year-old Edward was handsome, and this is confirmed by the two extant likenesses of him. One may have been painted when he was in Brussels in 1555 or it might be a copy of an original painted in 1568. It shows a slim young man with grey eyes, an aquiline nose and the auburn hair of the Plantagenets. An air of wariness and challenge is in his expression, and behind is a ruined tower, probably to denote his liberation. The second is a twentieth-century plaster cast of a medal dated to circa 1556. In profile, the face is similar to that in the portrait except it is more careworn and his thick head of hair more unruly.[8] Both portraits depict a strong, handsome face, and these physical attributes were enhanced by his learning. The Venetian ambassador described the 'very good literary education' he had received and noted his ability to speak several languages, while the French ambassador, Antoine de Noailles, declared him to be 'The handsomest and most agreeable gentleman in England.'[9] The imperial ambassadors sent a report to Charles V that also described Edward Courtenay. This was not polite flattery but an accurate account; it had to be. Although not stated explicitly, it was a warning, and it warned the emperor that Edward was a plausible candidate for the queen's hand:

> Yesterday, Courtenay, who was thrown into prison fifteen years ago, was released; and there is much talk here to the effect that he will be married to the Queen as he is of the blood royal. During his captivity he applied himself to all virtuous and praiseworthy studies, so he is very proficient, and is also familiar with various instruments of music. Thus his prison and confinement have not been grievous to him, but have been converted into liberty by his studiousness and taste for letters and science. There is in him a civility which must be deemed natural rather than acquired by the habit of society; and his bodily graces are in proportion to those of his mind. Several people say that the Queen has long since been married to a prisoner ...; we repeat this to your Majesty in order to render you as accurate an account as possible of the present state of opinion here, though we know that there is no truth in the saying.[10]

This situation immediately set Edward on a collision course with the Habsburgs as Charles V had already decided that the husband he wished his cousin to have was his own son, Philip of Spain. Charles viewed Mary's accession as a 'windfall', an opportunity to encircle France. As he had already decided to abdicate and pass Spain and the Netherlands to Philip, a match with England would enhance the security of those territories. While he couched his advice to Mary in terms of affection and desire for her happiness, in reality Charles V exploited her trust and reliance on him. This had taken root in the 1530s as a result of her father's rejection and threats, and she would always view Charles as a powerful protector whose 'good and trusty advice' she was prepared to follow. Determined to bring the marriage about, Charles was the consummate politician, and his approaches were subtle. He was very careful not to broach the idea of marriage to Philip too soon, and he revealed an understanding of

Mary's character that those around her seemed to lack. He did not want any criticisms made of Edward in her presence, until he was sure of her feelings, 'for if she took it into her head [to marry him] nothing would stop her, if she is like other women, and she would always bear you a grudge for your remarks. But you might touch on the greater advantages that would be offered by a foreign marriage, without insisting on the person on whom her choice might fall.'[11]

However, there were many on the council and in the country at large who abhorred the idea of a Spanish match, and this gave Edward powerful and influential backing. It is not surprising that the young man's hopes were raised when he had the support of his mentor, Stephen Gardiner, now Lord Chancellor and one of the queen's most important ministers. Not only that, Sir Robert Rochester, his nephew Sir Edward Waldegrave and Sir Francis Englefield all supported his marriage to the queen. This triumvirate had served Mary for many years, they were devoted servants who had been imprisoned on her behalf in 1551 and their opinions mattered. Rochester held the position of comptroller of the royal household and was a member of her Privy Council. Waldegrave, too, was a member of her council while his wife, Frances, was the daughter of Sir Edward Neville who had been beheaded with Edward's father. Waldegrave was a stalwart supporter of the earl and even considered leaving Mary's service over the marriage question. Englefield, the grandson of that same Sir Thomas who had advised Katharine Courtenay during her restoration, was also a member of the queen's Privy Council, and all three may have made Edward's acquaintance when they were imprisoned in the Tower for over six months.[12] Then there was Gertrude, in close contact with Mary, able to speak up for her son and a constant reminder of the trials and tribulations they had both endured on her behalf which required appropriate reward. In addition, Edward enjoyed support from further afield. The French were vehemently against the Spanish match as it would be detrimental to their interests while Venice, determined to guard its independence, also opposed it. These ambassadors, charming and flattering representatives of their masters, ruthlessly sought to use Edward as a way to derail the Habsburg marriage.

Despite these tensions at the highest levels, Edward initially comported himself well. On Sunday 13 August one of his first public outings was to church with his mother in St Pauls, but even this was not without drama. As Dr Gilbert Bourne delivered a sermon criticising the Protestant changes of the previous reign the crowd became incensed, shouting 'papist', and Bourne was unable to continue. Others went further with one man throwing a sword or dagger at him 'to kill him'. If it wasn't for the arrival of the mayor and 'that lord Courtenay and his mother, who were present, succeeded in quieting the uproar, it looked as if a public tumult might have followed'.[13] It is a testament to Gertrude and Edward's courage and skills of persuasion that they were prepared, and able, to calm the crowd considering they were identified with the Catholic, rather than the Protestant, faith. Two weeks later, the imperial ambassadors were able to report that Edward was scrupulous in his behaviour concerning overtures from the French ambassadors. Receiving letters of credence from Henry II, King of France, Edward 'sent them at once to his mother, that she might communicate their contents to the queen'. However, they also noted that the French ambassadors had 'feasted and banqueted' several members of the council and had invited Edward 'with the excuse that they believed him to be of the Council; thus making his acquaintance without arousing suspicions'. They were only too willing to inform the queen of this as part of on-going attempts to undermine her trust in him, and described the presentation of the letters as 'strange and intolerable behaviour' aimed at giving him 'credit and a taste for ruling'. They advised that 'distrust of the French is the best protection against their designs'.[14]

However, the queen was determined that Gertrude and Edward should receive appropriate recompense and was also keen to welcome the marchioness back into her inner circle. Renard reported in September that Gertrude 'is always welcome with the Queen, and usually sleeps with her', while the favour she enjoyed is evidenced by the approaches made to her.[15] Following the imprisonment of the duke of Northumberland his desperate wife, Jane, wrote to Anne, Lady Paget beseeching her to 'make my lady markes of Exiture my good lady' to intercede for her husband's life.[16] In this case Jane's pleas went unheard and Northumberland was executed on 22 August. William Parr, Marquis of Northampton, fared better. The estranged husband of Anne Bourchier, Gertrude's cousin, was imprisoned for his part in Northumberland's conspiracy, but if he were to be executed for treason it would jeopardise Anne's claims to her ancestral lands. Thus Gertrude, motivated by concern for her cousin's prospects, was one of those who successfully interceded with the queen for his pardon.[17] William Herbert, Earl of Pembroke, was fully involved in Northumberland's plot to divert the succession to the Grey line, but once Northumberland had left London he changed sides. The unimpressed queen was not convinced of his loyalty and he was placed under house arrest. Desperate to obtain her favour and regain his influence, he approached both Gertrude and Edward and on 13 August was admitted to the newly formed Privy Council. His gratitude was reported later that month, 'It has been discovered that the Earl of Pembroke gave a present of a sword and poniard to Courtenay besides a basin and ewer and several horses, worth in all more than three thousand crowns, to get back into the Council, and because Courtenay's mother had made his peace with the Queen.'[18]

Mary's generosity to the Courtenays is evidenced by a series of grants over September and October including a parliamentary act of restoration. On 3 September Edward was created earl of Devon 'with remainder to his heirs male' and granted an annuity of £20 from the petty customs in the port of London 'for the better maintenance of his estate'.[19] The following day, the commissioners responsible for selling the goods of attainted individuals were ordered to stop further sales 'because the Queen hath granted certain stuff to the Lady Marquess of Exeter and to the earl of Devon, her son'.[20] On 28 September Edward was finally granted part, but not all, of his father's estates for never again would 'the great inheritance belonging to the Earldom of Devon return to the family in its entirety'.[21] Nevertheless, it was a substantial grant with lands in several counties including Devon, Cornwall, Dorset, Buckinghamshire and Surrey valued at £1,242 6s 8d per year. Furthermore, Edward was to receive the issues from lady day last, which was 25 March 1553.[22] He was now able to set up his own household, and he established his main residence at Kew on the banks of the Thames, just nine miles from London and three miles from Richmond Palace. While in London he resided at Cannon Row, which lay in the shadow of Westminster. It was an exclusive address of several houses where prominent individuals lived including, in 1598, Ann Stanhope, Duchess of Somerset. Edward either had the free use of it or rented it from its owner Henry Radcliffe, second Earl of Sussex.

Further honours and recognition followed. In preparation for her coronation the queen created around twenty Knights of the Bath, of which Edward was one and his half-cousin, James, Lord Mountjoy, another. The newly created Earl of Devon was now appropriately girded to take part in the coronation. On Saturday 30 September Mary left the Tower and made her way to Westminster 'riding triumphantly in an open chariot to be seen'. In the chariot behind sat Princess Elizabeth and Anne of Cleves then 'rode on horseback four ladies of estate, apparelled in crimson velvet, and their horses trapped with the same: and, these great ladies were the Duchess of Norfolk, the Marchioness of Exeter, the Marchioness of Winchester, and the Countess of Arundel'. At the coronation feast in Westminster Hall, Edward bore the sword and the Earl of Westmorland the cap of maintenance, as they would do again at the opening of Parliament.[23]

Gertrude and Edward had good reason to be gratified at this first session of Parliament, which sat until 21 October. Only three acts were passed, one was a Treason Bill and the other two concerned the 'restoration in blood' of Gertrude and Edward. Nor was this the end of the queen's generosity for on 24 October, in response to a petition from Gertrude 'for the better support of her estate and rank', Mary granted her 'cousin' a swathe of manors in Devon, Dorset and Somerset. One of them, Marshwood, had been part of Catherine of

Aragon's dower where Gertrude's mother-in-law, Katharine, Countess of Devon, had enjoyed a pleasant visit in the summer of 1524. Another was Canford in Dorset, which would become one of Gertrude's favourite residences. Along with these manors an annual rent of £136 1s 4d out of Dunkeswell priory was also granted.[24] Not everyone was pleased by Mary's liberality, the imperial ambassador Renard being incredulous that these two acts of Parliament had been so prioritised when 'there were other more important matters waiting to be dealt with'. He actually questioned the queen about it, asking who had brought it forward as he believed 'that it would not have gone through so rapidly had it not been for the marriage question'. Mary replied that Edward and his mother, on Stephen Gardiner's advice, had requested it, and we know that Edward, in his mother's presence, had spent half-an-hour speaking to the queen about it on 6 October. However, Mary did not believe it had anything to do with the marriage question, but Renard was not convinced.[25]

Renard's ongoing suspicions about the activities of the French and Venetian ambassadors also continued, prompting him to exclaim angrily 'it is hardly to be believed how these ambassadors are plotting to prevent the match with his Highness'.[26] The Venetian ambassador, Giacomo Soranzo, wined and dined Edward who was a frequent visitor to the Venetian embassy.[27] The talk of marriage was incessant 'among the people, and quite publicly, too' and Edward, becoming overconfident, began to visit the embassy without obtaining royal permission.[28] In November, when Gertrude asked Mary for 'leave for her son to go and sup at the Venetian ambassador's ... in the company of the French ambassador', the queen retorted that 'he had gone often enough without leave, and that she hoped he would behave prudently in all respects, and do nothing inconsistent with his duty'.[29] These visits to the Venetian embassy would have been bittersweet as it was based in his father's former London residence at St Laurence Poultney, where Edward had spent time as a child and where his little gilt sword was found after his father's arrest.[30] Every visit would have reminded him of what he had lost, perhaps inspiring a self-righteous assumption that marriage to the queen was the least he deserved. In the middle of all this, the worst person possible made an appearance when Geoffrey Pole returned to England in September. Edward's reaction reveals that the trauma of that night in November 1538 was still with him. When he heard that Geoffrey had arrived in London, he threatened to kill him as the cause of his father's death and that of the Countess of Salisbury 'and he charged him with the crime'. The queen and council were informed of Edward's outburst, and so seriously did they take his threats that Geoffrey was moved to the house of 'a certain gentleman' and placed under armed guard for his own protection. Significantly, no action was taken against Edward, quite possibly because Mary sympathised with him and shared his views. She certainly did little to help Geoffrey, despite the fact that he had ten children to support and the family were in financial difficulties.[31]

It was during this period, September to October, when the traumatic memories of the past were most acute, and his belief never stronger that the crown matrimonial was within his grasp, that Edward went spectacularly off the rails. Mary's generosity convinced Edward, and others, that this signalled her intention to accept him as her husband, and the reaction of those around him made everything worse. Renard complained that he was 'beginning to give himself airs of importance, and he is courted and followed about by the whole Court; we have been told that some fall on their knee when speaking to him, as they do to the Queen, as if the marriage were a settled thing'. Edward probably didn't insist that they fall on their knees, but he didn't stop them from doing so either, and he was already living in a semi-regal manner revealed by the presence of a canopy of cloth of gold and crimson velvet at his Canon Row residence. His pride now became 'so odious and insufferable' that he 'is not as well thought of as he was' while jealous rivals such as his kinsman, Lord Thomas Grey, claimed that everyone was disgusted by his behaviour. He snubbed the imperial ambassadors, had the temerity to tell one of the council 'that no such marriage [to Philip] would take place' and offended Princess Elizabeth when marriage to her was mentioned by declaring that he would rather marry a 'simple girl' than her because she was a heretic and of 'doubtful lineage on her mother's side'.[32]

Reports of debauchery also began to emerge. The only contemporary evidence for Edward's dissolute behaviour comes from a letter written by the French ambassador Noailles on 17 October, but as he was supporting Edward's bid to marry the queen there is no reason to suspect he had fabricated these stories.[33] According to Noailles, he had been told by a gentleman of Edward's household that 'the Queen's opinion of him was poor as she had heard that he was engaging in many youthful follies, and even frequenting prostitutes and women of ill-repute'. Noailles prompted one of those close to Edward to 'advise him of these facts, and to consider the harm he was doing to his reputation, as well as the extent to which he was placing himself at risk of losing the greatest estate and fortune to which he could ever aspire'. But it was to no avail, Noailles continued, because 'he is so wilful that he will believe no one, and, like someone who has lived in a tower all his life and now enjoys great freedom, he can never have enough of its delights and has no fear of what he is being told'. Unless women had been smuggled into the Tower, we must believe that this healthy 27-year-old male had never had a sexual encounter before and was now making up for lost time. He was probably no different from many other young men in this period, including Philip who it is believed had a mistress during his first marriage. The problem for Edward was that he had to sow his wild oats in the public eye. The queen, it transpired, understood that Edward might need help to adjust to the outside world and had tried to help by appointing a gentleman to train and govern him. However, things had deteriorated to the point that he left Edward's company and refused to see him for over eight days. It is possible that this gentleman was Sir Francis Englefield, who did refuse to see Edward or go to court for several days stating he had a fever, which could have been a diplomatic illness.[34] Noailles also reported that the situation was putting a strain on his mother's relationship with the queen, and Gertrude was clearly at her wits' end 'his mother the Marchioness, who used to be privy to all the Queen's secrets, is imploring other people for help daily, which until now she had never done'. Queen Mary was a 37-year-old virgin who had told Renard in forthright terms that if Philip 'were disposed to be amorous, such was not her desire' because she was, Renard informed the emperor, 'of the age your Majesty knew of and had never harboured thoughts of love'.[35] Naturally, Edward's behaviour appalled her and Noailles was in despair. He was right to be concerned, on 21 October, not even a week after Noailles wrote to Henry II, Mary told Renard 'that she had no liking for Courtenay'.[36]

In reality, unbeknownst to Edward and his supporters, he never stood a chance of marrying her, and she had already decided against him as early as August. There were a number of reasons for this, one being that she didn't think he, or any other Englishman, was good enough for her, telling Renard 'it would not be honourable in her to choose one who was her vassal, subject and servant'. Emotionally, the match with Philip was the one her mother would have approved of, tying her more closely to her Spanish family, which, after the way her father had treated her, is understandable. Finally, to put it into modern day parlance, she simply didn't fancy Edward. She had declared that she was only marrying for the good of her kingdom and to do her duty, in which case the appearance of her husband should not have mattered, but it did. Mary was, after all, a Tudor, and finding her spouse attractive was all important. This is proven when she naively asked Renard if she could meet Philip first before committing herself. She had even planned how this might be done, suggesting that as she had heard he was soon to travel to Flanders, she 'thought he might perhaps pass through England … under colour of proceeding on his way to your Majesty'.[37] She also stated that she wanted to marry a man 'of the middle age' and that Edward at 27 was too young for her. However, she conveniently waived that obstacle aside to marry Philip who was one year younger than Edward. Despite being an attractive man, beauty is in the eye of the beholder and Edward didn't appeal to her, and this aversion grew when his dissolute behaviour came to light. Continual attempts to push her into marriage with this man made her agitated, stressed and, at times, physically ill. Those close to her like Gertrude, Rochester, Englefield and Waldegrave, failed to appreciate this when they should have done, and the marriage question ultimately damaged their relationships with the queen.

As Mary refused to commit herself one way or another, tensions continued to run high. False reports that marriage with Philip was actually being negotiated prompted Noailles to send a secret message to Edward on 7 September urging him to build up a party of supporters in the forthcoming Parliament to block it.[38] Within a day or two a delegation of the council comprising Edward's mentor, Gardiner, with Rochester, Englefield and Waldegrave spoke to the queen, and made every effort to persuade her to marry Edward explaining that 'he alone in the kingdom is worthy of the marriage'.[39] Attempts were then made to hold Parliament before her coronation, which Renard interpreted as an attempt to make her coronation dependent on her compliance with their wishes, one of which was to marry Edward. On 10 October, while Parliament was sitting, Renard formally proposed Philip to the queen who, although inclined to accept, was extremely worried about how her council and the people would react. To her credit she made clear that if Philip 'wished to encroach in the government of the kingdom she would be unable to permit it, nor if he attempted to fill posts and offices with strangers, for the country itself would never stand such interference'. Renard assured her on all points and dramatically described Philip as 'so admirable, so virtuous, prudent and modest as to appear too wonderful to be human'. Despite being presented with such a paragon, Mary was in agonies over making one of the biggest decisions of her life.[40]

Unaware of the proposal, on 21 October several members of her council including Gardiner, Rochester, Waldegrave, Englefield and Sir Richard Southwell, Master of the Queen's Ordnance, again tried to get clarity on the matter. In a three-pronged attack they encouraged Mary to consider marrying Edward explaining that he was 'the match that would be most welcome to the people' and that 'no foreigner had ever before been king of the country'. Once more the queen calmly, but firmly, stood her ground. Then finally, on 27 October, Renard was given audience by the queen and four members of her council including Gardiner. After dramatically stating that she had cried over two hours that day while praying God to inspire her decision, Mary declared that she 'believed she would agree' to marry Philip, paying courtesy to the fact that the council's concurrence was needed. She then asked to speak to Renard apart so she could inform him of what she had said to Edward, but 'she could not say any more without bursting into tears'. The queen had informed Edward in Gertrude's presence that she was not going to marry him, and this most difficult of conversations had upset her deeply. In early November it was reported that

Gertrude had fallen out of favour, although she remained at court, suggesting that her reaction to her son's rejection had not been temperate.[41]

On 29 October with just Renard and Susan Clarencius present, Mary promised to marry Philip before the Holy Sacrament, and while this spelled the very end of Edward's hopes, the climax came on 16 November when a delegation from Parliament, including Gardiner, came to speak to her about her marriage to Philip. Much to the queen's anger and indignation, their purpose was to persuade her, once again, to take an English husband. The next day, when Gardiner foolishly mentioned the marriage question yet again, the queen's patience snapped. Having made clear time and time again that she did not want to marry the Earl of Devon, she now exploded and left the man Henry VIII claimed only he could control, flummoxed and in tears. She accused him of putting the speaker up to the visit because he had used all Gardiner's arguments in favour of Edward, but she would tell him now so there was no misunderstanding, 'she would never marry Courtenay'. Gardiner replied 'with tears' that he had never instructed the speaker, 'although he had mentioned those considerations to him'. On the back foot, he admitted that he had been fond of Edward since they were in prison together, but the queen's sarcastic response left him speechless when she asked 'whether it would be suitable to force her to marry a man because the Bishop had conceived a friendship for him in prison'. After the dressing down was over, Gardiner declared 'that it would not be right to try to force her in one direction or another, and that he would obey the man she had chosen'.[42] He knew that the only way to retain his position and guard the country's interests was to accept her choice, and draw up a marriage treaty as favourable to England as possible. However, this was a decisive moment in more ways than one because as 'every avenue of constitutional opposition to her will was blocked', opposition to the Spanish match was 'driven underground and intensified'.[43]

In the aftermath of Mary's decision to marry Philip of Spain, Edward was fearful. He had shown open hostility to the Spanish match and to the Spanish ambassadors, yet Philip was to be his king and he was worried about his position. William Lord Paget, a former pupil of Gardiner's who was now his rival on council, was one of the few who had been in support of the Spanish marriage, and he began to make approaches to Edward as a way of ensuring it's acceptance. His proposition involved confirming Elizabeth as heir, thus securing the succession should Mary die childless, and marriage to Edward. Due to his popularity, this would please the people, prevent Elizabeth from intriguing and keep her in the old faith because if Edward 'who seemed to be a Catholic' were her husband, he would keep her in that religion. Edward met Paget in late November and they talked for over two hours. The disconcerted earl, confronted with the calm and forensic questioning of Paget, asserted that

Gardiner, Waldegrave, Englefield and Southwell 'had put it into his head that he might aspire to an alliance with the Queen, and urged him to press his suit in secret'. Edward himself 'had not thought of such a thing before, and now he feared the Queen's goodwill towards him had changed, that she was angry, that the husband of her choice would not be glad to see him, and that the Queen had heard evil reports of him'. Lacking his mother as intermediary due to her estrangement, Edward prayed Paget 'to assure the Queen, on his behalf, of his desire to continue her most humble and obedient, faithful servant, who would always remember that he owed her his life, honour, goods and liberty'.[44] Edward's father would have been appalled at his cowardice and the betrayal of his supporters, something the marquis would never have done, but part of what Edward said was true. He would never have aspired to the queen's hand if he had not been encouraged by more experienced individuals who knew the queen better than he. However, Paget's proposals came to nothing as neither Mary or the emperor trusted that, as a couple at liberty, Edward and Elizabeth would not be more of a threat. Although the marriage question was now settled, Edward was still not free of the swirling intrigues at court for he remained a useful tool for those who refused to accept the Spanish match.

On 21 January 1554 Edward received an urgent summons from Stephen Gardiner. Appearing before him in secret, he was questioned about a planned uprising against the queen's marriage. According to the historian Robert Tittler 'the pathetic Courtenay was made to tell all he knew', something with which Anthony Fletcher concurs, telling us that Gardiner 'managed to worm the gist of the plot out of the foolish and unreliable Courtenay', while a furious Noailles reported that 'this young fool of a Lord Courtenay' had revealed the plot. His disclosure was therefore blamed for dooming the rising to failure. The hypocrisy of Noailles' outrage is staggering considering that he, by early December, had told Paget that 'he did not believe the Queen would wish to marry without asking the opinion of the nobility, and hinting that if she did so he knew what the answer would be, because of the intrigues Courtenay had been carrying on with most of them'.[45] In truth, the failure of Wyatt's rebellion had begun much earlier than 21 January and blame for that lies more firmly at the door of others.

On 26 November, after news of the queen's marriage became known, a group of individuals met to discuss plans for a rising. This group included Sir Thomas Wyatt [son of the Henrician poet], Sir Peter Carew, Sir Edward Rogers, Sir James Croftes and, by December, Edward's kinsman the Duke of Suffolk.[46] Rogers hailed from Lopit, Devon, and may have had kinship links to Edward's family.[47] Also involved, but to a lesser extent, was Edmund Tremayne who also hailed from Devon and had recently entered Edward's service.[48] Sir Peter Carew came from a Devonshire family with longstanding links to the Courtenays. His father, Sir William, had attended the funeral of Sir William Courtenay and was among those who carried the coffin of Katharine, Countess of Devon, while his mother had been chief mourner at the countess' funeral. The plan agreed in December involved marrying Elizabeth to Courtenay and placing them on the throne in place of Queen Mary who was to be deposed; her assassination, though mooted, was rejected. As Edward's marriage to Elizabeth was at the centre of the plot, they naturally made contact with him. The intermediary between Wyatt and Edward was Rogers, while Edward communicated directly with Carew, it later emerging that he had a cipher carved on his guitar that they both used.[49] Having agreed their plan, the conspirators decided upon the method. There was to be a four-fold rising which would descend on London and the date chosen was 18 March. Each local rising was to be led by Croftes in Herefordshire, Wyatt in Kent, Suffolk in Leicestershire and Carew and Edward in Devon.[50] In addition, the French were to provide naval support, while the Venetian ambassador was also to play a part, it later being claimed that he supplied arms from one of the Venetian ships.[51] Edward, allegedly, began collecting arms at his London home along with 'disguises in which to fly with Carew to Cornwall'.[52] However, the rebels had already made their first mistake and, as Carew, Croftes and Wyatt were experienced military men and Edward was not, this was their mistake not his. It was imperative that each of the leaders had the confidence and support of the locality in order to raise troops, but Suffolk and Carew did not, and it was this, especially in Carew's case, that caused the conspiracy to unravel.

From about 1547 Carew had resided on his wife's lands in Lincolnshire, thus he had been absent from the county for some years. When he was sent back to Devon in 1549 to calm growing resistance to religious change, his sledgehammer approach turned 'a demonstration into a rebellion', and he became a figure of hatred. He was not the man to raise Devon now, and as he began to realise support was not forthcoming he became more vocal in his attacks on the Spanish to try and whip up backing for the plot. He 'made little effort to conceal his plans' while a wagon-load of armour was blatantly drawn through the streets by one of his servants in broad daylight.[53] With the Earl of Devon by his side, able to appeal to traditional Courtenay loyalty, he might do better. On 17 January, he begged Edward to come to Devon with all speed, telling him that 'all the inhabitants of the county would support him against the queen and the Spaniards' a guarantee he clearly couldn't make. In order to get Edward there, he placed post horses along the road from London to Devonshire, but Edward sensibly demurred.[54] In his absence, it might have been Carew who spread the rumour that the earl was secretly living in his house at Mohun's Ottery only awaiting the time to act.[55]

It didn't take long for rumours to reach the council that things were amiss in Devon, and on 2 January, the very day that Edward welcomed the imperial ambassadors to London and rode with them to Durham House before a sullen crowd, the council summoned Carew to appear before them. It is undeniable that Carew's reckless behaviour was the cause of the plot first coming to light because on 7 January Renard was aware that Carew 'who lives in the West somewhere between Cornwall and Devonshire, has been intriguing' and that the council had determined to imprison him once he returned to London.[56] By 18 January, Renard believed things were at such a crisis point that the French were readying their fleet and about to send soldiers, and when the rebels learned that Renard had laid this information before the queen, Wyatt left London for Kent, while Croftes remained to keep an eye on events.[57] When Gardiner summoned Edward before him, the rebels knew almost immediately and this forced them to act prematurely.

Gardiner, having learned the extent of Edward's involvement was afraid that he would be implicated as a known supporter of the earl, whom he also wished to protect no doubt as husband in reserve if the Spanish match failed to materialise. It took him two days to screw up the courage to tell Renard what Edward had said but watered it down sufficiently that the earl remained at liberty. He had been approached, Gardiner explained, by 'several people' who 'had attempted to influence him where religion and the marriage were concerned', but he had ignored them 'for his mind was made up to live and die in the Queen's service'.[58] Meanwhile, the rebels' plans began to fall apart and on 25 January Carew, realising his position was hopeless, abandoned the rising, took ship and sailed for France. The duke of Suffolk was unable to gather sufficient forces and also tried to flee, but he was forced to surrender. Croftes, realising that all was lost, made no attempt to raise Herefordshire and his inevitable arrest followed. Only Wyatt was able to raise a credible force, estimated at 3,000, but he, too, blundered. Instead of making straight for London where he enjoyed support, he diverted to take the unimportant Cooling Castle, and this gave London time to prepare. With Edward among her escort, the queen gave a rousing speech in the guildhall that won the Londoners' cautious loyalty. Then suddenly, at four o'clock in the morning, London was awakened to find that Wyatt had crossed the river and was approaching. There was 'much noise and tumult' and panic ensued with the Council having to meet at the queen's bedside. When Wyatt made his attempt to take London, marching from Knightsbridge to Ludgate, the Londoners response was muted. While they didn't desert to him, they didn't do much to stop him either and things must have seemed on a knife edge. Rumours flew, including reports that Wyatt had won and the earl of Pembroke had defected.[59] Renard contemptuously remarked that Edward and William

Somerset, earl of Worcester, 'showed no sign of fighting and distinguished themselves on this their first field by running off to Court crying that all was lost and the rebels were winning the day'. The ambassador viewed this as cowardice, but they were among many who were confused, while Edward had little to no military training so his anxiety is understandable. If Renard can be believed, his distress led to an extraordinary outburst to Matthew Stuart, Earl of Lennox, during which he ranted 'that he was as good a man as Pembroke', that he wouldn't obey him and that the queen had reprimanded him by telling him 'he was not doing his duty as he ought' even though, Edward declared, 'he was a good man and true in his allegiance'.[60] It would prove to be the case that fear often prompted the earl into outbursts of hysteria, which someone of more experience and emotional maturity could have controlled. Fortunately for Mary, by the end of the day, with an exhausted army and the gates of London still locked, Wyatt had no choice but to surrender. However, for Gardiner, the worst was not over.

Earlier, one of Noailles messengers had been captured and on 28 January his despatches were in Gardiner's hands. As he began to decipher them he saw, to his horror, Edward's name in connection with the rebellion. Therefore, when he passed the deciphered letter to the queen he left Edward's name blank, claiming he was unable to decipher that element. Renard was not convinced and after obtaining the original letter from the queen, he arranged his own decipherment and clearly saw Edward's name which 'showed that the object of the rebellion was to favour Courtenay, its author, that Elizabeth was levying troops in her part of the country and that some of the Council were in the plot'. Renard was furious, telling the queen 'that the Chancellor and other members of her Council had always favoured Courtenay, and I suspected that they approved of Wyatt's undertaking'. Renard then confronted the chancellor with the correctly deciphered letter, and a very uncomfortable Gardiner turned red with embarrassment.[61]

Renard now began to encourage Mary to arrest both Edward and Elizabeth, especially when Wyatt accused the earl of being involved and alleged that the plot had been organised in his and Elizabeth's interests. In light of such accusations, the council issued orders for his arrest and he was apprehended at Canon Row on 12 February. Escorted by a guard of 200, Edward was taken by boat to the Tower arriving half an hour after Jane Grey's execution.[62] Although Gertrude had remained at court following Mary's rejection of her son, she had withdrawn herself 'from the intimacy to which the Queen had admitted her' and ceased to speak to her 'about her son or any other topic'. Edward's arrest may have been the final straw that prompted a disillusioned Gertrude to leave court, which she had done by 17 February. Resenting the queen for her decision to marry

Philip, angry and frustrated at her son's behaviour, she was also fearful for his life. She was right to be concerned.[63] From this point onwards Renard strained every sinew to bring the earl to the block. He sincerely believed that Mary would never be secure while Edward and Elizabeth lived, and Charles V agreed.

From February onwards a series of interrogations took place; Sir James Croftes admitted that the French supported the rebellion but wouldn't incriminate Elizabeth; Edmund Tremayne refused to implicate either Elizabeth or Edward even under threat of torture,[64] William Thomas, one-time clerk of the Council, confessed that he and two others had planned to kill the queen, and Wyatt accused Edward before three witnesses of being 'as much a traitor as he, if not more', something Edward denied.[65] Other prisoners also accused Edward of being involved, and the queen and council believed 'he had heavy charges to answer and was guilty'. However, consenting to treason without committing any act did not invoke the death penalty, so the council's efforts focused on trying to discover whether he had committed any act, something which the resentful queen now supported 'as Courtenay had had no regard for her life or crown'. However, an increasingly outraged Renard was convinced that Gardiner, who was in overall charge of the interrogations, was using his position to protect Edward as 'every word of evidence against Courtenay comes to the Chancellor's ears'. Furthermore, one of Edward's servants visited another of the imprisoned conspirators, John Young, to persuade him not to accuse the earl while Waldegrave, who was sympathetic to Edward, was sent to examine Young. To Renard's shock, Young was released the next day. It does seem as if Gardiner was continuing to use his position to shield Edward, and on 3 March he was moved from the Bell Tower to the more comfortable tower over the gate, which Renard believed was done on Gardiner's orders without recourse to the Council.[66]

What Renard did not mention was the possibility that attempts were made to procure false evidence aimed at sending Edward to the block. On the scaffold before his execution on 11 April, Wyatt sensationally and publicly exonerated both Edward and Elizabeth, and it is possible that he had initially accused them in the hope of pardon.[67] This begs the question of just how far Edward was involved, and this uncertainty is typical of his life. He was touted as the husband of a Catholic queen, yet was the hope of the Protestants as husband to Elizabeth. This meant he had to remain guarded about his true religious faith. He played a delicate game by encouraging those who wished to use him as a focus for rebellion, without actually committing himself to them, and he would use this tactic for the rest of his life. If he was openly disloyal he would lose everything, and so on the surface he professed loyalty to Mary. But he had to hold out the possibility of support to the malcontents, otherwise they would simply replace him with someone else. Indeed, after Edward confessed all to

Gardiner and ostensibly supported the queen, it was reported that the rebels 'had got in his place someone else, who was to marry the Princess Elizabeth'.[68] He obviously knew of the plot, had corresponded with the rebels and might have acted if success seem certain, but in the end he did not and the information he gave Gardiner helped to foil the conspiracy. Thus, despite Renard's urging, neither Edward or Elizabeth could be brought to the block under the law, but they would remain prisoners.

On 19 May, Elizabeth was sent into house arrest at Woodstock Palace, Oxfordshire, and in the early hours of 25 May, probably to avoid any protests in his favour, Edward was escorted out of London under armed guard and taken to Fotheringhay Castle, Peterborough.[69] Leading the escort was 54-year-old Sir Thomas Tresham, a man so trusted by the queen that he had commanded a company of soldiers whose sole purpose had been to protect her during Wyatt's rebellion.[70] Edward had hunted within Tresham's deer park during his months of freedom and despite Tresham now being his gaoler, they would maintain a friendship following his release. He was fond of Tresham, later writing to enquire about his health during a period of illness and would even take Tresham's son into his service. This is the other side of Edward's character which is rarely considered and will be looked at in the next chapter. But for now, within the confines of Fotheringhay, he would have time to reflect in the company of a man he referred to as 'good Sir Thomas Tresham'.

Chapter 14

1555

Taking Leave

If wishing might take place, you should be there.

On 25 July 1554, Queen Mary married Philip of Spain in Winchester Cathedral with Edward's mentor, Gardiner, officiating. Gertrude should have been present on this great occasion, but evidence suggests that she did not return to court until the following year. Despite Philip's attendants describing Mary as old, flabby and badly dressed, his behaviour towards her was exemplary. Mary, starved of affection, developed genuine feelings for him, which were never reciprocated. Philip would be married and widowed four times and showed genuine grief for three of those wives, weeping and withdrawing himself from company. His honest but devastating reaction to Mary's death was summed up in five words, 'I felt a reasonable regret.'[1] Fortunately, Mary would never know, and in the autumn of 1554, when she believed she was pregnant, her joy was complete. However, there were persistent rumours that the French were trying to stir up trouble and had not given up on the idea of marrying Edward to Elizabeth. Renard's fears grew as the queen's confinement approached; what would happen if she died but her child lived? In that instance Philip was to become regent but during his absences would be required to rule through deputies, possibly Spaniards.[2] This would be unwelcome to many in England, and he had already heard that 'a number of people are plotting to make Courtenay King if anything happens to the Queen'. There was also gossip that Mary was not pregnant but planning to pass off another child as her own, while the regular burning of Protestants was very unpopular, all prompting Renard's gloomy observation, 'I have never seen the people in such an ugly mood as they are at present.' At the same time Edward, still hoping for freedom, begged the queen for pardon pledging that he would serve Charles V in 'whatever place he might be told'.[3]

Discussions about what to do with Edward intensified, until it was finally agreed to release him but send him out of the country before the queen entered her confinement. It would be too dangerous for the Earl of Devon to be close at hand should anything happen to the queen, and once the decision was made things moved quickly. Edward was to go to the emperor's court in Brussels, and on 8 April 1555 he left Fotheringhay after fifteen months imprisonment and travelled to court 'to kiss hands'.[4] Unbelievably, he was immediately presented with another marriage proposal, this time to 38-year-old Frances Grey, mother of Lady Jane Grey. Reportedly, Edward's rather ungentlemanly response was that he 'would rather leave the country than marry her'. Frances wouldn't have cared; she was unavailable anyway having married her much younger master of the horse Adrian Stokes in March![5] During a last conversation with Gardiner, Edward was assured that if he left now he would be able to return at his pleasure 'his absence at the moment of the delivery sufficing them'.[6] His desire to go to Italy was also under consideration. Barely able to take leave of his mother, who had dutifully arrived at Kew to supervise the inventorying of his households, he took ship to Calais where he arrived, suffering from sea sickness, on 8 May 1555.[7] Warned by his friends to go straight to the emperor's court to avoid suspicion, the breathless earl explained that as he had little more than the clothes he stood up in and only a small amount of furniture, he had to go to Antwerp first to see royal agent Thomas Gresham and get some ready cash.[8]

The last months of Edward's life were spent overseas, the result of which was a large amount of correspondence, some of which has been preserved. The most important letters fall into three different groups; those to his family, those to his friends and those to trustees who he had appointed to manage his estates, some of whom, like James Bassett, were also friends. The volume of correspondence is such that not all could be studied for this book, but those letters that have been, show a side of Edward that is often neglected. The concern shown by his family and friends, and the value that Edward placed on sincere friendship is both poignant and enlightening. No one who was simply a foolish and ambitious wastrel, as History's verdict implies, could have earned such affection and care.

His Family

Following his departure, Edward's capable mother took charge of closing down his houses in England until his return. Staying at Kew, she double-checked the inventory of that residence and left 'your house wholly furnished, every chamber as you left them'. She checked the Canon Row inventory brought by Edward's servant, John Walker, noting that the canopy of cloth of gold and crimson velvet had gone missing, remarking 'it is no marvel at such a time, though some things were missed'.[9] She entrusted the inventories and Edward's plate to Walker, before going on to Malsanger where she was staying. This impressive

Tudor manor house was owned by Sir William Warham, nephew of William Warham archbishop of Canterbury, and he seems to have put it at Gertrude's disposal. Located in Hampshire, it provided a base closer to London than her own residences. While the letter is businesslike and lacks warmth, Gertrude had always discharged her maternal duty to Edward. She had been involved in collecting issues from his estates during his imprisonment, and after he left England she attempted to regain her position at court, although she had little enthusiasm for it. In June she wrote that 'if my waiting can do you good, if I may get a chamber, I will wait, although my years require rest'.[10] On 6 August, Edward congratulated her on being called to the queen's Privy Chamber, 'I rejoice much madam to hear of your ladyship's good health and also to perceive … that the Queen's Majesty hath called you again into her Privy Chamber in such honourable wise as it appeareth her highness Doth greatly favour you.' This was understandable, Edward continued, as Gertrude had 'always bourne a true and faithful heart towards Her majesty'.[11] Gertrude's letters go on to reveal her gratitude for Mary's friendship, which appears to have resumed, perhaps helped by the absence of her son. In February 1556 William Ryce informed Edward that 'My Lady your mother is in very good health, and hath been lately at the court, where the Queen's highness made very much of her.'[12]

Nevertheless, Gertrude and Edward's letters convey a palpable tension between them. Perhaps a close relationship was not possible after all that had happened. Edward recognised that his parents' loyalty to Mary, which had led to his father's execution, was laudable, but did he also resent them, his mother in particular? She had committed the crime but walked free, while Edward, completely innocent, remained behind bars. Did Gertrude, in turn, feel a deep-seated guilt that was difficult to deal with? We cannot know, but their relationship was not an easy one. In October 1555 the queen herself sent an admonishment to Edward, via James Bassett, for not writing to his mother enough. Upon asking Gertrude whether she had received any letters from her son, she answered 'not this five or six weeks; whereat the Queen marvelled, for there had come letters to others since'.[13] Gertrude often complained of this, grumbling in June 'you have so much business you have no leisure to write with your own hand to your own mother: and seldom to hear from you'.[14] Bassett attempted to heal relations between them, telling Edward:

I conversed with my Lady your mother, in whom I found much motherly affection and great care … your Lordship shall not find all things true which you fear and suspect in her towards you. I wish earnestly your Lordship should with your often letters entertain her as is convenient, she being your mother, whereby no occasion be ministered by you of loss or decay of goodwill between you.[15]

Edward's naivety and thoughtlessness, which occasionally resulted in a rather blunt tone, would not have helped matters. In July 1555, despite having nothing much to write about, he told his mother that as a messenger happened to be with him, and he felt it was his duty, he had written this letter to her. He complained about his lack of money and informed her that he did 'sometimes go abroad unto the notable towns' to explore 'where I pass the time much to my contentation'. After ending the letter he remembered something else, and this reveals his sensitivity to perceived slights, and fondness for quoting proverbs and sayings which often appear in his letters. He complained about one of his mother's old servants, 65-year-old Sir William Daubeney, who had been a gentleman in his parents' household and keeper of one of the marquis' parks. It seems that Daubeney had been among those attending him during his imprisonment at Fotheringhay and had not shown him the same respect as Tresham had. He told Gertrude that 'since I saw him last he never would ask for me nor send to me nor write me commendations but I see the old expression is true in him Seldom seen soon forgotten'.[16] Despite Edward's complaints, Gertrude tried to obtain a prebend for her old servant that had fallen into her son's hands. In November 1555, Edward, still resentful over Daubeney's snub, informed her that he had already bestowed it upon one of his own servants in reward for their 'faithful and long service'. He then added that Daubeney was 'an old man' and 'unlearned'.[17]

Despite the apparent strain in their relationship, Gertrude was concerned for her son's welfare and prepared to indulge him, as revealed in the above letter of November 1555. In this, Edward, who was currently in Louvain, thanked her for agreeing to send her cook to him. As his own cook had died Gertrude's was, he explained, 'a most necessary man for my purpose'. Desperate for decent meals, he hoped that the cook would come as soon as possible in the company of Walter Prune, one of his most reliable messengers. However, so as not to leave his mother 'utterly destitute', in exchange he was sending one of his servants, a man called Herman Ring, to her. Ring had stepped into the culinary breach after the cook's death but appears not to have been as accomplished, as Edward felt the need to reassure his mother that he 'hath a good will to learn'![18] Mother and son exchanged tokens, and in one letter Edward showed concern when he regretted being unable to assist her being so far away 'in this time of your business … when I might have done your ladyship some service'.[19] Leaving Malsanger for her manor of Canford in September 1555 she told him

'If wishing might take place, you should be there', before urging him 'to avoid all ill and sinful company'.[20]

Gertrude wrote to Edward again in October and November 1555, and these are her last surviving letters to him, although not the last she wrote. They have a melancholy tone as she ponders her life and her son's situation. In October, she laments that 'seeing you be so far from me in a strange country, my motherly heart fears many perils that might happen to you', continuing that if he serves God 'his merciful goodness will give you grace to fly sin and evil counsel and company' which will be to the 'comfort of all your friends'. She informs him that she has been at Canford, which she likes, and 'I think you will when you see it.' She had concluded business there and purchased a number of 'bargains' that though chargeable to her, will be profitable to him. She still felt the need to stamp her maternal authority on her 29-year-old son though, and she warned him that he will only see those profits if 'you be to me as God and nature command you'. It seems she considered he hadn't been, complaining that she was currently in London to see the queen and to hear news of him, but when she spoke to his servant John Walker she received neither letter or token from him 'whereby I perceive slackness of duty'.[21]

On 22 October, Edward sent a flurry of letters concerning his imminent departure to Italy, including one to his mother, since lost. Her last surviving letter to him was written from Malsanger on 8 November 1555 in reply to that. In one sense Gertrude was pleased to receive the letter 'to perceive you do not forget your mother, who esteems you above her own life' but in another she was sorry that he was going so far away. She sincerely hoped that, before leaving, he would 'come into England to see the queen's highness and your poor mother, who has as little worldly comfort as ever woman had, saving only the goodness and comfort of the queen's highness'. She was so keen for him to come that she was sending a messenger to him to bring her news, and if there was any chance of him coming then she would remain at Malsanger to wait for him. After informing him of her ill health, 'I am at this present so pained with the cholic and the stone, that I have much ado to write', she again tells him she is 'praying daily for your short return into England'. She ends the letter with yet another plea for him to visit, 'If you come to England I trust I shall see you, or else I will shortly write to you if I be alive.'[22] Gertrude's pleas are all the more poignant because Edward, although wishing to come, was prevented from visiting England. He had left for Italy the day before she wrote this letter and she would never see him again.

Few sources survive for the rest of Edward's family but Reginald Pole, his father's second cousin, also showed concern for him. He, too, was worried about the company Edward kept and wrote to Girolamo Muzzarelli, the Vatican representative at Brussels, about a certain 'individual' that Edward had with him suggesting, diplomatically, that the Nuncio should make greater efforts to rid the young earl of 'this bad company'.[23] Furthermore, he marshalled friends such as the merchant and banker, Anthony Bonvisi, to help Edward. While in Europe Bonvisi conducted some of his financial affairs and provided loans at fair, perhaps even preferential, rates, prompting Bassett to write, 'I rejoice at the kindness Mr. Bonvisi showeth you.'[24] Michael Throckmorton, Pole's longstanding agent who was based in Mantua, Italy, was another. He lent Edward money, advised him on financial matters, introduced him to suitable merchants and invited him to Mantua. Warm relations certainly existed between Edward and his uncle, John Blount, son of Lord Mountjoy and his fourth wife Dorothy, who was around the same age. Soon after his arrival in Brussels, Edward urged Bassett to obtain a licence for his uncle to join him telling him 'he is I assure you a young man of a very good nature and very towardlye'.[25] It is not certain he made it to Brussels despite Bassett's efforts for he wrote to Edward in January the following year from England. He pledged his desire to do 'your Lordship service', told him of the terrible weather in England, the worst in living memory and ended the letter by describing himself as 'your Lordship's loving uncle to command'. Before returning to the earl, Blount willed the bearer of the letter to repair to Edward's mother and to Lady Berkeley to obtain more news and updates from his friends.[26] One of the first letters he wrote on arrival in Calais was to Lady Berkeley. This is most likely his aunt, Katherine, wife of Sir Maurice Berkeley. Katherine enjoyed a close relationship with Edward's mother who referred to her as 'my sister Katherine Barkeley' and left her a bequest in her will.[27] Like his uncle, John Blount, who was Katherine Berkeley's half-brother, she was concerned about Edward's welfare, and Edward's letter to her reveals that she had shown kindness to him. His letter is certainly warmer than those to his mother and, despite needing to leave for Antwerp, Edward took the time to write to her and wish her well for the delivery of the child she was then carrying 'beseeching God to send you a good delivery and me a good arrival'. Katherine and Edward had hunted together, and in his letter he lamented 'your broken bow' and thanked her for 'the pains that you took when I was with you'.[28] On 23 November 1555, before leaving for Italy, he thanked her for her 'gentle letters and token'. He also desired her to thank 'those unknown friends that wish me to know their mind for my well doing' and pledged that if he is not further away than Germany and Italy 'you shall often hear from me and I pray you I may do the like from you'. He ends prophetically by asking her to pray for him 'for the voyage will be somewhat dangerous'.[29]

During his six months of freedom in England, Edward did more than conspire and visit houses of ill repute; he formed lasting friendships. The correspondence with some of these friends show a deep emotional attachment and a longing for home.

His Friends

Thomas Smith, who may have held a minor position in Edward's administration, was one such friend.[30] Despite being a man of much lower rank, his friendship was deeply valued by the earl who corresponded with him regularly during his exile. On 29 May 1555, he gave Smith 'thanks for your friendship always borne towards me ... as one whom I would be very glad to hear as well of as of any friend I have'.[31] In a letter written on 1 July 1555, Edward expresses his pleasure that Sir Thomas Tresham has recovered from his sickness. Showing his longing for home, he tells Smith that if things had been different and he had remained in England, he wished that 'we might have been there this summer together practising with our crossbows among his deer supposing I should have shot better this year at my mark than I did last time'.[32] He expressed his desire to send Smith a goshawk if it could be arranged and asked him to 'send my hearty commendations to good Sir Thomas Tresham'. 'Thus' he tells Smith 'I recommend you to God sending unto you a thousand thanks for the great friendship I have found in you' and signs himself 'your Loving friend E. Devonshire'.[33]

Another friend was Henry Neville, Lord Abergavenny, son of Lord Bergavenny and the nephew of Sir Edward Neville who had been executed with Edward's father. The links with the past went further for his wife, Frances, was the daughter of the marquis' friend, Thomas Manners, earl of Rutland. Furthermore, Abergavenny's cousin, Sir Henry Neville, son of the executed Sir Edward, was a Protestant exile at Padua and when Edward arrived in Venice in 1556, Sir Henry joined his household.[34] Frances would become known as a writer of pious Protestant works, and although Abergavenny had been loyal during Wyatt's rebellion, secretly they probably sympathised with the earl's position. The friendship between Edward and Abergavenny is evidenced in another of his letters. Writing from Brussels in June 1555, no doubt due to the speed with which he was forced to leave England, Edward laments that he was not able to see him not being sure 'to find you at home'. He asks whether Abergavenny can procure for him 'bucks and does that doth graze' and ends the letter with longing 'I would spend an hundred pounds to have your company here one month for I lack such a companion but since that cannot be I remember you to God and trust one day to see you in England again with your broad dagger on your back thus I end and bid you most heartily farewell.'[35] It cannot be denied that the warmth of these letters contrast sharply with those sent to his mother.

His Agents

James Bassett headed the group that was appointed to look after Edward's affairs in England, which had been 'left in a raw case by means of my hasty departure'.[36] These individuals included the triumvirate who had supported his marriage to the queen, Sir Francis Englefield, Sir Robert Rochester and Sir Edward Waldegrave, and also the queen's solicitor, William Cordell. The most important of these, though, was James Bassett, son of Honor, Viscountess Lisle, from her first marriage. Despite being the same age as Edward, Bassett often adopted an avuncular tone in his letters, advised him on his behaviour and was not afraid to gently reprimand him. The earl allowed this because he knew Bassett's criticisms were prompted by concern. Bassett was keen to ensure that Edward showed appropriate courtesy, telling him after his departure, 'I did all your messages and commendations, according to your Lordship's letter, who all were most glad to hear of you ... every one by one, recommendeth them unto you. Your Lordship did well specially to name them, because they might see their names in your letter.'[37] In July 1555 he went so far as to admonish Edward. The earl believed Bassett had delayed writing to him, but it was due to the slow delivery of letters. Bassett wrote:

> I am glad my letters hath purged me of that fault you supposed to be in me, which was slowness in writing; and now I wish your Lordship would amend in yourself that which you reckoned a fault in me, and then you might ... satisfy such of your friends as may justly look sometime to hear from you by writing, as my Lord Cardinal [Pole] and other.[38]

He was conscientious and committed to protecting Edward's interests, and his loyalty and abilities meant he was valued by others. He had been a devoted servant to Stephen Gardiner, and when the chancellor died on 12 November 1555, it was Bassett who broke the news to Edward, having 'spent day and night altogether with him, until he died'.[39] The queen also appreciated Bassett's talents and appointed him to her Privy Chamber, used him as her private secretary and granted him Mohun's Ottery in Devon, confiscated from Sir Peter Carew.

Of course, Edward had to deal with his affairs from a distance with communications taking days. In one letter from his mother, she explained the delay in receiving one of his letters because 'my man was much troubled with his passage; for, being on the sea, there was a great fight between the Frenchmen and the Spaniards, so that the ship he was in was fain to turn back again to Calais'.[40] On another occasion Edward informed William Cordell that 'I have hitherto made you no answer, partly because it was long before your letter came to my hands.'[41] At times Bassett was left tearing his hair out. He had sincerely hoped that Edward would be allowed to return to England, even briefly, before setting out for Italy, explaining that it 'would have been an exceeding great furtherance to your affairs, for it is impossible for us to do to your contentation, inasmuch as you being absent cannot perceive so well our reasons that guide us'.[42] Sometimes, lacking the time to write everything in a letter, Bassett would have to trust that Edward's messenger, usually Walter Prune, would be able to remember all he had told him. This time lag meant problems could not be resolved swiftly, such as Edward's desperate need for funds for his journey to Italy. At one point, as he waited for replies to his numerous letters, he became uncharacteristically angry with his trustees. He complained that none of his instructions had been complied with and he was determined to discharge John Heydon who held a senior position in his administration, but within days he was thanking his trustees once again for the arrangements they had made for 'his supply on his travels'.[43] This group managed a range of affairs for the earl and were occasionally forceful in their advice, as when they refused to allow him to accept a loan on terms offered by Thomas Gresham, as they were so 'onerous' and 'ruinous'.[44] They did, on occasion, give conflicting advice, but this served to provide the earl with sensible options for his consideration. When Sir William Petre, the queen's secretary, expressed a wish to buy the manor of Whitford in Devon, part of the Courtenay estate, Sir Francis Englefield counselled that it were better for him to sell anywhere but in Devon. Bassett, however, advised that he should sell to Petre 'considering who he is, and that he may do him some pleasure'.[45] Consequently, Edward took Bassett's advice and reluctantly sold to Petre. Edward might be described as foolish by some, but he could not have chosen better than the trustees he appointed.

All of the above individuals played specific roles in Edward's life. His mother and his trustees provided practical assistance, but for emotional support he turned to his friends. For some reason that closeness, that candid expression, could not be replicated with his mother. Whether this might have changed if Edward had returned to England can never be known, for Edward's future, short as it was, lay overseas.

The earl finally reached Brussels on 16 May 1555 where lodgings were provided for him by the emperor.[46] On 19 May he was presented to Charles V and both played their parts perfectly. Edward 'demeaned himself very well' showing gratitude to Philip for interceding with the queen, which had allowed him to 'come to offer his services to the Emperor, the renown of whose Court was so great'. Charles replied that he was 'moved not merely by the King's and Queen's recommendation, but for the sake of the Earl's father, whose noble virtues were not unknown to him, and of whose ill fortune a great piece be thought was for the good will he bare to his welldoings'. Charles accepted Edward's service and would inform him of what was required, but in the meantime 'desired that he should take all pleasure which the Court could show him'.[47] Then, just ten days later, Edward wrote a desperate note to Bassett. To a standard letter that had already been prepared, he hastily inserted a note on a ripped piece of paper. On this the first words were 'I pray you consider my going into Italy' and he tells Bassett 'I have as much need in this case to use your friendship as ever I had in anything' and he recommends 'the trust of myself and my affairs to your hands'. He would write no more on this as the rest would be declared by his messenger.[48] The reason for this extraordinary behaviour is explained by a report, dated 6 June, of Federico Badoer the Venetian ambassador in Brussels. Edward had visited him with Sir John Mason, the English ambassador, and told him he was intending to travel to Venice but, Badoer continued 'from many indications I comprehend that he is in great fear for his life, and thinks of nothing but preserving it, without evincing suspicion of the Emperor'.[49]

Chapter 15

1555–1558

Canford

there will be less trouble in England, now that this inducement has been removed.

As spring became summer the queen remained in confinement, and towards the end of May 1555 there were rumours that the pregnancy was false. To her misery, this turned out to be the case and given her health and age, she was 39, it was considered unlikely she would ever have a child. This meant Elizabeth's accession was assured. As it was expected that she, like Mary, must marry and bear children Edward was once again the obvious choice, another foreign match being undesirable. Philip, however, was determined to retain authority in England until Mary's death but, as Elizabeth's future husband, Edward was a powerful focus for those discontented with the Marian regime. This threat to Habsburg influence in England led Charles V, probably with Philip's knowledge but not with Mary's, to plan Edward's permanent removal. It must be achieved without any blame attaching to the Habsburgs, which might compromise Philip's position, and so Charles' plan involved the earl's accidental death in a skirmish between his retinue and some locals.[1]

Despite Charles' experience of covert operations, the whole affair was bungled from the start. Edward, as early as May, suspected an attempt on his life was to be made, and he started telling people. This explains the increasing urgency of his requests to leave Brussels and why he enlisted several influential individuals to help him. These included James Basset, Dr Thomas Martyn, a staunch Catholic in Gardiner's service, and the English ambassador, Sir John Mason.[2] Bassett, convinced of Philip and Mary's goodwill, tried to sooth the earl's concerns and managed to obtain permission for him to leave Brussels from time to time to visit places nearby for his health.[3] Edward's request was given credence by a genuine health problem, which he described as a disease of the hip that had flared up during his last incarceration as the result of 'a great cold'.[4]

To lull him into a false sense of security and prevent him from embarrassing the Habsburgs by airing his fears, Philip's right-hand-man, Ruy Gomez, used Edward's mother and friends. Gertrude wrote to Edward in July telling him that 'Don Ruy Gomez ... by order of his King, let her know that he [Edward] has cause to be easy in his mind, as his Majesty loves him, and will soon show it'.[5] Yet within days, the first of four assassination attempts occurred when an 'intimate servant' of the earl was mortally wounded by a Spaniard. On two further occasions twelve Spaniards picked a quarrel with Edward's attendants and in one instance he was 'pursued to his own chamber'. Not only afraid, Edward was now angry, telling the Venetian ambassador he was going to Louvain for a few days 'not caring whether he had audience of the Emperor one week or another, he would have it on his return'. At the same time, he was sent a lifeline by the Duke of Ferrara whose secretary urged the earl to visit his duchy. As Ferrara led the anti-Habsburg alliance in Italy and was an ally and relation of the French king, this would not have gone unnoticed.[6] After his return from Louvain, Edward and his attendants were attacked for the fourth time while riding though Brussels and 'he wishing to favour his followers by reproving the Spaniards, they threatened him, so seeing a number of Spaniards hastening to the assistance of their countrymen ... he returned in haste to his lodging, and on the retreat ... four of his attendants were wounded, and some of the Spaniards also'. This prompted a visit to the Bishop of Arras where the earl 'made great complaint of the assaults to which his retinue had been four times subjected'. Arras was all concern but falsely attributed the blame to 'prostitutes, and disputes of that sort between menials'.[7]

Edward was not convinced, and it is no wonder he wrote to his friends longing to be back in England. Sir John Mason, who had a warm relationship with Edward, was angry on the earl's behalf. When a row broke out in late September over Philip's intention to give greater precedence to the Portuguese ambassador at the funeral of Charles V's mother, Mason snapped. Being told by Philip that neither ambassador was now to attend, Mason confronted the king with a retinue of Englishmen. He spoke vehemently, used 'foul language' and 'his haughty bearing was such that not only did he not dismount, but would not allow Lord Courtenay to alight'. Not only that, he had written to the Council in England 'that Lord Courtenay's servants had been maltreated by Spaniards at this court, and that the other English likewise were as ill looked on as possible, which, on his Majesty's return to England, might induce them to do some great harm to his retinue'. Philip and Ruy Gomez were furious with Mason, and when Edward refused to attend a supper organised by Arras, Philip did not invite him to join a hunt in honour of Charles V's sister, Maria, regent of the Netherlands.[8]

The assassination attempts had been disastrous failures, but Edward still had to be dealt with, especially as Philip had now left England. It was therefore agreed that Ruy Gomez would take over the arrangements and the assassination would occur far away in Venice. Accordingly, on 15 October 1555, Philip gave Edward licence to leave no doubt aware that 'his chief intention is to reside some time in Venice'.[9] Two days later, Ruy Gomez met Marco da Risano, the assassin he had hired for the job, and gave him instructions. In Venice, Gomez would send to Risano 'a person of mine' who will provide a description of Edward enabling Risano 'to discover his abode, and perform the service in his company, as he will have other companions' who, between them, will be carrying 'three harquebuses, each with three balls'. After the murder, as Risano knew Venice, he was to organise boats for their escape to Puglia. For this, he would be paid 1,000 crowns.[10] We know all this because Risano was either a Venetian spy or defected to the Venetian state in December 1555; but can we believe his testimony? He certainly knew all the facts, Gomez was in Brussels at that time, he knew Edward was going to Venice, there had been earlier attempts on Edward's life and the empire had not shied from assassination in the past, all giving credibility to his claims.

Unaware of Gomez's plans, but still in fear of his life, Edward began making rapid arrangements to leave Brussels. His request to visit England first to settle his affairs was met with refusal, despite his mother, his friends and even the queen herself, desiring it. He issued instructions for the sale of Whitford to Sir William Petre, as mentioned above, and closed down his household. Informing John Trelawney that as he was 'able to retain only a small number of attendants, he sends home his son, who has the heart of a gentleman'.[11] Unfortunately, the son of his friend, Sir Thomas Tresham, took the news of his discharge badly and departed 'in rage'. However, Edward's devotion to Tresham was unchanged and he assured him 'that betwixt you and me it breedeth no alterances at all, but that I am and shall be towards you in all points as your gentleness towards me hath bound me'.[12] Despite his affairs being unsettled, he left Brussels with just four horses and arrived at Louvain by 12 November where he would remain until the end of the month to complete arrangements.[13] His trustees were tasked with raising money for the journey and satisfying his creditors, and Bassett advised him to request Bonvisi, upon the bonds of his trustees, to give him credit of 6,000 ducats in Italy, which they would repay upon sight of the earl's bills.[14]

Then, just before he left Louvain something curious happened. Edward received and replied to a letter from Sir Philip Hoby, a Protestant who had gained licence to leave England. During his sojourn in Europe, Hoby had consorted with other disgruntled English exiles and Renard was convinced he was there to plot against Mary.[15] Hoby informed Edward that he was at Antwerp and, with Mason, was desperate to visit him at Louvain, but the weather had prevented it.[16] In reply, Edward sent a cryptic and highly suspicious letter. He writes:

The lets shall be very great, and my business very extreme, but we will have both our desires satisfied, *for I have also somewhat to do with Mr. G. bis;* but keep it very secret, for if I perform it [as I would you should not too assuredly look for it] I will so steal on you as no unnecessary man shall be privy thereunto, neither going, coming, nor remaining there.[17]

As Edward and Hoby corresponded, the so-called Dudley conspiracy was hatched in London involving conspirators in France and Italy.[18] This plot reportedly planned to rob the exchequer, murder the queen and replace her with Elizabeth and Edward.[19] It has therefore been claimed that this is what Edward and Hoby were to discuss, and the reference to extreme business was the earl's attempt to sell land worth £200 via his agent John Walker to fund the plot.[20] This accusation was made in March 1556 after the conspiracy was discovered and interrogations conducted.[21] Walker was one of Edward's most trusted servants who had provided 'faithful service to me both in my adversity and all other ways'.[22] If he had used anyone for such a task it is believable that he would have used Walker. However, when Walker was arrested in July 1556, he was only accused of concealing his knowledge of the plot, but not of involvement in it.[23] Furthermore, the only land sale that his trustees were aware of at this time was the sale of Whitford to Sir William Petre, and it is difficult to see how Edward could have arranged the sale of £200 worth of lands behind their backs. The letter is confusing and the meaning impossible to glean with any certainty. Indeed, it may have been full of false promises to keep Hoby dangling, but one thing is certain; it suggests clandestine activity. Considering the queen's clemency, this might be considered ungrateful; on the other hand, Edward could not be sure that Mary was non-complicit in the attempts on his life and may have believed that removing her, and thus her husband, was the only way to guarantee his safety.

It must have been with some relief that the Earl of Devon left Louvain at the end of November. Travelling east to Cologne, he then journeyed south to Mainz where he picked up 'his stuff' and was welcomed by 'Smonde Isenheubt who did him much pleasure' following a letter of introduction from failed cook, Herman Ring.[24] He continued south, hoping to stay at Spires [Speyer], but hearing people were dying of the plague there he journeyed onwards to the village of 'Rhinehouse' and then to Augsburg, were he arrived on 26 December. Significantly, he continued his correspondence with Hoby, thanking him for letters of introduction and sending commendations to Sir John and Lady Mason.[25] Edward finally reached Padua in early January and on 15 January the English Ambassador to Venice, Peter Vannes, invited him to the city.[26] Edward accepted and was treated with the greatest respect by the Signory who referred to him as the Marquis of Exeter, his Excellency and 'the most illustrious Lord Edward Courtenay, Earl of Devonshire'. They spent 128 ducats on refreshments and other things to formally welcome him, but more importantly, on 10 February, gave him and 15 servants licence to 'carry weapons in this city and in all our towns and places', which was increased to 25 servants the next day at Edward's request.[27] The Signory had no doubt informed Edward about the assassination which was to have occurred in Venice, prompting these precautions. Unlike his vulnerable position in Brussels, Edward was now accompanied by a retinue of twenty-five armed men. Delighted by his reception in Venice, he established his main residence there, renting a house for 250 ducats a year.[28] Along with money raised from land sales and loans, he was also granted credit with the merchants to the value of 3,000 or 4,000 crowns at the queen's command, a commendable act of generosity.[29] Perhaps to allay suspicions over his residence in Italy, or because of his genuine love of learning, he put down further roots by enrolling at Padua's University of Law, a university where Reginald Pole had also studied, and regally described himself as a noble Englishman from the royal family of the White Rose of Britain.[30]

As he settled in, letters from family and friends continued to show concern for him, especially as he was now surrounded by a community of disgruntled English exiles. On 23 February Anthony Browne, Lord Montague, the current owner of West Horsley, warned him to avoid temptation and prayed to God for His help. Although he recognised Edward's disposition tended towards godliness, nevertheless, he was 'a man and therefore frail'.[31] As this high-profile young man was being feted by the empire's enemies, Philip ordered his ambassador to Venice 'to watch him carefully and find out everything he is up to. If he leaves that place and proceeds towards Milan or Piedmont, you will immediately … let me know.'[32] The next day, 21 March, Edward left Venice for Ferrara, ostensibly to deliver a letter from Philip to the duke and arrived there on Sunday 22 March. Again, he was gratified by his reception telling Mason 'the Duke lodged me in his palace and entertained me I assure you very honourably', and when he left Ferrara urged him to return for a longer stay 'to the intent he might show me the pleasures and commodities of his state'.[33] What he didn't tell Mason about were the discussions he had with several English conspirators. These included the Earl of Bedford and Nicholas Tremayne, brother of his servant Edmund who had now joined his household in Venice. Nicholas was the spokesperson for the Dudley conspiracy rebels who were based in France and was acting as their contact with Edward. According to the report of the Venetian ambassador in England, written on 28 April, 'the Earl of Devonshire was invited and called to Ferrara by the Duke solely for the purpose of tempting and persuading him to withdraw to France and adhere to his most Christian Majesty, promising him honourable provision', but, he added, 'he has been considered sage, for not having inclined or given ear to any of the offers made him'.[34] Again, Edward was showing just enough interest to give them hope but not committing. Edward left Ferrara for Venice on Tuesday 24 March, the very day the Venetian ambassador in England reported that a plot recently discovered [the Dudley Conspiracy], was of much greater threat than originally suspected, as it 'was of greater circuit and extent than had been at first supposed'. As a result, the passage ports were closed and arrests took place revealing suspicions that Edward was involved. As noted, his agent John Walker was one, while another was arrested 'solely for having written letters to and received letters from Lord Courtenay'.[35] In mid-April Lord Paget arrived in Brussels to update Philip on matters in England and pass on information gleaned from the accused, including claims that the rebellion's objective was 'to make Lord Courtenay their king'.[36] The failed assassination attempts were coming back to haunt Philip.

Despite his caution in not committing openly to the rebels, Edward was nonetheless concerned about how he was viewed in England and wrote to Mason on 18 April that he was afraid he was 'not in good favour with the Queen, as his servant, Walker, has been imprisoned'.[37] A further letter from Edward to Mason on 2 May suggests he had been reassured he was not under suspicion, and he was further buoyed by Mason's intercession on Walker's behalf. Edward ends this letter with a pleasant account of the arrival in Venice of the Queen of Poland on 26 April which he witnessed first-hand. Bona Sforza, heir to the duchy of Milan, had married Sigismund I of Poland in 1517. Tensions developed with her son and heir after Sigismund's death, and on 1 February 1556, she left Warsaw for Padua. Held in high esteem in Italy, the 62-year-old queen's progress was treated like a state visit. Edward observed her arrival in Venice where she was met by the Signory and attended by a hundred of the 'fairest gentlewomen in Venice ... all apparelled in white and very rich in jewels'. Bona and her entourage, which included her ambassador and chief steward, Arturo Pappacoda, were conducted down the Grand Canal in a ceremonial barge amid fireworks and music while the canal and overlooking buildings thronged with spectators including Edward. It was a prophetic moment; did she spot the handsome, well-born earl? Did they make eye contact? We will never know, but the following year she was dead, poisoned by her trusted ambassador Pappacoda who had been bribed by the agents of Philip of Spain.[38]

The celebrations to welcome Bona Sforza had provided a brief respite for Edward, who was coming under increasing pressure from both the rebels and the Habsburgs. Following the collapse of the 'Dudley conspiracy' the rebels were losing ground, the King of France appeared to be cooling, they were running out of funds and it was now imperative that Edward commit himself. According to information provided by an English government spy, around 24 May Edward returned to Ferrara where he was visited by Henry Killigrew who hailed from Cornwall. Killigrew was now in the service of Francois de Vendome, Vidame of Chartres, one of the first leaders of the Protestant movement in France who was well connected enough to count Henri II as kin.[39] Killigrew carried a message from his master promising Edward that if he would go to France, the Vidame 'would provide for him three thousand crowns and any other thing he had beside should be at his commandment'. Killigrew also urged him not to return to England as 'it would cost him his life'. Edward thanked him for his friendship but replied that 'it was not for him to enter any king's realm upon any subjects promise'.[40] Frustrated, Killigrew returned to break the bad news to his compatriots while another conspirator fed up with Edward's prevarication, his servant Edmund Tremayne, had left his service in April. The earl was 'very sorry and ill satisfied' with 'Tremayne's foolish departing', especially as he was followed by Sir Henry Neville.[41]

On the other side was an equally frustrated Philip. As war with France appeared inevitable, he needed to be sure of English backing. For that, Mary must be secure on her throne as he knew there would be considerable hostility to providing military support to the Habsburgs. Therefore, the earl of Devon could not be allowed to continue as a focus for opposition.[42] Whether he was involved in conspiracy or not, Edward's name continued to be taken in vain to serve the purposes of others. In July a youth in Sussex attempted to impersonate him, in Ipswich a rising in support of Elizabeth and Edward occurred, and when Henry Killigrew returned to France he spread false rumours that Edward would soon arrive at the French court.[43] His role as a figure head was crucial, with Noailles stating that 'every hope of English liberty rested "in him alone"'.[44] In June, probably as a result of Philip's concerns, there were rumours that Edward was to be recalled to England but realising the danger, 'by no means will he go thither'.[45] In England, the queen was under considerable strain; she, too, feared assassination and was disillusioned with the opposition to her rule and the continuous plots. Combined with the lack of a child and the third failed harvest in a row, she must have wondered whether God was angry with her, and throughout July and August 'was in a condition bordering upon hysterical collapse'.[46]

Edward, too, was beginning to show signs of renewed stress, perhaps sensing that Philip was once again sharpening his claws. He wrote to Mason on 4 July 'I am right sorry to understand that any suspicions or evil rumours should be raised of me', assuring him that they 'are utterly without cause' and claimed that his letters were being opened in Flanders.[47] This is believable, for if any proof of treasonous activity were discovered Philip would have the perfect excuse to recall him to England.[48] Mason tried to reassure him, telling him, 'I think you will have lately heard from your queen the good opinion her highness hath of you.'[49] This letter from Mary was corroborated by the Venetian ambassador who was informed that she 'had written to Lord Courtenay, at Venice, to let him know that all the first and last charges brought against him had been found to be false, and that she loves and always shall love him in conformity with his station'. Mary further explained 'that she was induced to perform this office for the sake of truth, and that he may not continue to despair of the King's favour and of hers'.[50] The earl, however, was not reassured and the situation was difficult for both of them when he was the subject of so many rumours. This was perfectly demonstrated when the English ambassador in France wrote directly to the queen in August and repeated Killigrew's lies, telling her that Edward would soon join the rebels in France 'and that they have already taken some port in one of her Majesty's islands'.[51] To avoid suspicion, and no doubt in fear of his life once more, Edward began to live 'a life more solitary', surrounding himself only with Venetian gentlemen he trusted. These tensions might lie behind his furious outburst at the arrival in Padua of his servant Humphrey Michell without permission.

Michell was one of Edward's bailiffs and an able administrator who had enjoyed the earl's favour,[52] but on 16 June he wrote a grovelling letter of apology to his master who was then staying at Casa Marcello, a rural villa near Levada belonging to the Marcello family of Venice. Michell explained that if 'my repairing to your presence should have offended you I would not have attempted to do it. But being there in the company of a number of young gentlemen that offered themselves to attend your lordship at the waterside, I thought it also my bounden duty to do the like.' He assured him that he had always been careful 'not to disobey you' and that 'if the venturing of my life might stand your lordship in any stead I have been and ever shall be as ready to adventure the same' pleading for 'the remission of your most grievous displeasure against me'. So angry was Edward, that he refused to allow Michell into his presence, which is why he had to beg for forgiveness by letter. He lamented 'Alas my very good Lord I feel that in my coming hither I have done your Lordship very evil service' and ended with the prophetic words 'I pray God preserve your Lordship in health and keep you out of the hands of your enemies.'[53] It is not clear exactly why Edward was so angry. Was the earl worried that Michell was a spy or an assassin? It is possible, but a more likely explanation is that Michell, a Protestant and friend of Edmund Tremayne, had left England without licence thus placing Edward under more suspicion. Indeed, after Edward's rejection Michell transferred to the service of the earl of Bedford, another Protestant, and enjoyed his patronage during the reign of Elizabeth.[54] Michell's arrival clearly unnerved Edward who immediately left Padua and sequestered himself with his trusted Venetian attendants at Casa Marcello. He was right to be afraid, but in the end it was a sudden summer storm that delivered him into Philip's hands.

Edward's last weeks were described to Queen Mary by the English ambassador at Venice, Peter Vannes, and what follows is his account.[55] Around the end of August, Edward travelled to an island called Lio six miles from Venice to see his hawks fly. This area was a kind of waste ground without any houses on it, and during the visit he was 'suddenly taken with a great tempest of wind and rain'. The weather was so bad that he could not return in his gondola but had to travel to Venice in a searchers' boat that happened to arrive. He was soaked to the skin but, according to Vannes, refused to change into warmer garments. A few days later he told Vannes he had fallen on the stairs in his house. This might have been due to his hip problem, which could have flared up after getting so wet and cold on the journey back. However, he didn't feel any ill effects afterwards and decided to go to Padua. He travelled by coach and arrived on a Saturday night, probably Saturday 5 September. Vannes considered this was the worst form of transport to have taken as it was so shaky and bumpy. The next day the ambassador visited him and 'found him very weak'. This could have been due to nothing more than tiredness after the journey from Venice and perhaps a bit of a chill, but Vannes explained it as the beginning of a fever. Significantly, after the ambassador's visit Edward began to get worse and worse 'and entered in a continual great hot ague: and some time more vehement than at another'. According to Vannes, he avoided his friends and remained in the company of just two physicians, but it is equally possible that his friends were prevented from seeing him, and all the while Vannes was in regular personal contact with Edward and his household. Even as he lay ill, Edward worried about what people were saying about him, telling Vannes during one of his many bedside visits, 'that it had been reported unto him that some had said that he was better French than English: and if God did recover him and send him his health so that he might come to the knowledge of the misreporter he was minded to try that quarrel with his sword'. But Edward did not recover; in fact, his condition worsened and as the end approached the ever-present Vannes hovered over him, closely monitoring everything. He exhorted him to take communion and Edward answered in broken words:

that he was well content so to do: and in token thereof ... and in repentance of his sin he lift up his eyes and knocked himself upon the breast: and after I had suffered him to pause a good while I caused the sacrament to be brought, and after the priests godly exhortation he forced himself to receive the blessed communion: but his tongue had so stopped his mouth and his teeth so cloven together, that in no wise he could receive that same: And after this sort this gentleman is gone as I do not doubt to God his mercy.

Edward Courtenay, Earl of Devon, died on Friday 18 September 1556 aged 30. Within an hour Vannes sat down to write to the queen.

What can we make of all this? It is true that the plague was prevalent in Venice from July through to October, so could Edward have succumbed to this? Or did he develop a fever after getting wet at Lio as Vannes alleged, or is there a more sinister explanation? Although the evidence is circumstantial, Kenneth Bartlett has made a convincing case for the latter.[56] The Habsburgs had already made several attempts on Edward's life, and Philip was quite capable of ordering an assassination, which he would do the following year when he bribed Bona Sforza's ambassador to poison her. The English ambassador in Venice who, by nature of his position had easy access to Edward, was 68-year-old Peter Vannes, the Dean of Salisbury. He, like Philip, had form for this, having a year or two earlier hired assassins to murder Sir Peter Carew in Venice, an attempt that failed. He was also a man in need of money, mentioning his straitened circumstances in letters to the queen and to Sir William Petre.[57] He was present at the earl's bedside throughout and possibly controlling access to him. Furthermore, Vannes had been resident ambassador at Venice for a decade, yet at the very moment when an experienced ambassador was needed as war with France loomed, he suddenly requested his recall to England immediately after Edward's death. Was it to avoid discovery?

Compounding this were the mysterious circumstances surrounding Edward's letters, letters that would be extremely valuable to Philip. They would have contained the names of the earl's correspondents, some of whom were conspirators, details of the various plots about which he had been approached, and the involvement of states such as France and Venice. In Vannes' letter to Mary he alluded to 'all kind of writings and letters: that he [Edward] had either here or at Venice' which 'shall be put in assurance abiding for your commandment'.[58] He requested the then bailiff of Padua to seal them in a casket and hold them in custody, which was done in the presence of Edward's retinue, sealed with his seal and deposited in the Paduan archives. By 16 November Vannes, having heard from the queen, requested them from the newly appointed bailiff, but the Council of Ten instructed the bailiff not to hand them over, but to do so 'without showing that you have had any commission from us'. The Venetians realised how damaging they could be and acted accordingly. They ordered the bailiff to send the casket to them 'in a wrapper, in a cautious manner and secretly, without communicating it to anyone'. A carpenter was sent for to carefully open it at Venice, and the letters which they considered incriminating and politically sensitive were marked with a cross and removed. The rest were put back into the linen cover and stitched, placed in the casket which was carefully sealed and sent back to Padua as if it had never left. On 28 November, the Signory finally gave approval for the letters to be handed over to Vannes.[59] That the Signory took such action means they clearly had something to hide.

Vannes' account of Edward's death was the one most people accepted. The funeral oration delivered by the earl's fellow student at Padua, Thomas Wilson, mentioned illness and fever.[60] Four days after his death the Spanish ambassador at Venice wrote that he died 'of a fever, which carried him off in fourteen days'.[61] However, the earl's death sparked gossip in Padua that Queen Mary was behind it, causing Vannes to defend her honour.[62] More disturbing is an account by Pietro Bizzarri that appears in a book about the history of Genoa that he wrote in the late 1570s. As a member of the household of the earl of Bedford, there is every reason to believe that Bizzarri was part of Edward's circle in Padua and Venice. This means his account, like Vannes', is first-hand from someone on the spot when Edward died. According to him, Edward 'breathed his last surrounded by the deceits of his enemies, and not before he recognized their evil intentions and murderous hands ...'[63] If we are to accept the strong circumstantial evidence pointing to Edward's death by poison, the summer storm at Lio played right into his enemies hands. It is entirely possible that his soaking at Lio did give him a bit of a chill. While Vannes' assertion that he refused to change into warmer clothes is not credible, he would have been forced to remain in wet clothes during the six-mile journey back to his residence in Venice. As we have seen previously, catching a cold or chill tended to exacerbate his hip problem, a contributory factor perhaps to his fall on the stairs. Once in Padua, a little weak and under the weather, he was attended by four physicians and two surgeons, and in the presence of Vannes. Using the mild chill as a smokescreen, poison would give the effect of this chill developing into a full-blown fever. Fevers are contagious, which provided a useful pretext for keeping the earl's friends away. This was a far more subtle way of despatching him than by a clumsy quarrel with unruly Spaniards in Brussels or a murderous attack by thugs in Venice. This was done by stealth and executed with finesse by a 68-year-old cleric. The most distressing element is the claim that Edward knew what was happening to him but too late to extricate himself due to his weakened state. Whether Vannes acted alone or in league with the physicians is not known. He was keen to reassure Sir William Petre that the physicians and surgeons who had attended Edward were present at his postmortem and had been sworn and examined as to 'what kind of disease, and how it began and how it continued till the hour of the said Earl his death'.[64] But, as Bartlett correctly notes, the doctors could have been suborned by Vannes to provide the testimony he required.[65] The benefit of Edward's demise to the Habsburgs is clear, the Spanish ambassador at Venice noting that 'with his death his intrigues will cease and there will be less trouble in England, now that this inducement has been removed'.[66]

Edward Courtenay was buried in the Basilica of St Anthony at Padua on 21 September and an inscription 'Odoardo Courtenai, 1556' could still be seen in the nineteenth century. It is supposed that as the tomb was to be a temporary one, the epitaph composed for it exists in print only. It is believed that his remains were removed from St Anthony's at some point, but their fate remains unknown.[67] If Gertrude was at court when Vannes' letter arrived, the queen would have informed her personally, but how she took the news of her only son's death is not recorded. It probably prompted her retirement from court as she was not in the best of health and had said she needed rest. But she retained the queen's friendship and exchanged New Year's gifts with her in 1557, receiving £10 in cash and giving a gilt jug and salt.[68] Her remaining months were spent at her beloved manor of Canford. Located on the River Stour, it was just seven miles from Poole and the coast. As her health began to deteriorate, she drew up her will on 25 September 1557, a year after Edward's death. She requested that her body be buried in the church near to where 'it shall happen me to pass from this transitory life', made the traditional Catholic arrangements for masses and prayers to be said for her soul and for the distribution of charity. She ordered provision for her servants, each was to have a black coat, a year's wage and her house to be continued for forty days to provide meat, drink and lodging for them. Her linen was to be divided between her chamberers and two servants, Elizabeth Cotton and Agnes Reed, received cash bequests. One of her most unfathomable instructions was for £10 to be distributed among the poor to pray for her, her husband and her parents but no mention was made of her son. Vannes informed Mary that Edward had taken the wine but was unable to take the sacrament due to his swollen tongue and clamped jaw, but he believed he died 'a very good Christian man'. However, he appointed a Protestant to deliver Edward's funeral oration. It is possible that Gertrude was not convinced of his Catholic faith and suspected her son had Protestant leanings, in which case she may have felt it inappropriate to have Catholic prayers said for him. In addition to bequests to family members previously mentioned, she left two flagons of silver to Margaret, daughter and heir of Anthony Harvey. The capable and utterly loyal Harvey was appointed her sole executor, and to him she left the residue of all her goods and chattels, describing him as 'my trusty and well beloved friend'. Gertrude died between 26 December 1557 and 8 January 1558.[69] She was buried in the Minster Church of St Cuthburga, Wimborne Minster, where her tomb of Purbeck marble can still be seen. The brass shields on the side have been torn off, and part of the inscription of black lettering on brass that went around the top margin of the tomb has been lost. What remains translates as ' ... wife of the late Henry Courtenay, Marquis of Exeter and mother of Edward Courtenay, lately ea ...'. At least here, Edward is remembered.

Gertrude was an extraordinary woman who married into an extraordinary family, who lived through tumultuous times. Her mother-in-law was a princess of England, the last of the Plantagenet children of Edward IV. A woman of deep emotion, her composure and self-control sometimes belied the kindness and generosity which lay beneath. Her mother's daughter, she ran the massive estates of the earldom of Devon with energy and adeptness, completely undaunted by the challenge. Her son, Henry, was a man of rare virtues who demonstrated unfailing loyalty to his friends no matter the cost. His marriage to Gertrude was a happy one, he loved and respected her; he was right to. She was a capable woman whose courage and devotion to Mary matched his own. Intelligent and dynamic, she both inspired and reassured, traits that earned her the trust and admiration of men like Lord Montague, Sir Edward Neville and Sir Nicholas Carew. But Henry and Gertrude paid a terrible price for their beliefs and their son continued to pay that price, as his long imprisonment left him unable to cope with the pressures of freedom, ultimately leading to his exile and murder.

Over the winter of 1557 as her sickness worsened, Gertrude looked out from the windows of her manor at Canford; all was cold, reduced, stark, etched with the sharpness of winter. But when she closed her eyes she could remember summer; the vast landscape of open fields and lush foliage, the silken stream, the sounds of birds, splashes, leaves fluttering in the breeze. Her greatest wish had been for Edward to visit her here and her words hang in the air: 'I have been at Canford, the which I do not mislike, no more I think you will when you see it.'[70]

Appendix

The IHS Jewel and a Portrait of Gertrude, Marchioness of Exeter?

On 25 January 1547, an inventory of Princess Mary's jewels was taken. Among them was 'a Ihus set all with Diamonds with three pearls pendant'.[1] IHUS, or IHS, is a monogram representing Christ. This entry noted that it had been 'Restored to the lady markues of Exeeter', revealing she had previously owned it.

In Holbein's sketch and portrait of Jane Seymour, the IHUS brooch she wears on the front of her dress matches the description of Gertrude's brooch very closely. Furthermore, it is the same brooch worn by Catherine of Aragon in Horenbout's miniature of her dated to 1525. If it is the same brooch that was restored to Gertrude in 1547, she may have come into possession of it via a number of ways. Catherine of Aragon may have gifted it to her in gratitude for her service and loyalty, after which the marchioness might have presented it to Jane Seymour following her marriage to Henry VIII. Jane wears it in exactly the same place as Catherine had done in 1525, an appropriate tribute to a woman both she and Gertrude admired. Alternatively, as part of the queen's jewel collection Jane might have given it to Gertrude after becoming queen. Either way, it would have come back into royal hands following the marchioness's arrest, before passing to Princess Mary.

Among Holbein's sketches in the royal collection is an unidentified woman.[2] On her dress she wears a brooch similar to the IHUS brooch, except it has one large pearl pendant. It is not clear whether two further pearls were originally drawn as the sketch has been 'painfully disfigured by rubbing and retouching'.[3] The sitter is a woman of high status, the jewels on her gable hood almost identical to those on Jane Seymour's gable hood in the finished portrait of her referred to above, now held in the Kunsthistorisches Museum. The sitter is attractive with blue grey eyes, dark hair, strong features and a confident expression. As portraits of the Marquis and Marchioness of Exeter must have existed, it is tantalising to wonder whether this is a sketch of Gertrude Courtenay wearing her IHUS brooch, thus capturing her in her late twenties to mid-thirties.

Genealogical Trees

The Royal Descent of the Courtenays

Edward IV
b. 1442
d. 1483
= Elizabeth Woodville
b. c. 1437
d. 1492

Henry VII
b. 1457
d. 1509
= Elizabeth of York
b. 1466
d. 1503

Mary
b. 1467
d. 1482

Cecily, Viscountess Welles
b. 1469
d. 1507

Edward V
b. 1470

Margaret
b. 1472
d. 1472

Richard, Duke of York
b. 1473

Anne, Lady Howard
b. 1475
d. 1511

George
b. 1477
d. 1479

William Courtenay, Earl of Devon
b. c. 1475
d. 1511
= Katharine, Countess of Devon
b. 1479
d. 1527

Bridget, a nun at Dartford Priory
b. 1480
d. c. 1507

Arthur
b. 1486
d. 1502

Margaret, Queen of Scotland
b. 1489
d. 1541

Henry VIII
b. 1491
d. 1547

Mary, Queen of France &
Duchess of Suffolk
b. 1495
d. 1533

Mary I
b. 1516
d. 1558

Elizabeth I
b. 1533
d. 1603

Edward VI
b. 1537
d. 1553

Henry Courtenay, Earl of Devon,
Marquis of Exeter
b. 1498(/99)
exec. 1538

Margaret, Lady Herbert
b. 1498(/99)
b. 1519-1526

Edward
b. c. 1500
d. 1502

Edward Courtenay, Earl of
Devon
b. 1526
d. 1556

This genealogical tree was created using Family Historian genealogy software.

The Pole Descent

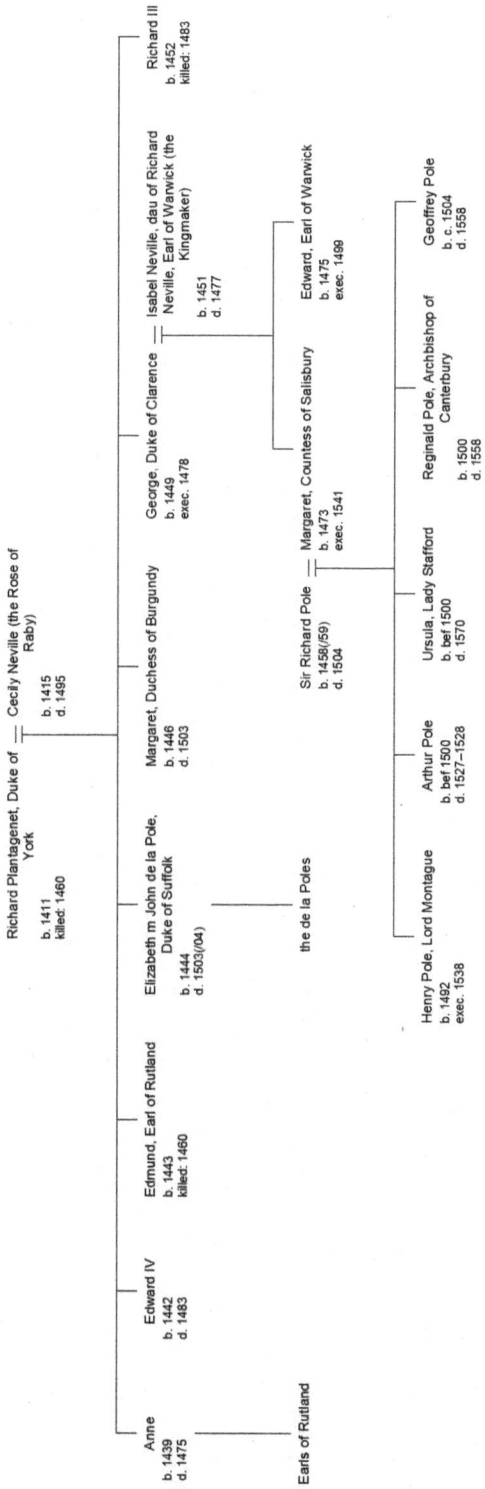

Richard Plantagenet, Duke of York
b. 1411
killed: 1460

Cecily Neville (the Rose of Raby)
b. 1415
d. 1495

Anne
b. 1439
d. 1475

Edward IV
b. 1442
d. 1483

Edmund, Earl of Rutland
b. 1443
killed: 1460

Elizabeth m John de la Pole, Duke of Suffolk
b. 1444
d. 1503/(04)

Margaret, Duchess of Burgundy
b. 1446
d. 1503

George, Duke of Clarence
b. 1449
exec. 1478

Isabel Neville, dau of Richard Neville, Earl of Warwick (the Kingmaker)
b. 1451
d. 1477

Richard III
b. 1452
killed: 1483

Earls of Rutland

the de la Poles

Edward, Earl of Warwick
b. 1475
exec. 1499

Margaret, Countess of Salisbury
b. 1473
exec. 1541

Sir Richard Pole
b. 1458/(59)
d. 1504

Henry Pole, Lord Montague
b. 1492
exec. 1538

Arthur Pole
b. bef 1500
d. 1527–1528

Ursula, Lady Stafford
b. bef 1500
d. 1570

Reginald Pole, Archbishop of Canterbury
b. 1500
d. 1558

Geoffrey Pole
b. c. 1504
d. 1558

This genealogical tree was created using Family Historian genealogy software.

The Grey Descent

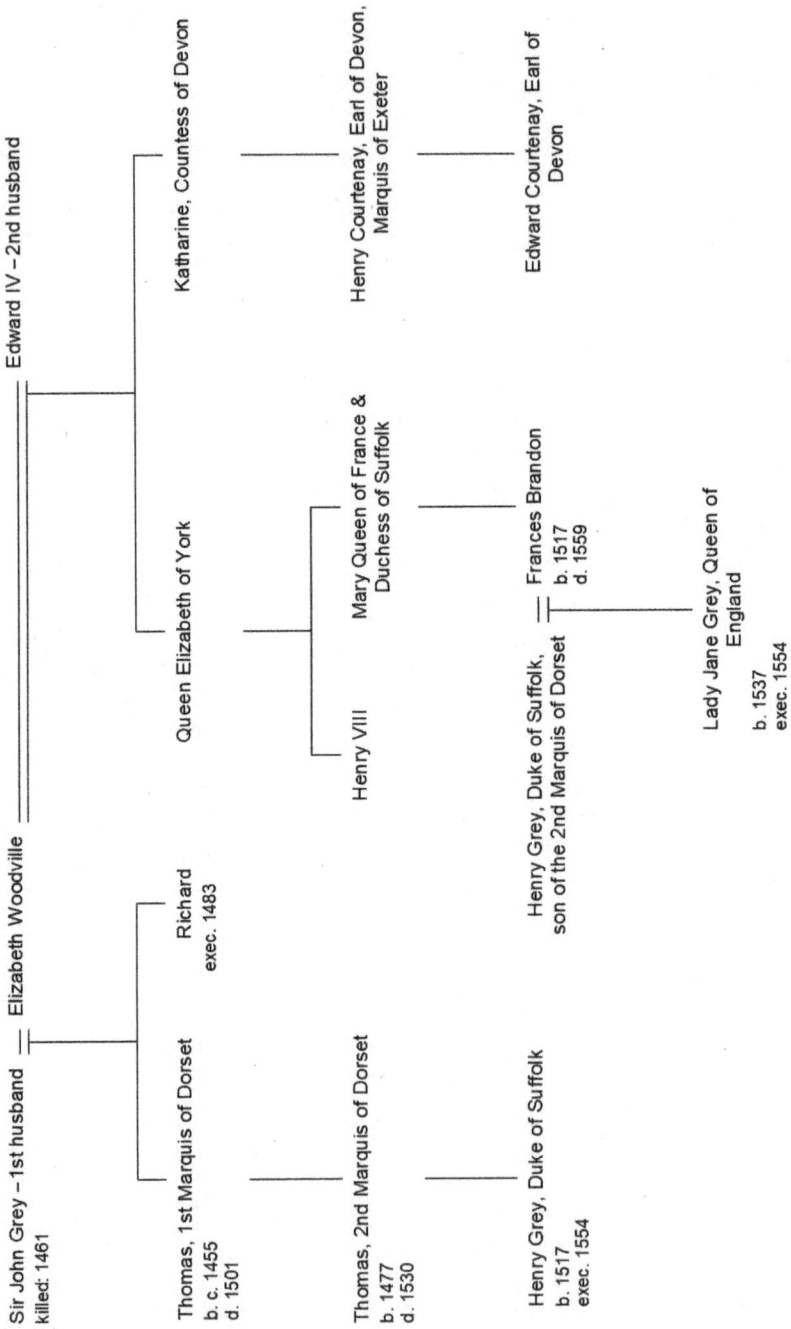

Sir John Grey – 1st husband
killed: 1461

═ Elizabeth Woodville ═

Edward IV – 2nd husband

Richard
exec. 1483

Thomas, 1st Marquis of Dorset
b. c. 1455
d. 1501

Queen Elizabeth of York

Katharine, Countess of Devon

Thomas, 2nd Marquis of Dorset
b. 1477
d. 1530

Henry VIII

Mary Queen of France &
Duchess of Suffolk

Henry Courtenay, Earl of Devon,
Marquis of Exeter

Henry Grey, Duke of Suffolk
b. 1517
exec. 1554

Henry Grey, Duke of Suffolk,
son of the 2nd Marquis of Dorset

Frances Brandon
b. 1517
d. 1559

Edward Courtenay, Earl of
Devon

Lady Jane Grey, Queen of
England
b. 1537
exec. 1554

This genealogical tree was created using Family Historian genealogy software.

The Blount Descent

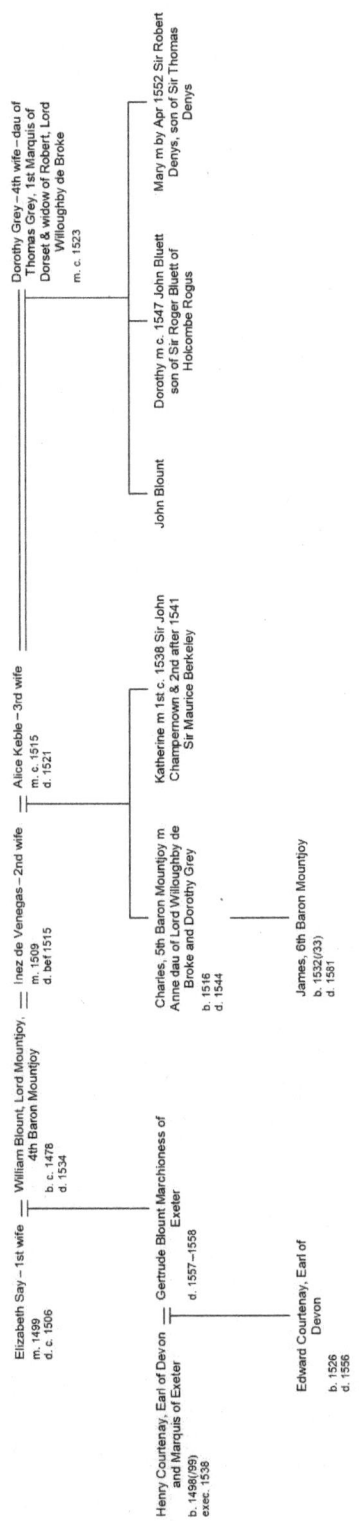

Elizabeth Say – 1st wife
m. 1499
d. c. 1506

William Blount, Lord Mountjoy, 4th Baron Mountjoy
b. c. 1478
d. 1534

Inez de Venegas – 2nd wife
m. 1509
d. bef 1515

Alice Keble – 3rd wife
m. c. 1515
d. 1521

Dorothy Grey – 4th wife – dau of Thomas Grey, 1st Marquis of Dorset & widow of Robert, Lord Willoughby de Broke
m. c. 1523

Henry Courtenay, Earl of Devon and Marquis of Exeter
b. 1498(/99)
exec. 1538

Gertrude Blount Marchioness of Exeter
d. 1557–1558

Charles, 5th Baron Mountjoy m Anne dau of Lord Willoughby de Broke and Dorothy Grey
b. 1516
d. 1544

Katherine m 1st c. 1538 Sir John Champernown & 2nd after 1541 Sir Maurice Berkeley

John Blount

Dorothy m c. 1547 John Bluett son of Sir Roger Bluett of Holcombe Rogus

Mary m by Apr 1552 Sir Robert Denys, son of Sir Thomas Denys

Edward Courtenay, Earl of Devon
b. 1526
d. 1556

James, 6th Baron Mountjoy
b. 1532(/33)
d. 1581

This genealogical tree was created using Family Historian genealogy software.

The Say Descent

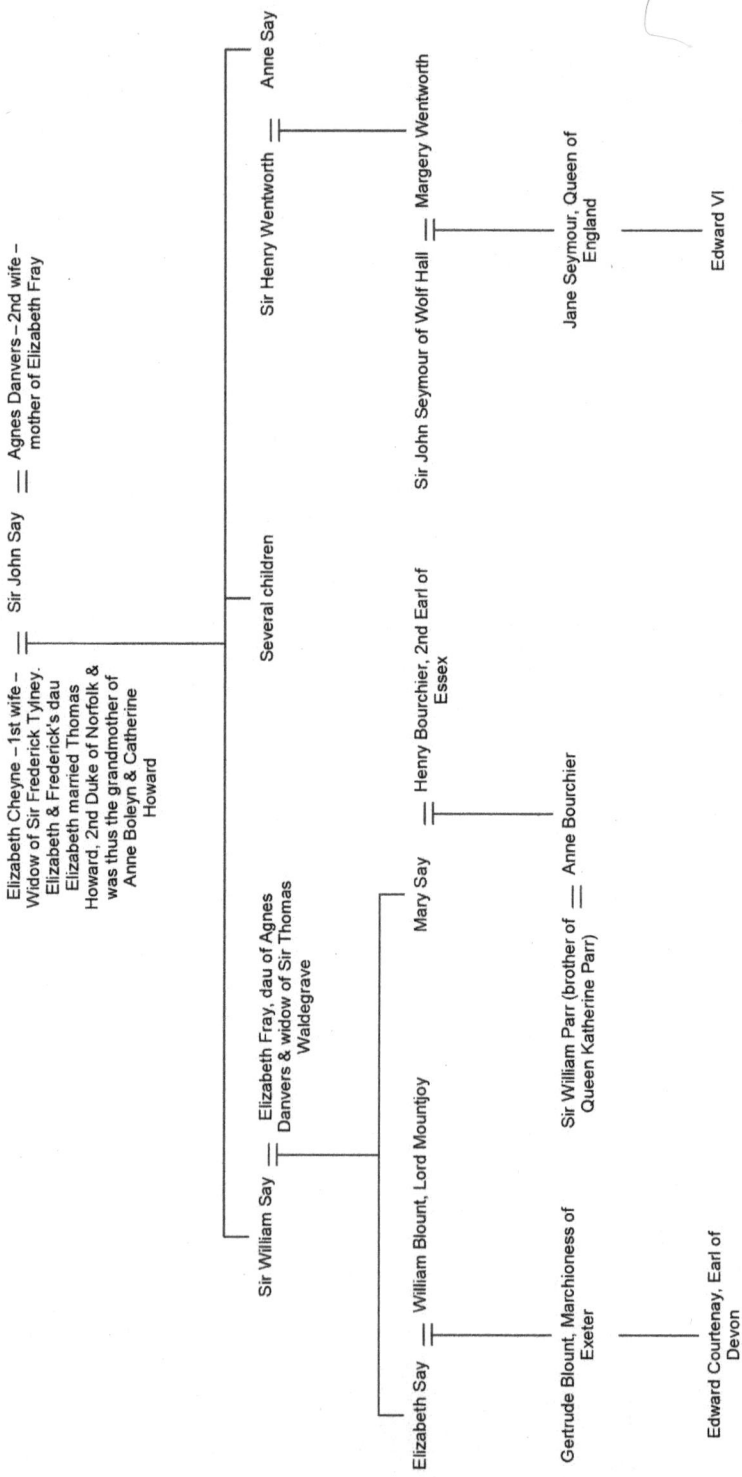

Sir John Say == Elizabeth Cheyne – 1st wife –
Widow of Sir Frederick Tylney.
Elizabeth & Frederick's dau
Elizabeth married Thomas
Howard, 2nd Duke of Norfolk &
was thus the grandmother of
Anne Boleyn & Catherine
Howard

Sir John Say == Agnes Danvers – 2nd wife –
mother of Elizabeth Fray

Sir William Say == Elizabeth Fray, dau of Agnes
Danvers & widow of Sir Thomas
Waldegrave

Several children

Sir Henry Wentworth == Anne Say

Mary Say == Henry Bourchier, 2nd Earl of
Essex

Sir William Parr (brother of == Anne Bourchier
Queen Katherine Parr)

Sir John Seymour of Wolf Hall == Margery Wentworth

Elizabeth Say == William Blount, Lord Mountjoy

Jane Seymour, Queen of
England

Gertrude Blount, Marchioness of
Exeter

Edward Courtenay, Earl of
Devon

Edward VI

This genealogical tree was created using Family Historian genealogy software.

Abbreviations

APC:	*Acts of the Privy Council of England.*
CCR:	*Calendar of the Close Rolls.*
CPR:	*Calendar of the Patent Rolls.*
CSP Dom:	*Calendar of State Papers Domestic Series.*
CSP Foreign:	*Calendar of State Papers Foreign.*
CSP Sp:	*Calendar of State Papers, Spain.*
CSP Ven:	*Calendar of State Papers, Venetian.*
Cokayne:	Cokayne, George Edward, *Complete Peerage of England, Scotland, Ireland, Great Britain and the United Kingdom*, Vols 1–8 (George Bell and Sons, London, 1887–1898).
Conspiracies:	Loades, David, *Two Tudor Conspiracies* (Cambridge University Press, 1965).
Gairdner, *Letters and Papers*:	Gairdner, James, *Letters and Papers Illustrative of the Reigns of Richard III and Henry VII*, Vols 1 and 2 (Longman, Green, Longman, and Roberts, 1861).
Exiles:	Garrett, Christina Hallowell, *The Marian Exiles* (Cambridge University Press, 1966).
Harbison:	Harbison, E. Harris, *Rival Ambassadors at the Court of Queen Mary* (Princeton University Press, 1940).
L&P:	*Letters and Papers, Foreign and Domestic, of the Reign of Henry VIII, 1509–1547*, (eds) Brewer, J.S., Gairdner, J., Brodie, R.H., Vols 1–12 (1862–1910).
LL:	Byrne, Marie St Clare, *The Lisle Letters*, Vols 1–6 (University of Chicago Press, Chicago, 1981).
Materials:	Campbell, William, *Materials for A History of The Reign of Henry VII*, Vols 1–2 (Rolls Series, London, 1873).
'Misfortune':	Bartlett, Kenneth, R., '"The Misfortune That Is Wished for Him": The Exile and Death of Edward Courtenay, Earl of Devon', *Canadian Journal of History*, 14 (1979).
Mackay:	Mackay, Lauren, *Inside the Tudor Court* (Amberley Publishing, Gloucester, 2014).
ODNB:	Oxford Dictionary of National Biography on-line.
PPE:	Nicolas, Harris Nicholas, *Privy Purse Expenses of Elizabeth of York: Wardrobe Accounts of Edward the Fourth* (William Pickering, London, 1830, reprint Frederick Muller Ltd, London, 1972).
Pierce:	Pierce, Hazel, *Margaret Pole, Countess of Salisbury, 1473–1541: Loyalty, Lineage and Leadership* (University of Wales Press, Cardiff, 2003).
VCH:	*Victoria County History.*

State Papers: *State Papers King Henry the Eighth*, Vol. 1, Pts 1 and 2 (John Murray, Albemarle Street, 1831).

TNA: The National Archives.

Westcott: Westcott, Margaret R., 'The Estates of the Earls of Devon, 1485–1538' (MA Diss., Exeter University, 1958).

In most cases spellings have been modernised.

Notes

Chapter 1

1. As Katharine was christened at Eltham she was almost certainly born there. From November 1478 to 11 February 1479 Edward IV was at Eltham on and off, but the longest period he was there was fourteen days between 17 January to 11 February, with just three journeys to Westminster in that period. The longest consecutive period of days he was there was six days between the 24 January and the 4 February, so it is likely that this was due to the birth of his daughter. After 11 February Edward did not return to Eltham for the rest of the year. Ashdown-Hill, John, *The Full Itinerary of Edward IV* (updated edition November 2017). Available for download: https://www.amberley-books.com/pub/media/wysiwyg/The_Full_Itinerary_of_Edward_IV_by_John_Ashdown-Hill_-_revised_29.11.2017.pdf

2. Mancini, Dominic, *The Usurpation of Richard III*, trans. Armstrong, C.A.J. (Alan Sutton Publishing, Gloucester, 1989), p. 65.

3. Jones, Michael (trans. and intro.), *Philippe de Commynes Memoirs The Reign of Louis XI 1461–83* (Penguin Books, Middlesex, 1972), pp. 184, 414.

4. Scofield, Cora L., *The Life and Reign of Edward IV*, Vol. 2 (Fonthill Media Ltd, Stroud, 2016, reprint), pp. 249–250.

5. Laten nails give a neater finish. *PPE*, p. 122. The item appears between 18 April and 29 September 1480.

6. Grose, Francis Astle and Thomas, Edward Jeffrey, The Antiquarian Repertory, Vol. 1 (London, 1807) pp. 305–306. For an account of her sister Bridget's christening at Eltham, which would have been similar to Katharine's, though perhaps with more attendees, see Condon, Margaret M., 'Princess and Nun: Bridget (1480–c.1507), the Youngest Daughter of Edward IV', *The Ricardian*, Vol. 32 (2022), pp. 124–126.

7. *Rymer's Foedera* Volume 12, (ed.) Thomas Rymer (London, 1739–1745), p. 110.

8. Hicks, Michael, *Edward V The Prince in the Tower* (Tempus Publishing Ltd, Gloucestershire, 2003) pp. 66–67; Ross, C., *Edward IV* (Eyre Methuen Ltd, London, 1991), p. 247.

9. *Rymer's Foedera* Volume 12, pp. 110, 148; Quoted in Scofield, *The Life and Reign of Edward IV*, Vol. 2, pp. 253, 329.

10. Mattingly, Garret, *Catherine of Aragon* (Jonathan Cape Publishers, Oxford, 1944), p. 15.

11. McKendrick, Melveena, *Ferdinand and Isabella* (American Heritage Publishing Co. Inc., New York, 1968) p. 95.

12. McKendrick, *Ferdinand and Isabella*, p. 134.

13. Grose and Thomas, *The Antiquarian Repertory*, Vol. 1, p. 306.

14. Scofield, *The Life and Reign of Edward IV*, Vol. 2, pp. 37–38.

15. Dockray, Keith (quoting Colin Richmond) *Edward IV from Contemporary Chronicles, Letters and Records* (Fonthill Media Ltd, Stroud, 2015), p. 213.

16. See Chapter 7.

17. It was claimed that Edward IV had previously promised marriage to Eleanor Butler in order to sleep with her, and once consummated it constituted a valid marriage. He then married widow Elizabeth Woodville in secret in 1464. His intention might have been the same, but when he arrived at the church Elizabeth's mother, a priest and witnesses were present, and the marriage went ahead. The fact that he married Elizabeth in secret without the knowledge of his council gave Gloucester's claims credence. Ashdown-Hill, John, *Eleanor The Secret Queen* (The History Press, Gloucester, 2010), pp. 101–103; 105–106; 135–136; 173–175.
18. Hicks, *Edward V The Prince in the Tower*, pp. 178–179.
19. Pronay, N., and Cox, J. (eds), *The Crowland Chronicle Continuations, 1459–1486* (Richard III and Yorkist History Trust, London, 1986), p. 163.
20. Horrox, R. and Hammond, P.W. (eds), *British Library Harleian Manuscript 433*, Vol. 3 (Richard III Society, London, 1979–1983), p. 190, f. 308b.
21. Strickland, Agnes, *Lives of the Queens of England*, Vol. 2 (Henry Colburn, London, 1854), p. 365.
22. Weir, Alison, *Elizabeth of York: The First Tudor Queen* (Jonathan Cape, London, 2013), pp. 116–117.
23. Sheppard Routh, Pauline '"Lady Scroop Daughter of K. Edward": an Enquiry', *The Ricardian*, Vol. 9, No. 121 (June 1993), pp. 411–412.
24. In 1486 the marriage was annulled after coming before the Consistory Court at York.
25. Hay, Denys (ed. and trans.), *The Anglica Historia of Polydore Vergil A.D. 1485–1537*, Camden Third Series Vol. 74 (London, 1950), p. 3.
26. Levine, Mortimer, *Tudor Dynastic Problems 1460–1571* (George Allen and Unwin Ltd, London, 1973), p. 137.
27. Levine, *Tudor Dynastic Problems*, p. 138.
28. Pierce, pp. 8, 10.
29. *Materials*, Vol. 1, p. 311.
30. Vergil, *The Anglica Historia*, p. 5.
31. *Materials*, Vol. 1, pp. 178–183.
32. *Materials*, Vol. 1, pp. 121–123.
33. Pronay and Cox, *The Crowland Chronicle Continuations*, p. 191.
34. Vergil, *The Anglica Historia*, p. 145; Pollard, A.J. *The Reign of Henry VII from Contemporary Sources*, Vol. 1 (Longmans, Green and Co., 1913), pp. 162, 231; Harvey, Anthony and Mortimer, Richard (eds), *The Funeral Effigies of Westminster Abbey* (The Boydell Press, Suffolk, 1994) pp. 45, 51, 6–7; Howgrave-Graham, R.P., 'The Earlier Royal Funeral Effigies: New Light on Portraiture in Westminster Abbey', *Archaeologia*, Vol. 98 (1961), p. 167. The effigy was supposed to resemble the deceased as closely as possible, including their stature.
35. Hobbins, Daniel (ed. and trans.) André, Bernard, *The Life of Henry VII* (Italica Press, New York, 2011), p. 34.
36. *PPE*, pp. 74–75, 78.
37. Robinson, Joseph Armitage, *Notes and Documents Relating to Westminster Abbey, No.4 The Abbot's House at Westminster* (Cambridge University Press, 1911), pp. 13, 22–23.
38. Henry VII's payment of £200 to his mother on 24 February 1486 who 'of late' had responsibility for the daughters of Edward IV probably signalled the end of that arrangement.
39. Penn, Thomas, *Winter King* (Allen Lane, London, 2011), pp. 21–22.
40. Hearne, Thomas (ed.), *Joannis Lelandi Antiquarii de Rebus Britannicis Collectanea*, Vol. 4 (London, 1770), pp. 204–207.

41. Vergil, *The Anglica Historia*, p. 19.

42. *Materials*, Vol. 2, pp. 142, 148.

43. *CPR*, 1494–1509, p. 369.

44. *Materials*, Vol. 2, pp. 225, 319, 322, 379, 555.

45. Hearne, *Joannis Lelandi Antiquarii*, Vol. 4, p. 249.

46. Conway, Agnes, *Henry VII's Relations with Scotland and Ireland 1485–1498* (Cambridge University Press, 1932), p. 8.

47. Conway, *Henry VII's Relations with Scotland and Ireland*, p. 10.

48. *Rymer's Foedera*, Vol. 12, p. 328.

49. Chalmers, Trevor, Stewart, James, duke of Ross *(ODNB)*.

50. Chalmers, Trevor, James IV *(ODNB)*.

51. Macdougall, Norman, James III *(ODNB)*.

52. Chalmers, James, duke of Ross.

53. Nichols, J., *A Collection of All the Wills Now Known to be Extant, of the Kings and Queens of England ...* (Society of Antiquaries, London, 1780), pp. 350–351.

54. *Vetusta Monumenta*, Vol. 3 (Society of Antiquaries, London, 1796), pp 75.

55. Sutton, Anne F. and Visser-Fuchs, Livia, 'The Royal Burials of the House of York at Windsor: II. Princess Mary, May 1482, and Queen Elizabeth Woodville, June 1492', *The Ricardian*, Vol. 11, No. 44 (March 1999), p. 455.

56. Roger, Euan C., '"To Be Shut Up": New Evidence for the Development of Quarantine Regulations in Early-Tudor England', *Social History of Medicine*, Vol. 33, No. 4 (November 2020) pp. 1081–1083.

Chapter 2

1. Vergil, *The Anglica Historia*, p. 75.

2. Gunn, Steven, J., Warbeck, Perkin [Pierrechon de Werbecque; alias Richard Plantagenet, duke of York] [c. 1473–1499] *(ODNB)*.

3. Nichols, John Gough, *Collectanea Topographica et Genealogica*, Vol. 1 (John Bowyer Nichols and Son, London, 1834), p. 22. The requirements of the indenture of marriage were completed by the Earl of Devon on 3 November 1495 in which Katharine was described as the wife of William Courtenay.

4. Given-Wilson, Chris, Brand, Paul, Phillips, Paul Seymour, Ormrod, Mark, Martin, Geoffrey, Curry, Anne and Horrox, Rosemary (eds), *Parliament Rolls of Medieval England* (Boydell & Brewer, Woodbridge, 2005), No. 17, p. 481.

5. *L&P*, Vol. 9, Item 479.

6. Madox, Thomas, *Formulare Anglicanum: or, a Collection of Ancient Charters and Instruments of Divers Kinds, Taken from the Originals* (Jacob Tonson and R. Knaplock, London 1702, reprinted by ECCO Print Editions) pp. 109–111.

7. *PPE*, p. 99.

8. Thomson, J.A.F., 'The Courtenay Family in the Yorkist Period', *Bulletin of the Institute of Historical Research*, Vol. 45, Issue 112 (November 1972), p. 235.

9. Cokayne, Vol. 3, p. 105.

10. Gunn, Steven, J., Courtenay, Edward, first earl of Devon [d. 1509] *(ODNB)*.

11. Vergil, *The Anglica Historia*, p. 107.

12. Hall, Edward, *Chronicle*, (ed.) Ellis, Henry (London, 1809; reprint published by Andesite Press), p. 484.

13. The Royal Window in Canterbury Cathedral was damaged during the English Civil War and the damaged window described in 1777. The heads of Princess Elizabeth and

Anne were lost, while Katharine, Cecily and Bridget's heads had survived. The hair of all five princesses was described as golden. The heads of the princesses were recorded in water colour in 1789 by Jacob Schnebbelie for the Society of Antiquaries. However, there are some inconsistencies between Schnebbelie's watercolours and other contemporary descriptions of the panels. Therefore, it cannot be regarded as an accurate representation of Katharine, but rather as a representation of the original head, now lost. The window has since been restored. I am extremely grateful to Geoffrey Wheeler for drawing my attention to this and to Elizabeth Dent for all her help and advice regarding the lost heads. Dent, Elizabeth, "'The goodly and glorious window … a piece in it kinde beyond compare": A History of the Royal Window, Canterbury Cathedral (ca. 1482–83)', MA Diss., University of York, 2012); pp. 17, 28–29, 50; Gostling, William, *A Walk in and About The City of Canterbury with Many Descriptions Not to Be Found in Any Description Hitherto Published* (Canterbury, 1777), pp. 339–340.

14. Archaeology Data Service: Oliver, George and Jones, Pitman 'The Will of Katharine, Countess of Devon, Daughter of Edward IV; Dated May 2, 1527', *Archaeological Journal*, Vol. 10 (1853), p. 56. https://archaeologydataservice.ac.uk/library/browse/issue.xhtml?recordId=1139191

15. Hearne, *Joannis Lelandi Antiquarii*, Vol. 4, p. 219.

16. Gairdner, *Letters and Papers*, Vol. 2, p. 291.

17. Starkey, David, *Henry Virtuous Prince* (Harper Press, London, 2008), pp 82–83.

18. Gairdner, *Letters and Papers*, Vol. 1, p. 391.

19. Gairdner, *Letters and Papers*, Vol. 1, p. 227; Fraser, Antonia, *A Survey of London Written in the Year 1598 by John Stowe* (Sutton Publishing, Gloucestershire, 2005), pp. 92, 292–293; Cokayne, Vol. 3, p 63. In 1598 Stowe referred to an ancient house on Warwick Lane which was built by an Earl of Warwick and which was once owned by 'Cecille Duchess of Warwick'. As part of the Warwick inheritance, it was likely in the hands of the crown through the minority of Edward, Earl of Warwick, or after 'the kingmaker's' widow settled her estates on the crown before her death in 1492/1493, enabling Henry VII to grant the use of it to the Earl of Devon.

20. TNA: C 54/ 396: I am very grateful to Dr David Wright for his assistance with the Latin translation of this document relating to the age of Henry Courtenay; Cleaveland, Ezra, *A Genealogical History of the Noble and Illustrious Family of Courtenay* (Exeter 1735; reprint Forgotten Books, London, 2018), p. 247. Cleaveland's work does contain some inaccuracies, but his description of a deed dated 1511–1512 in which Katharine describes her daughter as being aged above 13, correctly identifies the councillors to whom it is addressed, strongly suggesting that this deed existed. Pierce, Hazel, 'Margaret Courtenay, Lady Herbert: Edward IV's Elusive Granddaughter', *The Ricardian*, Vol. 35 (2025, forthcoming).

21. The three points should normally be removed on the death of the father. I am very grateful to Chris Broom and Ann Ballard of The Institute of Heraldic and Genealogical Studies for their advice on the Courtenay arms.

22. Head, David M., *The Ebbs and Flows of Fortune: The Life of Thomas Howard, Third Duke of Norfolk* (The University of Georgia Press, London, 2009), p. 21; Gunn, Steven J., 'The Courtiers of Henry VII', *English Historical Review*, Vol. 108, Issue 426 (January 1993), p. 33.

23. Gunn, S.J., 'The Courtiers of Henry VII, p. 33.

24. Gairdner, *Letters and Papers*, Vol. 1, p. 410.

25. Tremlett, Giles, *Catherine of Aragon: Henry's Spanish Queen* (Faber and Faber, London, 2010), p. 83.

26. He succeeded to the marquessate after his father, Katharine's half-brother, died in August that year.
27. For these celebrations see: Grose and Thomas, *The Antiquarian Repertory*, Vol. 2, pp. 289, 296, 298–299, 302–304, 306–310.
28. Hearne, *Joannis Lelandi Antiquarii*, Vols 4–5, pp. 259–263.

Chapter 3
1. Hall, *Chronicle*, p. 496.
2. Gunn, S.J., 'The Courtiers of Henry VII', *English Historical Review*, 108 (1993), p. 34.
3. Gunn, S.J., Bourchier, Henry, second earl of Essex [1472–1540] *(ODNB)*.
4. Hall, *Chronicle*, p. 495.
5. Cunningham, Sean, Pole, Edmund de la, eighth earl of Suffolk [1472?–1513] *(ODNB)*.
6. Cunningham, Sean, *Henry VII* (Routledge, Oxford, 2007), p. 188.
7. Cunningham, *Henry VII*, p. 188.
8. Cunningham, *Henry VII*, p. 189.
9. *Polydore Vergil*, p. 125.
10. Gairdner, *Letters and Papers*, Vol. 1, pp. 113–114.
11. Cunningham, *Henry VII*, p. 189.
12. *CPR*, 1494–1509, p. 223.
13. Seward, Desmond, *The Last White Rose* (Constable, London, 2010), p. 150.
14. Gairdner, *Letters and Papers*, Vol. 1, p. 134.
15. Gairdner, *Letters and Papers*, Vol. 1, p. 226–227; Hanham, Alison, 'Edmund de la Pole and the Spies, 1499–1509: Some Revisions', *Australian and New Zealand Association of Medieval and Early Modern Studies*, No. 6 (1988), pp. 109–112.
16. Gairdner, *Letters and Papers*, Vol. 1, pp. 183–184.
17. Gairdner, *Letters and Papers*, Vol. 1, p. 284.
18. Buchanan, Patricia Hill, *Margaret Tudor Queen of Scots* (Scottish Academic Press, Edinburgh, 1985), p. 12.
19. *PPE*, p. 25.
20. *PPE*, p. 20.
21. Weir, *Elizabeth of* York, pp. 365, 382.
22. Vergil, *The Anglica Historia*, p. 125.
23. Vergil, *The Anglica Historia*, p. 125.
24. Hall, *Chronicle*, p. 496.
25. *PPE*, p. 17.
26. Strachey, J. (ed.) and others, *Rotuli Parliamentorum*, Vol. 7 (1767–1777), p. i.
27. Orme, Nicholas, Conway, Sir Hugh [c. 1440–1518] *(ODNB)*.
28. Gairdner, *Letters and Papers*, Vol. 1, pp. 231–240.
29. Cokayne, Vol. 3, p. 112.
30. *CPR*, 1555–1557, Vol. 3, p. 164.
31. *CCR, 1500–1509*, Item 885, p. 330.
32. *L&P*, Vol. 1, Item 3324, No. 8.
33. *PPE*, pp. 63, 79, 11, 100, 70, 75–76.
34. Hearne, *Joannis Lelandi Antiquarii*, Vol. 5, pp. 373–374.
35. Weir, *Elizabeth of York*, pp. 389–390.
36. Harris, Barbara J., *Edward Stafford, Third Duke of Buckingham, 1478–1521* (Stanford University Press, California, 1986), pp. 49–50; *PPE*, p. 41.
37. *PPE*, p. 32.

38. *PPE*, p. 77.
39. *PPE*, p. 88.
40. Pollard, A.J. *The Reign of Henry VII from Contemporary Sources*, Vol. 1, p. 231.
41. *PPE*, p 96.
42. Hall, *Chronicle*, p. 497.
43. Grose and Thomas, *The Antiquarian Repertory*, Vol. 4, pp. 241, 242.
44. Penn, *Winter King*, pp. 112–113.
45. Jenkins, Susan and Blessley, Krista 'Royal Wooden Funeral Effigies at Westminster Abbey' *The Burlington Magazine*, 161 (January 2019), pp. 26, 28, 32; St John Hope, W.H., 'On the Funeral Effigies of the Kings and Queens of England', with a 'Note on the Westminster Tradition of Identification' by Robinson, Joseph Armitage, *Archaeologia*, 60 (1907), pp. 550–551; Harvey and Mortimer (eds), *The Funeral Effigies of Westminster Abbey*, p. 48.
46. Today only the head with a reconstructed nose, the top half of the body and the complete left arm survive and can be seen on display in Westminster Abbey.
47. An Angel was a gold coin with a depiction of St Michael, the archangel, on one side. Significantly, the Angel was introduced to the English coinage by Elizabeth and Katharine's father, Edward IV.
48. Grose and Thomas, *The Antiquarian Repertory*, Vol. 4, pp. 242–250.
49. Penn, *Winter King*, p. 113.
50. TNA: LC 2/1, 75v; Starkey, *Virtuous Prince*, p. 309.
51. *L&P*, Vol. 4, Item 1939, p. 863.
52. Starkey, *Virtuous Prince*, pp. 172–173.
53. Starkey, *Virtuous Prince*, pp. 118–119, 170.
54. BL: Add. MS 7099, f. 83 (payments), 1503: The Chamber Books of Henry VII and Henry VIII, 1485–1521: https://www.dhi.ac.uk/chamber-books/
55. Palgrave, Francis (ed.), *The Antient Kalendars and Inventories of the Treasury of his Majesty's Exchequer*, Vol. 3 (London, 1836), p. 395, items 17 and 23.
56. Starkey, *Virtuous Prince*, p. 310.
57. Hampton, W.E., 'The White Rose Under the First Tudors Part 2. Edmund de la Pole', *The Ricardian*, Vol. 7, No. 98 (September, 1987), p. 474.
58. Nichols, J.G. (ed.), *The Chronicle of Calais*, Camden Series, Vol. 35 (1846, reprinted Alpha Editions, 2019), pp. 5–6.
59. Nichols, *The Chronicle of Calais*, p. 6.
60. In August 1507 Katharine's sister Cecily died while her youngest sister Bridget died before 19 December. On that day Henry VII authorised the payment of 46 shillings and eight pence 'for a marblestone bought to lay upon my lady Bridget within the choir of Dartford'. E36/214 f. 111v: The Chamber Books of Henry VII and Henry VIII, 1485–1521: https://www.dhi.ac.uk/chamber-books/search/search.

Chapter 4
1. Penn, *Winter King*, p. 341.
2. *L&P*, Vol. 1, 11 (10).
3. Gunn, Courtenay, Edward, first earl of Devon (*ODNB*).
4. TNA: PROB11/16/15.
5. Starkey, *Virtuous Prince*, p. 278
6. Thomas, A.H., and Thornley, I.D. (eds), *The Great Chronicle of London* (1938) (Alan Sutton Publishing, Gloucester, repr. 1983), pp. 339–340.

7. *L&P*, Vol. 1, 82.
8. Jones, Michael K., and Underwood, Malcolm G., *The King's Mother* (Cambridge University Press, 1992), p. 236.
9. BL: Add. MS 21481, f.8v.
10. *L&P*, Vol. 1, 158 (19, 20).
11. *L&P*, Vol. 1, 104; *L&P*, Vol. 1, 158 (75).
12. TNA: SP/1/2, f.67.
13. BL: Harley MS. 69, f.5v; *L&P*, Vol. 1, Item 467, Appendix 9, Item 9.
14. Anglo, Sydney, *Spectacle, Pageantry, and Early Tudor Policy* (Oxford, 1869), p. 112; Anglo, Sydney, *The Great Tournament Roll of Westminster: A Collotype Reproduction of the Manuscript* (Oxford, 1968), pp. 51–52.
15. Anglo, *The Great Tournament Roll of Westminster*, pp. 52–53, 54.
16. Thomas and Thornley, *The Great Chronicle of London*, p. 370.
17. Anglo, *The Great Tournament Roll of Westminster*, pp. 54, 88; 89–90.
18. Anglo, *The Great Tournament Roll of Westminster*, pp. 113–114. William Courtenay also jousted against Henry Guildford and the earl of Wiltshire, but as these tilts were shared with Edward Neville it is difficult to know which scores belong to William and which to Neville.
19. Anglo, *The Great Tournament Roll of Westminster*, pp. 55, 115.
20. Anglo, *The Great Tournament Roll of Westminster*, p. 58.
21. *L&P*, Vol. 1, Item 734.
22. Westcott, p. 43, n. 3.
23. *L&P*, Vol. 1, Item 520.
24. *L&P*, Vol. 1, Item 749 (23).
25. Starkey, *Virtuous Prince*, p. 311.
26. Riordan, Michael, Englefield, Sir Thomas [1455–1514] *(ODNB)*.
27. Westcott, p. 90.
28. Hall, *Chronicle*, p. 520; Anglo, *The Great Tournament Roll of Westminster*, pp. 58–59.
29. *Polydore Vergil*, p. 126. The symptoms described above are those of pleurisy, which William must have experienced.
30. Westcott, pp. 89, 301.
31. Westcott, pp. 96, 100.
32. College of Arms: MS ff: 13.33b–13.35; 13.96–13.96b; I15.138–I15.140v. I am very grateful to Michael Peter Desmond O'Donoghue, *York Herald*, for his assistance with these sources.
33. College of Arms: MS f.13.35.

Chapter 5
1. *L&P*, Vol. I, Item 1083 (2).
2. BL: Lansdowne MS 978/98, f. 111v. *PPE*, p. xxvii.
3. *L&P*, Vol. 1, Item 3435.
4. *L&P*, Vol. 1, Item 3325.
5. Hall, *Chronicle*, p. 570.
6. Loades, David, *Mary Rose* (Amberley Publishing, Gloucester, 2012), p. 80.
7. Hall, *Chronicle*, p. 570.
8. *L&P*, Vol. 1, Item 3357.
9. Loades, *Mary Rose*, p. 84.
10. *L&P*, Vol. 1, Item 3387.

11. Loades, *Mary Rose*, pp. 92–94.
12. *L&P*, Vol. 1, Items 3334, 3435.
13. *L&P*, Vol. 2, Item 227.
14. *L&P*, Vol. 2, Item 222.
15. *L&P*, Vol. 2, Item 224.
16. In 1503 Brandon abandoned his betrothed, Anne Browne, who was pregnant with his child, in order to marry her much wealthier aunt, Margaret Mortimer, twenty years his senior. After financially plundering Margaret's lands, he had the marriage annulled and married Anne Browne who died in 1510. His flirtation with Margaret of Austria in 1513 caused a European scandal. Gunn, Steven J., *Charles Brandon, Duke of Suffolk, 1484–1545* (Basil Blackwell Ltd, London, 1988), pp. 28–30; Watkins, Sarah-Beth, *The Tudor Brandons* (Chronos Books, Hants, 2016), pp. 24–25, 28, 30–31.
17. *L&P*, Vol. 1, Item 1524 (5).
18. *L&P*, Vol. 1, Item 2537; Gunn, *Charles Brandon*, p. 20.
19. *L&P*, Vol. 1, Item 1948 (68).
20. *L&P*, Vol. 1, Items 2654, 2941.
21. *L&P*, Vol. 2, Items 660; 696.
22. Westcott, pp. 216–217.
23. *L&P*, Vol. 2, p. 1487.
24. Westcott, p. 217; CR/668: Description included in the on-line catalogue, Devon Heritage Centre.
25. *L&P*, Vol. 2, Item 696.
26. Gunn, *Charles Brandon*, p. 38.
27. Westcott, pp. 215–218.
28. Nicholas, Harris Nicolas, *Report on the Proceedings on the Claim to the Barony of L'isle, in the House of Lords* (William Pickering, Stevens and Sons, London, 1829), p. 12.
29. Gunn, *Charles Brandon*, p. 23.
30. *CPR*, 1494–1509, p. 486.
31. *L&P*, Vol. 1, Item 257 (40).
32. TNA: PROB 11/17/337.
33. TNA: PROB 11/17/293.
34. *L&P*, Vol. 1, Item 1602 (12); *L&P* Vol. 1, Item 1662 (26).
35. *L&P*, Vol. 3, Item 152.
36. Cleaveland, *A Genealogical History of the Noble and Illustrious Family of Courtenay*, p. 247.
37. *L&P*, Vol. 2, Item 167.
38. Ross, James, *The Foremost Man of the Kingdom: John de Vere, Thirteenth Earl of Oxford (1442–1513)* (The Boydell Press, Suffolk, 2015), p. 149.
39. Hearne, *Joannis Lelandi Antiquarii*, Vol. 4, p. 206.
40. Ross, *The Foremost Man of the Kingdom*, p. 158–160.
41. Cokayne, Vol. 6, p. 168.
42. *L&P*, Vol. I, Item 2964 (80).
43. Crawford, Anne, 'The Mowbray Inheritance', *The Ricardian*, Vol. 5, No. 73 (June, 1981), fn. 5, p. 339.
44. Gunn, *Charles Brandon*, p. 39.
45. *L&P*, Vol. I, Item 2964 (80).
46. Ross, *The Foremost Man of the Kingdom*, p. 160.
47. Clark, Nicola, *Gender, Family and Politics: The Howard Women, 1485–1558* (Oxford University Press, 2018), pp. 66–71, 69; Ellis, Henry (ed.), Transcript of an order made

by Cardinal Wolsey, as Lord Chancellor, for the regulation of the household expenses, and general management of the affairs of the young Earl of Oxford ...' *Archaeologia*, Vol. XIX (1821), pp. 62–65.

48. *L&P*, Vol. I, Item 3617; the dispensation was needed because bride and groom were descended from Jaquetta of Luxembourg and Richard Woodville, the great-grandparents of both.

49. Hughes, Jonathan, Somerset [formerly Beaufort], Charles, first earl of Worcester [c. 1460–1526] *(ODNB)*.

50. Pierce, p. 29.

51. Westcott, p. 215.

52. TNA: PROB11/16/15.

53. *L&P*, Vol. 2, Revel Accounts, pp. 1500, 1502.

54. Samman, Neil, 'The Henrician Court During Cardinal Wolsey's Ascendancy c. 1514–1529' (PhD Diss., Bangor University, 1988), p. 333.

55. She signed it 'By your aw … humble Dought … Margaret Courte…y'.

56. Clark, *Gender, Family and Politics*, p. 83.

57. TNA: PROB 11/16/15.

58. TNA: PROB 11/17/293.

59. *L&P*, Vol. 2, Revel Accounts, p. 1500.

60. There was a tradition that a monument to a deceased lady in Colyton Church, Devon, was that of Margaret. However, it has since been shown that the tomb is that of Margaret Courtenay, née Beaufort, wife of Thomas Courtenay fifth Earl of Devon. Radford, G.H., 'The Courtenay Monument in Colyton Church' *Report and Transactions of the Devonshire Association for the Advancement of Science, Literature, and Art*, Vol. 39 (July 1907), pp. 143–155.

61. *L&P*, Vol. 3, Item 152, pp. 49, 50.

62. *L&P*, Vol. 3, Item 152, p. 51.

63. In June 1520 three of the French king's gentlemen visited Henry VIII's daughter Princess Mary. One of the ladies attending the princess was 'the lady [Margaret], wife to the lord Herbert, countess of Worcester'. Margaret's name has been included in the abridged version of this letter printed in the *Letters and Papers*, but in the original manuscript it is blank. On balance the lady was more likely to be Margaret Courtenay's step-mother-in-law Eleanor, Countess of Worcester. *L&P*, Vol. 3, Item 896; Pierce, 'Margaret Courtenay, Lady Herbert: Edward IV's Elusive Granddaughter'.

64. Margaret Westcott has understandably assumed that the payment of 8s for the transport of four horses from Katharine to 'Mistress Margaret' in London in 1524 referred to her daughter. However, this was actually one of Katharine's servants who was known as Mistress Margaret, and who had been sent to Henry Courtenay's residence in London in 1524. Mistress Margaret was still serving Katharine in 1527 by which time Katharine's daughter had died. Furthermore, Margaret Courtenay's correct title was Lady Herbert and this is how her brother referred to her in 1519. Westcott, p. 257; TNA: E36/223, f. 38r, f. 33r; TNA: SP 1/46, f. 52.

65. Russell, Gareth, *Young, and Damned and Fair: The Life and Tragedy of Catherine Howard at the Court of Henry VIII* (William Collins, London, 2018), pp. 337, 343.

66. *Polydore Vergil*, p. 265.

67. Head, *The Ebbs and Flows of Fortune*, p. 21.

68. He ends a letter to Cromwell warning that if she is sent to him it 'might give me occasion to handle her otherwise than I have done yet'. Head, *The Ebbs and Flows of Fortune*, p. 252.

69. *L&P*, Vol. 20, Pt 2, Item, 496 (18); Cokayne, Vol. 6, p. 50.

70. BL: Cotton MS Titus B, fol. 390r–v, quoted in Clark pp. 85–86; *L&P*, Vol. 12, Pt 2, Item 976.

71. *L&P*, Vol. 2, Item 1573.

Chapter 6

1. Westcott, p. 98. The grant was a lease of lands and tenements in West Coker, Somerset, part of the earldom lands and therefore in Katharine's ownership.

2. Samman, 'The Henrician Court During Cardinal Wolsey's Ascendancy', pp. 74–76.

3. Westcott, Margaret R., 'Katherine, countess of Devon [1479–1527]' (*ODNB*).

4. Westcott, p. 54.

5. Westcott, p. 100; Baker, J.H., Pollard, Sir Lewis [d. 1526] (*ODNB*).

6. Westcott, pp. 96, 99, 100; Prince, John, *The Worthies of Devon* (London, 1810), p. 710.

7. *Statutes of the Realm*, Vol. 2 (London, 1816, reprinted 1963); Westcott, p. 46.

8. Charles Brandon, Duke of Suffolk also brought twelve cases. Westcott, pp. 100, 203; Rawcliffe, Carole, *The Staffords, Earls of Stafford and Dukes of Buckingham 1394–1521* (Cambridge University Press, 2008), p. 175.

9. *L&P*, Vol. 3, Item 2994 (27).

10. Westcott, p. 20.

11. Rodger, N.A.M., *The Safeguard of the Sea: A Naval History of Britain, 660–1649* (Penguin Books, London in association with the National Maritime Museum, 2004), p. 204.

12. *L&P*, Vol. 1, list 4, p. 751 does not include the number of men provided. List 3, p. 750, does provide the number but incorrectly ascribes 200 men to 'Lord Devon'. List 4 clearly states that men were provided by 'the Countess of Devon'.

13. *L&P*, Vol. 1, Item 3614, p. 1518.

14. *L&P*, Vol. 4, Item 895 (11), p. 391.

15. Breverton, Terry, *The Tudor Kitchen* (Amberley Publishing, Gloucester, 2017), p. 11.

16. *L&P*, Vol. 4, Item 771; TNA: E36/233; *L&P*, Vol. 3, Item 3370; TNA: SP1/28; *L&P*, Vol. 4, Item 3759; SP1/46, ff. 44–49. Where other sources are used these will be referenced.

17. https://www.tivertoncastle.com/index.php. The castle is open to the public and accommodation is available.

18. Westcott, p. 99; Westcott, Margaret, 'Surveying the Estates of Henry Courtenay, Earl of Devon, Marquis of Exeter and Traitor, 1543–4', in Gray, Todd, *Devon Documents, Devon & Cornwall Notes & Queries, Special Issue* (1996), p. 201.

19. Dugdale, James, *The New British Traveller*, Vol. 2 (London 1819, reprinted by General Books, Memphis, USA, 2012), p. 186.

20. Historic England: https://historicengland.org.uk/listing/the-list/list-entry/1384869?section=official-list-entry

21. Westcott, Margaret, 'Katherine Courtenay, Countess of Devon, 1479–1527', in Gray, Todd, Rowe, Margery and Erskine, Audrey (eds), *Tudor and Stuart Devon The Common Estate and Government: Essays Presented to Joyce Youings* (University of Exeter Press, 1992), p. 24; Westcott, p. 99; Westcott, 'Surveying the Estates of Henry Courtenay, Earl of Devon', p. 201.

22. Breverton, *The Tudor Kitchen*, pp. 47, 48, 12.

23. Westcott, p. 67.

24. Chandler, John, *John Leland's Itinerary: Travels in Tudor England* (Alan Sutton Publishing, Gloucestershire, 1998), p. 123.

25. *L&P*, Vol. 13, Pt 2, Item 354.

26. Lynn, Eleri, *Tudor Fashion* (Yale University Press, London, in association with Historic Royal Palaces, 2017), pp. 44, 47.
27. Westcott, pp. 304, 301.
28. Williams, Paul, 'The Trading Community of Exeter 1470–1570 with special reference to Merchants and Tailors Vol. 2 of 2 (PhD Thesis, University of Exeter, 2020), p. 453.
29. Lynn, *Tudor Fashion*, pp. 125–29, 173, 131.
30. Davidson, James, *The History of Newenham Abbey in the County of Devon* (Longman & Co., London, 1843), p. 97.
31. Pamela Y. Stanton, 'Sir John [iii] Arundell of Lanherne (*c.*1474–1545)', in 'Arundell family (*per.* 1435–1590)', *ODNB*; *LL*: Vol. 1, p. 307.
32. AR/24/17 via TNA Discovery: https://discovery.nationalarchives.gov.uk/details/r/3c15733e-0835-46db-a204-371dad60e892
33. Orme, Nicholas, Veysey [*formerly* Harman], John [c. 1464–1554] *(ODNB)*.
34. Worthy, Charles, *Devonshire Wills: A Collection of Annotated Testamentary Abstracts* (Bemrose & Sons Ltd, London, 1896), pp. 478, 481.
35. Westcott, p. 302
36. Baggs, A.P. and Bush, R.J.E., 'Parishes: Dowlish Wake', in *A History of the County of Somerset:* Vol. 4, (ed.) Dunning, R.W. (*VCH*, London, 1978), pp. 151–156; Orme, Nicholas, 'Sir John Speke and his Chapel in Exeter Cathedral', *The Devonshire Association for the Advancement of Science, Literature and Art, Report and Transactions*, Vol. 118 (1986), p. 28.
37. *L&P*, Vol. 2, Item 4570.
38. Westcott, pp. 52, 302, 304.
39. The lordship or manor of Marshwood traditionally formed part of the queen's jointure. In 1540 it would be granted to Anne of Cleves on her marriage to Henry VIII. *L&P*, Vol. 1, Item 94 (35), p. 49; *L&P*, Vol. 15, Item 144 (2), p. 52.
40. In the *Letters and Papers* edited version of her accounts, it states that she had three fools, Dick, Mug and Kit, but the words 'the fools' were mistaken for the word 'Kit'. Furthermore, references throughout her accounts never make mention of more than two fools. *L&P*, Vol. 4, Item 771.
41. Henry, Lord Daubenay, held lands in the west country including Somerset which were within proximity of Katharine's estates.
42. Sim, Alison, *Pleasures and Pastimes in Tudor England* (Sutton Publishing, Gloucester, 1999), p. 183.
43. History of Parliament: Carent, William [d. 1476], of Toomer in Henstridge, Somerset: https://www.historyofparliamentonline.org/volume/1386–1421/member/carent-william-1476
44. *Materials*, Vol. 2, p. 439.
45. Speight, Helen M., '"The Politics of Good Governance": Thomas Cromwell and the Government of the Southwest of England', *The Historical Journal*, Vol. 37, No. 3 (Sept. 1994), p. 631.
46. Westcott, 'Katherine Courtenay' in *Tudor and Stuart Devon*, p. 31.
47. Challen, W.H., 'Lady Anne Grey', *Notes and Queries*, Vol. 10, Issue 1 (January 1963), pp. 5–9.
48. Prince, *The Worthies of Devon*, p. 555.
49. Pierce, pp. 186–189.
50. *PPE*, p. 6; Westcott, pp. 78, 94; SP 1/138, f. 113.
51. Webb, Simon, *The History of Richard III by Thomas More* (Langley Press, Durham, 2015), p. 17.

Chapter 7

1. Oliver and Jones, 'The Will of Katharine, Countess of Devon', pp. 53–57.
2. Tremlett, *Catherine of Aragon*, p. 257.
3. Mattingly, *Catherine of Aragon*, p. 196.
4. Tremlett, *Catherine of Aragon*, pp. 263–264.
5. Tremlett, *Catherine of Aragon*, p. 238.
6. An earlier will, likely drawn up in 1515, survives in the National Archives: E 210/10166. Unlike the will signed in 1527, this will directed 'a tombe to be upon our burial or nigh there unto'. Another inclusion here, missing from the 1527 will, was the instruction to pray for the souls of 'all our brothers and sisters'. Katharine, alone of her sisters, is the only one known to have planned such a remembrance for their brothers, the princes in the Tower. Pierce, Hazel, 'A Remembrance of the Sons of Edward IV by their Sister Katharine Courtenay, Countess of Devon', *The Ricardian*, Vol. 35 (2025, forthcoming).
7. TNA: SP 1/46, f. 46.
8. TNA: SP 1/46, f.48.
9. Quoted in Starkey, David, *Six Wives: The Queens of Henry VIII* (Random House, London, 2003), p. 213.
10. *L&P*, Vol. 4, Item 3786.
11. Ives, Eric, *The Life and Death of Anne Boleyn* (Blackwell Publishing, Oxford, 2006), p. 111.
12. Sylvester, R.S., and Harding, Davis P., *Two Early Tudor Lives* (Yale University Press, London, New Haven, Connecticut, 1969), p. 69.
13. *L&P*, Vol. 4, Item 3563.
14. *CSP*, Sp, Vol. 3, Pt 2, Item 571, p. 822.
15. Murphy, Virginia, 'The Literature and Propaganda of Henry VIII's First Divorce', in MacCulloch, D. (ed.), *The Reign of Henry VIII: Politics, Policy and Piety* (Macmillan Press Ltd, London, 1995), p. 144.
16. College of Arms: Coll. Arm. MS I15 ff: 133v–137v. The account of Katharine's funeral.
17. The herald has recorded him as Sir John Speke, but this is an error.
18. History of Parliament on-line: https://www.historyofparliamentonline.org/volume/1509-1558/member/carew-george-1505-45
19. History of Parliament on-line: https://www.historyofparliamentonline.org/volume/1509-1558/member/champernon-%28chamberlain-chamborne%29-sir-arthur-1524-78
20. Pierce, pp. 59, 73, 81, 157; History of Parliament on-line: https://www.historyofparliamentonline.org/volume/1509-1558/member/carew-george-1505-45.
21. *L&P*, Vol. 4, Item 895 (11), p. 391.
22. TNA: E/36/223.
23. Cooper, J.D.P., Carew, Sir George [c. 1504–1545] *(ODNB)*. This reveals that Lady Joan Carew was alive in 1527.
24. History of Parliament on-line: https://www.historyofparliamentonline.org/volume/1509-1558/member/carew-george-1505-45.
25. TNA: E/36/223. In June 1524 Katharine sent her a buck.
26. In the inventory of Katharine's possessions at Tiverton in 1527, a saddle for Mug the fool was recorded.
27. In her will, Katharine directed that 'our body to be buridd in the new Chapell lately edefyed and bylded in the southe side of the churche of Seynt Peter, of Tyverton'. The Greenway chapel was built in 1517 on the south side of St Peter's Church, while the

Chapel of our Blessed Lady, the Courtenay chapel, was built much earlier and was located outside the church. It was described by Risdon in the seventeenth century as being 'in the Churchyard'. Welsford, A.E., *John Greenway 1460–1529 Merchant of Tiverton and London A Devon Worthy* (Tiverton, 1984), pp. 7, 18.

28. Oliver and Jones, 'The Will of Katharine, Countess of Devon', p. 56.
29. Pierce, pp. 92–96.
30. Mattingly, *Catherine of Aragon*, p. 11.

Chapter 8

1. Warrants to the Great Wardrobe, BL: Add. MS. 18,826, f.10; Add. MS. 18,826, f.19, dated 26 March 1511 described Henry as 'our right trusty and wellbeloved servant'; BL: Add. MS. 18,826, f.30; *L&P*, Vol. 1, Items 986, 1199.
2. Allen, P.S and H.M., *Letters of Richard Fox* (The Clarendon Press, Oxford, 1929), pp. 68–69. Katharine had asked Fox whether the king wished Henry to stay with her or go overseas. As Henry did not go, the king must have refused, and her request may have been calculated to ensure her son accepted her decision without complaint.
3. *L&P*, Vol. 1, Item 2227.
4. *L&P*, Vol. 3, Item 2612.
5. *L&P*, Vol. 3, Item 311.
6. *State Papers*, Vol. 1, Pt 1, p. 7.
7. *L&P*, Vol. 3, Item 386.
8. For the above see Walker, Greg, 'The 'Expulsion of the Minions' of 1519 Reconsidered', *The Historical Journal*, Vol. 32, No. 1 (March 1989), pp. 14, 10, 13, 8.
9. *L&P*, Vol. 2, Item 4409. A list survives of those included in the embassy but Henry Courtenay is not among them. As a cousin of the king, he would have been the most high-profile person there and named if he had been present. Other individuals included his relations and friends such as Lord Montague and Arthur Pole, Thomas Manners and Lord Leonard Grey, and this perhaps added to the confusion.
10. *L&P*, Vol. 3, Item 152.
11. *L&P*, Vol. 3, Items 14, 23; Brown, Rawdon, *Four Years at the Court of Henry VIII, Sebastian Giustinian*, Vol. 1 (Smith, Elder & Co, London, 1854), pp. 251, 253.
12. Although this would have been difficult as 134 ladies actually attended, the smaller number who directly served the queen and dined in her presence chamber with the King of France would all have been expected to be beautiful. Tremlett, *Catherine of Aragon*, p. 227; Richardson, Glenn, *The Field of Cloth of Gold* (Yale University Press, London, 2020), p. 146.
13. Starkey, *Virtuous Prince*, p. 62.
14. The ballad had Say, as one of those doomed to share Suffolk's fate, speak the following lines 'manus tue fecerunt me' ['Thy hands have made and fashioned me']. Nicholls, Francis Morgan, *The Hall of Lawford Hall* (London, 1891), pp. 126–127.
15. Roskell, J.S., *Parliament and Politics in Late Medieval; England*, Vol. 2 (The Hambledon Press, London, 1981), pp. 153, 160, 158, 169, 153.
16. Nicholls, *Lawford Hall*, pp. 151, 153.
17. TNA: PROB 11/6/459.
18. Nicholls, *Lawford Hall*, p. 135.
19. Kirby, J.L., Say [Fynys], Sir John [d. 1478] *(ODNB)*.
20. Nicholls, *Lawford Hall*, p. 163.

21. Bayne, C.G., completed by Dunham, William Hulse, *Select Cases in the Council of Henry VII* (Selden Society, London, 1958), p. xxi.
22. Roskell, *Parliament and Politics*, pp. 170–171.
23. *CCR, 1485–1500*, p. 23; *Materials*, Vol. 2, p. 398; *CCR, 1500–1509*, pp. 88, 314; *CPR, 1485–1494*, p. 387.
24. Fortescue, Thomas, Lord Clermont, *A History of the Family of Fortescue in all its Branches*, second edition (London, 1880), pp. 241, 242, 243.
25. Pollard, *The Reign of Henry VII from Contemporary Sources*, Vol. 2, p. 78.
26. Nicholls, *Lawford Hall*, p. 164.
27. Gairdner, James (ed.), *The Paston Letters* (Alan Sutton Publishing Ltd, Gloucester, 1983), Vol. 5, pp. 216–218.
28. Two sons who died young were also born to William, but it is not clear whether they were the sons of Genevieve or Elizabeth. TNA: PROB 11/24/102; C 142/10/29: IPM Elizabeth Say, late the wife of William Say: Essex. TNA on-line catalogue.
29. Gunn, Steven J., 'Henry Bourchier, Earl of Essex [1472–1540]' in Bernard, George W. (ed.), *The Tudor Nobility* (Manchester University Press, 1992), p. 145; TNA: C1/335/92, Blount v Bourchier, confirms that Elizabeth was the eldest daughter.
30. *CCR, 1485–1500*, p. 238.
31. Gunn, 'Henry Bourchier', in Bernard (ed.), p. 145.
32. Gunn, 'Henry Bourchier', in Bernard (ed.), p. 146.
33. TNA: C1/335/92: Blount v Bourchier.
34. *L&P*, Vol. 9, Item 481.
35. *PPE*, p. 29.
36. *CCR, 1500–1509*, p. 239.
37. TNA: PROB 11/25/473.
38. Horrox, Rosemary, Blount, Walter, first Baron Mountjoy [d. 1474] *(ODNB)*.
39. *Materials*, Vol. 2, p. 237.
40. Nicholls, *Lawford Hall*, pp. 207–208.
41. Starkey, *Virtuous Prince*, p. 129.
42. Borman, Tracy, *The Private Lives of the Tudors* (Hodder & Stoughton, London, 2017), p. 53.
43. Mackay, pp. 29, 95.
44. Carley, James P., Blount, Charles, fifth Baron Mountjoy [c. 1516–1544] *(ODNB)*.
45. Cokayne, Vol. 8, p. 150.
46. *L&P*, Vol. 3, p. 1358; Samman, 'The Henrician Court During Cardinal Wolsey's Ascendancy', p. 355.
47. *L&P*, Vol. 3, pp. 1539, 1551.
48. *L&P*, Vol. 11, Item 1217 (6).
49. Gertrude was sometimes referred to as 'the young countess of Devon' to distinguish her from her mother-in-law.
50. For the above account of the Field of the Cloth of Gold see: Richardson, *The Field of Cloth of Gold*, pp. 132, 210, 216.
51. *L&P*, Vol. 3, Item 906.
52. *L&P*, Vol. 3, Items 491, 528.
53. *L&P*, Vol. 4, Item 3105, p. 1407.
54. *CSP*, Ven, Vol. 4, No. 105.
55. *CSP*, Ven, Vol. 4, No. 188.

56. *L&P*, Vol. 5, Item 927; Miller, Helen, *Henry VIII and the English Nobility* (Basil Blackwell Ltd, Oxford, 1989), p. 85. In the *L&P* the marquis is identified as Dorset. This is incorrect as Thomas Grey, second Marquis of Dorset, died in 1530 and his son was only fifteen in 1532.

57. *A Collection of Ordinances and Regulations for the Government of the Royal Household* (Society of Antiquaries, London, 1790), p 154.

58. *L&P*, Vol. 3, Items 894, 901. In these two letters written 1 and 4 July 1520, Sir Richard Wingfield, English ambassador to France, asked Wolsey to request the king to remember Henry Courtenay's counterpart in France 'who is in the King's chamber here'. On 31 May 1521, as part of investigations into the Duke of Buckingham's treason, a letter was sent to the king's council addressed 'To my lord of Devonshire, his good lordship, … and to other of the King's most noble council'. *L&P*, Vol. 3, Item 1320.

59. Westcott, pp. 56, 238, 239.

60. *L&P*, Vol. 3, Items 2992 (3); 3062 (26).

61. For a description of the stannaries and how they worked see Westcott, pp. 223–224.

62. TNA: STAC 2/4/42.

63. *L&P*, Vol. 4, Item 2445.

64. *L&P*, Vol. 3, Item 2415 (6).

65. *L&P*, Vol. 3, Item 2415; Miller, *Henry VIII and the English Nobility*, p. 122; Institute of Historical Research, Reviews in History: Dr Hannes Kleineke, review of Justice and Grace: Private Petitioning and the English Parliament in the Late Middle Ages (review no. 665): https://reviews.history.ac.uk/review/665

66. Anstis, J. (ed.), *The Register of the Most Noble Order of the Garter* (1724), pp. 288–289; Harris, *Edward Stafford, Third Duke of Buckingham*, p. 187.

67. *L&P*, Vol. 4, Item 1792; Samman, 'The Henrician Court During Cardinal Wolsey's Ascendancy', p. 77.

68. *CSP*, Ven, Vol. 4, No. 682.

69. TNA: E 326/11649; *L&P*, Vol. 13, Item 754.

70. Whitley, Catrina Banks and Kramer, Kyra, 'A New Explanation for the Reproductive Woes and Midlife Decline of Henry VIII', *The Historical Journal*, Vol. 53, No. 4 (December, 2010), pp. 836, 837–838. Other symptoms include physical and mental decline which typically become manifest around the age of forty. They propose that this explains the deterioration in Henry's character from the 1530s demonstrated by his increasing paranoia and cruelty.

71. TNA: SP 1/80: The confession of Elizabeth Barton, the Nun of Kent.

72. TNA: E36/223; *L&P*, Vol. 4, Item 969 (2).

73. Clutterbuck, Robert, *The History and Antiquities of the County of Hertford*, Vol. 2 (London, 1821), p 134.

74. *L&P*, Vol. 4, Item 1792; Samman, 'The Henrician Court During Cardinal Wolsey's Ascendancy', p. 75.

75. TNA: SP/1/138, ff. 103 left, 115 left. Virginals had a keyboard and sound was produced by the plucking of strings, a regale was a small portable organ and a viol had five to seven strings and was played using a bow.

76. TNA: SP/1/138, ff. 111 right, 102 left, 115 right.

77. TNA: SP/1/138, ff. 105 left, 114 left.

78. TNA: SP/1/138, f. 95 right.

79. TNA: SP/1/138, f. 103 right.

80. TNA: SP/1/138, f. 112 left.

81. TNA: SP/1/138, ff. 105 right, 105 left.
82. *State Papers*, Vol. 1, Pt 1, CXLVIII, p. 302; CLVII, pp. 312–13.

Chapter 9
 1. Mackay, p. 62; Tremlett, *Catherine of Aragon*, p. 308.
 2. *CSP*, Sp, Vol. 4, Pt 2, No.1047.
 3. *CSP*, Sp, Vol. 4, Pt 2, No. 1073.
 4. Tremlett, *Catherine of Aragon*, p. 335.
 5. Quoted in Mackay, p. 98.
 6. Quoted in Pierce, p. 133.
 7. *CSP*, Sp, Vol. 4, Pt 1, No. 354. Chapuys' letter refers to the wife of the 'young Marquis'. As the only other marquis in England at this time was in his fifties, this must refer to Henry Courtenay's wife.
 8. West Horsley Place is owned by a charitable trust dedicated to repairing and conserving the landscape and buildings. Details of events and how to visit can be found on their website: https://www.westhorsleyplace.org/
 9. *L&P*, Vol. 13, Pt 2, Item 804, sixth examination of Sir Geoffrey Pole.
 10. Mackay, p. 119.
 11. Hawkyard, Alasdair, Neville, Sir Edward [b. in or before 1482, d. 1538] (*ODNB*); TNA: SP/1/138, f. 101 right.
 12. Lehmberg, Stanford, Carew, Sir Nicholas [b. in or before 1496, d. 1539] (*ODNB*.
 13. Chibi, Andrew A., Stokesley, John [1475–1539] *(ODNB)*.
 14. Starkey, David, *The English Court: From the Wars of the Roses to the Civil War* (Longman, London, 1987), p. 107; Ives, *The Life and Death of Anne Boleyn*, p. 109.
 15. At the time of Wolsey's fall, Chapuys identified Norfolk, Suffolk and Thomas Boleyn as 'the King's most favourite courtiers, and the nearest to his person … who transact all state business', Exeter is not mentioned. *CSP*, Sp, Vol. 4, Pt 1, No. 135; In 1546 Norfolk wrote about a conversation he had with Wolsey at Esher in 1529 in which Wolsey told him 'he had gone about fourteen years to have destroyed me; … by the setting upon of my lord of Suffolk, the marquis of Exeter, and my lord Sands; who said often to him, that if he found not the means to put me out the way, at length I should surely undo him'. It would date Wolsey's claim to 1515 when Exeter was only 16 or 17 years old and rather young to be used in intrigues against Norfolk. The most credible interpretation is that Exeter warned Wolsey about Norfolk's enmity. Burnet, Gilbert, *The History of the Reformation of the Church of England*, Vol. 6 (The Clarendon Press, Oxford, 1865), p. 277; finally, as Wolsey's political life hung by a thread in September and October 1529, Exeter did all he could to help him meet the king's demand to remove the Prior of Trywydreath from his position. Oliver, George, *Monasticon Dioecesis Exoniensis* (Longman, Brown, Green & Longmans, London, 1846), pp. 45–47; Orme, Nicholas, *VCH of Cornwall*, Vol. 2 (Institute of Historical Research, 2010), p. 294.
 16. *CSP*, Sp, Vol. 4, Pt 1, No. 354; Ives, *Anne Boleyn*, p. 135.
 17. *L&P*, Vol. 5, Item 238.
 18. *CSP*, Sp, Vol. 4, Pt 2, Item756.
 19. *L&P*, Vol. 13, Pt 2, Items 802; 804.
 20. Speight, '"The Politics of Good Governance"', p. 634.
 21. For Kendall see *L&P*, Vol. 8, Items 359, 224, 569; *L&P*, Vol. 5, Item 837.
 22. Because he was claiming that his daughter Princess Mary was illegitimate.
 23. *CSP*, Sp, Vol. 4, Pt 2, Item 788.

24. Cokayne, Vol. 5, p. 400.
25. *L&P*, Vol. 13, Pt 2, Item 961; Rose-Troup, Frances, *The Western Rebellion of 1549* (London, 1913, reprinted Forgotten Books, London, 2018), p. 25.
26. *CSP*, Ven, Vol. 4, Item 694.
27. Miller, *Henry VIII and the English Nobility*, pp. 64–65.
28. Ives, *Anne Boleyn*, p. 140.
29. Geoffrey's mother later testified that if Montague had not prevented him, Geoffrey 'would have gone in warfare' but she did not know in whose service. In 1535 Chapuys informed the emperor that long ago Geoffrey had told him 'that he wished to go to Spain' but Chapuys dissuaded him 'believing the service he might render to Your Majesty would be next to nothing when compared with the damage that might result to him and his people in case of discovery'. *L&P*, Vol. 13, Pt 2, Item 818; *CSP*, Sp, Vol. 5, Pt 1, No 165.
30. *L&P*, Vol. 13, Pt 2, Item 804, sixth examination of Sir Geoffrey Pole.
31. *CSP*, Sp, Vol. 4, Pt 2, No. 1024; Knecht, R.J., *Francis I* (Cambridge University Press, 1988), pp. 226–227.
32. Mackay, p. 95.
33. TNA: SP/1/80, ff. 142–145. The Confession of Dame Elizabeth Barton.
34. Mackay, p. 93.
35. Pierce, p. 103.
36. TNA: SP/1/80, ff. 142–145. The Confession of Dame Elizabeth Barton.
37. *State Papers*, Pt 2, pp. 398, 400.
38. *LL*: Vol. 1, No. 34, p. 515.
39. *CSP*, Sp, Vol. 4, Pt 2, No. 1127.
40. *State Papers*, Pt 2, pp. 408–409.
41. *L&P*, Vol. 13, Pt 2, Item 830, p. 342.
42. *L&P*, Vol. 6, Item 1468.
43. Wood, M.A.E., *Letters of Illustrious Ladies of Great Britain*, Vol. 2 (London, 1846), pp. 98–101.
44. Exeter had been at Horsley when the nun visited, recovering from the sickness which had prevented him from attending Anne Boleyn's coronation. Gertrude's servant, Constance Bontayne, stated in 1538 that she didn't know if Exeter was at Horsley when the nun was there, then admitted that 'on better remembrance' he was at Horsley and testified to gossip in the house concerning the nun's words. *L&P*, Vol. 13, Pt 2, Item 802.
45. Watt, Diane, 'Barton Elizabeth [*called* the Holy Maid of Kent, the Nun of Kent] (c. 1506–1534)] (*ODNB*).
46. Pierce, pp. 101–102.
47. Tremlett, *Catherine of Aragon*, p. 388; *State Papers*, Pt 2, p. 417.
48. *L&P*, Vol. 7, Item 83.
49. Chambers, R.W., *Thomas More* (The Harvester Press, Sussex, 1981), p. 304.
50. *L&P*, Vol. 7, Items 690, 726; *CSP*, Sp, Vol. 5, Pt 1, No, 68.
51. *L&P*, Vol. 7, Item 257.
52. *L&P*, Vol. 13, Pt 2, Item 804, seventh examination of Sir Geoffrey Pole.
53. Pierce, p. 112.
54. *L&P*, Vol. 7, Item (22) 1498; *CSP*, Sp, Vol. 5, No. 109; Mackay, p. 122.
55. *LL*, Vol. 2, Nos. 412, 419; Vol. 4, No. 836.
56. *CSP*, Sp, Vol. 5, Pt 1, No. 156; Whitley and Kramer, 'Reproductive Woes', p. 831.
57. *L&P*, Vol. 8, Item 1105.

58. *CSP*, Sp, Vol. 5, Pt 1, No. 156.
59. *L&P*, Vol. 9, Item 766.
60. *L&P*, Vol. 9, Item 776.
61. *CSP*, Sp, Vol. 5, Pt 1, Nos. 229, 230.
62. *CSP*, Sp, Vol. 5, Pt 2, No. 1.

Chapter 10
1. TNA: PROB/11/7/374. The will of John Blount, grandfather of Gertrude Courtenay.
2. *L&P*, Vol. 13, Pt 2, Item 779.
3. *CSP*, Sp, Vol. 5, Pt 2, No. 3.
4. Mackay, p. 154.
5. *CSP*, Sp, Vol. 5, Pt 2, No. 9.
6. *CSP*, Sp, Vol. 5, Pt 2, No.13.
7. *L&P*, Vol. 10, Items 282, 495.
8. Norton, Elizabeth, *Jane Seymour Henry VIII's True Love* (Amberley Publishing, Gloucester, 2009), p. 18; Loades, David, *Jane Seymour: Henry VIII's Favourite Queen* (Amberley Publishing, Gloucester, 2013), p. 31.
9. *CSP*, Sp, Vol. 5, Pt 2, No. 43.
10. *CSP*, Sp, Vol. 5, Pt 2, No. 47.
11. *CSP*, Sp, Vol. 5, Pt 2, No. 61.
12. *CSP*, Sp, Vol. 5, Pt 2, No. 48.
13. For the fall of Anne Boleyn see Ives, *The Life and Death of Anne Boleyn*, pp. 307–308, 313.
14. *L&P*, Vol. 10, Item 601.
15. *CSP*, Sp, Vol. 5, Pt 2, No. 55.
16. Ives, *The Life and Death of Anne Boleyn*, p. 317.
17. *L&P*, Vol. 11, Item 7.
18. *L&P*, Vol. 14, Pt 1, Item 190.
19. *L&P*, Vol. 13, Pt 2, Item 979 (15, 17).
20. Pierce, pp. 106–107; *L&P*, Vol. 10, Item 975.
21. Dodds, M.G. and R., *The Pilgrimage of Grace and the Exeter Conspiracy*, Vol. 1 (Cambridge University Press, 1915), pp. 241, 243.
22. MacCulloch, D., *Thomas Cromwell: A Life* (Penguin Books, London, 2018), p. 385.
23. *L&P*, Vol. 11, Item 755.
24. *L&P*, Vol. 11, Item 776.
25. *L&P*, Vol. 11, Item 793.
26. *L&P*, Vol. 11, Item 800.
27. *L&P*, Vol. 11, Item 822.
28. *L&P*, Vol. 13, Pt 2, Item 765.
29. Quoted in Dodds, *The Pilgrimage of Grace and the Exeter Conspiracy*, Vol. 1, pp. 259–260.
30. *L&P*, Vol. 11, Item 887.
31. *L&P*, Vol. 11, Item 1217 (6); Miller, *Henry VIII and the English Nobility*, p. 234.
32. *L&P*, Vol. 13, Pt 2, Item 804, Sir Geoffrey Pole's fifth examination.
33. Pierce, pp. 112–113.
34. Childs, Jessie, *Henry VIII's Last Victim: The Life and Times of Henry Howard Earl of Surrey* (Jonathan Cape, London, 2006), pp. 114–115.
35. *L&P*, Vol. 12, Pt 2, Item 51.
36. *LL*, Vol. 3, Nos. 798, 818, Vol. 4, No. 910.
37. Mayer, T.F., Pole, Reginald [1500–1558] (*ODNB*).

38. *L&P*, Vol. 13, Pt 2, Items 766, 804 second examination of Sir Geoffrey Pole.
39. *L&P*, Vol. 13, Pt 2, Item 804 third examination of Sir Geoffrey Pole.
40. *L&P*, Vol. 13, Pt 2, Items 828, 2, examination of Morgan Wells, 829, 2, examination of John Collins.
41. *L&P*, Vol. 13, Pt 2, Item 765.
42. *L&P*, Vol. 13, Pt 2, Items 797, 804 fifth examination of Sir Geoffrey Pole.
43. *L&P*, Vol. 13, Pt 2, Item 827, 1, examination of John Collins.
44. *L&P*, Vol. 13, Pt 2, Items 772, 804 third examination of Sir Geoffrey Pole.
45. *L&P*, Vol. 11, Item 860.
46. *L&P*, Vol. 12, Pt 2, Item 973, iii.
47. *LL*, Vol. 4, No. 870.
48. Madden, Frederick, *Privy Purse Expenses of the Princess Mary* (London, 1831, reprinted by Forgotten Books, London, 2015), p. 14.
49. *L&P*, Vol. 12, Pt 2, Item 242.
50. *L&P*, Vol. 12, Pt 2, Item 298.
51. Pierce, pp. 112–113.
52. *State Papers*, Pt 2, pp. 570–571.
53. Wood, *Letters of Illustrious Ladies*, Vol. 2, p. 263.
54. *L&P*, Vol. 12, Pt 2, Item 1060.
55. *L&P*, Vol. 12, Pt 2, Item 1151, 2.
56. A bearward took care of bears and other animals, training them for displays of entertainment such as dancing and baiting etc.
57. *L&P*, Vol. 13, Pt 2, Item 804, 4, examination of Sir Edward Neville.
58. *L&P*, Vol. 13, Pt 2, Item 961, 2.
59. Baker, J.H., Montagu, Sir Edward [1480s–1557] *(ODNB)*.
60. *L&P*, Vol. 13, Pt 1, Item 358.
61. *L&P*, Vol. 13, Pt 1, Item 371.

Chapter 11

1. *L&P*, Vol. 13, Pt 1, Item 852. Lawford was the nearest of the Exeters' Say properties to Claydon in Suffolk, where the letter describing these events was written.
2. The History of Parliament on-line, Hull, John II [by1503–49], of Larkbeare, Devon: https://www.historyofparliamentonline.org/volume/1509–1558/member/hull-john-ii-1503-49
3. TNA: E36/223.
4. *L&P*, Vol. 13, Pt 1, Item 1192.
5. Pierce, pp. 117–121.
6. *L&P*, Vol. 13, Pt 2, Items 771, iii, 804, fourth examination of Sir Geoffrey Pole; Pierce, p. 137.
7. Mayer, T.F., Helyar, John, [1502/3–1541?] *(ODNB)*; Mayer, T.F., Crofts [Croft], George [d. 1539?] *(ODNB)*.
8. Blanchard, Ian, Gresham, Sir Richard [c. 1485–1549] *(ODNB)*; *L&P*, Vol. 12, Pt 1, Item 817; Pierce, p. 124; The History of Parliament on-line, Gresham, Sir Richard [by 1486–1549], of London: https://www.historyofparliamentonline.org/volume/1509-1558/member/gresham-sir-richard-1486-1549
9. Murphy, B., *Bastard Prince Henry VIII's Lost Son* (Sutton Publishing, Gloucestershire, 2001), p. 75.
10. *L&P*, Vol. 13, Pt 2, Item 217.

11. Pierce, pp. 122–124.
12. Quoted in Pierce, p. 137.
13. Pierce, p. 128.
14. *L&P*, Vol. 13, Pt 2, Item 695, 3. No. 36.
15. Quoted in Pierce, pp. 128–129.
16. *L&P*, Vol. 13, Pt 2, Item 796.
17. *L&P*, Vol. 13, Pt 2, Item 804, third examination of Sir Geoffrey Pole.
18. *L&P*, Vol. 13, Pt 2, Item 702, No. 1, 2.
19. *L&P*, Vol. 13, Pt 2, Item 702, No. 3.
20. Hamilton, William Douglas, *A Chronicle of England During the Reigns of the Tudors by Charles Wriothesley, Windsor Herald*, Vol. 1 (Camden Society 1875), p. 88.
21. *L&P*, Vol. 13, Pt 2, Item 804, fourth examination of Sir Geoffrey Pole.
22. *L&P*, Vol. 13, Pt 2, Items 765, 6 Nov, 695, No. 2.
23. *L&P*, Vol. 13, Pt 2, Items 772, 802, 829, No. 2, 827, No. 3, 828, No. 2.
24. TNA: SP/1/138, f. 113 right.
25. *L&P*, Vol. 13, Pt 2, Items 779, 827, No. 3, ii, 772, 956.
26. *L&P*, Vol. 13, Pt 2, Items 804, fifth and seventh examinations of Sir Geoffrey Pole, 830, 5, ii, No. 4, 955, 6, 11; *CSP*, Sp, Vol. 5, Pt 2, 43a.
27. Pierce, p. 136.
28. *L&P*, Vol. 13, Pt 2, Items 817, 797, No. 4, 802, 702, Nos, 2, 3, 827, No. 1.
29. *L&P*, Vol. 13, Pt 2, Item 771, iii.
30. TNA: SP/1/138 f. 116 left. Mrs Couper referred to George Gatte as one Gates.
31. TNA: SP/1/138 f. 111 right. Elys was also yeoman and groom of the marquis' chamber and held several positions as bailiff.
32. *L&P*, Vol. 13, Pt 2, Item 820, No. 1.
33. *L&P*, Vol. 13, Pt 2, Item 961, No. 2. This document is very mutilated and much is illegible.
34. *L&P*, Vol. 13, Pt 2, Item 979, Nos. 15, 17.
35. *L&P*, Vol. 13, Pt 2, Item 979, Nos. 7, 11.
36. *L&P*, Vol. 13, Pt 2, Item 979, No. 5.
37. Pierce, pp. 156–157.
38. *L&P*, Vol. 13, Pt 2, Item 986, No. 6.
39. Hamilton, *A Chronicle of England During the Reigns of the Tudors by Charles Wriothesley*, p. 92.
40. Pierce, pp. 142–143.
41. Knecht, *Francis I*, p. 292.
42. Pierce, pp. 160, 161.
43. Pierce, pp. 164.
44. *L&P*, Vol. 13, Pt 2, Item 1134.
45. *LL*, Vol. 5, p. 285, 286.
46. *CSP*, Ven, Vol. 5, No. 806.
47. *L&P*, Vol. 13, Pt 2, Item 732.

Chapter 12
1. *L&P*, Vol. 13, Pt 2, Item 805, No. 7.
2. *L&P*, Vol. 14, Pt 1, Item 290, No. 3.
3. MacCulloch, *Thomas Cromwell*, p. 474; Webb, Peter, 'John and Jasper Horsey – Two Tudor Opportunists, Part 1' *Proceedings of the Dorset Natural History and Archaeological Society*, Vol. 100 (1978, published 1979), p. 29.

4. She served Gertrude throughout her imprisonment in the Tower and as her testimony did not make her a traitor in Gertude's eyes, then neither should Horsey's.
5. *L&P*, Vol. 13, Pt 2, Item 827, No. 2.
6. Webb, 'John and Jasper Horsey', Part 2', pp. 24, 25.
7. *L&P*, Vol. 14, Pt 1, Item 37; TNA: SP/1/138, f. 95 right.
8. *L&P*, Vol. 14, Pt 1, Item 403 (60).
9. *L&P*, Vol. 15, Items 733 (11), 942 (58).
10. *L&P*, Vol. 15, Item 937; SP/1/138, f. 109 right.
11. *L&P*, Vol. 19, Pt 1, Item 864.
12. *L&P*, Vol. 21, Pt 1, Item 643, f. 58, p. 311.
13. *L&P*, Vol. 14, Pt 2, Item 189.
14. *L&P*, Vol. 14, Pt 1, Item 290, Nos. 3, 8.
15. *L&P*, Vol. 14, Pt 1, Item 280.
16. Hamilton, *A Chronicle of England During the Reigns of the Tudors by Charles Wriothesley*, p. 93.
17. *L&P*, Vol. 14, Pt 1, Item 532.
18. *L&P*, Vol. 14, Pt 1, Item 37.
19. *L&P*, Vol. 14, Pt 1, Item 806.
20. *L&P*, Vol. 21, Pt 2, Item 554.
21. *L&P*, Vol. 14, Pt 1, Item 867, Cap. 15.
22. *L&P*, Vol. 14, Pt 1, Items, 1091, 989.
23. *L&P*, Vol. 13, Pt 2, Item 1176.
24. *L&P*, Vol. 14, Pt 2, Item 780 (32).
25. *L&P*, Vol. 16, Item 380; *L&P*, Vol. 15, Item 436 (87).
26. TNA: SP/1/164, f. 108, L; *L&P*, Vol. 15, Item 686.
27. James, Susan, Parr, Anne [née Bourchier], seventh Baroness Bourchier [1517–1571] *(ODNB)*.
28. *L&P*, Vol. 14, Pt 1, Item 651 (52).
29. Madden, *Privy Purse Expenses of the Princess Mary*, pp. 111, 145.
30. *L&P*, Vol. 8, Item 802 (10, 11).
31. TNA: SP/1/130, f. 105.
32. If the letter referred to Katharine's biological mother, Alice Kebel, rather than her stepmother this would mean the plate and jewels were secretly delivered to Exeter no later than 1521 when Alice Kebel died, and when Lord Mountjoy was still alive, which seems unlikely. Furthermore, no evidence of lands assigned for this purpose has been found.
33. Sil, Narasingha P., Denny, Sir Anthony [1501–1549] *(ODNB)*. Trim, D.J.B., Champernowne, Henry [1537/8–1570] *(ODNB)*.
34. Riordan, Michael, Henry VIII, privy chamber of [act. 1509–1547] *(ODNB)*.
35. TNA: PROB 11/40/8: The will of Gertrude Courtenay, Marchioness of Exeter.
36. TNA: PROB 11/30/653. The will of Charles, Lord Mountjoy.
37. The History of Parliament on-line, Blount, Sir Richard [by 1506–64], of Mapledurham, Oxon. and Dedisham, nr. Slinfold, Suss: https://www.historyofparliamentonline.org/volume/1509–1558/member/blount-sir-richard-1506-64
38. *APC*, Vol. 2, p. 104; Vol. 3, p. 235; Vol. 4, p. 206.
39. Submitted to Thomas Goodrich, Bishop of Ely and Chancellor of England. He assumed the chancellorship on this date, meaning the action must have taken place afterwards. Heal, Felicity, Goodrich [Goodryck], Thomas [1494–1554] *(ODNB)*.

40. TNA: C/1/1298, ff. 42, 43, 44, 45.
41. *L&P*, Vol. 15, Item 487.
42. Pierce, p. 178.
43. *LL*, Vol. 6, p. 176.
44. *L&P*, Vol. 16, Item 1011.
45. *L&P*, Vol. 17, Item 880, f. 44.
46. *L&P*, Vol. 21, Pt 2, Item 775, ff. 96, 97.
47. *APC*, Vol. 1, p. 447.
48. *CSP*, Sp, Vol. 8, Nos. 199, 275.
49. TNA: SP/1/225, ff. 21 left, 22.
50. *L&P*, Vol. 21, Pt 2, Item 475, No. 78.
51. *CSP*, Sp, Vol. 9, pp. 192–206.
52. *CSP*, Sp, Vol. 9, pp. 45–53.
53. Babington, Churchill, intro., *The Benefit of Christ's Death* (Bell & Daldy, London, 1855), dedication to the Duchess of Somerset.
54. Armstrong, C.D.C., Gardiner, Stephen [1495x8–1555] *(ODNB)*.
55. Armstrong, Gardiner, Stephen *(ODNB)*.
56. Loach, Jennifer, *Edward VI* (Yale University Press, London, 2002), pp. 161–162.

Chapter 13
1. Elton, G.R., *England Under the Tudors* (Methuen & Co. Ltd, 1971), p. 215; Harbison, p. 58; Overell, M. Anne, 'Nicodemite's Progress: Edward Courtenay', in *Nicodemites: Faith and Concealment Between Italy and Tudor England* (Brill, Leiden, 2018), p. 101.
2. Edwards, J., *Mary I England's Catholic Queen* (Yale University Press, 2011), pp. 98–99.
3. Nichols, J.G. (ed.), *The Chronicle of Queen Jane*, Camden Society, Vol. 49 (1850, reprinted Alpha Editions, 2019), p. 14.
4. MacCulloch, D., 'The Vitae Mariae Angliae Reginae of Robert Wingfield of Brantham', *Camden Miscellany*, XXVIII, Camden Fourth Series, Vol. 28 (1983), p. 271.
5. *CSP*, Sp, Vol. 11, pp. 150–162, 109–127.
6. Edwards, *Mary I England's Catholic Queen*, p. 149.
7. *CSP*, Sp, Vol. 11, pp. 48–56.
8. The painter has been identified as Antwerp artist Stephen van der Meulen. It is dated, but not certainly, to 1568. As Edward was resident in Brussels in 1555 and did visit Antwerp, it may have been painted at that time. The inscription to the right of Edward refers to his imprisonment, release by Mary and the suspicion in which he was held. The plaster cast is in the National Portrait Gallery. Strong, Roy, *The English Icon: The Elizabethan and Jacobean Portraiture* (The Paul Mellon Foundation for British Art, London, 1969), pp. 119, 120, 130.
9. *CSP*, Ven, Vol. 5, No. 934; Quoted in Muller, James Arthur, *Stephen Gardiner and the Tudor Reaction* (Macmillan & Co. Ltd, London, 1926), p. 236.
10. *CSP*, Sp, Vol. 11, pp. 109–127.
11. *CSP*, Sp, Vol. 11, pp. 162–176.
12. Hughes, Jonathan, Rochester, Sir Robert [c. 1500–1557] *(ODNB)*; Loomie, A.J., Englefield, Sir Francis [1522–1596] *(ODNB)*; Weikel, Ann, Waldegrave, Sir Edward [1516/17–1561] *(ODNB)*.
13. *CSP*, Sp, Vol. 11, pp. 162–176.
14. *CSP*, Sp, Vol. 11, pp. 183–197.
15. *CSP*, Sp, Vol. 11, pp. 211–229.

16. Gunn, Steven J., 'A Letter of Jane, Duchess of Northumberland, in 1553', *The English Historical Review*, Vol. 114, Issue 459 (November 1999), p. 1270.
17. *CSP*, Sp, Vol. 11, pp. 197–211; James, Parr, Anne [née Bourchier] (*ODNB*).
18. Sil, Narasingha P., Herbert, William, first earl of Pembroke [1506/7–1570] (*ODNB*); *CSP*, Sp, Vol. 11, pp. 183–197.
19. *CPR*, 1553–1554, p. 170.
20. *APC*, Vol. 4, p. 339.
21. Westcott, p. 71.
22. *CPR*, 1553–1554, pp. 250–257; Archer, Ian W., Courtenay, Edward, first earl of Devon [1526–1556] (*ODNB*).
23. Strype, John, *Ecclesiastical Memorials*, Vol. 3, Pt 1 (Oxford, 1822), pp. 53–54, 57.
24. *CPR*, 1553–1554, pp. 81–82.
25. *CSP*, Sp, Vol. 11, pp. 308–316; Leyde, A., *Ambassades de Messieurs de Noailles en Angleterre*, Vol. 2 (1763), p. 219.
26. *CSP*, Sp, Vol. 11, pp. 352–363.
27. *CSP*, Sp, Vol. 11, pp. 250–261, fn. 11.
28. *CSP*, Sp, Vol. 11, pp. 197–211.
29. *CSP*, Sp, Vol. 11, pp. 352–363.
30. *CSP*, Sp, Vol. 11, pp. 302–308, fn. 8.
31. *CSP*, Sp, Vol. 11, pp. 238–250; Pierce, p. 183.
32. *CSP*, Sp, Vol. 11, pp. 302–308; 285–302.
33. Leyde, *Ambassades de Messieurs de Noailles*, pp. 219–220.
34. Simon Renard reported on 4 November that Edward had 'been three times to see Inglefield and ask whether he feels well enough to go to Court; for Inglefield has a fever and is melancholy because his wife has left him and is now living a carnal life. This keeps him in his house, out of which he has not ventured for several days; and the air is very cold and variable.' Although this letter was written on 4 November, three weeks after Noailles' letter, and suggests that Englefield was currently keeping to his house, it might not be the incident referred to by Noailles. However, it could represent the on-going deterioration of Edward and Englefield's relationship. *CSP*, Sp, Vol. 11, pp. 331–337.
35. *CSP*, Sp, Vol. 11, pp. 285–302.
36. *CSP*, Sp, Vol. 11, pp. 308–316.
37. *CSP*, Sp, Vol. 11, pp. 285–302.
38. Harbison, pp. 78–79.
39. *CSP*, Sp, Vol. 11, pp. 229–238.
40. *CSP*, Sp, Vol. 11, pp. 285–302.
41. Harbison, p. 93; *CSP*, Sp, Vol. 11, pp. 308–316; 316–331.
42. *CSP*, Sp, Vol. 11, pp. 363–374.
43. Harbison, p. 93.
44. *CSP*, Sp, Vol. 11, pp. 387–407.
45. Tittler, Robert, *The Reign of Mary I* (Longman, London, 1990), p. 19; Fletcher, Anthony, *Tudor Rebellions* (Longman, London, 1990), p. 1990; Harbison, pp. 126–127; *CSP*, Sp, Vol. 11, pp. 407–423.
46. *Conspiracies*, pp. 15–16.
47. *Exiles*, p. 272.
48. Bartlett, Kenneth, R., 'The English Exile Community in Italy under Queen Mary I [1553–1558]' (PhD Thesis, University of Toronto, 1978), p. 296.

49. Nichols, *Chronicle of Queen Jane*, p. 69; *CSP*, Sp, Vol. 12, pp. 129–147.
50. *Conspiracies*, p. 21.
51. *CSP*, Sp, Vol. 12, pp. 100–123.
52. *Conspiracies*, p. 22; *CSP*, Sp, Vol. 12, pp. 93–100.
53. Cooper, J.D.P., Carew, Sir Peter [1514?–1575] (*ODNB*); Fletcher, *Tudor Rebellions*, p. 70; *Conspiracies*, p. 38.
54. *CPR*, 1554–1555, pp. 292.
55. *Conspiracies*, p. 38.
56. *CSP*, Sp, Vol. 12, pp. 1–20.
57. *Conspiracies*, p. 24.
58. *CSP*, Sp, Vol. 12, pp. 36–50.
59. *Conspiracies*, pp. 71, 73.
60. *CSP*, Sp, Vol. 12, pp. 82–93.
61. *CSP*, Sp, Vol. 12, pp. 66–82.
62. Nichols, *Chronicle of Queen Jane*, p. 59.
63. *CSP*, Sp, Vol. 12, pp. 36–50, 100–123.
64. *Exiles*, pp. 309–310.
65. *CSP*, Sp, Vol. 12, pp. 129–147.
66. *CSP*, Sp, Vol. 12, pp. 147–164; Nichols, *Chronicle of Queen Jane*, p. 67.
67. *Conspiracies*, p. 92.
68. *CSP*, Foreign, No. 155.
69. Nichols, John Gough (ed.), *The Diary of Henry Machyn*, Camden Society (1848), p. 64.
70. Carter, P.R.N., Tresham, Sir Thomas [c. 1500–1559] (*ODNB*).

Chapter 14

1. *CSP*, Sp, Vol. 13, No. 502, pp. 435–442.
2. 'Misfortune', p. 8.
3. *CSP*, Sp, Vol. 13, No. 161, pp. 143–153.
4. *CSP*, Ven, Vol. 6, No. 49, pp. 35–51.
5. *CSP*, Sp, Vol. 13, No. 178, pp. 153–168.
6. *CSP*, Ven, Vol. 6, No. 67, pp. 51–59.
7. TNA: SP/11/5, f. 73.
8. *CSP*, Ven, Vol. 6, No. 73, pp. 59–72.
9. Wood, *Letters of Illustrious Ladies*, Vol. 3, pp. 302–303.
10. TNA: SP/11/7, f. 17; Wood, *Letters of Illustrious Ladies*, Vol. 3, p. 304.
11. TNA: SP/11/6, f. 3.
12. *CSP*, Ven, Vol. 6, No. 409, pp. 346–361.
13. *CSP*, Ven, Vol. 6, No. 259, pp. 221–237.
14. Wood, *Letters of Illustrious Ladies*, Vol. 3, p. 303.
15. *CSP*, Ven, Vol. 6, No. 259, pp. 221–237.
16. TNA: SP/11/5, f. 124; SP/1/138, f.109 right.
17. TNA: SP/11/6, f. 98.
18. TNA: SP/11/6, f. 98.
19. TNA: SP/11/6, f.3.
20. Wood, *Letters of Illustrious Ladies*, Vol. 3, p. 305.
21. Wood, *Letters of Illustrious Ladies*, Vol. 3, pp. 306–307.
22. Wood, *Letters of Illustrious Ladies*, Vol. 3, pp. 308–309.
23. *CSP*, Ven, Vol. 6, No. 292, pp. 250–267.

24. *CSP*, Ven, Vol. 6, No. 94, pp. 71–82.
25. TNA: SP/11/5, f. 73.
26. TNA: SP/11/7, f. 5.
27. PROB 11/40/8: Gertrude Courtenay, Marchioness of Exeter.
28. TNA: SP/11/5, f. 73.
29. TNA: SP/11/6, f. 107, 108L.
30. TNA: SP/11/7, f. 17.
31. *CSP*, Ven, Vol. 6, No. 111, pp. 82–93.
32. Tresham's deer park was at his seat, Rushton Hall, Northamptonshire. This charming residence still stands today and is a hotel and spa.
33. TNA: SP/11/5, f. 125.
34. Bartlett, 'The English Exile Community in Italy', p. 281.
35. TNA: SP/11/5, f. 121.
36. TNA: SP/11/5, f. 94.
37. *CSP*, Ven, Vol. 6, No. 94, pp. 72–82.
38. *CSP*, Ven, Vol. 6, No. 159, pp. 125–138.
39. *CSP*, Ven, Vol. 6, No. 286, pp. 250–267.
40. Wood, *Letters of Illustrious Ladies*, Vol. 3, p. 305.
41. *CSP*, Ven, Vol. 6, No. 147, pp. 110–124.
42. *CSP*, Ven, Vol. 6, No. 286, pp. 250–267.
43. *CSP*, Dom, Vol. 6, Nos. 69–71, 73–74, p. 73.
44. *CSP*, Ven, Vol. 6, No. 286, pp. 250–267.
45. *CSP*, Ven, Vol. 6, No. 259, pp. 221–237.
46. *CSP*, Ven, Vol. 6, No. 84, pp. 72–82.
47. *CSP*, Foreign, No. 360, pp. 165–173.
48. TNA: SP/11/5, f. 93.
49. *CSP*, Ven, Vol. 6, No. 123, pp. 93–110.

Chapter 15
1. 'Misfortune', p. 9.
2. *CSP*, Dom, Vol. 5, No. 27; *CSP*, Ven, Vol. 6, No. 145, pp. 110–124.
3. *CSP*, Ven, Vol. 6, No. 135, pp. 93–110.
4. TNA: SP/11/5, f. 94.
5. *CSP*, Ven, Vol. 6, No. 165, pp. 138–145.
6. *CSP*, Ven, Vol. 6, No. 173, pp. 145–163; 'Misfortune', pp. 12–13.
7. *CSP*, Ven, Vol. 6, No. 187, pp. 163–175.
8. *CSP*, Ven, Vol. 6, No. 222, pp. 188–198.
9. *CSP*, Ven, Vol. 6, No. 248, pp. 214–221.
10. *CSP*, Ven, Vol. 6, No. 328, pp. 283–301.
11. *CSP*, Dom, Vol. 6, No. 46.
12. TNA: SP/11/6, f. 80.
13. *CSP*, Ven, Vol. 6, No. 273, pp. 237–250, No. 8, pp. 1–13.
14. *CSP*, Ven, Vol. 6, No. 286, pp. 250–267.
15. Bell, Gary M., Hoby, Sir Philip [1504/5–1558] (*ODNB*); 'Misfortune', p. 9.
16. *CSP*, Ven, Vol. 6, No. 284, pp. 250–267.
17. *CSP*, Ven, Vol. 6, No. 285, pp. 250–267. The meaning of 'Lets' is obstruction, hindrance. The words in italics were inserted in Edward's own hand.
18. *Conspiracies*, p. 179.

19. *CSP*, Ven, Vol. 6, No. 461, pp. 412–424; Archer, Courtenay, Edward, first earl of Devon (*ODNB*).
20. 'Misfortune', p. 9.
21. *CSP*, Dom, Vol. 7, No. 39; *Conspiracies*, p. 199.
22. TNA: SP/11/8, f. 78.
23. *CPR*, 1555–1557, Vol. 3, pp. 402–403.
24. *CSP*, Foreign, No. 444, pp. 198–200.
25. TNA: SP/11/6, f.125, f. 127.
26. *CSP*, Dom, Vol. 7, No. 2.
27. *CSP*, Ven, Vol. 6, Nos. 385, 386, pp. 333–345, No. 417, pp. 361–376.
28. *CSP*, Sp, Vol. 13, No. 272, pp. 268–271.
29. TNA: SP/69/9, f. 139.
30. Andrich, Io. Aloys, *De Natione Anglica Et Scota Iuristarum Universitatis Patavinae* (Patavii, 1892), p. 131.
31. TNA: SP/11/7, f. 19.
32. *CSP*, Sp, Vol. 13, No. 262, pp. 258–259.
33. TNA: SP/11/7, f. 81.
34. Bartlett, Kenneth, R., 'The English Exile Community in Italy and the Political Opposition to Queen Mary I', *Albion*, Vol. 13, No. 3 (Autumn, 1981), p. 235; *CSP*, Ven, Vol. 6, No. 466, pp. 412–424.
35. *CSP*, Ven, Vol. 6, Nos. 434, 440, pp. 377–395.
36. *CSP*, Ven, Vol. 6, No. 460, pp. 412–424.
37. *CSP*, Dom, Vol. 8, No. 16.
38. TNA: SP/11/8, f. 78; Ray, Meredith K., *Twenty-Five Women Who Shaped the Italian Renaissance* (Routledge, Oxford, 2024), pp. 66, 73, 74.
39. Miller, Amos C, *Sir Henry Killigrew: Elizabethan Soldier and Diplomat* (Leicester University Press, 1963), p. 21.
40. *Conspiracies*, p. 262; *CSP*, Foreign, No. 509, pp. 227–231.
41. TNA: SP/11/8, f. 78; *CSP*, Sp, Vol. 13, No. 272, pp. 268–271.
42. 'Misfortune', p. 21.
43. Harbison, p. 302; *CSP*, Foreign, No. 519, pp. 232–242.
44. Harbison, pp. 294–295.
45. *CSP*, Ven, Vol. 6, No. 504, pp. 472–484; *CSP*, Sp, Vol. 13, No. 272, pp. 268–271.
46. Loades, David, *Mary Tudor: A Life* (Basil Blackwell Ltd, Oxford, 1989), p. 266.
47. TNA: SP/11/9, f. 30.
48. 'Misfortune', p. 21.
49. TNA: SP/11/9, f. 38.
50. *CSP*, Ven, Vol. 6, No. 555, pp. 534–551.
51. *CSP*, Foreign, No. 523, p. 245.
52. *CSP*, Dom, Vol. 6, No. 68.
53. TNA: SP/11/9, f. 20; For Casa Marcello: https://www.camarcello.it/en/main-house/history/
54. Bartlett, 'The English Exile Community in Italy under Queen Mary I, pp. 277–278.
55. TNA: SP/69/9, ff. 138–140, pencil.
56. 'Misfortune', pp. 22–24.
57. TNA: SP/69/9, f. 139, pencil; *CSP*, Foreign, No. 546, pp. 260–273.
58. TNA: SP/69/9, f. 139, pencil.

59. *CSP*, Ven, Vol. 6, Nos. 708, 710, 716, 717, pp. 788–804, Nos. 729, 730, 731, 734, 736, pp. 812–831.
60. Strype, *Ecclesiastical Memorials*, p. 420 ['aegritudine confectus'], p. 425 ['ex duplici febre tertiana mortuus'], p. 425.
61. *CSP*, Sp, Vol. 13, No. 283, pp. 275–280.
62. TNA: SP/69/9, f. 81.
63. 'Misfortune', p. 26, fn. 144; Bartlett, Kenneth, R., Bizzarri [Bizari], Pietro [b. 1525, d. in or after 1586] *(ODNB)*.
64. TNA: SP/69/9, f. 81.
65. 'Misfortune', p. 26, fn. 144.
66. *CSP*, Sp, Vol. 13, No. 283, pp. 275–280.
67. *CSP*, Ven, Vol. 3, Preface, pp. vii–xlvi.
68. Loades, *Mary Tudor: A Life*, p. 359.
69. TNA: PROB 11/40/8: her will was signed by witnesses on 26 December 1557 and proved at London on 8 January 1558.
70. Wood, *Letters of Illustrious Ladies*, Vol. 3, p. 306.

Appendix

1. Madden, *Privy Purse Expenses of the Princess Mary*, p192.
2. RCIN 912257: https://www.rct.uk/collection/search#/2/collection/912257/an-unidentified-woman
3. Parker, K.T., *The Drawings of Hans Holbein in the Collection of His Majesty the King at Windsor Castle* (The Phaidon Press, Oxford, 1945), p. 43.

Bibliography

Primary Sources

British Library
Harley MS. 69, f.5v: The booke of certaine triumphes.
Lansdowne MS 978/98, f. 111v: Katharine Courtenay's vow of chastity.

Warrants to the Great Wardrobe
Add. MS. 18,826, f.10, 13 December 1510.
Add. MS. 18,826, f.19, 26 March 1511.
Add. MS. 18,826, f.30, 2 July 1511.

College of Arms
Ms I3 ff. 33b–35, ff. 96–96b and Ms I15 ff. 138–140v: Funeral of Sir William Courtenay, buried as Earl of Devonshire.
Ms I15 ff. 133v–137v: Funeral of Katharine Courtenay, Countess of Devon.

National Archives
C 54/ 396: Indenture between Henry VIII and Henry Courtenay, Marquis of Exeter.
LC 2/1, 75L: Payments relating to the household of Prince Henry, son of Henry VII.
SP/1/2, f.67: Letter of Sir Richard Carewe to Thomas Ruthall, Bishop of Durham.
C1/335/92: Blount v Bourchier.
STAC 2/4/42: Benet v Lowre, tinwork dispute.
E 326/11649: Indenture between John Medam, one of the king's master carpenters, and Henry Courtenay, Marquis of Exeter.
SP 1/80: Confession of Elizabeth Barton, Nun of Kent.
SP/1/138: Inventory of goods at Horsely and Coombe and a list of the Marquis of Exeter's Servants.
SP/1/164: List of articles given from the royal wardrobe.
SP/1/130: Letter from the Marquis of Exeter to Cromwell re Katherine Blount's dowry.
C/1/1298: Evelegh v Marchioness of Exeter.
SP/1/225: Letter from the Council in London to the Council with the king including a letter from Edward Courtenay.
SP/69/9: Peter Vannes' letters re the death of Edward Courtenay.
Correspondence to and from Edward Courtenay:
SP/11/5: May–July 1555.
SP/11/6: August–December 1555.
SP/11/7: January–March 1556.
SP/11/8: May 1556.

SP/11/9: June–July 1556.
Katharine Countess of Devon, household accounts and inventory:
SP 1/28: Michaelmas 1522–3, State Papers General Series Henry VIII.
E 36/223: Michaelmas 1523–4, Exchequer, Lord Treasurer's Remembrancer's Books.
SP 1/46, ff. 44–49: Tiverton Castle Inventory.
Wills:
E 210/10166: An early will of Katharine Countess of Devon.
PROB 11/16/15: Edward Courtenay, Earl of Devon (1509).
PROB 11/40/8: Gertrude Courtenay, Marchioness of Exeter.
PROB 11/17/337: Sir Thomas Knyvet.
PROB 11/17/293: Muriel Knyvet née Howard.
PROB 11/6/459: Sir John Say.
PROB 11/24/102: Sir William Say.
PROB 11/25/473: William Blount, Lord Mountjoy.
PROB 11/7/374: John Blount, Lord Mountjoy.
PROB 11/30/653: Charles, Lord Mountjoy.

Printed Primary Sources

Acts of the Privy Council of England, (ed.) Dasent, John Roche, Vol. 1 1542–1547, Vol. 2
    1547–1550 (London, 1890); Vol. 3 1550–1552 (London, 1891); Vol. 4 1552–1554, Vol.
    5 1554–1556 (London, 1892).
Calendar of the Close Rolls, Henry VII, Vol. 1, 1485–1500, (ed.) Ledward, K.H., *Vol.* 2,
    1500–1509, (ed.) Latham, R.A. (London, 1955, 1963).
Calendar of the Patent Rolls, Henry VII, Vol. 1 1485–1494, Vol. 2 1494–1509 (London,
    1914, 1916).
Calendar of the Patent Rolls, Philip and Mary, Vol. 1 1553–1554, Vol. 2 1554–1555, Vol. 3
    1555–1557 (Liechtenstein, 1970).
Calendar of State Papers Domestic, Edward VI, Mary and Elizabeth, 1547–80, Vols 5–14, (ed.)
    Lemon, Robert (London, 1856).
Calendar of State Papers Foreign, Mary 1553–1558, (ed.) Turnbull, William B. (London, 1861).
Calendar of State Papers, Spain, 1485–1558, Vols 1–13, (eds) Bergenroth, G.A., De Gayangos,
    P., Mattingly, G., Hume, M.A.S., Tyler, R. (London, 1862–1954).
Calendar of State Papers, Venetian, 1202–1580, Vols 1–7, (eds) Brown, R., Bentinck, G.C.,
    Brown, H.F. (London, 1864–1890).
A Collection of Ordinances and Regulations for the Government of the Royal Household (Society
    of Antiquaries, London, 1790).
Letters and Papers, Foreign and Domestic, of the Reign of Henry VIII, 1509–1547, (eds) Brewer,
    J.S., Gairdner, J., Brodie, R.H., Vols 1–12 (1864–1920).
State Papers King Henry the Eighth, Vol. 1, Pts 1 and 2 (John Murray, Albemarle Street, 1831).
Statutes of the Realm, Vol. 2 (London, 1816, reprinted 1963).
Rotuli Parliamentorum, (ed.) Strachey, J., and others, 6 Vols (1767–1777).

Other Primary Sources

Allen, P.S and H.M., *Letters of Richard Fox* (The Clarendon Press, Oxford, 1929).
Andrich, Io. Aloys, *De Natione Anglica Et Scota Iuristarum Universitatis Patavinae* (Patavii,
    1892).
Anglo, Sydney, *The Great Tournament Roll of Westminster: A Collotype Reproduction of the
    Manuscript* (Oxford, 1968).
Anstis, J. (ed.), *The Register of the Most Noble Order of the Garter* (1724).

Babington, Churchill, intro., *The Benefit of Christ's Death* (Bell & Daldy, London, 1855).

Bayne, C.G., completed by Dunham, William Hulse, *Select Cases in the Council of Henry VII* (Selden Society, London, 1958).

Brown, Rawdon, *Four Years at the Court of Henry VIII, Sebastian Giustinian*, Vols 1 and 2 (Smith, Elder & Co, London, 1854).

Byrne, Marie St Clare, *The Lisle Letters*, Vols 1–6 (University of Chicago Press, Chicago, 1981).

Campbell, William, *Materials for A History of The Reign of Henry VII*, Vols 1–2 (Rolls Series, London, 1873).

Clutterbuck, Robert, *The History and Antiquities of the County of Hertford*, Vol. 2 (London, 1821).

Cokayne, George Edward, *Complete Peerage of England, Scotland, Ireland, Great Britain and the United Kingdom* (George Bell and Sons, London, 1887–1898).

Hall, Edward, *Chronicle*, (ed.) Ellis, Henry (London, 1809; reprint published by Andesite Press).

Hay, Denys (ed. and trans.), *The Anglica Historia of Polydore Vergil A.D. 1485–1537*, Camden Third Series Vol. 74 (London, 1950).

Gairdner, James, *Letters and Papers Illustrative of the Reigns of Richard III and Henry VII*, Vols 1 and 2 (Longman, Green, Longman, and Roberts, 1861).

Gairdner, James (ed.), *The Paston Letters* (Alan Sutton Publishing Ltd, Gloucester, 1983).

Given-Wilson, Chris, Brand, Paul, Phillips, Paul Seymour, Ormrod, Mark, Martin, Geoffrey, Curry, Anne and Horrox, Rosemary (eds), *Parliament Rolls of Medieval England* (Boydell & Brewer, Woodbridge, 2005).

Grose, Francis, Astle, Thomas and Edward, Jeffrey, *The Antiquarian Repertory*, Vols 1–4 (Edward Jeffrey, London, 1784–1808, reprinted by Forgotten Books London, 2017–2018).

Hearne, Thomas (ed.), *Joannis Lelandi Antiquarii de Rebus Britannicis Collectanea*, Vols 4 and 5 (London, 1770).

Madox, Thomas, *Formulare Anglicanum: or, a Collection of Ancient Charters and Instruments of Divers Kinds, Taken from the Originals* (Jacob Tonson and R. Knaplock, London 1702, reprinted by ECCO Print Editions).

Mancini, Dominic, *The Usurpation of Richard III*, trans. Armstrong, C.A.J. (Alan Sutton Publishing, Gloucester, 1989).

Nicholas, Harris Nicolas, *Report on the Proceedings on the Claim to the Barony of L'isle, in the House of Lords* (William Pickering, Stevens and Sons, London, 1829).

Nicolas, Harris Nicholas, *Privy Purse Expenses of Elizabeth of York: Wardrobe Accounts of Edward the Fourth* (William Pickering, London, 1830, reprint Frederick Muller Ltd, London, 1972).

Nichols, John Gough, *Collectanea Topographica et Genealogica*, Vol. 1 (John Bowyer Nichols and Son, London, 1834).

Nichols, John Gough (ed.), *The Diary of Henry Machyn*, Camden Society (1848).

Nichols, J.A., *Collection of All the Wills Now Known to be Extant, of the Kings and Queens of England ...* (Society of Antiquaries, London, 1780).

Nichols, J.G., (ed.), *The Chronicle of Calais*, Camden Society, Vol. 35 (1846, reprinted Alpha Editions, 2019).

Nichols, J.G., (ed.), *The Chronicle of Queen Jane*, Camden Society, Vol. 49 (1850, reprinted Alpha Editions, 2019).

Nicholls, Francis Morgan, *The Hall of Lawford Hall* (London, 1891).

Oliver, George, *Monasticon Dioecesis Exoniensis* (Longman, Brown, Green & Longmans, London, 1846).

Palgrave, Francis (ed.), *The Antient Kalendars and Inventories of the Treasury of His Majesty's Exchequer*, Vol. 3 (London, 1836).

Pronay, N., and Cox, J. (eds), *The Crowland Chronicle Continuations, 1459–1486* (Richard III and Yorkist History Trust, London, 1986).

Rymer's Foedera Volume 12, (ed.) Thomas Rymer (London, 1739–1745).

Strype, John, *Ecclesiastical Memorials*, Vol. 3, Pt 2 (Oxford, 1822).

Thomas, A.H. and Thornley, I.D. (eds), *The Great Chronicle of London* (1938) (Alan Sutton Publishing, Gloucester, reprinted 1983).

Vetusta Monumenta, Vol. 3 (Society of Antiquaries, London, 1796).

Wood, M.A.E., *Letters of Illustrious Ladies of Great Britain*, Vols 1–3 (London, 1846).

Secondary Sources

Anglo, Sydney, *Spectacle, Pageantry, and Early Tudor Policy* (Oxford, 1869).

Archer, Ian W., Courtenay, Edward, first earl of Devon [1526–1556] *(ODNB)*.

Armstrong, C.D.C., Gardiner, Stephen [1495x8–1555] *(ODNB)*.

Ashdown-Hill, John, *Eleanor The Secret Queen* (The History Press, Gloucester, 2010).

Baggs A.P. and Bush, R.J.E., 'Parishes: Dowlish Wake', in *A History of the County of Somerset*, Vol. 4, (ed.), Dunning, R.W. (VCH, London, 1978).

Baker, J.H., Pollard, Sir Lewis [d. 1526] *(ODNB)*.

Baker, J.H., Montagu, Sir Edward [1480s–1557] *(ODNB)*.

Bartlett, Kenneth, R., '"The Misfortune That Is Wished for Him": The Exile and Death of Edward Courtenay, Earl of Devon', *Canadian Journal of History*, Vol. 14 (1979).

Bartlett, Kenneth, R., 'The English Exile Community in Italy and the Political Opposition to Queen Mary I', *Albion*, Vol. 13, No. 3 (Autumn, 1981).

Bartlett, Kenneth, R., Bizzarri [Bizari], Pietro [b. 1525, d. in or after 1586] *(ODNB)*.

Bell, Gary M., Hoby, Sir Philip [1504/5–1558] *(ODNB)*.

Blanchard, Ian, Gresham, Sir Richard [c. 1485–1549] *(ODNB)*.

Borman, Tracy, *The Private Lives of the Tudors* (Hodder & Stoughton, London, 2017).

Breverton, Terry, *The Tudor Kitchen* (Amberley Publishing, Gloucester, 2017).

Buchanan, Patricia Hill, *Margaret Tudor Queen of Scots* (Scottish Academic Press, Edinburgh, 1985).

Burnet, Gilbert, *The History of the Reformation of the Church of England*, Vol. 6 (The Clarendon Press, Oxford, 1865).

Carley, James P., Blount, Charles, fifth Baron Mountjoy [c. 1516–1544] *(ODNB)*.

Carley, James P., Blount, William, fourth Baron Mountjoy [c. 1478–1534] *(ODNB)*.

Carter, P.R.N., Tresham, Sir Thomas [c. 1500–1559] *(ODNB)*.

Chambers, R.W., *Thomas More* (The Harvester Press, Sussex, 1981).

Chandler, John, *John Leland's Itinerary: Travels in Tudor England* (Alan Sutton Publishing, Gloucestershire, 1998).

Challen, W.H., 'Lady Anne Grey', *Notes and Queries* Vol. 10, Issue 1 (January 1963).

Chalmers, Trevor, Stewart, James, duke of Ross *(ODNB)*.

Chalmers, Trevor, James IV *(ODNB)*.

Chibi, Andrew A., Stokesley, John [1475–1539] *(ODNB)*.

Childs, Jessie, *Henry VIII's Last Victim: The Life and Times of Henry Howard Earl of Surrey* (Jonathan Cape, London, 2006).

Clark, Nicola, *Gender, Family and Politics: The Howard Women, 1485–1558* (Oxford University Press, 2018).

Cleaveland, Ezra, *A Genealogical History of the Noble and Illustrious Family of Courtenay* (Exeter 1735; reprint Forgotten Books, London, 2018).

Condon, Margaret M., 'Princess and Nun: Bridget (1480–c.1507), the Youngest Daughter of Edward IV', *The Ricardian*, Vol. 32 (2022), pp. 124–126.

Conway, Agnes, *Henry VII's Relations with Scotland and Ireland 1485–1498* (Cambridge University Press, 1932).

Cooper, J.D.P., Carew, Sir George [c. 1504–1545] *(ODNB)*.

Cooper, J.D.P., Carew, Sir Peter [1514?–1575] *(ODNB)*.

Crawford, Anne, 'The Mowbray Inheritance', *The Ricardian*, Vol. 5, No. 73 (June, 1981).

Cunningham, Sean, *Henry VII* (Routledge, Oxford, 2007).

Cunningham, Sean, Pole, Edmund de la, eighth earl of Suffolk [1472?–1513] *(ODNB)*.

Davidson, James, *The History of Newenham Abbey in the County of Devon* (Longman & Co, London, 1843).

Dockray, Keith, *Edward IV from Contemporary Chronicles, Letters and Records* (Fonthill Media Ltd, Stroud, 2015).

Dodds, M.G. and R., *The Pilgrimage of Grace and the Exeter Conspiracy* Vols 1 and 2 (Cambridge University Press, 1915).

Dugdale, James, *The New British Traveller*, Vol. 2 (London 1819, reprinted by General Books, Memphis, USA, 2012).

Edwards, J., *Mary I England's Catholic Queen* (Yale University Press, 2011).

Ellis, Henry (ed.), 'Transcript of an order made by Cardinal Wolsey, as Lord Chancellor, for the regulation of the household expenses, and general management of the affairs of the young Earl of Oxford...' *Archaeologia*, Vol. 19 (1821).

Elton, G.R., *England Under the Tudors* (Methuen & Co. Ltd, 1971).

Fletcher, Anthony, *Tudor Rebellions* (Longman, London, 1990).

Fortescue, Thomas, Lord Clermont, *A History of the Family of Fortescue in all its Branches*, second edition (London, 1880).

Fraser, Antonia, *A Survey of London Written in the Year 1598 by John Stow* (Sutton Publishing Ltd, Gloucestershire, 2005).

Garrett, Christina Hallowell, *The Marian Exiles* (Cambridge University Press, 1966).

Gostling, William, *A Walk in and About The City of Canterbury with Many Descriptions Not to Be Found in Any Description Hitherto Published* (Canterbury, 1777).

Gunn, Steven J., *Charles Brandon, Duke of Suffolk, 1484–1545* (Basil Blackwell Ltd, Oxford, 1988).

Gunn, Steven J., 'Henry Bourchier, Earl of Essex [1472–1540]' in Bernard, George W. (ed.), *The Tudor Nobility* (Manchester University Press, 1992).

Gunn, Steven J., 'The Courtiers of Henry VII', *English Historical Review*, Vol. 108, Issue 426 (January 1993).

Gunn, Steven J., 'A Letter of Jane, Duchess of Northumberland, in 1553', *The English Historical Review*, Vol. 114, Issue 459 (November 1999).

Gunn, Steven, J., Warbeck, Perkin [Pierrechon de Werbecque; alias Richard Plantagenet, duke of York] [c. 1473–1499] *(ODNB)*.

Gunn, Steven, J., Courtenay, Edward, first earl of Devon [d. 1509] *(ODNB)*.

Gunn, Steven, J., Bourchier, Henry, second earl of Essex [1472–1540] *(ODNB)*.

Hamilton, William Douglas, *A Chronicle of England During the Reigns of the Tudors by Charles Wriothesley, Windsor Herald*, Vols 1 and 2 (Camden Society 1875, 1877).

Hampton, W.E., 'The White Rose Under the First Tudors Part 2. Edmund de la Pole', *The Ricardian*, Vol. 7, No. 98 (September, 1987).

Hanham, Alison, 'Edmund de la Pole and the Spies, 1499–1509: Some Revisions', *Australian and New Zealand Association of Medieval and Early Modern Studies*, No. 6 (1988).

Harbison, E., Harris, *Rival Ambassadors at the Court of Queen Mary* (Princeton University Press, 1940).

Harris, Barbara J., *Edward Stafford, Third Duke of Buckingham, 1478–1521* (Stanford University Press, California, 1986).

Harvey, Anthony and Mortimer, Richard (eds), *The Funeral Effigies of Westminster Abbey* (The Boydell Press, Suffolk, 2003).

Hawkyard, Alasdair, Neville, Sir Edward [b. in or before 1482, d. 1538] *(ODNB).*

Head, David M., *The Ebbs and Flows of Fortune: The Life of Thomas Howard, Third Duke of Norfolk* (The University of Georgia Press, London, 2009).

Heal, Felicity, Goodrich [Goodryck], Thomas [1494–1554] *(ODNB).*

Hicks, Michael, *Edward V The Prince in the Tower* (Tempus Publishing Ltd, Gloucestershire, 2003).

Hobbins, Daniel (ed. and trans) André, Bernard, *The Life of Henry VII* (Italica Press, New York, 2011).

Horrox, R., Blount, Walter, first Baron Mountjoy [d. 1474] *(ODNB).*

Horrox, R. and Hammond, P.W. (eds), *British Library Harleian Manuscript 433*, 4 Vols (Richard III Society, London, 1979–1983).

Howgrave-Graham, R.P., 'The Earlier Royal Funeral Effigies: New Light on Portraiture in Westminster Abbey', *Archaeologia*, Vol. 98 (1961).

Hughes, Jonathan, Rochester, Sir Robert [c. 1500–1557] *(ODNB).*

Hughes, Jonathan, Somerset [formerly Beaufort], Charles, first earl of Worcester [c. 1460–1526] *(ODNB).*

Ives, Eric, *The Life and Death of Anne Boleyn* (Blackwell Publishing, Oxford, 2006).

James, Susan, Parr, Anne [née Bourchier], seventh Baroness Bourchier [1517–1571] *(ODNB).*

Jenkins, Susan and Blessley, Krista 'Royal Wooden Funeral Effigies at Westminster Abbey', *The Burlington Magazine*, Vol. 161 (January 2019).

Jones, Michael (trans. and intro.), *Philippe de Commynes Memoirs The Reign of Louis XI 1461–83* (Penguin Books, Middlesex, 1972).

Jones, Michael K., and Underwood, Malcolm G., *The King's Mother* (Cambridge University Press, 1992).

Kirby, J.L., Say [Fynys], Sir John [d. 1478] *(ODNB).*

Knecht, R.J., *Francis I* (Cambridge University Press, 1988).

Lehmberg, Stanford, Carew, Sir Nicholas [b. in or before 1496, d. 1539] *(ODNB).*

Levine, Mortimer, *Tudor Dynastic Problems 1460–1571* (George Allen and Unwin Ltd, London, 1973).

Leyde, A., *Ambassades de Messieurs de Noailles en Angleterre*, Vol. 2 (1763).

Loach, Jennifer, *Edward VI* (Yale University Press, London, 2002).

Loades, David, *Two Tudor Conspiracies* (Cambridge University Press, 1965).

Loades, David, *Mary Tudor: A Life* (Basil Blackwell Ltd, Oxford, 1989).

Loades, David, *Mary Rose* (Amberley Publishing, Gloucester, 2012).

Loades, David, *Jane Seymour: Henry VIII's Favourite Queen* (Amberley Publishing, Gloucester, 2013).

Loomie, A.J., Englefield, Sir Francis [1522–1596] *(ODNB).*

Lynn, Eleri, *Tudor Fashion* (Yale University Press, London in association with Historic Royal Palaces, 2017).

MacCulloch, D., 'The Vitae Mariae Angliae Reginae of Robert Wingfield of Brantham', *Camden Miscellany*, 28, Camden Fourth Series, Vol. 29 (1983).

MacCulloch, D., *Thomas Cromwell: A Life* (Penguin Books, London, 2019).

Macdougall, Norman, James III *(ODNB).*

Mackay, Lauren, *Inside the Tudor Court* (Amberley Publishing, Gloucester, 2014).

Madden, Frederick, *Privy Purse Expenses of the Princess Mary* (London, 1831, reprinted by Forgotten Books, London, 2015).

Mancini, Dominic, *The Usurpation of Richard III*, trans. Armstrong, C.A.J. (Alan Sutton Publishing, Gloucester, 1989).

Mattingly, Garret, *Catherine of Aragon* (Jonathan Cape Publishers, Oxford, 1944).

Mayer, T.F., Crofts [Croft], George [d. 1539?] *(ODNB)*.

Mayer, T.F., Helyar, John, [1502/3–1541?] *(ODNB)*.

Mayer, T.F., Pole, Reginald [1500–1558] *(ODNB)*.

McKendrick, Melveena, *Ferdinand and Isabella* (American Heritage Publishing Co. Inc., New York, 1968).

Miller, Amos C., *Sir Henry Killigrew: Elizabethan Soldier and Diplomat* (Leicester University Press, 1963).

Miller, Helen, *Henry VIII and the English Nobility* (Basil Blackwell Ltd, Oxford, 1989).

Muller, James Arthur, *Stephen Gardiner and the Tudor Reaction* (Macmillan & Co. Ltd, London, 1926).

Murphy, B., *Bastard Prince Henry VIII's Lost Son* (Sutton Publishing, Gloucester, 2001).

Murphy, Virginia., 'The Literature and Propaganda of Henry VIII's First Divorce', in MacCulloch, D. (ed.), *The Reign of Henry VIII: Politics, Policy and Piety* (Macmillan Press Ltd, London, 1995).

Norton, Elizabeth, *Jane Seymour Henry VIII's True Love* (Amberley Publishing, Gloucester, 2009).

Orme, Nicholas, Conway, Sir Hugh [c. 1440–1518] *(ODNB)*.

Orme, Nicholas, Veysey [formerly Harman], John [c. 1464–1554] *(ODNB)*.

Orme, Nicholas, *VCH of Cornwall*, Vol. 2 (Institute of Historical Research, 2010).

Orme, Nicholas, 'Sir John Speke and His Chapel in Exeter Cathedral', *The Devonshire Association for the Advancement of Science, Literature and Art, Report and Transactions*, Vol. 118 (1986).

Overell, M. Anne, 'Nicodemite's Progress: Edward Courtenay', in *Nicodemites: Faith and Concealment Between Italy and Tudor England* (Brill, Leiden, 2018).

Parker, K.T., *The Drawings of Hans Holbein in the Collection of His Majesty the King at Windsor Castle* (The Phaidon Press, Oxford, 1945).

Parker, Geoffrey, *Imprudent King: A New Life of Philip II* (Yale University Press, London, 2014).

Penn, Thomas, *Winter King* (Allen Lane, London, 2011).

Pierce, Hazel, *Margaret Pole, Countess of Salisbury, 1473–1541: Loyalty, Lineage and Leadership* (University of Wales Press, Cardiff, 2003).

Pierce, Hazel, 'A Remembrance of the Sons of Edward IV by their Sister Katharine Courtenay, Countess of Devon', *The Ricardian*, Vol. 35 (2025, forthcoming).

Pierce, Hazel, 'Margaret Courtenay, Lady Herbert: Edward IV's Elusive Granddaughter', *The Ricardian*, Vol. 35 (2025, forthcoming).

Pollard, A.J., *The Reign of Henry VII from Contemporary Sources*, Vols 1–3 (Longmans, Green and Co., 1913).

Prince, John, *The Worthies of Devon* (London, 1810).

Radford, G.H., 'The Courtenay Monument in Colyton Church', *Report and Transactions of the Devonshire Association for the Advancement of Science, Literature, and Art*, Vol. 39 (July 1907).

Rawcliffe, Carole, *The Staffords, Earls of Stafford and Dukes of Buckingham 1394–1521* (Cambridge University Press, 2008).

Ray, Meredith K., *Twenty-Five Women Who Shaped the Italian Renaissance* (Routledge, Oxford, 2024).

Richardson, Glenn, *The Field of Cloth of Gold* (Yale University Press, London, 2020).

Riordan, Michael, Henry VIII, privy chamber of [act. 1509–1547] *(ODNB)*.

Riordan, Michael, Englefield, Sir Thomas [1455–1514] *(ODNB)*.

Robinson, Joseph Armitage, *Notes and Documents Relating to Westminster Abbey, No.4 The Abbot's House at Westminster* (Cambridge University Press, 1911).

Rodger, N.A.M., *The Safeguard of the Sea: A Naval History of Britain, 660–1649* (Penguin Books, London, in association with the National Maritime Museum, 2004).

Roger, Euan C., '"To Be Shut Up": New Evidence for the Development of Quarantine Regulations in Early-Tudor England', *Social History of Medicine*, Vol. 33, No. 4 (November 2020).

Rose-Troup, Frances, *The Western Rebellion of 1549* (London, 1913, reprinted Forgotten Books, London, 2018).

Roskell, J.S., *Parliament and Politics in Late Medieval England*, Vol. 2 (The Hambledon Press, London, 1981).

Ross, C., *Edward IV* (Eyre Methuen Ltd, London, 1991).

Ross, James, *The Foremost Man of the Kingdom: John de Vere, Thirteenth Earl of Oxford (1442–1513)* (The Boydell Press, Suffolk, 2015).

Russell, Gareth, *Young and Damned and Fair: The Life and Tragedy of Catherine Howard at the Court of Henry VIII* (William Collins, London, 2018).

St John Hope, W.H., 'On the Funeral Effigies of the Kings and Queens of England', with a 'Note on the Westminster Tradition of Identification' by Robinson, Joseph Armitage, *Archaeologia*, Vol. 60 (1907).

Scofield, Cora L., *The Life and Reign of Edward IV*, Vols 1 and 2 (Fonthill Media Ltd, Stroud, 2016, reprint).

Seward, Desmond, *The Last White Rose* (Constable, London, 2010).

Sheppard Routh, Pauline '"Lady Scroop Daughter of K. Edward": an Enquiry', *The Ricardian*, Vol. 9, No. 121 (June 1993).

Sil, Narasingha P., Denny, Sir Anthony [1501–1549] *(ODNB)*.

Sil, Narasingha P., Herbert, William, first earl of Pembroke [1506/7–1570] *(ODNB)*.

Sim, Alison, *Pleasures and Pastimes in Tudor England* (Sutton Publishing, Gloucester, 1999).

Speight, Helen M., '"The Politics of Good Governance": Thomas Cromwell and the Government of the Southwest of England', *The Historical Journal*, Vol. 37, No. 3 (Sept. 1994).

Starkey, David, *The English Court: From the Wars of the Roses to the Civil War* (Longman, London, 1987).

Starkey, David, *Six Wives: The Queens of Henry VIII* (Random House, London, 2003).

Starkey, David, *Henry Virtuous Prince* (Harper Press, London, 2008).

Strickland, Agnes, *Lives of the Queens of England*, Vol. 2 (Henry Colburn, London, 1854).

Strong, Roy, *The English Icon: The Elizabethan and Jacobean Portraiture* (The Paul Mellon Foundation for British Art, London, 1969).

Sutton, Anne F., and Visser-Fuchs, Livia, 'The Royal Burials of the House of York at Windsor: II. Princess Mary, May 1482, and Queen Elizabeth Woodville, June 1492', *The Ricardian*, Vol. 11, No. 44 (March 1999).

Sylvester, R.S. and Harding, Davis P., *Two Early Tudor Lives* (Yale University Press, London, 1969).

Thomson, J.A.F., The Courtenay Family in the Yorkist Period', *Bulletin of the Institute of Historical Research*, Vol. 45, Issue 112 (November 1972).

Tittler, Robert, *The Reign of Mary I* (Longman, London, 1990).

Tremlett, Giles, *Catherine of Aragon: Henry's Spanish Queen* (Faber and Faber, London, 2010).

Trim, D.J.B., Champernowne, Henry [1537/8–1570] *(ODNB)*.

Walker, Greg, 'The "Expulsion of the Minions" of 1519 Reconsidered', *The Historical Journal*, Vol. 32, No. 1 (March 1989).

Watkins, Sarah-Beth, *The Tudor Brandons* (Chronos Books, Hants, 2016).

Watkins, Sarah-Beth, *Margaret Tudor Queen of Scots* (Chronos Books, Hants, 2017).

Watt, Diane, 'Barton Elizabeth [called the Holy Maid of Kent, the Nun of Kent] [c. 1506–1534)] *(ODNB)*.

Webb, Peter, 'John and Jasper Horsey – Two Tudor Opportunists, parts 1 and 2', *Proceedings of the Dorset Natural History and Archaeological Society*, Vol. 100 (1978, published 1979).

Webb, Simon, *The History of Richard III by Thomas More* (Langley Press, Durham, 2015).

Loomie, A.J., Englefield, Sir Francis [1522–1596] *(ODNB)*.

Weir, Alison, *Elizabeth of York: The First Tudor Queen* (Jonathan Cape, London, 2013).

Weir, Alison, *The Lost Tudor Princess: The Life of Lady Margaret Douglas* (Ballantine Books, New York, 2015).

Welsford, A.E., *John Greenway 1460–1529 Merchant of Tiverton and London A Devon Worthy* (Tiverton, 1984).

Westcott, Margaret, 'Katherine Courtenay, Countess of Devon, 1479–1527', in Gray, Todd, Rowe, Margery and Erskine, Audrey (eds), *Tudor and Stuart Devon The Common Estate and Government: Essays Presented to Joyce Youings* (University of Exeter Press, 1992).

Westcott, Margaret, 'Surveying the Estates of Henry Courtenay, Earl of Devon, Marquis of Exeter and Traitor, 1543–4', in Gray, Todd, *Devon Documents, Devon & Cornwall Notes & Queries*, Special Issue (1996).

Westcott, Margaret R., 'Katherine, countess of Devon [1479–1527]' *(ODNB)*.

Whitley, Catrina Banks and Kramer, Kyra, 'A New Explanation for the Reproductive Woes and Midlife Decline of Henry VIII', *The Historical Journal*, Vol. 53, No. 4 (December 2010).

Worthy, Charles, *Devonshire Wills: A Collection of Annotated Testamentary Abstracts* (Bemrose & Sons Ltd, London, 1896).

Theses and Dissertations
Bartlett, Kenneth, R., 'The English Exile Community in Italy under Queen Mary I [1553–1558]' (PhD thesis, University of Toronto, 1978).

Dent, Elizabeth, '"The goodly and glorious window … a piece in it kinde beyond compare": A History of the Royal Window, Canterbury Cathedral [ca. 1482–83]' (MA Diss., University of York, 2012).

Samman, Neil, 'The Henrician Court During Cardinal Wolsey's Ascendancy c. 1514–1529' (PhD Diss., Bangor University, 1988).

Westcott, Margaret R., 'The Estates of the Earls of Devon, 1485–1538' (MA Diss., Exeter University, 1958).

Williams, Paul, 'The Trading Community of Exeter 1470–1570 with Special Reference to Merchants and Tailors Vol. 2 of 2' (PhD Thesis, University of Exeter, 2020).

On-line Resources
Archaeology Data Service:

Oliver, George and Jones, Pitman, 'The Will of Katharine, Countess of Devon, Daughter of Edward IV; Dated May 2, 1527', *The Archaeological Journal*, Vol. 10 (1853): https:// archaeologydataservice.ac.uk/library/browse/issue.xhtml?recordId=1139191

Archives and Cornish Studies Service.

AR/24/17: via TNA Discovery: https://discovery.nationalarchives.gov.uk/details/r/3c15733e-0835-46db-a204-371dad60e892

Ashdown-Hill, John, *The Full Itinerary of Edward IV* (updated edition November 2017): https://www.amberley-books.com/pub/media/wysiwyg/The_Full_Itinerary_of_Edward_IV_by_John_Ashdown-Hill_-_revised_29.11.2017.pdf
British History Online: https://www.british-history.ac.uk/
Casa Marcello: https://www.camarcello.it/en/main-house/history/

The Chamber Books of Henry VII and Henry VIII, 1485–1521
https://www.tudorchamberbooks.org/edition
BL Add. MS 7099, f. 83: 7 September 1503.
E36/214 f. 111v: 19 December 1507.
Add. MS 21481, f. 8v: 1 July 1509.

Devon Heritage Centre.
CR/668: Covenant by Katharine, Countess of Devon. On-line catalogue: https://devon-cat.swheritage.org.uk/records/CR/668
Historic England:
Tiverton Castle: https://historicengland.org.uk/listing/the-list/list-entry/1384869?section=official-list-entry

History of Parliament Online
Blount, Sir Richard (by 1506–1564), of Mapledurham, Oxon. and Dedisham, nr. Slinfold, Suss: http://www.histparl.ac.uk/volume/1509-1558/member/blount-sir-richard-1506-64
Carent, William (d. 1476), of Toomer in Henstridge, Somerset: https://www.historyofparliamentonline.org/volume/1386-1421/member/carent-william-1476
Carew, George (by 1505–45), of Mohun's Ottery, Devon: https://www.historyofparliamentonline.org/volume/1509-1558/member/carew-george-1505-45
Champernown, Sir Arthur (c. 1525–1578), of Modbury and Dartington, Devon: https://www.historyofparliamentonline.org/volume/1558-1603/member/champernown-sir-arthur-1525-78
Gresham, Sir Richard (by 1486–1549), of London: https://www.historyofparliamentonline.org/volume/1509-1558/member/gresham-sir-richard-1486-1549
Hull, John II (by 1503–1549), of Larkbeare, Devon: https://www.historyofparliamentonline.org/volume/1509-1558/member/hull-john-ii-1503-49

Jenstad, Janelle. The Agas Map. *The Map of Early Modern London*, Edition 7.0, edited by Janelle Jenstad, U of Victoria, 05 May 2022: mapoflondon.uvic.ca/edition/7.0/map.htm.
National Archives:
C 142/10/29: IPM Elizabeth Say, late the wife of William Say: Essex. via TNA Discovery.
Institute of Historical Research, Reviews in History:
Dr Hannes Kleineke, review of Justice and Grace: Private Petitioning and the English Parliament in the Late Middle Ages (review no. 665): https://reviews.history.ac.uk/review/665
Oxford Dictionary of National Biography on-line.

Royal Collection
RCIN 912257: https://www.rct.uk/collection/search#/2/collection/912257/an-unidentified-woman

Index